D1083075

Studies in eighteenth-century music; a tribute to Karl Geiringer on his seventieth birthday. Edited by H. C. Robbins Landon. In collaboration with Roger E. Chapman. New York, Oxford University Press, 1970.

425 p. music, port. 25 cm. $14.00

"A selected bibliography of the works of Karl Geiringer ...": p. [407]–419.

1. Music—Addresses, essays, lectures. 2. Music—History and criticism—18th century. I. Geiringer, Karl, 1899– II. Landon, Howard Chandler Robbins, 1926, ed. III. Chapman, Roger Eddington, 1916–

ML55.G24S8 1970b   780'.94   70–17848
                                                MARC

Library of Congress   70 [4]   MN

STUDIES IN EIGHTEENTH-CENTURY MUSIC

BY KARL GEIRINGER

THE BACH FAMILY
BRAHMS: HIS LIFE AND WORK
HAYDN: A CREATIVE LIFE IN MUSIC
JOHANN SEBASTIAN BACH
MUSICAL INSTRUMENTS

Karl Geiringer

STUDIES IN EIGHTEENTH-CENTURY MUSIC

A TRIBUTE TO
KARL GEIRINGER
ON HIS SEVENTIETH BIRTHDAY

EDITED BY H. C. ROBBINS LANDON
IN COLLABORATION WITH ROGER E. CHAPMAN

NEW YORK
OXFORD UNIVERSITY PRESS
1970

Music Setting by John B. Barkwith

Printed and bound in Great Britain

FOREWORD

It is with the greatest pleasure that we honour the seventieth birthday of our former teacher, Professor Karl Geiringer. Many of his colleagues, in Europe and in America, have gathered together to present this Festschrift, the contents of which we decided to limit to the eighteenth century, one of Karl Geiringer's special periods. If the international list of contributors bears eloquent witness to Karl Geiringer's stature as a scholar, it perhaps does a little less than justice to his extraordinary merits as a teacher, about which we would like to add a personal word.

Having been fortunate enough in the early post-war years to have studied with Karl Geiringer at Boston University, we can attest to his brilliant and compelling method of teaching. Whether it was a class in Schubert for a hundred undergraduate students having little or no technical knowledge of music, or whether it was a specialized seminar for advanced students dealing, let us say, with Mozart's symphonies, Karl Geiringer always found the right level, the right tone and the right way in which to bring the subject close to the students' hearts. Another factor of Karl Geiringer's teaching should be stressed here (since it cannot, in the nature of a Festschrift, be otherwise revealed): his uncompromising efforts to combine musical theory, or if you will musicology, with practical music-making. We remember with vivid pleasure, even after an interval of nearly a quarter of a century, how one day an entire undergraduate class was handed music to Dufay's *Gloria ad modum tubae,* in the performance of which the editor played one of the trumpet parts on a valveless D-trumpet, reconstructed from an old E-flat Confederate Army bugle. We all were expected to, and in fact did, participate in the College orchestra and/or choir; and we were encouraged, if (as was the case with the editor) we played in the orchestra, to perform on as many instruments as possible. We also recall that Karl Geiringer materially assisted us when the editor and his co-student Samuel Adler (now at the Eastman School of Music, Rochester) wished to form our own Collegium Musicum.

Karl Geiringer himself used to like to play viola in a quartet which he made up of his students; he also very often conducted the orchestra, for instance to illustrate his own brilliant lecture series on Haydn at the Boston Public Library in 1946–47.

All these were things that vastly reduced the fatal gap between musicology and the practical world of music, and his former students owe him an eternal debt for his efforts in this direction. Not for Karl Geiringer the chalk and blackboard alone: we made music at every conceivable opportunity.

We would like to add one final word. Karl Geiringer was a native Austrian and as Custodian of the famous Archives at the Gesellschaft der Musikfreunde in Vienna had already made a distinguished name for himself as a scholar, when he left his native country in 1938 to go, first to England, and then to America. In company with many distinguished central European scholars, such as Alfred Einstein, Curt Sachs and Leo Schrade, he brought the standards and traditions of the Old World to us in the New, and not only greatly enriched the lives of the American universities but succeeded in bringing us even closer to Europe and European thinking. Since most of us are engaged in working with some aspect of the vast tradition of European musical culture, it is obvious that the presence, in America, of men like Karl Geiringer revolutionized American scholarship in general and musicology in particular.

Professor Geiringer now lives and teaches at Santa Barbara in California which is—if we may be permitted to make a personal remark—as delightful a place for a distinguished European scholar to finish a long and distinguished career as we can possibly imagine.

It is a well-known fact that many scholars are constantly aided and abetted by their wives. Mrs. Irene Geiringer, herself a trained historian, has always collaborated with Karl Geiringer, generally in the role of an unseen partner. In a very real sense, therefore, this is a Festschrift in her honour as well.

Buggiano Castello,   H.C.R.L.
August 1969

CONTENTS

A*

STUDIES IN EIGHTEENTH-CENTURY MUSIC

CONTENTS

GERALD ABRAHAM

SOME EIGHTEENTH-CENTURY POLISH SYMPHONIES

Whereas the symphonies of Czech-born composers of the eighteenth century—though, it is true, more those of the emigrants to Mannheim, Paris and Italy than those of their compatriots (such as J. A. F. Miča) who stayed at home—are historically famous, the Polish symphonies of the same period remain almost unknown in the West. Indeed they have until recently been largely unknown even to Polish musicians. When in 1932 Henryk Opieński was writing about eighteenth-century Polish symphonists,[1] he was able to name in addition to the two he was dealing with—Wojciech Dankowski (c. 1762–c. 1820) and Jan Wański the elder (1762–after 1800)—only two others: Jakub Gołąbek (c. 1739–89) and Antoni Milwid (dates unknown). Since the War, thanks very largely in the first place to the researches of Tadeusz Strumiłło, who died tragically young, the picture has altered enormously. At a Round Table of the Congress of the International Musicological Society at Salzburg in 1964 Hieronim Feicht spoke of the great number of early Polish symphonies now known and of the employment in some of them of Polish folk-themes. And at Bydgoszcz two years later Jan Węcowski read a paper[2] summing up the then state of research, with a valuable appendix in the form of a catalogue of non-Polish eighteenth-century symphonies preserved in Polish libraries. At the same time reliable publication began. In 1951–52 the conductor Jan Krenz had published 'practical' versions of one of Dankowski's two D major Symphonies, and Milwid's in C major as a 'Sinfonia concertante' for oboe and symphony orchestra, but the first Polish symphony to appear in a scholarly text was one (dated 1771) by a totally unknown composer, A. Haczewski, which Strumiłło printed in the musical appendix to his *Źródła i początki romantyzmu w muzyce polskiej* (Cracow, 1956). Then three of Goląbek's symphonies and two of Wański's were published in Szweykowski's series *Źrodła do historii muzyki polskiej* (Cracow, 1962) and in 1964 the same general editor embarked on a special series of *Symfonie polskie* in which works by Paszczyński, Pietrowski, Pawłowski, Orłowski, Namieyski, Bohdanowicz and others have already appeared.

Not one of these names is likely to be familiar to any Western musician who has not interested himself in Slavonic culture. These were not composers working in the wider context of European music and contributing to its main stream, like Mysliveček and Jírovec (Gyrowetz) and Vaňhal. Some, like Haczewski and 'Giacomo' Pasczyński, are totally unknown, surviving only in single symphonies to which their names are attached. Karol Pietrowski has left a 'Veni Creator' for three solo voices, two violins, two trumpets and continuo and a 'Jesu Corona Virginum' for soprano and the same instruments in addition to his two symphonies, but neither his dates nor anything else about him is known. Milwid is slightly less shadowy; he was a member of the church *kapela* at Czerwińsk and composed Masses and other church music. Goląbek belonged to the *kapela* of Cracow Cathedral. Wański was a violinist at Poznan and wrote operas and church music. Dankowski was a prolific composer of church music, which turns up all over the place, and in 1792 played the viola in the orchestra of the German theatre at Lwów under Elsner. Practically all were local musicians who composed for the local vocal/instrumental *kapela*. And according to J. Kitowicz,[3] symphonies were sometimes played by the *kapele* in church, at aristocratic houses before balls and at marriages and other festivities. Symphonies thus written by the local composer for the local band for the great house in the neighbourhood must clearly not be judged by international standards, but if studied sympathetically for what they are, these unpretentious—sometimes quite primitive—works of art offer a great deal of interest.

Two of the most primitive are the already mentioned D major Symphony of Haczewski and the Symphony in the same key by Bazyli Bohdanowicz,[4] found in the library of the Theological Seminary at Sandomierz and probably also dating from the 1770s since Bohdanowicz emigrated to Vienna in 1780 and became a viola-player at Karl Marinelli's Leopoldstadt Theatre. Haczewski's is scored for 2 flutes, 2 horns and strings, Bohdanowicz's for 2 oboes, 2 horns[5] and strings. In both the weakest movement is the first; the invention is extremely poor, though

Bohdanowicz's second subject shows that he was acquainted with Mannheim idioms and to keep it going he employs a device he uses later almost *ad nauseam:* the echoing of first-violin phrases by the seconds at the same pitch or an octave lower. The pseudo-development is no more than a brief, pointless modulation in Haczewski, practically non-existent in Bohdanowicz. But both become a little more interesting in the later movements, which in each include a polonaise. Indeed Haczewski's central movement—he has only three—is the *alla polacca:*

in the middle section of which the flute, mostly solo, has an independent part. The flutes in thirds dominate the entire minor middle section of the finale, a 2/4 ternary *allegretto* which suggests a krakowiak. In Bohdanowicz's Symphony the 'Polonese' is an additional movement to the usual scheme: slow movement (without tempo marking) for strings only; minuet and trio; 'Polonese'; and 3/8 *presto moderato* finale in sonata form, with a substantial development of 45 bars. The second strain of his polonaise:

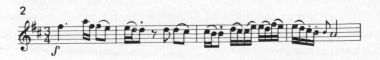

shows a striking relationship to Haczewski's, and the syncopated openings of most of the melodic phrases of his slow movement are related rhythmically to those of the polonaise and melodically to the second strain of its trio.

Pietrowski's two symphonies[6] and Namieyski's[7]—all three in D—

represent a rather more sophisticated type of symphony, though the cling-
ing to D major, an easy key for the violins as well as the brass (which are
always crooked in D, although the horns appear in F in the modern
scores), suggests that they were written for not particularly skilful
players. Indeed the only score of Namieyski's Symphony known for a
long time was in the parish-church music at Grodzisk in Poznania,
though another, anonymous, copy (dated 1834) turned up later in the
library of the Monastery of the Pauline Fathers at Częstochowa; an inscription on the Grodzisk manuscript tells us that the church acquired it
'from the papers of Stanis. Ścigalski', presumably a relative of Franciszek
Ścigalski, himself the composer of a 'Symphonia grande' (as well as a
number of liturgical works), from which Strumiłło published the slow
movement in the musical appendix to his *Żródła i początki romantyzmu.*
We know even less of Namieyski than we do of Pietrowski, not even his
Christian name or other compositions by him, though the making of a
copy as late as 1834 suggests that his Symphony enjoyed some little
reputation. The existence of two copies also provides an association, if
not exactly a link, with a composer of whom we know rather more: the
Silesian-born Jakub Gołąbek, member of the Cathedral *kapela* at Cracow
from about 1774 until his death on March 30, 1789.[8] For his Symphony
(II) in D was also 'offered to the Church in Grodzisk by Stani. Ścigalski',
a copy of his C major Symphony was found in the Pauline Monastery at
Częstochowa, and a list of symphonies—also dated 1834—in the same
Monastery includes both Namieyski's Symphony and symphonies in D
and C by Gołąbek, no doubt the Grodzisk D major and the C major we
know.

Of these three—Gołąbek, Namieyski and Pietrowski—Gołąbek was
probably the oldest. He writes for the same orchestra as Bohdanowicz,
except that in the finale of the C major Symphony he exchanges the oboes
for flutes, but with much more enterprise. His wind are more independent
of the strings and in the finale of D major (I), for which he provides a
bassoon part, he has a long passage for wind only. That he had a penchant
for the wind is apparent also from his C major Partita for clarinets, horns
and bassoon.[9] Thematic invention was not his strong point; his first
subjects are all fanfare-like and, as Muchenberg points out, all his insipid
second subjects are cast in the same rhythmic, and nearly the same
melodic, mould. Muchenberg has no difficulty in finding a number of
Mannheim affinities; indeed Węcowski's catalogue shows that the
Mannheimers and Czechs—and early Haydn—were well known in

Poland ('Hayden is a very good composer', someone has written on one of the Grodzisk scores), but not Sammartini or Monn, the Bach brothers hardly at all, and not Mozart. (Mozart's operas were known but not his symphonies.) Gołąbek's first-movements are typical of the mid-century formal experiments before the general acceptance of sonata-form. In his D major (I) the first subject is extended and followed by wandering modulations which return to a fresh tonic theme before the dominant second-subject appears; the 'development' is hardly more than a tonal interruption and the recapitulation is a mere 24 bars in which the second subject never reappears at all. Indeed Gołąbek never does bring back the second subject in his recapitulations. In the exposition of D major (II) it is the second subject which is allowed to expand, but the recapitulation is even shorter, a mere eight-bar reference to the first subject, followed by a 34-bar coda which refers back at one point in the bass to a passage heard twice in the development. In the C major occurs something like a true development, in the sense of ideas being worked through a series of harmonies; the recapitulation is, as usual, very brief.

Gołąbek's slow movements differ considerably: a short binary *andante* (still in D major), a *rondeau andante* so-called (really a binary-form theme with two variations), and in the C major an extended binary movement on a theme of a much less conventional type, rather suggesting a sentimental song of the day, with an odd little imitative interruption. So with the finales—for all three symphonies are three-movement compositions: D (II) ends with an *allegro molto* in binary form, the C major with a 3/8 *prestissimo* sonata-rondo, while D (I) concludes some conventional *presto* variations with a highly unconventional coda:

Namieyski's five-movement symphony, with two minuets-and-trios
employs pairs of flutes and horns; clarinets in D may be substituted for
the flutes but they are treated exactly like oboes, being written almos
entirely in their upper register, with total neglect of the chalumeau sound
and of all the instrument's other special qualities. Namieyski's themes are
more shapely than Gołąbek's and the whole Symphony shows a much
more assured command of technique; it could easily take its place beside
all but the best Mannheim or J. C. Bach symphonies—and would pass
unnoticed among them, since it lacks personal or national traits. The
opening theme of the sonata-form finale:

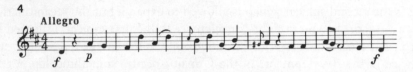

is particularly attractive; the 28-bar development is entirely based on
scale-idea from the second member of the first subject.

Pietrowski can be associated with Namieyski and Gołąbek in that one
of his symphonies, both again in D major, was found in the Grodzis
archives. But he differs from them by betraying the unmistakable in
fluence of Mozart. The opening theme of the *allegro* of (I), the Grodzis
symphony, has a likeness to that of the *Zauberflöte* overture which was
pointed out by Strumiłło[10] and is too close to be accidental. This *allegro*
moreover, has a 12-bar *grave* introduction which is far from Mozartea
but could have been suggested by Mozart, and the development begin
by taking up an idea from the codetta as Mozart so often does. Somethin
like *durchbrochene Arbeit* occurs later:

and real harmonic tension is built up before the recapitulation. One curiosity of the exposition is that, while arrival in the dominant area is marked by the appearance of a new theme, most of the 'second subject' is built on the first theme. The *andante* variations on a binary theme and the minuet-and-trio are much more Haydnish, but the very attractive *presto* sonata-form finale has a distinct flavour of *Nachtmusik*.

Pietrowski's Symphony (II) has no slow introduction and the chief interest of the material of the first *allegro* is that the second subject is a sort of free inversion of the first:

But the development has all the features of that in (I), except that the recapitulation is less skilfully approached, and both slow movement and minuet run on parallel lines to the companion work. But the finale is quite *sui generis*, a *prestissimo* in a free form for which I can think of no model. It begins in the tonic minor:

passes through a fugato in F major, travels as far afield as E minor, and reaches the tonic major only at bar 142—rather more than half-way through the movement. One idea after another is picked up and discarded until, just before the end, the first violins (always unaccompanied) begin to throw out the first two bars of Ex. 7 in the major; finally they do it twice, *pp*, and the symphony ends with tutti tonic chords.

Such experiments as this and the 'farewell' end of Gołąbek's D major

(I) are naturally rare. But by no means all these early Polish symphonies run on conventional lines. Milwid's lost Symphony in B flat minor was entitled 'Bieda ruska' ('Russia's woe) and is said to have been based on Belo-Russian folk-melodies; the second movement was a *dumka*. The two symphonies by Wański, in D and G, published by Florian Dąbrowski,[11] are as the autograph title-page tells us 'Two Symphonies from Opera Overtures', the operas in question being his *Pasterz nad Wisłą* (The Shepherd by the Vistula) and a work, *Kmiotek* (The Peasant), produced at Radomicko in the winter of 1786–87, which was not mainly his composition though he may have written the overture for it. The main *allegro* theme of the *Pasterz* Symphony again has a whiff of *Die Zauberflöte* and again there is a short *adagio* introduction. Both are well-written four-movement works for a pair of flutes, one horn only and strings, but one would like to know the original overtures and whether the conversion to symphonies was effected simply by adding *andante*, minuet and finale in each case; unhappily all the opera music has disappeared. Another D major Symphony by Wański,[12] preserved like them in the Archiepiscopal Archives at Gniezno, a four-movement work with no wind other than flutes, shows much less resource, and Opieński wrote very unenthusiastically[13] about yet another D major Symphony in three movements, now apparently lost. Dankowski's E flat Symphony[14] is unusual in several ways: *e.g.* the substitution of fresh material for the original first-subject in the recapitulation (an area in which the Poles were often unorthodox—Wański's G major Symphony recapitulates the first subject after the second). But its most striking feature is the free treatment of the wind (two clarinets, bassoon and two horns): the antiphony of strings only and wind only at the very beginning and in several later passages, the interplay of clarinets and violins at the beginning of the *adagio*, the predominance of clarinets and horns in the minuet, the episode for wind only in the *rondeau* finale. In fact Dankowski treats the wind as a self-contained group equally important with the strings; it was not for nothing that he indicated on his title-page that the clarinets and horns were '*obligée*'.

Although Opieński could justly claim that the *adagio maestoso* introduction of Dankowski's D major Symphony is a polonaise, and one can point to examples of the old folk-polonaise in Haczewski and Bohdanowicz, none of these—nor Haczewski's krakowiak—has a very pronounced national flavour. For that, the Polish symphony had to wait for a foreign-born musician, though one who became a very true and loyal

Pole: Elsner, the future mentor of Chopin. Of Elsner's eight symphonies, the earliest that has survived is the seventh, in C major, opus 11, performed in Warsaw on April 22, 1805, and published by André of Offenbach the same year. Here, as the trio of the minuet, he inserted a true mazurka—with the sharpened fourth of the major scale which is one of the hallmarks of Polish folk-melody:[15]

That is the historic link between Poland's early symphonists and her greatest composer.

NOTES

1 'Symfonje A. Dankowskiego i J. Wańskiego', *Kwartalnik muzyczny*, no. 16 (1932), p. 685.

2 'La musique symphonique polonaise du XVIIIe siècle', *Musica Antiqua Europae Orientalis: Acta Scientifica Congressus* (ed. Zofia Lissa) (Warsaw, 1966), p. 334.

3 *Opis obyczajów za panowania Augusta III* (Wrocław, 1951). Quoted by Węcowski, *op. cit.*, p. 342.

4 *Symfonie polskie*, VI. The earliest recorded Polish symphony is one by Jacek Szczurowski (1718–after 1773), dating from about 1740 but still undiscovered; the earliest surviving one is an anonymous *Symphonia a 2 Violini Alto Viola con Organo* which Węcowski discovered at Raków Opatowski (Węcowski, *op. cit.*, p. 335).

5 In D, not F as in the printed score.

6 *Symfonie polskie*, II.

7 *Ibid.*, V.

8 The highly condensed English, French, German and Russian summaries of Bohdan Muchenberg's admirable and extensive preface to the scores of Gołąbek's three surviving symphonies, *Źródła do historii muzyki polskiej*, III (Cracow, 1962), all give the wrong date March 27th. At least one other Symphony of his—in D and dated 1783, mentioned by Opieński, *op. cit.*, p. 687 (footnote)—disappeared during the last War. Węcowski has discovered two more, in B flat and D, which have not yet been published (*op. cit.*, p. 338).

9 *Źródła do historii muzyki polskiej*, IV, and *Music in Old Cracow* (ed. Szweykowski) (Cracow, 1964), p. 288.

10 'Do dziejów symfonii polskiej', *Muzyka* (1953), 5–6, p. 38.

11 *Źródła do historii muzyki polskiej*, V.

12 Printed in *Muzyka staropolska* (ed. Hieronim Feicht) (Cracow, 1966), p. 289.

13 *Op. cit.*, p. 690.

14 *Muzyka staropolska*, p. 322. Unfortunately the D major work described by Opieński is available only in Krenz's modernization which makes serious consideration impossible.

15 Quoted from Alina Nowak-Romanowicz, *Józef Elsner* (Cracow, 1957), p. 49.

OTTO E. ALBRECHT

ENGLISH PRE-ROMANTIC POETRY IN SETTINGS BY GERMAN COMPOSERS

Ever since, at the age of fifteen, I made the pleasurable discovery that Schubert's *Ave Maria* was not set to the same text as the *Ave Maria* of Mr Bach-Gounod (although audiences of that day were all too frequently exposed to the Schubert song with the Latin text plus Wilhelmi's obbligato), I have not ceased to be fascinated by the great number of German *Lieder* settings of English poetry. Many have become popular beyond their deserts, while others have remained (not always justly) unknown. These songs are far too numerous to discuss in a contribution of this nature, and I shall restrict myself to poems written before 1800. Even with this limit I proposed to omit from consideration Shakespeare, who would require a volume to himself, and whose effect upon composers has already been the subject of several studies.[1] The hundreds of settings of Robert Burns and the numerous *Lieder* based on the Ossianic poetry of James Macpherson will likewise be omitted, since both are so closely identified with the Romantic movement on the Continent.[2]

For some time I wondered that no publisher had brought out a comprehensive collection of German *Lieder* set to English texts, but it soon became apparent that in very few cases had the composers seen the original English poems, and that the German translations they used were almost always in a metre so different from the original that it would be impossible to sing them in English without drastic changes in either text or music. An attractive anthology could nevertheless be put together, printing the music with the German text and the original English poem opposite.

A considerable number of these English texts are anonymous and belong to the Anglo-Scottish border ballads. These date chiefly from the sixteenth and seventeenth centuries and were collected and published in the eighteenth. The principal collections from which the German poets drew was the famous one by Bishop Percy.[3] The definitive edition is of course the work of Child,[4] whose numbers have served since to identify the ballads. It may come as a surprise to learn that as many as thirteen of the Child ballads have been set by German composers, and some of them several times. The composers, with few exceptions, do not seem to have been familiar with Percy's collection. Their source was either Johann Gottfried Herder, who began to publish his collections of foreign folk poetry as early as 1774, or poets such as Goethe, Bürger, Freiligrath, Fontane, Geibel, and others less well known.

Perhaps the best known of the ballads that have attracted *Lieder* composers is *Edward* (Child 13B). Herder had already expressed his enthusiasm for this magnificent ballad before his first collection of translations appeared.[5] It was quickly set to music by Karl Siegmund von Seckendorff (1744–85), who altogether set ten of Herder's translations from the English in his three volumes of songs.[6] Another contemporary setting appears in the collection of Josef Anton Steffan (Stěpan) (1726–97).[7] These are both eclipsed by the splendid setting by the master of the ballad, Karl Loewe.[8] It is well known that both Loewe and Schubert set Goethe's *Erlkönig* as their opus one; few realize that Loewe's opus 1 contains three songs, including *Edward*. Loewe, at the age of 22, displays his complete mastery of the ballad in these two songs, and his *Edward* is far superior to Schubert's *Altschottische Ballade* (Deutsch 923),[9] a setting of the same text, of which two slightly different versions were written a year before his death. The only composition that approaches Loewe's is the duet setting of Brahms.[10] That this poem had haunted him ever since, twenty years earlier, he had subtitled his bleak and powerful piano *Ballade* (opus 10, no. 1) 'nach der schottischen Ballade Edward' is apparent in a letter to Otto Dessoff shortly after the duet was published.[11] Like many of Brahms' songs for two voices it is not a true duet, since the two voices do not overlap. The reputation of Adolf Jensen as song-writer has suffered a great decline since the early years of this century, but some of his better songs are the least known; they are to be found in the more than thirty songs on English texts written in the last years of his life. His *Edward*[12] belongs in this group, but it is not to be compared with the Loewe or Brahms settings.

The Bonny Earl of Murray ('Ye Highlands and ye Lawlands') (Child 181A) is the source of Herder's poem *Murrays Ermordung*, which appears in an early group of eight songs by Brahms,[13] otherwise devoted to rather archaic settings of six German folk-songs and a poem by Thibaut de Navarre.[14] Two other translations of this ballad are known to me in musical settings. Karl Friedrich Gisbert, Freiherr von Vincke (1813–92), furnished the German version for a group of songs by Moritz Weyermann (1876–?).[15] *Der schöne Graf von Murray* is the only one I have so far identified; the remainder appear to be nineteenth-century poems. A third translation is by Theodor Fontane (1819–98), who more than any German poet after Herder concerned himself with Anglo-Scottish ballads.[16] Five of Fontane's ballads are found in settings by Martin Plüddemann (1845–97), in his day a well-known singer and song composer. *Lord Murray* is no. 5 in this group.[17] The others are no. 1, *The Mermaid* (Child 285); no. 2, *Sir Hugh, or the Jew's Daughter* (Child 155B); no. 3, *Fair Margaret and Sweet William* (Child 74);[18] no. 4, *Lord Maxwell's Last Goodnight* (Child 195). All five of these ballads were composed between 1893 and 1895, but none has kept a place in the repertoire. Fontane has marked them all 'frei nach dem Englischen', with the result that they cannot be sung to the English text. Fontane is also the translator of *Thomas the Rhymer* (Child 37C), which Loewe used for one of his better-known songs, with its effect of tinkling fairy bells.[19]

Jamie Douglas (Child 204) includes in most versions a song whose first appearance in print antedates the published ballad by fifty years. This is *Waly, waly, gin love be bony*, and, translated by Herder as *O weh, o weh*, appears in two eighteenth-century *Lieder*. Seckendorff's setting[22] is followed very quickly by one by Johann Friedrich Reichardt.[21] It seems to have been neglected by later composers except for the song by the prolific Wilhelm Taubert (1811–91).[22]

One of Jensen's sets of songs to Anglo-Scottish poems was devoted to Allan Cunningham, as translated by Freiligrath.[23] The first of this group, however, is the anonymous *Baron of Brackley* (Child 203), which, to be sure, appeared in Cunningham's collection,[24] but also in various other sources of the same period.

Sweet William's Ghost (Child 77), translated by Herder as *Wilhelm's Geist*, was used by Seckendorff,[25] and seems to be the only setting of this gruesome ballad. Likewise, the best known of all the ballads in the United States, *Bonny Barbara Allan* (Child 84), in Fontane's translation, is found only in a setting by Fritz Kögel, a nineteenth-century composer otherwise unknown to me.

One of the rare ballads that are humorous rather than tragic is *Get up and bar the door* (Child 275). Translated by Goethe with the title *Altschottisch*, appearing later as *Gutmann und Gutweib*, it was first set by Loewe[26] and much later by Hugo Wolf,[27] as one of his less successful songs. A third setting is by the Swiss musicologist composer, Alfred V. Heuss (1877–1934).[28] Humour of a sort is also characteristic of *Our Goodman, or The Merry Cuckhold and the kind Wife* (Child 274B). Translated by Friedrich Ludwig Wilhelm Meyer (1759–1840), it was set to music by Friedrich Hurka (1762–1805) as *Des Pächters Rückkehr; Bänkelsängerlied*.

A number of anonymous poems of the eighteenth century or earlier, other than Child ballads, were used by *Lieder* composers. The familiar song, known incorrectly as *Lady Anne Bothwell's Lament* ('Balow, my babe, lye still and sleipe'), was published with the title *Wiegenlied* by Herder in 1774. It appeared in Wieland's *Teutscher Merkur* in 1779 with Seckendorff's music, in the following year in a setting by Christoph Rheineck (1748–97),[29] and a little later in a group of songs by Franz Christoph Neubauer (1760–95).[30] The poem must have exercised a great fascination upon Reichardt, for his *Wiegenlieder für gute deutsche Mütter*[31] offers no less than four different settings. No. 14, as *Wiegenlied einer unglücklichen Mutter*,[32] is followed by *Chanson d'une malheureuse mère*, translated by Mr Berquin. This, in turn, is followed by no. 16, to a different melody but to the original English text, as *Lady Anne Bothwell's Lament*. Looking back to no. 10 of the *Wiegenlieder*, we are astonished to find a fourth tune, this time to a translation by Klamer Schmidt (1746–1824), beginning 'Schlaf süss und hold, mein trautes Kind'. The Schmidt translation is also used by J. A. P. Schulz (1747–1800) in his *Lieder im Volkston*.[33] Nearly a hundred years after this cluster of *Lieder* Brahms uses the first line of Herder's translation ('Schlaf sanft, mein Kind, schlaf sanft und schön') as a motto for his *Intermezzo* in E flat.[34] Three more settings of Herder's text by minor song composers are listed in Challier.[35]

Two more well-known English ballads, not found in Child, were set by Loewe. Of *The Blind Beggar's Daughter of Bednall-Green*[36] he made two versions in 1834, to a translation by Grand-Duke Carl of Mecklenburg-Strelitz (1785–1837). In translating *The Nut-Brown Maid*[37] Herder uses only seventeen of the original thirty stanzas, and Loewe omits four of Herder's.

'Over the mountains and over the waves', with the refrain 'Love will find out the way' in Herder's translation found a quick response in the eighteenth century. Seckendorff's setting of 1779 appears as *Die Gewalt der Liebe*[38] and Reichardt[39] uses Herder's title, *Weg der Liebe*. Carl Friedrich Zelter's *Macht der Liebe* (1797) I know only from a reference in Wittmann's study.[40] Herder had divided his translation into two parts, and this is respected by Brahms in his duet[41] as well as by Max Bruch.[42]

The Lament of the Border Widow ('My love he built me a bonny bower'), as translated by Freiligrath, is set to music by Jensen and ascribed to Scott, although it is much earlier.[43] The composer presumably was not aware that Scott's *Minstrelsie of the Scottish Border* contained largely folk-songs which he had merely collected. Another source of Herder's translations is John Aikin, from whom he borrowed an anonymous poem, *The Mad Maiden* ('One morning very early').[44] This is Herder's *Lied eines wahnsinnigen Mädchen* and was set by Johann Philip Christian Schulz (1773–1827)[45] and by a B. von Dahlberg.[46] *The Gaberlunyie-Man* ('The pauky auld carle came oer the lee') is printed as an appendix to *The Jolly Beggar* (Child 279), and both poems have been attributed, rather implausibly, to James V of Scotland, since both the first printed version and the earliest mention of a connection with the royal Stuart date from around 1724. Herder's *Bettlerlied* appears in Seckendorff's collection[47] and in a setting by Arnold Mendelssohn, which I have not seen. Probably the earliest translation I have found is by Friedrich von Hagedorn (1708–54), who rendered the anonymous poem 'This is the wine, which in olden time' as *Der Mischmasch* ('Der Weintrunk erhält') in 1729. This appears in some of our oldest musical settings of English verse, by Johann Valentin Görner (1702–62),[48] Friedrich Wilhelm Marpurg (1718–95)[49] and Friedrich Wilhelm Weis (1744–1826).[50] There is also a later version by Albert Methfessel (1785–1869).[51]

Two more anonymous English poems, as translated by Herder, remain to be mentioned. *The Pilgrim* ('Oh! happy, happy groves, Witness of our tender loves')[52] appears in Herder's *Volkslieder* as *Das Thal der Liebe* ('O seelig, seelig Thal').[53] Reichardt[54] and Rust[55] promptly set this poem to music, and two more songs by A. Kiel[56] and Philip Wolfrum (1854–1919)[57] appear much later. Herder found the original English of his *Billiges Unglück* ('Wem Gott das selt'ne Glück verlieh')[58] in Allan Ramsay's collection *The Ever Green*.[59] The single musical setting is by Reichardt.[60]

Aside from the anonymous poems, which are difficult to date with any exactness, the oldest English poem of which I have found a German setting is by Sir Henry Wotton (1568–1639). This, *The Character of a Happy Life* ('How happy is he born or taught'), was translated by Herder in his *Volkslieder* (1778) and three years later was set to music by J. F. Reichardt as *Der Glückliche*.[61] This song, exceptionally, may be sung in English, since Herder respected the metrical scheme of the original.

Many commentators on Schubert's *Lieder* have devoted an extended chapter to his settings of English poems, but few have mentioned what is, aside from the familiar three lyrics from Shakespeare's plays, the oldest poem of the group. This is a fragment of a long poem, *The Mistresse*, by Abraham Cowley (1618–67). The first four lines of the section, *The Inconstant*, beginning 'I never yet could see that face', were translated by Joseph Franz von Ratschky (1715–1810) and set by Schubert in 1815 as *Der Weiberfreund* (Deutsch 271).[62] The identification of the text, made about 1950 by the Norwegian Schubert specialist, Odd Udbye, is recorded by the late Otto Erich Deutsch.[63]

Our third seventeenth-century poem is by Sir Charles Sedley (1639–1701), and tracking it down presented some amusing difficulties. Starting with Joseph Haydn's earliest solo song, *Das strickende Mädchen*,[64] ascribed to Herder, it was easy to trace his source to the famous collection of Thomas d'Urfey, *Wit and Mirth or Pills to Purge Melancholy*.[65] Here the compiler states that *The Knotting Song*, as it is known, is the work of one Sir Charles Sydney. Supposing this to be some relative of Sir Philip whom I did not remember, I searched in vain in a number of reference works. Giving up the problem and picking up Day and Murrie[66] a few days later in search of something unrelated, I was pleasantly surprised to discover *The Knotting Song* to be the work of Sir Charles Sedley.[67] First published in the *Gentlemen's Journal* for 1694, it was quickly set to music by Henry Purcell[68] in the following year. In Herder's translation it was first set by Haydn, then in 1782 by Steffan,[69] followed by Wilhelm Pohl (? –1807).[70]

Chloe resolved, a Ballad, by John Hoadly (1711–76), had been set to music by a Dr. Green as early as 1743. The poem, published by Herder as *Das Mädchen am Ufer*,[71] quickly found a number of *Lieder* settings. The first was anonymous, in a Swiss collection.[72] In quick order followed settings by J. F. Reichardt,[73] Steffan,[74] Friedrich Wilhelm Rust (1739–96),[75] Pohl,[76] Johann Friedrich Hugo, Baron von Dalberg (1760–1812),[77] and

Johann Karl Gottlieb Spazier (1761–1805).[78] The Challier catalogue[79] adds two more nineteenth-century versions.

Thomas d'Urfey the anthologist (1653–1723) becomes d'Urfey the poet in Herder's *Landlied* ('Meine Schäfchen morgens früh').[80] This is an abridged version of a lyric in d'Urfey's opera *The Kingdom of the Birds*, better known as *Wonders in the Sun*. The opera, performed in London in 1706, is a pasticcio. Whincop says 'It had several ballads in it that took very much with the common people',[81] which doubtless accounts for the author's reprinting it in his *Wit and Mirth*.[82] Using only three of the original nine stanzas, Herder makes the poem into a dialogue between a shepherd and shepherdess, softening thereby the inescapable overtones of 'Old Macdonald had a farm'. The German poem quickly became popular too and we find seven settings in the twenty years after its publication. Seckendorff's and Steffan's songs both appear in 1782, in their collections already mentioned,[83] Wilhelm Pohl's[84] in 1785, and an anonymous setting in 1793.[85] These are followed by Reichardt's song in his *Wiegenlieder*,[86] a version by Johann Christian Queck[87] and one by J. P. C. Schulz.[88] I have not seen the song by Hilarius von Siegroth.[89]

Colley Cibber (1671–1757), the Restoration actor-manager and poet-laureate, known for his improvements of Shakespeare, is represented here by a single song. This is *The Blind Boy* ('O say what is that thing call'd Light?'), translated by Jakob Nikolaus Craigher (1797–1855) as *Der blinde Knabe*, and composed by Schubert in 1825 (Deutsch 833)[90] in two slightly different versions. Craigher's poem is not found in his published works, and Deutsch assumes that the translation was made expressly for Schubert. The subject is perhaps a little too sentimental for modern taste, and it is not one of Schubert's great songs, but it can be sung to the original English words.

William Oldys (1696–1761) is represented here by a poem which, exceptionally, was set directly in its original English. This is his 'On a fly drinking out of his cup', which Paul Hindemith included in his set of English songs.[91] Alexander Pope (1688–1744) was likewise exceptional in having his ode, *The Dying Christian to his Soul*, published in English along with Herder's translation, in a setting by Dalberg.[92] The well-known setting of this ode, of course, is Schubert's *Verklärung* (Deutsch 59),[93] written when the composer was only 16.

Allan Ramsay (1686–1758), known as the author of the text of one of the earliest ballad operas, *The Gentle Shepherd* (1729), contributes one poem that, in a translation by Ludwig T. Kosegarten (1758–1818), attracted sixteen composers. This is *Ann thou were my ain Thing* ('Wenn du wärst mein eigen'). The best known of this large group of songs is that by Loewe.[94] Friedrich Wollank (1782–1831),[95] Christian Friedrich Johann Girschner (1794–1860),[96] Heinrich Marschner (1795–1861)[97] and Carl Gottlieb Reissiger (1798–1859)[98] are all roughly Loewe's contemporaries. Of the song-writers active after the death of Schubert we should mention Reissiger's brother Friedrich August (1809–83),[99] Franz Kücken (1810–82),[100] Josefine Lang (1815–80),[101] and the Anglo-German composer Heinrich Hugo Pierson (1815–73).[102] The others may be found in Challier's Catalogue.

William Shenstone (1714–63) is the author of *The Princess Elizabeth, alluding to a story recorded of her when she was prisoner at Woodstock, 1554.* His thirteen stanzas are reduced to five in Herder's translation, which begins with the third stanza of the English poem, 'Will you hear how once repining'. This is set by Rust,[103] who begins his *Elisabeth's Trauer im Gefängnis* with Herder's second stanza. The only other setting I have found is by Loewe.[104]

Tobias Smollett (1721–71) seems an unlikely name in this company, but in the diverse collection of songs found in the refreshingly shorter compositions of Johann Rudolf Zumsteeg (1760–1802) I ran across his *Lied* beginning 'Leb wohl du Strom, so sanft und schön',[105] without mention of author or translator.[106] At the foot of the page was the reference 'Aus Peregrine Pikle'. A quick look at Smollett's novel located the lyric 'Adieu ye streams that smoothly flow' in Chapter 18, and reference to several German translations produced Zumsteeg's text in the translation by W. C. S. Mylius.[107] Knapp[108] notes several musical settings of this poem in England but the Zumsteeg song seems to have escaped his notice.

A Scotch woman who seems to have written but a single poem also joins this select company. This is Jane Elliot (1727–1805), famous in Scotland as the author of *Lament for Flodden* ('I've heard them lilting at our ewe-milking'). A translation by Gerhard Anton von Halem (1752–1819), 'Hier tönten sonst frühe beim Melken der Kühe', is used by Ludwig Berger (1777–1839),[109] well known for having anticipated Schubert in setting to music Wilhelm Müller's *Schöne Müllerin*. Another translation of the Elliot poem, by Fontane, *Die Blumen des Waldes* ('Ich hörte sie singen'), appears in the collection of songs by Fritz Kögel.[110]

Bishop Percy, whose *Reliques of Ancient English Poetry* furnished so many poems for German authors, includes in his collection *The Friar of Orders Gray*.[111] This is a thing of shreds and patches indeed, in which he rescues fragments of old ballads from Shakespeare's plays and with generous passages of his own forms them into 'a little TALE, which is here submitted to the Reader's candour'. The poem is reprinted by Ronald S. Crane,[112] who identifies the borrowings, amounting to one quarter of the text. In a translation by Gottfried August Bürger (1748–94), the author of *Lenore*, perhaps the most famous of German poetic ballads, it found five musical settings in the last two decades of the eighteenth century. As *Der Bruder Graurock und die Pilgerin* it appeared first without music in the *Vossischer Musenalmanach* for 1778, and then was composed in turn by Georg Wilhelm Gruber (1729–96),[113] Johann André (1741–99),[114] Georg Friedrich Wolf (1761–1814),[115] Carl Wilhelm Glösch (1732–1809),[116] and Carl Gottlieb Werner.[117]

Freiligrath, in his translations of Sir Walter Scott, failed to distinguish between original poems and those which Scott collected and published in his *Minstrelsie of the Scottish Border*. Jensen, in his Scott songs, unwittingly includes a poem which Freiligrath took from the *Minstrelsie*, but which is actually by Robert Cunningham-Graham (1735–97). Scott uses the author's refrain as the title of the song, *O tell me how to woo thee*. The first line is 'If doughty deeds my lady please'. Jensen follows Scott in using the refrain for his title, *O sag' mir wie dich frei'n*.[118]

If Joseph Haydn's first song, *Das strickende Mädchen*, was originally an English song which he had never seen, he compensated for it by producing thirteen more which were published in England and with the original English texts. All of these were furnished him by his friend Anne Hunter (1742–1821), the wife of the distinguished surgeon, John Hunter. The first set of *Six Original Canzonettas*[119] acknowledged Mrs. Hunter as the author of the texts. They are, in order, *The Mermaid's Song*, *Recollection*, *A Pastoral Song* (the familiar 'My mother bids me bind my hair'), *Despair*, *Pleasing Pains*, and *Fidelity*. The second series,[120] however, indicates the author for only two; the third is a translation from Metastasio and the fourth *She never told her love*, from *Twelfth Night*. Some years ago it occurred to me to find out if there were discrepancies between the text as printed in Haydn's songs and in the published poems of Mrs. Hunter.[121] There were virtually none, except that Mrs. Hunter had chosen to call most of her poems 'Song'. As I was about to put the volume aside, my eye caught *The Wanderer*, the supposedly anonymous no. 2 of the second set of songs. Further investigation turned up *The Spirit's Song*, generally regarded as Haydn's best solo song. Apparently no one had thought in the last 150 years to consult Mrs.

Hunter's poems as a source.[122] *The Spirit's Song* poses a problem in that the first edition proclaimed it as the work of Shakespeare. It seems highly unlikely that Mrs. Hunter would have tried to pass off her poem as Shakespeare's, but perhaps she did not bother to tell her friend that she was the author.[123] Did the publisher, who must have known better, expect it would have a better sale with an illustrious name attached? It remains to be said that *O tuneful voice*, inspired by Haydn's departure from London after his second visit, in 1795, was also written by Mrs. Hunter.[124] The authorship of the three remaining songs in the second set of *Canzonettas* is still uncertain. I should like to think that Anne Hunter may also be the author of these (*Sailor's Song*, *Piercing Eyes*, *Content*). It may well be that for *The Wanderer* and *The Spirit's Song* she did not wish to acknowledge her authorship in 1795, but reconsidered her judgement when her volume of poems was ready for publication in 1802. In case of these three songs she may still have thought in 1802 that they were below the level of those she chose for publication. It seems unlikely that another 150 years will pass before their authorship is cleared up.

One more song remains to be listed, and this too involves a false ascription. Robert Franz set seventeen poems of English or Scotch origin to music, nearly all by Robert Burns. One of those ascribed to him is, however, not his work but is by Susanna Blamire (1747–94).[125] This is *What ails this heart o' mine*, translated as *Was pocht mein Herz so sehr?*[126] Another song, which Franz indicates only as Scottish, *Dies und das* ('Wie traurig sind mir Mädchen dran?')[127] I have so far been unable to identify.

Limitations of space have precluded doing much more than enumerating the English poets and the many ballads and lyrics that over the years have stimulated German translators and composers. Certainly no other influence from outside the borders of the German-speaking countries has been so great. If the poetry of the English Romantic movement and its impact on German song-writers is studied in turn, the picture will be complete and doubtless even more impressive.

NOTES

1 Among the most recent is *Shakespeare in Music*, ed. P. Hartnoll. London, 1964.

2 I expect to devote later studies to both Ossian and Burns, and to the English romantic poets as well.

3 Thomas Percy, *Reliques of Ancient English Poetry*, 3 vols. London, 1765.

4 Francis J. Child, *English and Scottish Popular Ballads*, 5 vols., Boston, 1882–98. A convenient abridgement in one volume was edited by G. L. Kittredge in 1904. Attention

should be called to the complete edition of the tunes of the ballads now in progress: B. H. Bronson, *The traditional tunes of the Child ballads*. Princeton, 1959– *.

5 *Von Deutscher Art und Kunst* (1733). His *Werke*, Bd. 5. Berlin, 1891, p. 174.

6 *Volks- und andere Lieder*. Sammlung 1–2. Weimar, 1779; Sammlung 3. Dessau, 1782.

7 *Sammlung deutscher Lieder für das Klavier*. 4te Abteilung. Wien, 1782. *Edward* and the three other Steffan songs hereinafter referred to were reprinted in *Denkmäler der Tonkunst in Österreich*, Bd. 54, Wien, 1920.

8 *Drei Balladen*, opus 1. Berlin, 1824.

9 Opus 165, no. 5. Wien, C. A. Spina [*c.* 1864].

10 *Balladen und Romanzen für zwei Singstimmen*, opus 75, no. 1. Berlin, 1877. Although it lies outside the scope of this study, mention might be made of Tchaikovsky's duet setting of the same text, opus 46, no. 2.

11 *Brahms Briefwechsel*, Bd. XVI. Berlin, 1922, p. 191.

12 *Vier Gesänge aus 'Stimmen der Völker' von J. G. Herder*, opus 58. Breslau, 1876, no.3.

13 *Lieder und Romanzen*, opus 14, no. 3. Leipzig, 1861.

14 Herder's version is also used in no. 11 of Friedrich Grimmer's *Zwanzig Balladen und Romanzen im Volkston*. Leipzig, 1877. I have not seen the song by Alexander Winterberger (1834–1914), his opus 11, no. 6.

15 *Sechs Gesänge aus einer Sammlung englischer und schottischer Poesien*, opus 14, no. 2. Leipzig, n.d.

16 It should be observed that Fontane's *Archibald Douglas*, set to music so effectively by Loewe (opus 128), is an original poem and not a translation from the English.

17 *Balladen und Gesänge*. 8 vols. Nürnberg, 1893–97. Bd. 6, Fontane.

18 This ballad has also been set by A. Becker in his opus 39.

19 *Thomas der Rhymer, altschottische Ballade*, opus 135a. Braunschweig, 1867.

20 *Op. cit.*, Zweyte Sammlung, p. 24.

21 *Oden und Lieder*, Berlin, 1781. vol. III, p. 14. Reprinted in W. K. Jolizza, *Das Lied und seine Geschichte*. Wien, 1910, p. 335.

22 *Schottisches Lied*, opus 46, I, 2.

23 *Vier Balladen von Allen Cunningham*, opus 51. Breslau, 1875.

24 *The Songs of Scotland, ancient and modern*, 4 vols. London, 1825.

25 *Op. cit.*, Erste Sammlung, p. 26.

26 Opus 9, Heft VIII, no. 5. Leipzig, 1834.

27 *Gedichte von Goethe*. Wien, 1890. No. 13.

28 *Zwei heitere Balladen von Goethe*, opus 15. Leipzig, 1919.

29 *Zweite Lieder-Sammlung*. Memmingen, 1780, p. 6.

30 *Gesänge mit Begleitung des Klaviers*. Zürich, 1788. p. 14.

31 Leipzig, 1798.

32 Reprinted in Friedländer, *Das deutsche Lied im 18. Jahrhundert*. 3 vols. Stuttgart, 1902. I, 2 no. 138. Also in Jolizza, *op. cit.*, p. 337.

33 Dritter Theil. Berlin, 1790, p. 48.

34 *Drei Intermezzi für Pianoforte*, opus 117, no. 1. Berlin, 1892.

35 *Ernst Challier's grosser Lieder-Katalog*. Berlin, 1885–1914.

36 *Des Bettlers Tochter von Bednall Green*, in his *Werke*, Bd. 2. Leipzig, 1889, p. 150.

37 *Das nussbraune Mädchen*, opus 43, no. 3. Berlin, 1835.

38 *Op. cit.*, Zweyte Sammlung, p. 4.

39 *Oden und Lieder*. 3 vols. Berlin, 1779–81. Vol. III, p. 18. This does not include the second part, 'Die gordischen Knoten'.

40 G. Wittmann, *Das Klavierbegleitete Sololied C. F. Zelters*. Giessen, 1936, p. 33.

* . . . 1959– indicates last volume not yet published.

41 *Drei Duette für Sopran und Alt*, opus 20, nos. 1–2. Berlin, 1861.

42 *Lieder und Gesänge*, opus 49. Berlin, 1882.

43 *Sechs Gesänge von Scott*, opus 52. Breslau, 1875, no. 6.

44 J. Aikin, *Essays on song-writing*. London, 1774, p. 76.

45 *Volkslieder*, opus 5. Leipzig, n.d., no. 6.

46 Probably a misprint in Challier for Baron von Dalberg.

47 *Volks- und andere Lieder*, Zweyte Sammlung. Weimar, 1779, p. 16 (Bettellied).

48 *Sammlung neuer Oden und Lieder*, vol. 2. Hamburg, 1744, no. 16.

49 *Musikalische Allerley*. Berlin, 1761, no. 18.

50 *Lieder mit Melodien*. Lübeck, 1775. Vol. I, p. 29.

51 *Allgemeines Commers- und Liederbuch*. Rudolfstadt, 1818.

52 Thomas d'Urfey, *Wit and Mirth, or Pills to purge Melancholy*. 4th ed. 6 vols. London, 1719–20. Vol. V, p. 148.

53 Herder's *Werke*. Vol. XXV, p. 336.

54 *Oden und Lieder*. Vol. III. Berlin, 1781, no. 13.

55 *Oden und Lieder. Erste Sammlung*. Dessau, 1784, p. 27.

56 Opus 22, no. 1.

57 *Lieder und Gesänge, 3tes Heft*, opus 15. Wien, [c. 1904], no. 4.

58 Herder's *Werke*. Vol. XXV, p. 509.

59 2 vols. Edinburgh, 1724. vol. I, p. 204.

60 *Oden und Lieder*. Vol. III, p. 8.

61 *Ibid.*, p. 5.

62 First published in Schubert's *Werke*, Series XX, no. 128, in 1895.

63 Schubert, *Thematic Catalogue*. London, 1951, p. 121.

64 *XII Lieder*. Wienn, 1781, no. 1. In Haydn's *Lieder*, ed. P. Mies, München, 1960 (*Werke*, Reihe XXIX, Bd. 1), the text is credited to Sedley for the first time on information supplied by the present writer.

65 4th ed. 6 vols. London, 1719–20. Vol. V, p. 148.

66 C. L. Day and E. B. Murrie, *English Song-Books, 1651–1702*. London, 1940.

67 d'Urfey's false ascription seems less puzzling when we read that he was presented to Sir Philip Sidney, third Earl of Leicester, by Sir Charles Sedley, C. L. Day, *The Songs of Theodore d'Urfey*. Cambridge, Mass., 1933, p. 20.

68 *Thesaurus Musicus*, Book III. London, 1695, p. 5.

69 *Op cit.*, no. 6. Friedländer's statement in his edition of Haydn's songs (*Werke*, Series 20, Bd. I, Leipzig, 1932, p. vii), that Haydn found the text in Steffan's collection, is clearly false, since the latter appeared in 1782. Reprinted in *D.T.O.*, Bd. 54, no. 24.

70 *Lieder mit Melodien fürs Klavier*. Breslau, 1785.

71 Herder, *Werke*, vol. XXV, p. 169.

72 *Fortsetzung auserlesener moralischer Oden und Lieder*. Zürich, 1780.

73 *Oden und Lieder, Dritter Theil*. Berlin, 1781, p. 15.

74 *Sammlung deutscher Lieder*, Vierte Abteilung. Wien, 1782, no. 6. Reprinted in *D.T.O.*, Bd. 54, no. 6.

75 *Oden und Lieder*, Erste Sammlung. Dessau, 1784, p. 4.

76 *Lieder mit Melodien*. Breslau, 1785, no. 19.

77 *Lieder*. Mainz, 1790.

78 *Lieder am Klavier*. Leipzig, 1799.

79 *Op. cit.*, p. 431.

80 Herder's *Werke*, vol. XXV, p. 420.

81 Thomas Whincop, *A compleat list of all the English dramatic poets*. London, 1747.

Quoted in O. G. Sonneck, *Catalogue of opera librettos printed before 1800*. 2 vols. Washington, 1914. Vol. 1, p. 1157.

82 Vol. II, p. 214 (1719 ed.).

83 Seckendorff, *op. cit.*, *Dritte Sammlung*, p. 12. Steffan, *op. cit.*, no. 7.

84 *Lieder mit Melodien*, Breslau, 1785.

85 *Fünfzig Melodien zu den fünfzig auserlesenen Liedern*. Lemgo, 1793.

86 *Op. cit.*, no. XVIII.

87 *Mildheimisches Liederbuch*, Gotha, 1799, no. 407.

88 *Op. cit.*, opus 5, no. 1.

89 Opus 1, no. 16.

90 One version first published as a supplement to the *Wiener Zeitschrift für Kunst*, 1827, the other in his *Werke*, series XX, no. 468 (1895).

91 *English songs*, no. 4. Mainz, 1914.

92 Opus 14. London, [c. 1795].

93 Schubert's *Nachlass*, Book 17, no. 4. Wien, 1832.

94 Opus 9, Heft IV, no. 1. Leipzig, 1828.

95 Opus 1, no. 2. Leipzig, n.d.

96 Opus 27, no. 4.

97 Opus 92, no. 1.

98 Opus 107, no. 1. Leipzig, n.d.

99 Opus 15, no. 6. Berlin, n.d.

100 Opus 17, no. 1.

101 Opus 23, no. 2.

102 Opus 23, no. 4.

103 *Oden und Lieder*, Erste Sammlung. Dessau, 1784, p. 18.

104 *Lied der Königin Elisabeth*, opus 119. Berlin, 1854.

105 *Kleine Balladen und Lieder*, 7 vols. Leipzig, vol. VI, p. 27.

106 Ludwig Landshoff, *J. R. Zumsteeg*, Berlin, 1902, regards the text as anonymous.

107 *Peregrine Pickle, neu übersetzt*. 4 vols. Berlin, 1785.

108 'Smollett's verses and their musical settings in the 18th century', *Modern Language Notes* XLVI (1931), 224–32.

109 *Neun deutsche Lieder*, opus 17. Berlin, 1825, no. 9. *Klag' Gesang nach der Schlacht*.

110 *Fünfzig Lieder*. Leipzig, n.d., no. 49.

111 *Reliques* (1765 cd.), vol. I, part II, no. 18.

112 *A Collection of English Poems 1660–1800*. New York and London, 1932, pp. 868, 1246.

113 *Bürgers Gedichte*. Nürnberg, 1780. II, p. 30.

114 *Lieder und Gesänge beym Clavier*. Berlin, 1780. 3tes Heft, p. 70.

115 *Lieder mit Melodien*. Nordhausen, 1781, p. 6.

116 Berlin, Rellstab [c. 1795].

117 In Krigel's *Quartalschrift, Apollo*. Dresden, 1796.

118 *Sechs Gesänge von Scott*. Breslau, 1875, no. 5.

119 London, 1794.

120 *Original Canzonettas, second set*. London, 1795.

121 Anne Hunter, *Poems*. London, 1802.

122 Mrs. Hunter's authorship of these two songs is first acknowledged in print in Haydn's *Lieder*, ed. P. Mies (see note 64), on information supplied by the present writer.

123 *Des Geistes Gesang (The Spirit's Song)*. *Gedicht von Shakespeare*. Wien, 1804. The German translation is anonymous.

124 *O süsser Ton* (*O tuneful voice*). Leipzig, 1806. The German translation is by **Daniel** Jäger (1762–1802).
125 *Poetical Works*, ed. H. Lonsdale. London, 1842.
126 Opus 9, no. 1.
127 Opus 30, no. 5.

PUTNAM ALDRICH

'RHYTHMIC HARMONY' AS TAUGHT BY JOHANN PHILIPP KIRNBERGER

'I hold the method of Johann Sebastian Bach to be the best and only one; it is to be regretted that this great man never wrote anything theoretical about music, and that his teachings have reached posterity only through his pupils. I have sought to reduce the method of the late Johann Sebastian Bach to principles, and to lay his teachings before the world to the best of my powers, in my *Art of Pure Composition*,'[1]

wrote Johann Philipp Kirnberger in 1782. Few musicians would disagree with the first statement of this quotation. Whether the *Kunst des reinen Satzes*[2] [*Kunst*] is, in truth, a 'reflection of Bach's practical teaching', as Spitta suggests,[3] may be open to some doubt in view of the short period of time that Kirnberger is known to have spent with Bach as his pupil. Be that as it may, the present writer has been enlightened and stimulated by Kirnberger's teaching methods as they are set forth in the *Kunst* and in *Die wahren Grundsätze zum Gebrauch der Harmonie* [*Harmonie*].[4]

Of particular value for the analysis and performance of the music of Bach as well as for the teaching of harmony and counterpoint are Kirnberger's ideas on the subject of rhythm. During his lifetime Kirnberger was known primarily for his theory of the fundamental bass (which differed from Rameau's) and for his concept of essential and non-essential dissonances. Only recently has attention been directed to his attitude toward rhythm as it is revealed in a lesser known work entitled *Recueil d'Airs de danse Caractéristiques Pour servir de modèle aux jeunes Compositeurs et d'Exercice à ceux qui touchent du Clavecin*.[5] The Preface to this collection has been published, with commentary, in an English translation by Newman Powell.[6] The following excerpt is evidence of

37

Kirnberger's concern for rhythm in both composition and performance:

'Each of these dance types has its own rhythm, its phrases of equal length, its accents at the same places in each motif. . . .

If one neglects to practise the composition of characteristic dances, one will only with difficulty or not at all achieve a good melody. Above all, it is impossible to compose or to perform a fugue well if one does not know every type of rhythm; and therefore, because this study is neglected today, music has sunk from its former dignity, and one can no longer endure fugues, because through miserable performance which defines neither phrase nor accents, they have become a mere chaos of sounds.'[7]

In his *magnum opus* [*Kunst*] Kirnberger's discussion of rhythm appears only in the third section of Chapter IV in Part II. The reader will have covered more than 350 pages of the work before he even finds out what Kirnberger means by 'rhythm'. The reason for the late appearance of such an important subject is evidently that the author believed that all musical materials (tones, scales, intervals, chords, keys) and compositional processes (voice leading, cadences, modulation, metre, note values and tempo) must be thoroughly understood before the apprentice composer is ready to tackle rhythm, which is the basis for the construction of an entire musical composition.

Kirnberger explains that the term *Rhythmus* is used in two senses. Sometimes it is applied to the components of rhythm (*rhythmische Beschaffenheit*) such as tempo, metre and note values. 'Through tempo and metre', he says, 'the piece gets its character, whereby a gentle or violent, a sad or joyful sentiment is expressed' [*Kunst* II, 137]. But these have been treated in previous chapters. Kirnberger himself uses *Rhythmus* in the second sense, that is, as a structural force that organizes the phrases, periods and sections that go to make up the form of a complete composition:

'Whoever has even a moderate sense of hearing will have noticed that the greatest strength of music comes from its rhythm. Through rhythm the melody as well as the harmony of several measures are bound together into a single phrase so that the hearing grasps them all at once. And then several short phrases are again gathered together into a larger whole, forming one main sentence at the end of which comes a point of rest

which enables us likewise to understand these several phases all at once.
. . . Just as in spoken discourse only at the end of a sentence has one
grasped its meaning, and through this meaning one is more or less satisfied
according as it is a more or less complete sentence, so it is with music.'
[*Kunst* II, 137]

The musical equivalents of the sentences and clauses of spoken or
written discourse are called by Kirnberger *Abschnitte* and *Einschnitte*,
which may be translated 'periods' and 'phrases'. The period clearly
corresponds to the sentence, since it comes to a complete stop, expressed
in music by a full cadence. Phrases are divisions and sub-divisions of
periods. Kirnberger's definition of phrase is not categorical, but it is
revealing in that it establishes a specific relationship between rhythm and
harmony:

'Each period generally consists of a greater or smaller number of
phrases, which are not cut off or separated from each other as they would
be by cadences, but are nevertheless divided from each other by smaller
points of repose. These small points of repose are marked in the
melody by caesuras or rests, but in the harmony they are produced by
restful chords, especially by dominant chords. Wherever the little point
of repose occurs, at least a new consonant chord must be heard. One
can also use cadence chords, but they must be weakened by inversions
or dissonances so that the pause will not be too noticeable and the ear
will maintain its anticipation of the harmony that is to follow.' [*Kunst* II,
142]

This passage and the one quoted above reveal a number of significant
concepts: (1) the essential quality of rhythm is that it articulates the
structure by means of points of repose or resting places in the flow of
the music; (2) such resting places are obtained in melody by means of
temporal pauses of some sort, but (3) in harmony they are inherent
in the nature of the chords and intervals used. Some chords and intervals
(i.e. consonances) must be regarded as intrinsically restful or static;
others (inversions and dissonances) as non-restful or dynamic. Furthermore, (4) the criterion for determining the degree of motion or rest
inherent in chords and intervals is their effect upon the hearing of the
listener.

Once these principles are accepted, it becomes evident that in order
to plan the rhythmic organization of a work, the composer should be

aware of the relative degree of motion or repose that is imparted to the listener's perception by the various sonorous materials to be used. The attentive reader of Part I of the *Kunst* will have noticed that each category of musical materials and processes has been presented and explained in relation to how it affects the ear of the listener.

Harmony, as taught by Kirnberger, can be regarded as basically rhythmic, and 'rhythmic harmony' seems an appropriate name for this phenomenon, though Kirnberger did not use the term himself. 'Harmonic rhythm' has been defined as the rate of speed at which changes of harmony occur during the course of a piece. 'Rhythmic harmony' has no specific temporal implications, but refers to the quality of movement or rest transmitted through individual harmonies or progressions. The assumption upon which Kirnberger bases his theory of rhythmic harmony is extremely simple: that perfect or complete harmony implies repose to the listener because his ear is satisfied and expects no further movement; imperfect or incomplete harmony implies movement because the ear is not satisfied and cannot rest. The ramifications of this principle, however, will be seen to be pertinent to almost every aspect of composition, analysis, and even to the performance of eighteenth-century music. By following through Kirnberger's exposition, it is possible to situate every interval, chord and harmonic progression in a hierarchy of rhythmic functions. The following summary, extracted from various portions of the *Kunst* and *Harmonie* is given partially in direct translation and partly, to save space, in paraphrase of Kirnberger's text.

Intervals [*Kunst* I, 23 ff.]. Melodic intervals are classified as easy (*leicht*) or difficult (*schwer*); harmonic intervals as consonant or dissonant. Experience teaches us that intervals that are consonant in harmony are the easiest in melodic progression. Therefore, one must find out the degree of consonance and dissonance of each interval. This is determined by the ratios of the vibrating strings that produce them. The most consonant intervals are those whose ratios are the easiest to grasp. The ratio of the unison (1 : 1) is the easiest of all for the ear to grasp, just as the equality of two adjacent lines is the easiest relation for the eye to perceive. The unison is therefore the most consonant interval. Next to the unison, the perfect octave (ratio 1 : 2) is the most concordant interval; for the ear hears two, but not two *different* tones (*zwei aber nicht zweierley Töne*). Then follow the still perfect 5th (ratio 2 : 3) and 4th (3 : 4), and, in order of decreasing consonance, the major 3rd (4 : 5), the minor 3rd (5 : 6), the major 6th (3 : 5) and the minor 6th (5 : 8). All other intervals are dissonant, and give no immediate pleasure or satisfaction to the ear. The ratio of the major 2nd (8 : 9), for instance, is too hard for the ear to perceive, just as the eye can scarcely discern the fact that of two adjacent lines one is one ninth [*sic*] longer than the other. In a Table on page 19 of *Kunst* I all intervals, diatonic and chromatic, are classified according to the ratios that produce them.

Consonant Triads. Kirnberger's system of instruction is based on a synthesis of vertical harmonic progressions derived from thoroughbass practice[8] and a linear counterpoint consisting essentially of figurations of chord progressions. Every melody, he believes, is accompanied by a harmony suited to it. Even when listening to a single voice, as in an aria, one hears various accompanying tones. Thus, every musical composition is based on a series of chords. The whole of harmony consists of two basic chords from which all others are derived—namely, the consonant triad and the essential dissonant seventh chord [*Harmonie*, pp. 2 and 3]. 'The consonant triad can take three forms: major, minor or diminished. (See Example 1a.)

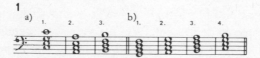

The first, with major 3rd, perfect 5th and octave over the root, has the most perfect (*vollkommenste*) harmony and brings about the greatest restfulness (*Beruhigung*). It is therefore used at the beginning of a piece to announce the key and at the end of a piece or section where, through its perfection, it produces complete rest. The minor triad is somewhat less perfect, but can still be used to begin or end a piece. The diminished triad is not perfect enough to set the tonality or to end a piece or even a phase [*Kunst* I, 34].

Inversions [*Kunst* I, 39]. The 3rd or the 5th of a triad may be used as the bass note, in which case the chord is said to be an inversion (*Verwechslung*). The consonant triad with the root (*Grundton*) in the bass produces the most perfect harmony and is most satisfying to the ear. The 6-chord, or first inversion, is not so complete, and the ear expects and awaits a chord with more perfect harmony. It can be used at the end of a phrase but not as the final chord of a period. The six-four chord, or second inversion, is the least perfect of the consonant chords; a phrase can neither begin nor end with it [*Kunst* I, 39].

The Harmonic period [*Kunst* I, 91 ff.].

'Chords, in music are like words in speech. Just as a number of connected words expressing a complete thought make a sentence, a number of connected chords ending with a cadence make a harmonic period; and as a number of connected sentences make a paragraph, a number of connected periods make a complete piece (or section) of music.'

Chords can have two kinds of connection with each other: a general or broad relation and a particular or narrow relation. The general relation is that they belong to the same mode and key and that the ear perceives this. This demands that the first chord in the series should impress upon the ear a certain diatonic scale in a major or minor mode and that the following chords, their roots as well as their intervals, should belong to this scale.

The narrow relationship of chords requires that the root of each successive chord should be closely allied to that of the preceding chord. The closest relationship between two tones occurs when they form the interval of a perfect 5th, for it is well known that every tone carries with it the sensation of its fifth. The lower sound of the 5th is the fundamental; the upper is dependent. When the bass descends a 5th, the 5th returns to its source. The relationship existing between two 5ths also exists between their harmonies.

The best, that is to say, the most connected progression of the fundamental bass is, therefore, the fall of a 5th or the rise of a 4th. The rising 5th is also a close connection (though not so close) because the 5th, being already contained in the first chord, prepares the ear for the second. In *Harmonie* (p. 50 f.) Kirnberger gives a list of the best, or in his terms the 'most natural', progressions for the fundamental bass: first, motion by 5ths and 4ths, secondly by 3rds and 6ths, and the weakest by rising 2nds.

Example 2 shows four different settings of a harmonic period on the same fundamental bass.[9] The connection of the chords is 'natural', since the bass moves in 4ths and 5ths with one descending 3rd. Examples 2a and 2b use only consonant triads in root position. Even in these simple harmonizations a rhythmic difference can be observed, arising from the dispositions of the intervals forming the chords. Example 2a is faulty because 'in the upper voice only perfect consonances are heard against the bass, so that the hearing is satisfied with each chord as if it were the end, and has no reason to expect anything further' [*Kunst* I, 146]. The second example (2b) is more dynamic, for the 3rds between the outer voices are not restful (*beruhigend*) and further progress is therefore expected. The third example (2c) brings the chords into a still closer relationship through the use of inversions, whose imperfect harmony 'arouses the expectation that more consonant chords will follow. The most beautiful continuity of harmonies is that in which the hearing is continually awaiting a more perfect harmony, which will not arrive until the end of the whole period' [*Kunst* I, 93].

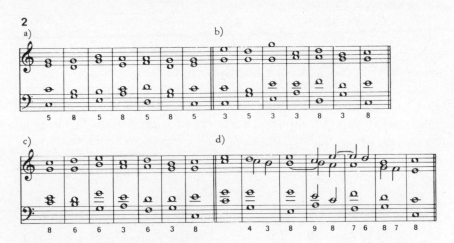

Non-essential (*zufällige*) *dissonances* [*Kunst*, I, 27–30]. Sometimes, in order to arouse in the hearing a desire for a certain harmony the tones of the chord are not sounded all at once against the bass. Instead, one or more tones of the preceding chord are held over, forming dissonances and making the ear wait for their resolution. These suspension dissonances must be resolved before the fundamental bass moves on to another harmony. They are called 'non-essential' because they can be omitted without causing any errors or ambiguities in the basic harmonic progression. Example 2d shows 4ths, 7ths and 9ths that are heard on the strong beat *instead* of the consonances to which they resolve. They do not belong to the chords with which they are heard, their sole value being their rhythmic capacity for leading the ear from one harmony to the next.[10]

Essential (*wesentliche*) *dissonances* [*Kunst*, I, 30]. Seventh chords and their inversions are necessary and can be called essential because they do not take the place of consonances but maintain a place of their own as chords. Like non-essential dissonances they must be prepared and resolved, but whereas suspensions resolve to the same harmony with which they are heard, seventh chords cannot resolve until the harmony changes. The rhythmic distinction is that suspensions make the ear wait for their resolution on a weak beat, while seventh chords prevent the ear from resting on the present harmony and carry it to that of the next root tone, regardless of whether the latter appears on a strong or weak beat. It will be noted that in Example 2d the seventh in bar 5 is non-essential but the seventh in bar 6 is essential.

The essential seventh chord can take four forms, as shown in Example 1b: No. 1, minor 7th with perfect 5th and major 3rd: No. 2, minor 7th with perfect 5th and minor 3rd: No. 3, minor 7th with diminished 5th and minor 3rd: No. 4, major 7th with perfect 5th and major 3rd.

The first is the least imperfect; it adds only a minor 7th to the major triad. No. 2 is more imperfect because the minor 3rd is less perfect than the major 3rd. No. 3 is still more imperfect because the diminished 5th is less perfect than the perfect 5th. No. 4 is the most dissonant, because the major 7th is more dissonant than the minor 7th. Inversions of seventh chords are imperfect in the same order—that is, the first second and third inversions are progressively less perfect and more dissonant.

Cadences [Kunst I, 94–100].

'If a period is to be all in one key the last chord must be the tonic triad. As in a sentence of speech one anticipates the last word before it is actually spoken, and one perceives that now the completion of the sense is about to take place, so in the perfect cadence of a harmonic period the feeling of the last chord is awakened beforehand. Therefore, the most perfect cadence will be that in which the penultimate chord will be the fifth of the tonic, and this cadence will have the greatest perfection if the penultimate chord contains the 7th, because for its resolution the final tonic will become absolutely necessary [Example 3a]. . . . The final cadence will be somewhat less perfect if, instead of the dominant, the penultimate chord is based on the subdominant [Example 3b]. It sometimes happens that this cadence is combined with the foregoing perfect cadence, thus confirming the complete repose with a double close' [Example 3c].

In a long period, smaller points of rest occur in the harmonic progression, so that the hearing is not completely satisfied but is required to

11

remain in suspense for some time. Strictly speaking, the ear finds some rest in every consonant triad, because this harmony is so perfect that it does not demand anything further. One can, therefore, make a little resting place without any further organization. This little rest is more noticeable when the triad is on a tone that forms a perfect consonance with the tonic, especially when this tone is approached by a consonant skip. In this case the repose is so noticeable that it is called a half cadence [Example 3d].

A third type of cadence occurs when an unexpected progression is heard after the dominant, which is followed by a chord other than the tonic; this is called by the Italians *Inganno*, or deceptive cadence (Example 3e).

The three types of cadence can be modified in many ways by which the feeling of rest is weakened, and thereby a great variety of resting places is obtained solely through cadential harmonic progressions, as follows: (1) inversion of the penultimate dominant; (2) inversion of the cadence chord itself; (3) delaying the cadence chord to a weak beat, thus producing the 'feminine' cadence that is characteristic of Gavotte rhythms [*Kunst*, I, 142]; (4) inclusion of the dissonance of a seventh in the cadence chord.

The fourth method is capable of almost indefinite extension. 'The first and most characteristic (*vornehmste*) effect of the seventh is that it postpones the repose or ending of a period that would otherwise be felt' [*Kunst*, I, 60]. In Example 4, for instance, three cadences are avoided

prior to the final cadence on A: namely, measure 3 would be a half cadence on G, measure 4 a perfect cadence on C, and measure 7 a half cadence on E if the chords did not contain sevenths. Example 4 also illustrates the functions of each of the four types of seventh chord shown in Example 1b. Approaching a cadence the harmony becomes progressively more perfect. Therefore, the proper positions of the four progressively more dissonant seventh chords are progressively farther away from the cadence. The most consonant seventh, No. 1, immediately precedes the final cadence and the expected cadence on C in bar 4. The No. 1 sevenths in bars 3 and 7 are preceded by No. 2 and No. 3 respectively, while the most dissonant No. 4 sevenths are farthest removed from any real or expected cadence [*Harmonie*, p. 6, n. 1].

The practical application of Kirnberger's theory of rhythmic harmony is eloquently illustrated in twenty-six different harmonizations of a single period of the chorale melody, *Ach Gott und Herr, wie gross und schwer sind mein begangne Sünden* [*Kunst* II, 22 ff.]. The articulation of the period into three phrases is already established by fermate in the melody. Kirnberger's intention is to show a great number of ways in which the articulation points may be varied by giving them more, less, or no rest at all, solely through choice of harmonic progressions. Space does not permit the quotation of all twenty-six examples but the first four arrangements, shown in Example 5 will demonstrate the principles involved.

The harmonization of the first example follows literally the pauses marked by the fermate through the use of dominant and tonic chords with perfect consonances in measures 2 and 4. These chords, however, create too great a feeling of rest on the words *Herr* and particularly on *schwer*, where the sense of the text is incomplete. This would induce the singers to stop too long at these points, thereby dragging out the performance unduly. The harmony also lacks variety, since only tonic, dominant and subdominant chords are used.[11] The harmony of No. 2 is better suited to the text, for the imperfect consonances and deceptive cadences in bars 2 and 4 suggest that a continuation is expected. This setting also acquires more harmonic variety than No. 1 by introducing three new chords in bars 2, 4 and 7.

Example 5, No. 3 introduces a foreign dominant chord in the first full bar, which immediately awakens the heightened attention of the listener. The continued use of C♯, F♯ and E-natural causes the key of B flat to waver, and keeps the listener in doubt as to the tonality until the final cadence in D minor, which is still weak enough to ensure continuity to the next phrase of the chorale. The inversions of seventh chords in bars 1, 3, 4, 6 and 7 produce a dynamic harmony throughout the period.

In the fourth example the 6–5 chord in the second bar completely cancels any harmonic pause on the word *Herr* in spite of the cadential quality of the melody. The first two phrases are thus contracted into one. The 4–2 chord in bar 3 binds together the words *gross und schwer*, as is fitting for the expression of the text.

In all twenty-six examples of the chorale setting the rhythmic harmony is adjusted to the sense of the words insofar as the points of rest correspond to the caesures and clauses of the text. Yet each version projects a slightly different interpretation of the text, arising from the various *degrees* of motion and rest implied by the harmony.

In the absence of a text the composer is not bound by any rule governing the length of phrases and periods except when he is employing dance rhythm [*Kunst*, II, 140]. As Kirnberger apprises us, however, in the

Receuil d'airs de danse quoted at the beginning of this essay, dance rhythms permeate all types of music in the Baroque era—even fugues and sacred music.[12] The musician who has followed Kirnberger's advice to practise the composition and performance of characteristic dances will have observed that the chorale *Ach Gott und Herr* is actually based on the rhythm (although not, of course, the tempo) of the bourrée. A characteristic rhythm for the bourrée is a phrase eight beats long, beginning with an up-beat and ending with a definite stop on beats 7 and 8. The eight-beat phrase is often broken into two parts, with a temporary resting place on beats 3 or 4 or both. The dancers move, more or less alternately, on the level of the pulse (or division of the beat) and on that of the beat. If the chorale in question were to serve as a bourrée it would be written with a different metre and smaller note values, as shown in Example 6.

The beat would be on the level of the half-note, and the eight-beat phrase would be divided into two similar step patterns, as indicated by the brackets. (L and R stand for left foot and right foot, T (thesis) for a pause with feet together.) The points of articulation, or rest, marked with a cross, would be the same as in the chorale.[13]

These outward features of the bourrée are easy enough to discern and to imitate, as are the structural features of many other dances that were popular in the early eighteenth century, such as the gavotte, rigaudon, minuet and passepied. To achieve any degree of refinement in the inner structure, however, or to write twenty-six correct but different bourrées on the same tune one would need to be familiar with many dances of the same type, and to give due consideration to rhythmic harmony as well as to *rhythmische Beschaffenheit*.

There appears, in *Harmonie* (pp. 52–103), a detailed analysis of J. S. Bach's Fugue in B minor from the *Well-Tempered Clavier* I—a piece which 'up to this day has seemed insoluble to the great men of our time' (notably Marpurg). This is, indeed, a *tour-de-force* of harmonic analysis.[14] It elucidates the synthesis of thoroughbass and counterpoint that is the major premise of all of Kirnberger's teaching. It also presents a breakdown of the hierarchy of rhythmic functions of chords and intervals by splitting them into three separate levels of harmonic perfection and imperfection.

The first six bars, containing the first entries of subject and answer are reproduced in Plate I. Directly under the keyboard score of the Fugue as Bach wrote it appears another keyboard score containing a figured *continuo* bass with its realization in complete four-part harmony. This thoroughbass 'accompaniment' is not purely theoretical but is set in a practical texture that could be played on a second harpsichord simultaneously with the Fugue. It represents the continuous series of chords that Bach presumably had in mind before he selected from them the notes suitable to construct the individual contrapuntal melodies of the fugue.

On the staff below this realization the mildest form of harmonic imperfection—that arising from inversions of chords—is subtracted, leaving a fundamental bass composed of the root tones of all the harmonies. Here the figures pertaining to inversions are eliminated, but those indicating nonessential dissonances and seventh chords are retained. Some of the figures are necessarily changed; a tone that is a 6 for an inversion becomes a 3 in relation to the root; the sharp 4th of a third inversion becomes the sharp 3rd of the root, etc.

On the lowest staff the figures referring to non-essential dissonances are eliminated, leaving only the roots of consonant triads and essential seventh chords, and confirming Kirnberger's postulate that 'all of harmony consists of only two basic chords from which all others are derived'. The reader may at first be disconcerted to find that the root tone frequently does not appear at all in the *continuo* realization. In most cases this results from Kirnberger's consistent interpretation of the diminished seventh (which is not recognized as a chord) as a non-essential 9th over a seventh chord whose root is a 3rd below the bass and not heard.

If anyone wonders by what means short of reading Bach's mind this fundamental bass could have been arrived at, the answer is actually quite simple. Kirnberger starts with the assumption that Bach thought exclusively in terms of harmonies whose roots move 'naturally'—that is, by 4ths and 5ths, with occasional descending 3rds and rising 2nds [*Harmonie*, p. 43]. This being the case, Kirnberger claims that the interpretation given here provides the *only* fundamental bass that will solve the apparent harmonic difficulties (*Schwierigkeiten*) involved in obtaining correct resolutions for all the seventh chords. [*Harmonie*, p. 53.]

Plate 1

With such an analysis the rhythmic functions of the harmonies can be followed from chord to chord in great detail. The sevenths on the lowest staff obviously represent the strongest rhythmic activity, since every essential seventh or sequence of sevenths inevitably leads to some sort of cadence on the next note that lacks a figure, which always stands for a consonant chord. The non-essential dissonances indicated on the staff above modify the rhythm by postponing the moment of repose (e.g. the 4-♯ suspensions on beat 1 of bars 2 and 5, and the 6–5 suspensions on the last beats of bars 2 and 5). The *continuo* bass is fully figured. When the non-essential dissonances of the staff below it have been subtracted it specifies the inversions of triads and seventh chords. If one remembers that first, second and third inversions are progressively less perfect, the precise degree of relative perfection of each successive harmony, and consequently the degree of motion and/or repose imparted to the rhythm by each harmony become apparent.

Kirnberger has demonstrated how the concept of rhythmic harmony can be applied to the teaching of composition, and how analysis of eighteenth-century works along these lines can lead to a clearer understanding of their inner structure. Judging from the remarks quoted above from the Preface to his *Recueil* it appears that performing musicians of 1777 had already lost contact with the musical style of the generation of J. S. Bach: '. . . one can no longer endure fugues because through miserable performance which defines neither phrase nor accents they have become a mere chaos of sounds'.

This description, unfortunately, seems equally applicable to many performances of Baroque music that we hear today. The twentieth-century motoric concept of rhythm has led to a uniformity of motion which obliterates the 'small points of repose' that Kirnberger considered essential to permit the listener to grasp the sense of individual phrases, accents and periods. Everything that Kirnberger has to say about rhythm leads one to the conclusion that such motoric, rhythmically undifferentiated performances of Bach and other baroque composers are distortions of the true Baroque style. I have found, in my teaching experience, that if the performer adjusts his temporal execution to the harmonic qualities that he has discovered through analysis the component elements of phrases and periods will be more clearly delineated, and that the performance will gain immeasurably in rhythmic vitality.

NOTES

1 Johann Philipp Kirnberger, *Gedanken über die verschiedenen Lehrarten in der Komposition als Vorbereitung zur Fugenkenntnis* (Berlin: G. J. Decker, 1782). Quoted in Eng. trans. in H. T. David and A. Mendel, *The Bach Reader*, rev. ed. (New York, 1951), p. 262.

2 Johann Philipp Kirnberger, *Die Kunst des reinen Satzes in der Musik* (2 vols.; Berlin and Königsberg: Decker & Hartung, 1774–76).

3 Philipp Spitta, *J. S. Bach* (Eng. ed. reprint; New York, 1951), III, 117.

4 Johann Philipp Kirnberger, *Die wahren Grundsätze zum Gebrauch der Harmonie* (Berlin and Königsberg: Decker & Hartung, 1773).

5 Subtitle, 'Partie I, consistant en XXVI pièces' (Berlin: J. J. Hummel, n.d.). The titles of the twenty-six pieces, their keys and time signatures are quoted in Siegfried Borris-Zuckerman, *Kirnbergers Leben und Werk und seine Bedeutung im Berliner Musikkreis um 1750* (Berlin, 1933), pp. 58, 59.

6 Newman W. Powell, 'Kirnberger on Dance Rhythms, Fugues, and Characterization,' in *Festschrift Theodore Hoelty-Nickel* ([Valparaiso, Indiana] Valparaiso University, 1967), pp. 65–76.

7 Powell's translation, *ibid.*, p. 69.

8 As an introduction to the *Kunst*, Kirnberger subsequently published an instruction book in thoroughbass: *Grundsätze des Generalbasses als erste Linie zur Composition* (Berlin, 1781).

9 Example 2 is based upon the models given in *Kunst*, I, 93, 146. Kirnberger's original models have here been slightly altered in order to adjust them all to the same fundamental bass.

10 Note, however, that other contemporary theorists (e.g., Marpurg) apply the term 'non-essential' to dissonant passing notes, changing notes, etc., which Kirnberger considers ornamental and treats in the section on *verziehrten oder bunten Contrapunkt* [*Kunst*, I, 189 ff.]. Kirnberger's 'non-essential' suspensions, on the other hand, are regarded as 'essential' by Marpurg and others. *Cf.* 'The Harmonic Theories of Kirnberger and Marpurg' by Joyce Mekeel, in *Journal of Music Theory*, Yale University, New Haven, IV, 2 (November 1960), 169–93.

11 Kirnberger regards the diminished 6–3 chord in bar 3 of this example as a 6–4–3 chord of which the 4th is missing but understood [*Kunst*, I, 47, 69–70]. In more modern parlance he attributes to this chord a 'dominant function'.

12 Kirnberger is by no means the only eighteenth-century writer to make this observation. *Cf.*, for instance, Johann Mattheson's discussion of the use of dance rhythms in composition, and his examples of the transformation of a chorale melody into various types of dances, in *Der vollkommene Capellmeister* (1739), pp. 161 ff.

13 The rhythm and dance movements of the bourrée and other court dances are described by Meredith Ellis in 'The Dances of J. B. Lully' (unpublished Ph.D., dissertation, Stanford University, 1967).

14 It appears that this analysis was actually worked out, under Kirnberger's supervision, by his pupil, J. A. P. Schulz. *Cf.* J. Mekeel, *op. cit.*, p. 183, n. 4.

EVA BADURA-SKODA

CLEMENTI'S 'MUSICAL CHARACTERISTICS' OPUS 19

The Haydn Yearbook 1963–64 issued among the smaller reports a very short article by Alan Tyson, 'Clementi as an imitator of Haydn and Mozart' (p. 90 f.), in which Tyson referred to Clementi's opus 19. This work was printed for the first time in 1787 under the following title: 'Clementi's Musical Characteristics or A Collection of Preludes and Cadences for the Harpsichord or Piano Forte Composed in the Style of Haydn, Kozeluch, Mozart, Sterkel, Vanhal and The Author . . .'.

Tyson started his article with a brief description which we would like to repeat here: 'Each of the composers mentioned on the title is represented by two "preludes", each of some forty or fifty bars, and one "cadence" (cadenza) of perhaps half that length. The material itself is somewhat desultory. Runs and arpeggios abound, and there are frequent modulations and changes of tempo. But none of the pieces contains a sustained melody, and though there is a measure of thematic play in some of the preludes, the phrases are only fragmentary and are usually quickly abandoned. It is therefore hard to find an internal association between either preludes or cadences and any particular works of the composers in question.' We wholeheartedly agree with Tyson when he then continues: 'Our reaction is bound to be one of disappointment . . .'.

In spite of this judgement we consider it worthwhile to draw attention again to Clementi's opus 19, mainly for two reasons:

1. Clementi, himself an interesting musician, must have had a reason to compose this work which, by the way, was printed quite often during his lifetime: eleven issues appeared, published by Longman & Broderip, London, August 1787; Boyer, Paris, 1788 (Affichement December 1787);

53

Imbault, Paris, 1788; Schott, Mainz, c. 1789–90; André, Offenbach, c. 1789–90; Le Duc, Paris, 1791; Artaria, Vienna, 1793; Longman, Clementi & Co., London, 1799(?); Muzio Clementi & Co., London, after 1801; Cappi, Vienna, 1804; Breitkopf & Haertel, Leipzig, after 1807 (as part of the 'Complete Edition' which this firm had started not only for Haydn and Mozart but also Clementi).[1] If we do not suspect Clementi to have written and published his opus 19 merely for commercial reasons, faking knowledge of the 'Extempore-Style' of his well-known colleagues, we have to assume that he must have met and heard personally all the composers mentioned in the title. This opens some new aspects on biographical data for the lesser-known composers among those mentioned.

2. Since the many known accounts of Clementi's personality and character do not give us any reason to doubt his reliability, and since there also can be no doubt that in the eighteenth century the terms 'Preludes and Cadences' referred usually to extempore-playing, we should consider this set of pieces as one of the few examples of written-down improvisation such as were customary at that time. The question of how much we are confronted merely by Clementi's own improvisational style and how much he was able to imitate his colleagues (and was even interested in this) is another point. Perhaps our initial disappointment with this work comes from the impression that Clementi was neither successful in being humorous nor successful in imitating the various composers' styles as we know them today. But he tried to be both as we want to prove later.

Starting with the biographical investigations and the questions when and where Clementi might have met the composers involved, we want to refer with regard to Haydn to an article by Georges Saint-Foix, 'Clementi and Haydn' (*The Musical Quarterly*, XVIII, 1932), in which Saint-Foix expresses the opinion that both masters must have met in Vienna in 1781–82. A letter from Haydn to Artaria in 1783 served as a basis for this conviction. Haydn wrote: 'Many thanks for the pianoforte Sonatas by Clementi, they are very beautiful; if the author is in Vienna, please present my compliments to him when opportunity offers.' During the winter Haydn usually was able to stay a short time in Vienna. For the winter in question, however, it seems that he came to Vienna only in December. Letters of Haydn to Zürich and Donaueschingen are dated: 'Vienna, 3rd. December 1781'.[2] A letter to Artaria dated January 4, 1782, however, was already written from Eszterháza but the content makes it clear that he had just left Vienna. Therefore, it is possible that Haydn met Clementi before he left for Hungary since Clementi's arrival must have taken place before or on December 24th, the day of the competition with Mozart before the Emperor. Clementi's and Haydn's meeting might well have occurred in a private home where it is also more likely to believe that Haydn sat down at a piano or another keyboard instrument to improvise or demonstrate a composition. Among Haydn scholars it is usually pointed out that Haydn neither considered himself a virtuoso on the piano nor appeared in public as such. However, we do know that he could play the piano well and that he did improvise. According to Dies his daily routine was to sit down at the piano immediately after breakfast and to improvise (*er phantasierte solange*) until he had found those musical thoughts needed for his intentions which he then wrote down, and Griesinger reports Haydn's remark: 'I was not a bad clavier player.'[3]

There is little reason to doubt that Clementi met Kozeluch. Both must have been interested in becoming acquainted with each other since both were well-known piano virtuosi and Kozeluch apparently liked to give musical *soirées* in his home. O'Kelly, who came to Vienna in 1783, recalls in his *Reminiscences* (1826) his first meeting with Mozart at Kozeluch's home:

'...I went one evening to a concert of the celebrated Kozeluch's, a great composer for the piano-forte, as well as a fine performer on that instrument. I saw there the composers Vanhall and Baron Dittersdorf; and, what was to me one of the greatest gratifications of my musical life, was there introduced to that prodigy of genius—Mozart. He favoured the company by performing fantasies and capriccios on the piano-forte. His feeling, the rapidity of his fingers, the great execution and strength of his left hand, particularly, and the apparent inspiration of his modulation, astounded me. After his splendid performance we sat down to supper, and I had the pleasure to be placed at table between him and his wife...'[4]

During his following stay in Vienna in 1802, and possibly also in 1807, Clementi gave piano lessons to Kozeluch's daughter Barbara.[5] Kozeluch's house might also have been the place where Clementi met Vanhal.

Mozart's and Clementi's competition at the Imperial Court is a well-known story. According to Clementi, shortly after his arrival in Vienna he received an invitation to play for the Emperor on the *forte piano*, and, when entering a room of the castle, was introduced to Mozart. Both were asked to play. Clementi started and, after first playing a free fantasy (*nachdem er eine zeitlang praeludiert hatte*), played a sonata.[6] When later asked by his pupil Berger about Mozart's and his own playing, he commented: 'I never before had heard anybody playing so full of *esprit* and grace; I was especially surprised about his [Mozart's] adagio playing and some of his extemporized variations, for which the Emperor had chosen the subject and which we had to vary alternatingly, accompanying each other'. Whether he heard Mozart's extempore playing on another occasion than this is not known for sure. But Mozart gave a concert in the [Burg-?] Theater on March 3, 1782, in which he played not only parts of *Idomeneo* and a piano concerto but also a free fantasy. According to O. E. Deutsch, he did this latter especially because of Clementi who then gave up the idea of giving a public *Akademie* himself.[7] The Emperor Joseph must have been impressed by both players. Dittersdorf reported in his autobiography a conversation which the Emperor started about this competition, and a whole year later Count Zinzendorf wrote in his diary that the Emperor had again spoken about this event.[8]

New light is shed on the biography of Clementi as well as that of Sterkel through Clementi's 'Musical Characteristics' if we take for granted that Clementi must have met Sterkel personally. Sterkel spent the years from 1779 until 1782 in Italy from where he returned to Mainz in the autumn of 1782. As we know from a number of unpublished letters from Sterkel to Artaria and Padre Martini, which are now kept in Viennese libraries,[9] Sterkel spent the early spring of 1782 in Venice, from where he wrote to Artaria that he hoped to meet him personally after Easter in Rome. His next preserved letter to Artaria is dated September 28, 1782, and was mailed from Milan. Sterkel had just arrived there and had to tell Artaria that the latter's letter mailed to Naples had missed him since he had to leave Naples already on May 13th. Sterkel soon had to rush back to Mainz; he had to travel via Tyrol and Augsburg, and not—as he had hoped—via Venice and Vienna.[10] From this correspondence we can guess that Sterkel spent some days in May and perhaps the greater part of the summer in Rome. It is there that he most likely met Clementi, who had not visited his parents and his home town since 1766, when at the age of 14 he followed an English gentleman to London. Until now the only known event in Clementi's biography in 1782 after he had left Vienna in May was a stay in Lyons, where he played on August 29th and where he might afterwards have spent some time before returning to London,[11] where we find him in 1783. Since he did not return to the Continent before publishing his opus 19, he could have heard Sterkel's playing only in Italy.

The second reason to investigate Clementi's opus 19 more thoroughly than done before is partly connected with our lack of evidence and sufficient knowledge of the art of improvisation as cultivated in Haydn's and Mozart's time. Only a few attempts of contemporary observers who tried to preserve this art are known, and most of them only left us verbal descriptions and no music.[12] Therefore we should not overlook the few hints Clementi's opus can give us. Even more interesting is the question of Clementi's motivation for composing his opus 19 and whether it was meant—at least partially—as a *compositio humoris causa*.

Now it is time that the reader gets an impression of Clementi's 'Preludes'. Therefore, one of the preludes 'alla Mozart' is reproduced herewith (pp. 57f.) It proves that Clementi indeed tried to imitate

Preludio à la Mozart I

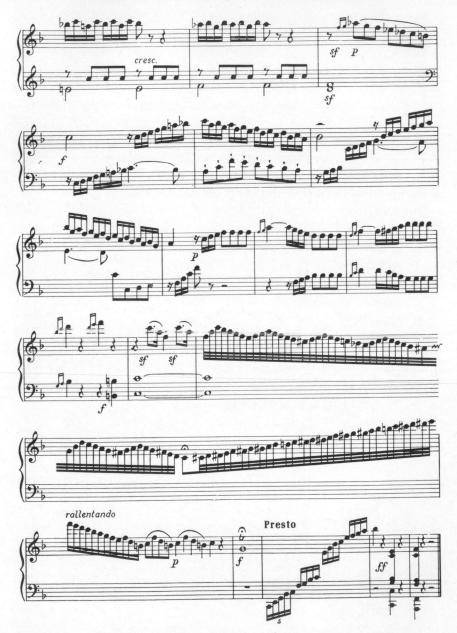

Mozart's style though with only limited success. Scattered around are
Mozartean sounding motifs and figures otherwise not found in Clementi's
works in such an accumulation. We are, however, more reminded of

Beethoven than of Mozart when, in the *Preludio II alla Mozart*, we come across a passage like this:

It justifies the observation of Saint-Foix that Beethoven learned from Clementi and not only vice versa. (Regarding Mozart, where Saint-Foix repeatedly claimed the same, his statements are less convincing.)

In the *Cadenza alla Mozart* Clementi clearly uses a subject known from the first movement of the A major Concerto, K. 414, which, by the way, Mozart employed a second time in the cadenza of the Concerto K. 488:[13]

What had Clementi in mind when writing these preludes and cadenzas? Were the pieces meant as parodies, as banter, or did he seriously study the style of his famous contemporaries and then feel that he should convey his knowledge through a publication and should make money from it? That an influence of the style of the Viennese masters on Clementi was observed by the contemporaries, we know from Cramer's *Magazin der Musik*, where we read: '. . . His [Pleyel's] pleasant cantabile on the piano is not as difficult as Clementi's or Mozart's sorceries [*Hexereien*];

he is more natural than they without violating the rules of good composition. Of Clementi it is certain that during his stay in Vienna he learned from many German composers, mainly Haydn, Mozart and Kozeluch; for from this time onward his newest works exhibit German character and a more correct treatment of middle parts . . .'[14]

In order to answer the above question, an analysis of one or another piece will be helpful. Let us, for example, take the *Preludio II alla Haydn*. It starts with a C major arpeggio and a little motif:

No well-known Haydn work begins this way. One cannot immediately recognize this motif as being taken from a Haydn piece unless one *wants* to find a relationship of this commonplace, but not especially Haydnesque, motif with one of his themes. In that case one could mention the Finale of Haydn's Symphony No. 73, 'La Chasse', which was composed *c*. 1781 and issued in London in 1786 by Forster ('The celebrated La Chasse in all its parts . . .'):

While playing not only this but all Clementi Preludes it is most disturbing for the musicians of today that the preludes fall apart into too small sections. In this specific prelude the next three bars have little to do with the opening motif. The following bars (6–7) show a rhythm which

already reminds us of the well-known Haydn C major Sonata which most of us have played as piano students (maybe the only Haydn sonata— shame on our teachers!). The matter becomes more obvious in the following bars and clear in bars 29–31. The model for this banter of Haydn was the 1st movement of the Sonata Hob. XVI/35. Clementi ('alla Haydn'): bars 29–31

Haydn: bars 13–14

The many Alberti figures in triplets found in this sonata are also imitated by Clementi, though they were normally not used as often by Haydn as by other composers at that time. And now the main motif is recognized as a paraphrase of Haydn's motif in bars 20–21.:

Instead of the expected *forte* chord in C major, Clementi finished the piece with a *pianissimo* ending, a repetition of the opening three bars. This 'persiflage' of a Haydn sonata, which had just become popular in Vienna being the first and easiest sonata of a collection issued by Artaria in 1780, also indicates Clementi's humorous intent.

In the copy of the André print of Clementi's opus 19 which is owned by the Austrian National Library, there are some handwritten changes in this prelude. After the opening three bars there are inserted four bars of rests with the indication '*Andante*' (the tempo for the whole piece is *Allegro*). The fourth bar again starts with an '*Allegro*'. The same insertion of rests and the tempo changes are found after bar 8. One can imagine that a performance of the Prelude in this way created a funny effect.

That the contemporaries realized the comic intentions Clementi

apparently wanted to achieve in his opus 19 we know from a review
which was issued in Bossler's *Musikalische Korrespondenz der teutschen
Filharmonischen Gesellschaft*[15]:

'We can take this collection of preludes for nothing other than a humorous
parody. A new product in its way! It is only desirable that it is not
imitated by those who do not have the genius of a Clementi. . . . That the
author imitated the favourite manners of the composers in question and
imitated them well, everybody can assume from the title alone. In order
to give our readers the possibility to get an idea of these preludes we
shall reproduce the one on page 8 [*Preludio alla Kozeluch*] and we shall
leave it to the impression of each reader to solve this musical enigma.'

The funniest effect and perhaps the best results in being humorous
Clementi reached in imitating Sterkel, whose peculiar style of playing was
parodied by more than one famous composer: we know that Beethoven
also was tempted to imitate Sterkel whom he visited in 1791. Wegeler
reports about this visit:

'Beethoven at that time had never heard a great excellent piano player
and did not know the fine shading [*Nuancierungen*] in treating the
instrument—his playing was rough and hard [*rauh und hart*]. Then he
came on a trip from Bonn to Mergentheim . . . to Aschaffenburg where he
was brought to Sterkel by Ries, Simrock and the two Rombergs. At the
request of the visitors Sterkel played. His playing was light and very
pleasant and, as Father Ries expressed it, somewhat lady-like. Beethoven
stood beside him with the tensest concentration. Then he was asked to
play . . . To the great surprise of all listeners, he did this perfectly and
exactly in the same pleasant manner which he had observed with Sterkel.'

Simrock also recalled this event in a letter to Schindler:

'. . . to the great surprise of all from Bonn who were present who had
never heard him [Beethoven] play in this way, he played completely in
the manner of the *Kapellmeister* with the utmost grace, brilliance and
lightness . . .'[16]

In Clementi's preludes 'alla Sterkel' we repeatedly find the indications
'*Allegro ma con Espressione*', '*Allegretto dolce e con molto espressione*', etc.,
and dynamic markings also change rapidly. After only one bar of '*Allegro
molto*' come 7 bars of '*Allegretto ma grazioso e dolce*'. The last bar is
marked '*Rallentando con espressione*'. In *Preludio II* we again find

'*Presto*' and changes of *forte* and *piano* signs four times per bar, and again '*Con molto grazia*' indications among passage work which is strikingly meaningless. And Sterkel could not possibly have been pleased with the homage paid to him by Clementi in the last five bars of the second prelude:

It seems that Clementi had more respect for Vanhal and Kozeluch than for Sterkel. He apparently remembered Vanhal mainly for still using too many of the traditional virtuoso harpsichord effects, while Kozeluch was teased with a meaningless, funny-sounding afterthought which ends *Preludio I*. This prelude in E flat major starts with a 'Grave' and brings in bar 3 a motif (repeated in bars 10 and 11), which seems to stem from Kozeluch's Sonata opus 15/2 in G minor.

Clementi, *Preludio I alla Kozeluch*:

Kozeluch, Sonata in G minor opus 15/2, first movement, bar 10 (and others):

The subject in the following 'Allegretto' in 6/8 rhythm in Clementi's prelude seems to be a reminiscence of the main subject of the second movement of Kozeluch's Sonata.

In the imitation of his own playing Clementi's sense of humour also comes out, but only if interpreted with wit and effective imitation of his showing off with virtuoso brilliance. We have to realize that the way of interpretation was—and is—most responsible for creating such effects. Clementi belongs in general to those composers who need brilliant performers to bring out the otherwise hidden excellence of their works. There have always been musicians who fascinated their audiences more than they moved them. The merits of their compositions are more easily spoiled by uninspired performances. Especially in this collection of free fantasies[17] and cadences, brilliant piano playing is needed desperately to guarantee a success. Maybe this was the reason why Clementi, when revising his opus 19 for the 'Complete Edition' of his works in 1807 added many brilliant passages, runs in octaves, etc. (The autograph of this revision is preserved in the Library of Congress, Washington.) It seems that while altering he was interested in achieving brilliant rather than humorous effects, neglecting even more than before proper stylistic imitations, and thus not increasing the value of his pieces. (The revised text was not used for the 'Complete Edition'.)

About his playing before the Emperor, Clementi remarked to Berger in 1806 that before coming to Vienna he had trained himself mainly in virtuoso playing and in brilliant passages in parallel thirds which were not in use before his time. We find indeed a long passage in parallel thirds in *Preludio II alla Clementi*:

Berger continues his report: 'It is worth mentioning that it is characteristic of Clementi to insert longer and very interestingly composed thematic episodes [*Zwischenspiele*] and cadenzas at the places of fermatas of his sonatas. This might have been the reason why he chose to play a sonata at the competition . . .'[18] Mozart's and Clementi's way of improvisation must have differed considerably. When Mozart played his sonatas, we now believe—and we have good reasons for doing so—that he did not insert cadenzas at most of the fermatas, and, in the rather exceptional cases, when he might have done it, he probably kept his fermata ornamentations much shorter than Clementi's. On the other hand, when Mozart announced a free fantasy in his concert programmes, we might assume that he played much longer and more elaborate pieces in a stricter form than his Italian contemporaries. As it was stated by listeners of Beethoven that he liked the rondo form for his extemporized pieces, we can guess that Mozart favoured the variation form. One hint in this direction we get from his report about the competition with Clementi:[19] '. . . He [Clementi] improvised and then played a Sonata . . . I improvised and played variations . . .' Perhaps Mozart's piano variations are those works known to us wherein we can get the closest impression of what he played when improvising. However, it must be stated that the Fantasies for Piano of Mozart which he wrote down afterwards showed strongly the influence of the old toccata form, especially K. 394 and 395 which, by the way, were called by Mozart 'preludio'. The unfinished C minor Fantasy K. 396 has the form of a sonata exposition. Only in Mozart's last piece for mechanical organ do we find a variation of an E flat major Andante subject.

In the eighteenth century many collections of cadenzas, preludes or capriccios were written (and some of them also published) which show a structure similar to Clementi's opus 19. These collections served the purpose of supplying those dilettante performers lacking skill in composing with effectful sounding preludes and cadenzas, the former needed, for example, for trying out an instrument, etc., the latter for insertion in concertos, sonatas and arias. These cadenzas were more or less unthematic but used commonly known motivic material and, therefore, could be played or sung everywhere. Best known today are the collections of specifically difficult violin cadenzas such as those of Locatelli, Tartini or Campagnioli; but usually the cadenza collections contained much easier, less virtuoso pieces, such as those of Ferdinand Kauer (contemporary print in the Austrian National Library, Music Department, Vienna). It is well possible to imagine that Clementi's opus 19 was published for a reason similar to the above-mentioned cadenzas and capriccios, maybe even suggesting to the customers that the pieces could help them in finding suitable ideas for 'improvised' cadenzas in the works of the composers mentioned in the title. The title-page of the André edition might be understood this way ('Preludes dan diferrens tons . . . dans le goût de Haydn Kozeluck etc.'). And this pragmatic purpose might have guided Clementi in 1807 when he was revising his old opus.

NOTES

1 For the English editions see A. Tyson, *Thematic Catalogue of the Works of Muzio Clementi*, Tutzing 1967, p. 57. (The British Union Catalogue dates the Longman, Clementi & Co. issue as 1799?); for the French edition see Cari Johansson, *French Music Publisher's Catalogues of the Second Half of the Eighteenth Century*, Stockholm 1955, vol. I, facsimilia 38, 76 and 101, vol. II, p. 131; the edition of Schott (copy in Österreichische Nat. Bibl. MS 42373) has the publisher's number 96; André's edition with the number 295 contains only the Preludes. The title reads: *Preludes dans diferrens [sic] tons pour le Clavecin ou Piano Forte, composee dans le goût de Haydn Kozeluck etc. par Clementi*. The copy owned by the Österr. Nat. Bibl. (Sign.: S A 86 D78) shows some handwritten alterations; in Artaria's edition, which copies the French title, the words 'et l'Auteur' are missing from the title, but Preludes and Cadenzas 'alla Clementi' are included (other omissions and printing mistakes shows the specific carelessness of Artaria's engraver); the Cappi edition was known to Pohl, who mentioned it in his biography of Haydn, vol. II, p. 295 n.; Breitkopf & Härtel issued Clementi's opus 19 in vol. XII, p. 36.

2 See H. C. R. Landon, *The Collected Correspondence and London Notebooks of Joseph Haydn*, London 1959, pp. 42 and 33.

3 See V. Gotwals, *Joseph Haydn Eighteenth-Century Gentleman and Genius*, a translation of the *Biographische Notizen über Joseph Haydn* by G. A. Griesinger and the *Biographische Nachrichten von Joseph Haydn* by A. C. Dies, Madison, 1963, pp. 204 and 63.

4 Quoted after O. E. Deutsch, *Mozart Die Dokumente seines Lebens*, Kassel, 1961, p. 454. (Translated by the Author.)

5 See J. G. Reichardt, *Vertraute Briefe, geschrieben auf einer Reise nach Wien 1808/09*, 2 vols., edited by G. Gugitz, vol. II, p. 21 n.

6 For this and the following quotation, see M. Unger, *Muzio Clementis Leben*, Langen-salza 1914, p. 27 f.

7 Deutsch, *op. cit.*, p. 176. Deutsch does not give a source for this statement. Though no public concert of Clementi is known, he must have played at least in private homes where Dittersdorf had an opportunity to hear him. See also Mozart's letter to his father dated January 23, 1782. The remark of Deutsch that Clementi left Vienna soon after Mozart's concert in March is not quite correct since we know from Mozart's letter dated May 8, 1782, that Clementi was still staying in Vienna but intended to leave on the following day.

8 For Dittersdorf see p. 110 of the edition Erfurt 1816. The diary of Count Zinzendorf was used by O. E. Deutsch; see *op. cit.*, p. 184.

9 Mss. in the Vienna Stadtbibliothek (I. N. 70688–I. N. 70696) and in the Handschriften-Abt. der Österr. Nat. Bibl. (VII 109).

10 See above, letter to Padre Martini.

11 See Unger, *op. cit.*, p. 33.

12 A noticeable exception to the rule is Mozart's K. 528a (Anh. C 27 .03), the attempt of a priest who had heard Mozart and who tried to write down an extemporized 'Fuga' which

Mozart played on an organ of a monastery near Prague. The 57-bar torso is reproduced in *Die Musik*, vol. X (1910), p. 106 f.

13 A. Tyson tried to prove that there was a possibility for Clementi to have known Mozart's A major Concerto K. 448—an unnecessary attempt, since this subject stems obviously from the already printed concerto K. 414. An error of Tyson's must be his claim that there is 'another apparent allusion' between the *Preludio II alla Mozart* and the Rondo K. 485; at least I cannot discover any resemblance.

14 Translated from the German. See 2. Jg., 2. Haelfte, p. 138 f., as an excerpt from a letter.

15 No. 4 (July 28, 1790); translation by the author.

16 Both quotations after L. Schiedermair, *Der junge Beethoven*, Leipzig, 1925, p. 213 f.

17 In H. Chr. Koch's 'Musikalisches Lexikon' of 1802 we find the following explanation of the term 'Praeludiren': 'to play a prelude. One uses this expression partly for the usual prelude of the organist before playing the hymns [*Choralgesaenge*] and partly to designate any extemporized fantasy' (translated from the German by the author). Many treatises were written to teach the beginning musicians in the art of improvisation, e.g. by Grétry; 'Méthode simple pour apprendre à préluder'.

18 See Unger, *op. cit.*, p. 29.

19 Letter to his father from January 22 1782. Mozart's sharp remarks about Clementi's somewhat shallow virtuosity can be considered as a justified judgment from his point of view and were certainly not a matter of jealousy as still claimed in MGG vol. 2, col. 1488.

IRMGARD BECKER-GLAUCH

JOSEPH HAYDN'S *AVE REGINA* IN A

———

C. F. Pohl mentions in his 'Chronological-Thematic list of Joseph Haydn's works composed in the years 1766–90' under B.m. 'Smaller Works of Church Music' twenty-one compositions.[1] Among the works of this kind 'evidently belonging to the time before the seventies'[2] (m. 5–10) he lists an *Ave Regina* in A (m. 7) which he briefly characterizes as an 'occasional work of the better kind'.[3] While Alfred Schnerich's list[4] of the 'Smaller Sacred Works' is clearly based on Pohl's, J. P. Larsen was the first to take a critical attitude toward Pohl's catalogue[5] by scrutinizing the source material available. The work under discussion is mentioned by Larsen as one of those existing in 'good copies' and he lists the Gesellschaft der Musikfreunde in Vienna as owner of the source.[6] In the list of Haydn's works compiled in *Die Musik in Geschichte und Gegenwart*, Larsen and H. C. R. Landon count the *Ave Regina* in A among the sacred works the authenticity of which may be claimed with great probability.[7]

The recent Haydn literature does not supply any more information on this work, except for references to three new sources subsequently to be dealt with in our study. Karl Geiringer,[8] whose study on the 'Small Sacred Works by Haydn in the Esterházy archives at Eisenstadt' offers the most significant contribution to this hardly explored area of Haydn's output, had no reason to mention the *Ave Regina* in A, as the work is not to be found among the copies in the Eisenstadt Castle or in the Archives of St. Martin, the Eisenstadt *Stadtpfarrkirche*.[9] The tradition regarding this work must therefore have started at another place.

A clear proof for the authenticity of the work is not available. No autograph has been preserved nor is the work mentioned in Haydn's so-called *Entwurf-Katalog* ('draft catalogue'), mostly autograph, or in the 'list of all those compositions that, as nearly as I can remember, I composed from my 18th to the 73rd year' which Haydn had compiled by his copyist and servant, Johann Elssler.[10]

Since the Haydn Institute began in 1955 systematically to build up its collection of source material,[11] no less than eleven contemporary copies of the *Ave Regina* in A have been unearthed.[12] All of them employ a solo soprano, mixed chorus, two violins and organ (mostly with violone). A few local peculiarities of the setting will later be mentioned.

Our main question is at first: which composer is indicated in these manuscripts. The name of 'Giuseppe Haydn' ('Giuseppe Hayden') is supplied by five sources:

(1) Vienna, Gesellschaft der Musikfreunde, I. 7841;
(2) Vienna, Austrian National Library, Music division, S.m. 23 108;
(3) Mariazell (Styria), Benedictine Priory, Ms. 300;[13]
(4) St. Florian (Upper Austria), Augustine Prebendary Monastery, 6/227a (listed in the catalogue also under 229a); and
(5) Ljubljana, Yugoslavia, University Library, Mus. N 794.[14]

To these handwritten parts may be added a single score

(6) in the Austrian National Library, Vienna, Music division, S.m. 15 785, with the indication 'Jos. Haydn' as author.

The word 'Haydn' ('Hayden') without Christian name is to be found in two manuscripts:

(7) Lilienfeld (Lower Austria), Cistercian Monastery, 256; and
(8) Budapest, Hungarian National Library Széchényi, Ms. mus. IV 74.[15]

No composer is mentioned on the title page of the copy in

(9) Kremsmünster (Upper Austria), Benedictine Monastery, Ser. F, Fasc. 5 No. 143.

The original title page is lost in

(10) Melk (Lower Austria), Benedictine Monastery, III. 98.[16]

It proved impossible to trace a manuscript known in 1950 to the former Haydn Society of Boston-Vienna, from

(11) Geras (Lower Austria), Premonstrant Monastery.

In view of those sources we may consider as assured Joseph Haydn's authorship of the work. In the numerous lists of Michael Haydn's works available in photographic copies to the Haydn Institute the work is not mentioned at all. A manuscript dated 1759 and preserved at Mariazell of an 'Ave Regina [in A] /â/Soprano Solo/Violinis 2^bus^/Organo/Cum/ Violone/Auth^re^ Sig^re^ Giov: Michael Hayden'[17] refers to another work, without a chorus.

A surprising feature of Joseph Haydn's work is the use of two different antiphons of B.M.V. as text. We find 'Ave Regina coelorum' in the manuscripts mentioned under (1), (3) and (10); 'Salve Regina, Mater misericordiae' in those mentioned under (4) to (7), (9) and (11); both texts together in the manuscript (2), originally as 'Salve' and subsequently changed to 'Ave' in (8). Though the question regarding the original text would seem to be answered by the preponderance of 6–8 'Salve Regina' manuscripts as compared to 3 'Ave Regina' sources, a closer scrutiny has revealed that only the 'Ave Regina' represents the original text. In the following two examples 'Ave Regina' was inserted as first text, 'Salve Regina' as second.

The arbitrary word repetitions, the errors in declamation (especially with 'Jesum') and the meaningless textual interpretation (*cf.* the crotchet rest between 'benedictum' and 'fructum' breaking up the connection) clearly reveal that the 'Salve Regina' text cannot have been the original one.

On the strength of this statement we allot significance of the first rank to those sources which use only the 'Ave Regina' text: the copies in Vienna (Gesellschaft der Musikfreunde) (1), Mariazell (3) and Melk (10), while those manuscripts using both texts—Austrian National Library (2) and Budapest (8)—should be considered to be of secondary importance.

Among the above-mentioned sources only the Mariazell manuscript is dated and this together with a most significant subsequent entry on the cover referring to a donation.[18] It reads: 'Obtulit Don[um] Tenorista /R:R P:P: Michaelensiu[m] Vienna,/et filia ejusde[m] 11 annoru[m]/ belle decantavit. 7̄6̄3̄.' Accordingly the owner of the manuscript received it in the year 1763 as a present from a tenor who was associated with St. Michael's—or more clearly with the Barnabites at St. Michael's[19]—in Vienna and whose 11-year-old daughter sang this *Ave Regina* beautifully.

The tenor, whose name is not mentioned, was in all likelihood Johann Michael Spangler who on Haydn's sudden expulsion from the Vienna Cantorei, offered him shelter.[20] Spangler was from 1749 to about 1764 tenorist at St. Michael's in Vienna next to which stands the Michaelerhaus in which Haydn resided for some time in the seventeen-fifties. Spangler's oldest daughter, Maria Magdalena Rosalie, was born on September 4, 1750.[21] The performance of the *Ave Regina* by the 11-year-old girl which is mentioned with such praise in the entry referring to the donation of 1763, must therefore have taken place around 1761–62. We know that Joseph Haydn engaged in 1768 this daughter of his benefactor as third descantist for the Esterházy court musicians. In the same year the 17-year old sang at the premiere of Haydn's *Dramma giocoso Lo speziale* on August 5th the demanding part of Grilletta.[22] As Haydn entrusted her with other important assignments, she must have been a highly gifted singer.

We might add that Haydn himself was not unknown in Mariazell. When he undertook a pilgrimage to the miraculous shrine of the Virgin in Mariazell[23] around 1750, he succeed in drawing attention to his musical abilities.

As point of departure for dating the *Ave Regina* in A the following is to be considered: before 1763 (according to the entry about the donation), before 1761–62 (according to indication of Magdalena's age). Examination of the Mariazell material points to an even earlier origin.

Several watermarks in the parts written by different copyists date from the fifties. That in the tenor part is, for example, identical with a watermark found by Eineder for 1754.[24] The watermarks of other papers even point to *c.* 1750, 1751, 1753.[25] According to the watermarks, the manuscripts in Kremsmünster and Lilienfeld may likewise have originated in the fifties.[26] The fact that not only one, but three manuscripts of different origin are available on paper proved to have been used in the seventeen-fifties, assures an approximately correct dating. Thus the *Ave Regina* in A may have been composed and circulated as early as the middle fifties. As the two manuscripts in Kremsmünster and Lilienfeld belong to the 'Salve' version, it seems evident that the textual change was carried out at an early stage.

The work's early origin deduced from the sources is fully confirmed by its style.

Haydn's *Ave Regina* in A starts with a large coloratura aria in *Andantino*, 2/4 time. Here one idea rises organically from the other; an unending flow of meaningful variety denotes in this work Haydn's early style. As in the two arias of the *Salve Regina* in E, whose autograph Haydn subsequently dated with 1756, here, too, we have not a *da capo* aria, but a kind of recapitulation free of any schematism. In the A major piece, for instance, the return of the thematic material by the orchestra is introduced in A minor, capped by the long-held high E of the solo soprano. As a contrasting middle section of the three-part composition[27] there follows a short choral piece 'Gaude Virgo gloriosa' in 4/4 Allegro, enlivened by the violin figures surrounding it. The choral setting which at first is homophonic, is later loosened by imitatory entrances, to which suspensions add harmonic spice. As in the *Salve Regina* in E the work is concluded by a piece for solo soprano and chorus: in the *Ave Regina* an *Adagio* in 3/4 time. Apart from the contrast between the soulful *cantilena* of the solo soprano and the warm *tutti* sound of the chorus, another feature here creates diversity of impression. The clearly cut contours of the *unisono*—particularly significant in interludes of Haydn's early works[28]—powerfully detach themselves from the broken chords of the accompanying *pizzicato* strings and lead from the soprano solo to the entrance of the chorus.

In his book on Joseph Haydn's Masses, C. M. Brand[29] designates the chapter devoted to the *Salve Regina* in E as Haydn's 'Italian period'. To be sure, in the work under discussion Haydn has largely adopted characteristic features of the Neapolitan style he encountered in various guises as Porpora's accompanist and copyist. However, he recast them into a powerful personal idiom. Here he advanced into areas of musical expression which may be termed as unconventional.

Like the *Salva Regina* in E the *Ave Regina* in A may—according to its stylistic character—have originated while Haydn studied with Porpora, thus around the middle seventeen-fifties.

The *Ave Regina* in A, as yet unpublished,[30] was a favourite in the eighteenth-century repertoire of sacred music. This is proved by the numerous manuscripts in existence. The work was even commercially available at an early date, for the Viennese copy of the Gesellschaft der Musikfreunde (1), dated according to the watermarks[31] from the middle sixties—show a price indication of '3f'(=3 Florins). The copy at Geras (11) has the date of 1773. The latest seems to be the copy of the score in the Austrian National Library (6) which, according to the nature of the penmanship, probably originated around 1800.

The Mariazell manuscript is the only one to reveal on the cover various performance dates from 1765–1826.[32] At an early stage 2 trombones were added[33] in Mariazell to the original setting in order to support the contralto and tenor parts of the chorus. Among the parts in the Austrian National Library (2) there is also one for tenor trombone. In the manuscript of St. Florian (4) the work shows a subsequent adaptation for tenor solo instead of soprano solo.[34] According to the remark on the title-page 'Ex Rebus Anton Stoll /R[egens] Chori Baadae' the parts were originally the property of Anton Stoll, the teacher and choral conductor in Baden near Vienna, for whom Mozart in all likelihood composed his famous *Ave verum* (K. 618).[35]

NOTES

1 C[arl]F[erdinand] Pohl: *Joseph Haydn*. 2. Band. Leipzig, 1882 [*Anhang*], p. 10 f. Here is the only thematic list of such Haydn works which has so far appeared in print.

2 *loc. cit.*, p. 334.

3 *loc. cit.*, p. 334.

4 Alfred Schnerich: *Joseph Haydn und seine Sendung*. 2. Auflage. Zürich-Leipzig-Wien, 1926, p. 194. In this list, which lacks numbers and thematic incipits, Schnerich's Nos. [5–25] correspond to Pohl's Nos. 1–21. Schnerich's Nos. [1–4] refer to works treated by Pohl only in the text of his monography.

5 Jens Peter Larsen: *Die Haydn-Überlieferung*. Copenhagen 1939, p. 289 f.

6 Pohl too, keeper of the Society's archives, knew only this source (as is revealed in his handwritten card index preserved in the Gesellschaft der Musikfreunde), and so did Robert Eitner (*cf.* his *Biographisch-Bibliographisches Quellen-Lexikon der Musiker und Musik-*

gelehrten christlicher Zeitrechnung bis Mitte des 19. Jahrhunderts, 2. verbesserte Auflage, vol. 5, Graz, 1959, p. 67).

7 Article on Haydn in vol. 5, Kassel and Basel, 1956, col. 1891. In Grove's *Dictionary of Music and Musicians*, 5th Edition, London–New York, 1954, vol. IV, p. 169, the *Ave Regina* in A is listed under the doubtful works.

8 Karl Geiringer: 'The small sacred works by Haydn in the Esterházy archives at Eisenstadt', in *Musical Quarterly*, XLV, New York, October 1959, pp. 460 ff. Karl Geiringer: 'Sidelights on Haydn's activities in the field of sacred music', in *Bericht über die internationale Konferenz zum Andenken Joseph Haydns, veranstaltet von der Ungarischen Akademie der Wissenschaften*. Budapest 7.–22. September 1959, ed. by B. Szabolcsi and D. Bartha. Budapest, 1961, pp. 49 ff. Karl Geiringer: 'Joseph Haydn als Kirchenmusiker. Die kleineren geistlichen Werke des Meisters im Eisenstädter Schloss' in *Kirchenmusikalisches Jahrbuch*, 44. Jahrgang, Cologne, 1960, pp. 54 ff.

9 Likewise there is no indication about the work in 'Inventarium /uiber die hochfürstlich/ Esterházyschen Kirchen = Musicalien/zu Eisenstadt/Anno 1858' (so-called Zagitz list, original in Princely Esterházy Archives, Eisenstadt) or in the 'Kirchen Musicalien /Inventarium /Ddo 5ten October 1837' of the Eisenstadt Stadtpfarrkirche. (Original lent to the Austrian National Library, Vienna.)

10 Cf. Jens Peter Larsen: *Drei Haydn Kataloge in Faksimile*. With introduction and supplementing thematic list. Copenhagen, 1941.

11 Cf. Georg Feder: 'Die Überlieferung und Verbreitung der handschriftlichen Quellen zu Haydns Werken' (1. Folge) in *Haydn-Studien, Veröffentlichungen des Joseph Haydn-Instituts, Köln, hg. von Georg Feder*, Band I, Heft 1. München-Duisburg, 1965, p. 3 ff. In English translation in: *The Haydn Yearbook*, IV, Wien-London-Zürich-Mainz-Milano, 1968, pp. 102 ff.

12 The following remarks are based on this collection of sources. For stimulating discussions about this work the author is greatly indebted to Dr. Georg Feder, director of the Joseph Haydn Institute. She extends her thanks for description of certain manuscripts to him, to her colleagues Dr. Günter Thomas and Dr. Horst Walter, as well as to Dr. Friedrich W. Riedel, formerly director of the R.I.S.M. central office at Kassel, and Prof. Dr. Hellmut Federhofer, Mainz (formerly Graz, Styria), for permitting us to examine, in 1958, his card catalogue of Haydniana in Mariazell.

13 Cf. Renate Federhofer-Königs: 'Zur Musikpflege in der Wallfahrtskirche von Mariazell/Steiermark', in *Kirchenmusikalisches Jahrbuch*, 41. Jahrgang, Cologne, 1957, p. 132.

14 Cf. G. Feder *loc. cit.*, p. 32 f.

15 Cf. *Haydns Werke in der Musiksammlung der Nationalbibliothek Széchényi in Budapest, herausgegeben anlässlich der 150-sten Jahreswende seines Todes 1809–1959*, Budapest, 1959, p. 101, no. 109.

16 The original title was not subsequently replaced by a calligraphic copy as happened frequently with manuscripts in Melk. The late Ernst Fritz Schmid noted around 1935 on the cover 'J. Haydn /Ave Regina'.

17 Cf. R. Federhofer-Königs *loc. cit.*, p. 132, where, owing to the survey-like character of the report on the rich holdings of the Mariazell church, the source could only briefly be mentioned.

18 The following remarks on the Mariazell manuscript were first made by the author within a lecture on 'New Research on Haydn's sacred music' given at the annual meeting of the members and curators of the Joseph Haydn Institute on May 8, 1967. The lecture will appear in vol. II of the Haydn Studies quoted in footnote 11 above.

19 Cf. C. F. Pohl: *Joseph Haydn*, 1. Band. Berlin, 1875, p. 119.

20 Pohl, *loc. cit.*, p. 117 f.

21 Pohl *loc. cit.*, p. 118.

22 *Cf.* Joseph Haydn *Werke*, ed. by the Joseph Haydn Institute, Cologne. Series XXV, vol. 3, München-Duisburg, 1959, preface.—Johann Harich: 'Esterházy-Musikgeschichte im Spiegel der zeitgenössischen Textbücher', in 'Burgenländische Forschungen', hg. vom Burgenländischen Landesarchiv, Heft 39. Eisenstadt, 1959, p. 32. Article Spangler, in *Die Musik in Geschichte und Gegenwart*, vol. 12. Kassel-Basel-London-New York, 1965, Column 975.

23 *Cf.* Pohl, I, p. 121 f.

24 Georg Eineder: 'The Ancient Paper-Mills of the Former Austro-Hungarian Empire and Their Watermarks.' Hilversum MCMLX, no. 297.

25 Watermarks resembling those in Eineder, *loc. cit.* no. 757, 41,772.

26 Watermarks resemble those in Eineder, *loc. cit.* no. 334 (proved for 1753) and 43 (proved for 1757).

27 Alois Fuchs in his 'Themathisches Verzeichniss/der/sämmtlichen Compositionen/von/ Joseph Haydn/. . . Wien 1840' (Berlin, Deutsche Staatsbibliothek, Mus. ms. theor. K. 606, fol. 61r), mentions erroneously: 'consists of 4 movements'.

28 *Cf.* Joseph Haydn: *Hymnus de Venerabili* I–IV, ed. by Irmgard Becker-Glauch. First edition. Munich-Duisburg, 1965. The composition considered as lost originated about the time of Haydn's *Stabat Mater* (1767).

29 Carl Maria Brand: *Die Messen von Joseph Haydn*. Würzburg-Aumühle, 1941, pp. 16 ff.

30 First edition by author in preparation.

31 Identical with Eineder's no. 1693 (proved for 1764).

32 R. Federhofer-Königs who did not quote the entry regarding the donation, mentions as first legible date of performance the year 1766. However, the year 1765 is to be seen five times, 1766 four times, 1769 five times; up to 1774 there are altogether twenty-one performances dates; from 1808(?) to 1826, six more. Regarding the title the following note should be made: The original title read only: 'Ave Regina . . .'. The words 'Salve vel' written above it were added subsequently. The two soprano parts (the older has four pages, the later seven pages) contain, however, only the text of the 'Ave Regina'.

33 Watermarks of these two parts similar to Eineder's no. 772 (proved for 1753).

34 The original 'Soprano Solo' and 'Tenore-Ripi[eno]' are not available any more.

35 Cf. *Chronologisch-Thematisches Verzeichnis sämtlicher Tonwerke Wolfgang Amade Mozarts . . . von Dr. Ludwig Ritter von Köchel. 6. Auflage, bearbeitet von Franz Giegling, Zürich, Alexander Weinmann, Wien, Gerd Sievers, Wiesbaden.* Wiesbaden, 1964, p. 705.

WOLFGANG BOETTICHER

ON VULGAR MUSIC AND POETRY FOUND IN UNEXPLORED MINOR SOURCES OF EIGHTEENTH-CENTURY LUTE TABLATURES

After Johannes Wolf[1] had first investigated the source material, the author honoured in this volume presented the basic iconographic study on lute instruments[2] as well as a specific terminological study,[3] which helped to direct the attention of scholars to the lesser members of the lute and guitar families. The most important representatives in the ultimate phase of tablature, *i.e.* the eighteenth century, were the *Colascione* (*Galichon*) and the diminutive forms of a 'small' lute (*lutina*), the *Mandürchen* or *Mandora*, the *Quinterne* as a smaller guitar-type and the *Cittern*. Regarding the description of these instruments and their rubrication we may refer to Curt Sachs.[4] We know that for these lesser representatives of the lute and guitar families a small size was by no means the rule. The Colascione had an unusually long neck combined with a comparatively small body. Striking is, however, its small number of strings (number of courses) which presupposes a less advanced technique of playing. This may have been equally the case with the other subordinate members of the group. This feature has in certain cases led to the formation of a specific repertoire characterized by certain sociological aspects: while the tablatures of lute, theorbo and angelica (usually equipped with a large number of strings) refer mainly to use in aristocratic circles, those of the subordinate instruments may exhibit pieces taken from vulgar music, a fact that has not yet been sufficiently explored. The author, stimulated by Geiringer's former research, should therefore like to discuss a few handwritten tablatures which present the rare case of an origin in artisan-farmer circles. They are largely missing in the classic source collections established by J. Wolf and R. Eitner. As a matter of fact they were not even quoted completely in a more recent catalogue[5] attempted by this author. The entire body of lute and guitar tablatures including all subordinate forms will before long be presented with the most important bibliographical data.[6] Some of the internal problems not likely to be discussed in such a catalogue are to form the subject of this report, the rest to be dealt with in a subsequent study. We limit ourselves at present to manuscripts from a repertoire largely in German language.

By and large features of vulgar art were not lacking in earlier lute practice. The intavolator dealt also with the *cosa bassa* and the craftsman's approach of a middle-class citizenry is clearly noticeable in such prints as those by H. Gerle and H. Neusidler. On the other hand a significant cooperation by scholars may be noticed (V. Galilei, J. B. Besardus). In the late phase of lute composition during the first half of the eighteenth century a 'lower' social stratum may be observed only in rare, hidden cases, such a connection being hardly plausible in view of the highly advanced performances on the main instrument with its 11–14 courses.

We should like first to direct attention to some galichon tablatures not listed by Wolf, but treated by R. Lück in his valuable unprinted dissertation.[7] The MS. 39 of the State and City Archives of Amberg (Upper Palatinate) seems to come from the old holdings of the Salesian Monastery which in the year of secularization, 1804, also offered two galichons for auction. The 191 movements written around 1730 are close to, partly even in direct accordance with, the two MSS. 1272, 1 and 1272, 2 of the Prince Fürstenberg Library at Donaueschingen in which 23 and 22 suites are presented (246 and 188 movements), written around 1735 and originating at Biberach near Wertingen (environs of Augsburg). To these may be added MS. A.R. 778 of the former Proske Library which is held at Regensburg: 48 movements from a somewhat later time (1750–60) arranged only at the beginning in the manner of suites. All these sources display as a common feature aspects of an origin in middle-class, non-aristocratic circles. Of course one finds there the favourite French-type dances such as Minuet, Bourrée, Gavotte and—as a typical feature of these tablatures—more antiquated forms such as Intrada, Praeambulum, Fantasia, Ciacona. However, there is a striking appearance of grotesque dances from the area of South German vulgar music. They appear partly under the heading 'German Dance' and the subtitle 'The merry hanswurst', 'Silly Peterl', 'Master Hammerle' (a marionette figure), and more rarely with the Italian designation '*Arlequinate*' (which after 1720 is often to be found in tablatures for plucked instruments). Even under as neutral a title as 'Trio' a vulgar theme is hidden (Incipit: 'Foolish Liesel'). The beginning of other songs reveals criticism of the time (*Cupido du bankhrter* [=bankrotter] *Bue*—'Cupid thou bankrupt boy'). The lack of knowledge of French which as a rule is unusual in tablatures— is revealed by the spelling the rather awkward writer employs: he writes *Bahbiet* (for Babette), *Franquez* (for Français), *Palletto* (for ballet); the latter movement has the subtitle 'Hanswurst and Columbina'. Expressions used in Italian comedy are more familiar to him ('H. Signore Pantaleone'). By and large there is a substantial occurrence of simple song-types outside the minuet-form.

Other galichon manuscripts deal with a more artistic setting for ensembles. They prove that the instrument, which was in demand because of its sharper tone, was really at home in courtly circles. We might mention the *Serenate* from the former private collection of the Saxonian king at Dresden[8] and a fascicle at Brussels[9] containing fragments of a movement which employs a duo of galichons. The instrument which, according to a description in 1650 was equipped with 2–3 courses, while it boasted 6 courses in 1740, flourished but briefly; there are no representative prints in existence.

Not much insight is provided by mandora tablatures which, though destined for an instrument with a flatter, smaller body, require playing on 8 courses. The repertoire of MS. 3242 of the State and University Library, Hamburg (burned in 1943) keeps to the conventional Aria, Variatio, Menuet, Marche, Capriccio. Likewise the German arias in Ms. mus. 40146 of the Berlin State Library (among others the graceful movement *Die Grasmücke*—'The warbler') and MS. mus. 40179 in the same collection (with *Salzburger Mädl*—'Girl from Salzburg') as well as mus. D 189 at the Moravian Museum at Brno (ČSSR) had their origin in a higher-class stratum. Merely a manuscript (still for 6-course mandora) of the Augsburg City Library, marked Tonkunst 290, includes vulgar pieces such as *Dienerl mein* ('My little servant') and *Steh mein Mützerl* ('Stay my little cap'). It is rather significant that mandora tablatures frequently supply extensive treatises regarding the technique of playing (*cf.* MS. Augsburg, Tonkunst 590; MS. Munich, Bavarian State Library, mus. pract. 509 with beautifully painted *Fundamento*, etc.). Similarly the so-called *Hamburger Cithrinchen* (little cittern of Hamburg) was, according to the evidence of manuscripts preserved, hardly used by the 'lower classes'.[10]

All the more interest is aroused by a discovery relating to the cittern. There are but few manuscripts for this instrument which had a flatter body and was mostly equipped with 4 courses. On the other hand prints before 1700 are by no means lacking,[11] and the use of the *cetula* already mentioned by J. Tinctoris is frequently attested (M. Praetorius, M. Mersenne, A. Kircher). English sources of *c.* 1590–1670 constitute an important group of their own.[12] To the same period belong the German manuscripts which display a repertoire with no specific differences. The MS. by David Samenhammer for 4-course cittern, dated 1590 and preserved in the Thorn, Poland, *Gymnasialbibliothek* presents next to German song movements (partly with 'after-dance') pieces such as the 'Beautiful Psalms' from Lobwasser's Cantionale. The tablature of the Castle-Library at Mikulov (ČSSR),[13] lost since a long time, comprises the usual suite movements. The *Tabulatur Buch auff der Cythar* (with 6 courses) of 1592 (burned in 1944) of the Saxonian Duke Hans Georg[14] has to be eliminated though several secular songs were included.[15] A late follower is J. W. Bunsold's *Evangelisches Choral-Buch* ('Evangelical Book of Chorales') dated 1765 for an enlarged instrument (13 courses), MS. Berlin State Library, mus. 40145. Within this group we may ascribe to the eighteenth century the manuscript of the Brussels Bibliothèque du Conservatoire royal 5622[16], hardly known so far, which is still based on the classic 4-course cittern (tuned g c' e' g') and employs the Italian numeral system; however, with the top line corresponding to the highest string, a specific type that was not new.[17]

The volume in pasteboard binding contains 91 sheets, fol. 2–46 comprising the tabulated movements, fol. 47–51r and 52v–91 text only (with numbered stanzas); fol. 51v, 52r remained empty and were formerly pasted together with sealing wax. We find incipits of sacred and secular German songs, with the latter prevailing (52 against 39). A few of the secular incipits have the additional designation of *Dantz* or *Menuet*. A 'Prussian March' is the only movement lacking a text. Among the secular pieces the group of pastoral idylls is noteworthy. There are also songs about animals (*Kein schöner Thierle als ein Schneck*—'No fairer animal than a snail'; *Ach wie sanft ruh ich bei meinem Vieh*—'Oh how gently do I rest next to my cattle'; *Ey jagt mir doch die Käfer weg*—'Oh, do drive the beetles away from me'); hunting songs, some dealing with domestic life (*Ist mir nicht mein Nudelbritle brochn*—'Isn't my rolling-pin broken') and—as probably the most curious find—a song movement by a journeyman weaver, the incipit of which matches the complete text in the second

79

part of the manuscript. Already the beginning is unusual; it paraphases Psalm 130 (*De profundis clamavi*). The stanzas read:

(1) Aus der Tiefe rufe ich, will dan niemand hören mich,
hört mich brafen webers knap, muß immer machen
knip knap knap, knip knap knap.

(2) Morgens wan ich früh aufsteh und in meinen keller geh,
eh ichs Stieglein trip trap trap, muß ich schon machen
knip knap knap, knip knap knap.

(3) Sing alsdan ein Morgen Lied, daß ich Lust Zur Arbeit krieg,
Spuhlen läßt man mir herab, daß ich kan machen
knip knap knap, knip knap knap.

(4) Knip knap das wer alle Tag, so lang als ich Essen mag,
muß ich brafer webers knap, immer machen
knip knap knap, knip knap knap.

(5) Komt der Sontag dan herbey, bin ich von dem knip knap frey,
kriech ich aus meiner gruft herfür Zu dem braun und wei=
sen Bier, knip knap knap, knip knap knap.

(6) Dorten wan ich Spielleuth hör, denk ich kein knip knap mehr,
lustig munter ist der Sohn, biß versofen ist der Lohn,
knip knap knap, knip knap knap.

(7) Solt ich ohn mein knip knap stehn, müßt ihr all ohn Hemder
gehn, Hemder ist das Schönst am Leib, Hemder Zier an Man
und Weib, knip knap knap, knip knap knap.

(8) Wan mein knip knap ausgemacht, Ziereter mit grosem Pracht,
den Tauf Stein und den altar und die Schwartze Todten bahr,
knip knap knap, knip knap knap.

(9) Sieh nur an die Priester schafft, wie sie Pranget so Lob
hafft, auf der Cantzel uns Zum Preiß, in der Leinwand
rein und weiß, knip knap knap, knip knap knap.

(10) Kayser, König, Herr und Knecht, Zieret unser knip knap recht,
er hab was er woll vorn Stand, komt mein knip knap in sein
Hand, knip knap knap, knip knap knap.

(11) Wan ich geh die Stieg hinab, denk ich an mein kühles Grab,
dorten werd ich armer knap nimmer machen
knip knap knap, knip knap knap.

(12) Dieses Liedlein hat gedicht und den webern zugericht
einer, der offt Tag und Nacht selbsten knip knap hat genacht,
knip knap knap, knip knap knap.

(13) Vivat brafer Webers Gsell, deine Cammen richtig stell,
Schlage Stoltz und Prächtig an, Jungfer wollen weber hahn,
knip knap knap, knip knap knap.

(14) Führe Tritt und Streich Zugleich, dieses macht den Meister
reich, Samstag bringet Sielber Geld, Lebewohl in dieser Welt,
knip knap knap, knip knap knap.

Among the gracefully flirting rococo pastorales this 'Weaver Song'
occupies a place of its own, especially so as the grotesque dances we
noted in galichon tablaturas, are lacking in this manuscript. Here we
do not find the usual mocking verse about an 'opprobrious trade',[18]
rather a proud testimony for a certain guild with allusions to high-ranking
persons.[19] Part of the tools are named exactly.[20] Another noteworthy fact
is that this trade song with the working refrain (describing a monotonous
activity) was made by a weaver himself, but is not free of social criticism—
even of his own person. The movement presented with a limited rhythmic
indication[21] only, reads in transcription:

Aus der Tie-fe ru-fe ich will dan nie-mand hö-ren mich,
hört mich bra-fen we-bers Knap muss im-mer ma-chen
Knip Knap Knap, Knip Knap Knap.

The primitive structure (the folkloristic substance of which may be
discussed in another study on song types in lute tablaturas around 1750)
conforms with the secular text supplied by the main writer who was

responsible for the intavolated and literary sections and may also have somewhat contributed to certain movements.[22]

The picture is completed by a 9-stanza song in praise of cittern playing which is likewise noted in the tablature. We are herewith quoting stanzas 1 and 5–7.

(1) Kommet her ihr Hirten Knaben und ergötzet euer Gemüth,
    die da Lust zum Singen haben und euch in her Music übt,
    setzt euch nieder, laßt uns singen, ich will meine Zitter
    Stimmen, ja wir wollen das gesang Zieren mit der Zitter Klang.

(5) Israel war sehr erschrocken, vor dem Riesen Goliath,
    der sie feindlich angesprochen und auch sehr Verhönet hat,
    da nahm David einen Stein, schleudert in ins Haupt hinein,
    daß er muß Zur Erden fallen, jetz hat nun ein end seyn
    prahlen.

(6) Was wolt ihr Vom Riesen sagen, es muß gar der der Teufel fort,
    wan er thät die Harpfen schlagen, an sein Vorig Höllen orth,
    ey so will bemühen mich, daß ich auch so emsiglich
    meinen Morgen und Abend Seegen auf der Zitter kan ablegen.

(7) Mancher aber mag sein Spotten, mir gefällt der Zitter Klang,
    der welt ränk und ihre Poßen Lieb ich nicht in dem Gesang,
    ich will Davids Lieder Borgen und vertreiben meine Sorgen
    mir Zur Lust und Gott Zum Preiß, diß soll syn mein Zitter
    weiß.

In spite of the attempt to use a biblical symbol a certain primitive quality is noticeable in the language used.

The 4-course cittern was hit with a plectrum and because of the metal strings employed differed in sound from the lute. Yet the writer noted in several instances the fingering (right hand up to the ring-finger). The doubles included ('in a different manner') testify to a flexible repertoire. Its selection of arias from the guild circles[23] supply interesting insight, also regarding the older literature for the singspiel, and various concordances will still have to be investigated. The 'weaver song' certainly had noteworthy followers.[24]

The era of sensibility which witnessed the rise of a liberalized middle class, had its impact on lute tablatures. The sequences of the favourite galant-courtly dances—anyway only loosely connected with the suite structure—were interrupted by vulgar-histrionic pieces and grotesque dances. In this connection one should recall that the regulatory function of brief grotesque dances reaches back to the earliest tablaturas (the 'after-dance' in a tighter metre, foreign national types, *etc.*). In a late period one even notices aspects of modern industrialization, the professional view of the weaver being supported by the proud conception of the hunter. At the same time the ideas of the Enlightenment made playing on the cittern appear as an act of humanizing power, this concept being conveyed by the picture of Orpheus victorious and the friendship of shepherds. This points to a significant recolouring of the repertoire which in a few border zones was spreading to the realm of vulgar music.

NOTES

1 J. Wolf, *Handbuch der Notationskunde* II, Leipzig, 1919, pp. 47 ff., 66 ff., 95 ff., 112 ff. 117 f., 119 f., 123, 125, 129, 145 f.; sources regarding guitar tablaturas, pp. 209 ff.

2 K. Geiringer, *Die Flankenwirbelinstrumente in der bildenden Kunst der Zeit zwischen 1300–1550*. Dissert. Vienna, 1923. *Vorgeschichte und Geschichte der europäischen Laute bis zum Beginn der Neuzeit*, in: ZfMw X, Leipzig, 1927–28, pp. 560 ff.

3 K. Geiringer, *Der Instrumentenname 'Quinterne' und die mittelalterlichen Bezeichnungen der Guitarre, Mandola und des Colascione*, in: AfMw VI, Leipzig, 1924, pp. 103 ff.

4 C. Sachs, *Reallexikon der Musikinstrumente*, Berlin 1913.

5 In his *Studien zur solistischen Lautenpraxis des 16.–18. Jahrhunderts*, inaugural dissertation, Berlin, 1943 (typewritten), appendix pp. 342–83; *cf.* also the author's articles '*Laute*' and '*Gitarre*' in: MGG VIII, col. 366–71 and IV, col. 196–98.

6 By the author in *Catalogue RISM*, manuscripts, vol. VII, Lute and Guitar Tablaturas. Munich-Duisburg, 1969.

7 R. Lück, *Ein Beitrag zur Geschichte des Colascione aund seiner süddeutschen Tondenkmäler im 18. Jahrhundert*, Dissert. Erlangen, 1954 (typewritten); by the same author, *Zwei unbekannte Basslauten -Instrumente, der italienische Colascione und der deutsche Galichon*, in: Neue Zeitschr. f. Musik CXXVI, 1, Mainz 1965, pp. 10–13.

8 Now at Dresden, *Sächsische Landesbibliothek*, Music Division. Here are works of the Bavarian Duke Clemens Franz de Paula (k722–70) in MSS. 2701/V/1 and—in an old copy—2701/V/la; moreover music by Giuseppe Antonio Brescianello (1721–51 chief conductor in Stuttgart, better known in his time through his violin concertos) in MSS. 2364/V/2 and —likewise in an old copy—2364/V/1; and music by a certain Johann Paul Schiffelholz (active in Ingolstadt and Regensburg) in MSS. 2806/V/1–4. A few anonymous suites in MSS. 2806/V/5, 2/5/5–7 belong to the same circle. Eitner's assumption (*Quellenlex*. IX, 22) that Schiffelholz invented the galichon, is not correct.

9 Brussels, Bibl. du Conservatoire royal MS. 15. 132, pasted in with a different size as fol. 46–49. This MS. was not yet accessible to R. Lück.

10 We might mention the MSS. Hamburg, *Staats-und Universitätsbibliothek* 3241 (burned in 1943) for 5 courses with operatic arias from local productions; MS. Berlin *Staatsbiblio-*

thek mus. 40267 (though with a *Galler Bauren Tantz*—peasant dance from St Gall). MS. mus. 40275 shows but few intavolated insertions of this kind.

11 In French and Italian manner. 4 courses: Viaera 1564; Ballard 1565; Vreedman 1568; Phalese 1570, 1582; Kärgel 1578; Valerius 1626. 6 courses: Kärgel—Lais 1578.

12 Especially the prints: Holborne 1597, Alison 1599, Morley 1599, Robinson 1609, Rosseter 1609, Morley 1611, Leighton 1614, Playford, 1650, 1652, 1666. Among the MSS. those not mentioned by J. Wolf: London Brit. Mus. Add. 30513 and Cambridge Univ. Libr. Dd. 4.23, Dd. 14.24, are the most important. *Cf.* the valuable contribution by Thurston Dart, *The Cittern and its English Music*, in: *Galpin Society Journal*, I, London, 1948 pp. 1–18.

13 Nikolsburg, former Libr. of Princess Dietrichstein. The MS. for 6-course cittern had been exhibited in 1892 at the Vienna World Exposition. I was recently (October, 1968), able to find it in the Brno (ČSSR) State Archives among foreign holdings and should like to express my thanks to the staff. The MS. contains in its second part a German lute tablature, a fact overlooked by J. Wolf.

14 The MS. was described, with the help of an autopsy, in this author's survey, *op. cit.* (1943), p. 349, under the reference number Mus. 2 307. It was held in the division of manuscripts, not in the music division, of *Sächsische Landesbibilothek*, Dresden.

15 In the so-called Nauclerus tablature dated 1615, preserved in Berlin *Staatsbibliothek* MS. mus. 40141, I see only in rare instances (fol. 151v. 152) entries for 4-course cittern.

16 New reference number F.[ond] A.[ancien] VI, 6. Missing in J. Wolf, *op. cit.*, and in this author's survey (1943). The MS. is inaccurately quoted by A. Wotquenne, *Catalogue de la bibliothèque du Conservatoire royal de musique de Bruxelles* . . . II, Brussels, 1902, p. 265 ('tablature chiffrée italienne ou allemande'). It might be mentioned in this connection that Wotquenne at another place reported with minute details on another lute tablature of the Brussels collection. (*Notice sur le manuscrit 704*. . . . in:L'Annuaire du Conservatoire . . . XXIV, Brussels 1900, pp. 178 ff.)

17 As early as 1578 at Kärgel, though with a different tuning.

18 As for instance in the 'Song of the linenweavers': . . . *nehmen keinen Lehrjungen an, der nicht sechs Wochen lang hungern kann*'–'accept no apprentice who cannot remain hungry for six weeks' (F. K. Freiherr v. Erlach, *Die Volkslieder der Deutschen* . . . I, Mannheim.) (1834, p. 508.)

19 'King and Emperor' are mentioned in another weaver-song of the time (L. Pinck, *Verklingende Weisen* . . . I, Kassel-Metz, s.a. [1926], p. 167). Variants in F. W. Freiherr v. Ditfurth, *Deutsche Volks-und Gesellschaftslieder des 17. und 18. Jahrhunderts*, Nördlingen, 1872.

20 The hand-loom framing was operated in the '*Keller*' (cellar) from a low *Sitz* (seat), reached by a '*Stiege*' (steps). The weaver operated with his feet the so-called '*Ersten*' and '*Zweiten Tritt*' (first and second treadle); these were wooden battens hard to move. The '*Kamm*' (comb) had to be 'set right' by hand. The '*Lade*' (hand-loom) then had to be touched 'proudly and magnificently' ('*stolz und prächtig angeschlagen*'). Thanks to it the '*Schütze*' (shuttle) was thrown back and forth by means of a '*Stock*' (stick). With his hands the weaver accomplished this '*Streich*' (stroke). This was also designated as '*Schuss*' (weft): the horizontal group of threads was crossed at right angles with the other called '*Kettle*' (warp). It is interesting to note that related expressions were used for hunting. In 1733 John Kay invented a device for the automatic back- and forth-motion of the '*Schütze*' (shuttle).

21 Only 2/8 groups (though moved sideways) are marked. According to the 'Menuet' of this collection notes not given a specific value should be considered as quarter or half notes. Tablature lines are only at the end of phrases; they do not indicate the metre.

22 Names and dates are missing. On the flyleaf it reads: '*Johanna Friederica/Heppe/veuve Antoine Laget*'. The linguistic version points to an origin in Southern Germany middle of the eighteenth century.

23 *e.g. 'Bin ich nicht des Metzgers sey*[*n*]*Sohn*'—'Am I not the butcher's son'.

24 Heinrich Heine ('Lied der schlesischen Weber'—'Song of Silesian Weavers, 1844'); Gerhard Hauptmann's drama 'The Weavers', 1892; Käthe Kollwitz's cycle of graphic art 'A revolution of weavers', 1895–96.

ANDRES BRINER

THE EARLY ZÜRICH
NEUJAHRSBLÄTTER

The Zürich *Collegia musica*, united 1812 as the *Allgemeine Musikgesell-schaft*, are responsible for a periodical publication, which stands, in origin and composition, apart from the rest of eighteenth-century periodica. The account given in the leading British music dictionary sums up nearly the most basic facts: 'The earliest Swiss Collegium musicum was the *Gesellschaft ab dem Musiksaal*, founded in 1613, which began to issue New Year's sheets in 1685. These unique documents of middle-class musical culture have appeared without interruption down to the present day'.[1] The *Gesellschaft ab dem Musiksaal* united virtually all music amateurs of the town until the beginning of a second *Collegium musicum* in 1679. Its musical meetings started and closed with the singing of protestant psalms. In between, the members, puritanical towns-people as well as the few noblemen present, indulged in the singing of secular part-songs. In the eighteenth century instrumental music came to play an ever more important part in these musical gatherings. The library of the *Allgemeine Musikgesellschaft*, whose catalogue has recently been published, gives an insight into the music acquired by the Zürich *Collegia musica* in the eighteenth century.[2]

The origin of the New Year's sheets is connected with a local tradition which seems to antedate the formation of the *Collegia musica*. It was, however, continued by them in various forms. According to this tradition, New Year's Day was an occasion for a particularly long and festive musical event, to which the children of the participating adults were invited. Before it all could start, they brought wood to warm the com-paratively large room in which the festivity took place and they received in turn from the organizing group a gift adapted to their tastes and needs. This exchange, appropriately called the 'Stubenhitzen', took on larger proportions once the *Gesellschaft ab dem Musiksaal* had built the large hall which, from 1684 on, conferred its name to the earliest *Collegium musicum*. The first New Year's publication served as a model for the publication of both major *Collegia musica* throughout most of the eighteenth century. It features a handsomely-worked etching as title vignette, followed by texts in Latin and German and ending with the parts of a newly and locally composed song. The contents were, for many years to come, spread over eight pages. Originally, as its last sentence uniformly says, intended for the 'kunst- und tugendliebende Jugend in Zürich', the New Year's sheets seem to have equally aroused the interest of the adults. The part-songs, of a changing number of voices, styles and structures, could have been mastered by adolescents only under the instruction of a music master and were most probably sung in conjunction with the adult members of the *Collegia*.

One of the earliest sources on the 'Stubenhitzen', from the year 1742, does not mention the New Year's publications, but sheds some light on the origin of the publications from the second *Collegium musicum*, founded in 1679. This *Collegium, Gesellschaft zur deutschen Schule*, started publication in 1713, *i.e.* again shortly after being helped by the town authorities to move into a proper 'Musicsaal' of their own. The 'Stubenhitzen' mentioned in this source must have been financial contributions, or at least material gifts in addition to donations from the parents of the children. It reads: 'Auf der Teutschen Schul hat sich seit etlichen Jahren zusammen gethan eine Anzahl junger Herren und Burgeren, geist- und weltichen Stands, diesen hat die Obrigkeit Anno 1702 in gemeldter Teutschen Schul einen Saal bauen lassen, woselbst auch ein fein Orgel-Werk von 8 Registern, jedoch mindrer Gattung zu finden, von Jacob Messmer, von Reinegg gemacht.—Anno 1711, den 21. Dezember, ist denen Herren Musicanten auf der teutschen Schul bewilligt worden, Stubenhitzen, gleich andern Gesellschafften, einzusamlen.'[3]

A later source from 1780 mentions the New Year's sheets as 'Musicalische Neujahrs-Stücke', a name by which they were known from their origin. By that time the sheets had changed in format and content in order to conform with the ideals of the Enlightenment. The sheets of the last decades of the century are easily read and equally easily appreciated. They are local contributions to the song and spirit of the new era, one of 'reason' and individual feeling, and they have been justly recognized for just that.[4] By 1780 they had also gained some recognition outside the town. The source proudly mentions the foreigners who have heard of both the concerts of the *Gesellschaft ab dem Musiksaal* and the New Year's publications. It first speaks of the weekly musical meetings of the 'auf dem eigentlichen Music-Saal sich befindliche löbliche Music Gesellschaft' and goes on to say that 'zugleich sich auch theils durch ihre schöne Concerte, theils durch ihre Musicalische Neujahrs-Stücke, welche jährlich sinth Anno 1685 im Druck erscheinen, nicht nur bei Einheimischen, sondern auch bey Fremden schon mehrmalen verrühmt gemacht hat'.[5] The publications of the second half of the century contain many a worthy verse and a well-worked song. And yet their content is obvious to the point of being poor, compared to the early sheets.

The *Neujahrsblätter* or *Neujahrsstücke* of the early years do present some problems. They are filled with an imagery, both pictorial and verbal, that goes back to the sixteenth and early seventeenth century. A brief description of the first sheet of 1685 may serve as an introduction. Its title reads: 'Musicalische Neu-Jahr-Gedichte, Gott zu Ehren und zur Vermehrung der Freuden in Gott einer ehr-, kunst- und tugenliebenden Jugend in Zürich von der Gesellschaft der Vocal- und Instrumental-Music ab dem Musiksaal daselbst zum andern Mahl aufgelegt'. Its title vignette shows Arion riding on a dolphin in the lake of Zürich, with the town clearly visible in the background. Also on the title page is the motto of the Collegium, 'Musica noster amor'. The purpose of music-making is then put into the words 'ut relevet miserum fatum solitosque labores'. The following German poetry begins with the verses:

> Diess ist der Musik nutz:
> Sie kann in diesem Leben
> Uns zu betrübter Zeit
> in Gott Erquickung geben;
> Versüssen B'ruffs-Geschäft:
> Bei Glückes vollem Lauf
> In Gottes süssem Lob
> Uns lieblich halten auf.

The part-song in this earliest of the sheets is printed on page 4 (Cantus I) and page 5 (Cantus II); a figured bass part runs underneath from page 4 to page 5. The text of the eight stanzas leads up to the final consideration:

Wird herbei das Stündlein rucken,
Das zum Sterben dir bestellt,
Hilf Gott, dass wir wohl abtrucken,
Und aus dieser schnoeden Welt,
Da nur Sünd ist, Angst und Qual,
Kommen in den Freudensaal.
Sterbt fröhlich, ihr Kinder, ihr Schwestern, ihr Brüder,
Wir sehen uns dörten in Ewigkeit wieder.

The spiritual background of this publication is obviously far removed from the enlightened minds of Johann Caspar Lavater and Hans Georg Nägeli, both later contributors to the publications. There is no reason in common history or mythology for Arion riding on a dolphin in the lake of Zürich. The Greek singer and composer must have been saved by the animal close to the island of Lesbos and not in the cold waters of a Teutonic lake. The ensuing texts seem strangely unrelated to the illustration. It is only after studying all aspects of the pictorial image as well as of the texts and the music that one realizes the central theme of the publication, the act of *salvation*. To enlightened thinking (as we still basically share it today) there is little purpose in reminding the adolescent at the turn of the year that he is doomed to die as anybody else. In the eyes of the anonymous authors of this New Year's publication, however, there was much purpose in bringing death before the eyes of their young readers in an effort to bring home the ultimate hope of the Christian: life after death. To 'die happily' ('Sterbt fröhlich') is the moral of their New Year's message. They spare no efforts, from this point on, to put the assembled paraphernalia of humanistic learning into the service of their educational aim. They seize on the story of the salvation of Arion not because they believe in any direct link of the mythological figure with their town, but because they are eager to insert any idol of pagan origin into a Christian framework.

Thus, the problem in reading the *Neujahrsblätter* of the early times is mostly one of finding the link between imagery, texts and music and appreciating it in terms of the educational aim of the authors. Ever so often it is just one word or one detail in the title vignette which gives the clue. One is quickly drawn by the riddle to be solved, the challenge of filling out a crossword puzzle whose dimensions are those of biblical knowledge and humanistic learning. Thus in 1701, when a new town hall was built, the mythological figure is that of Amphion, playing his harp. The biblical quotations are centring in the idea of spiritual (as opposed to mere technical) building and the Latin verse contains twice the word 'aedificat' which can be found in front of a representation of the new town hall. The text reads:

'Templa, Forumque, Domos, Pietas, Prudentia, Virtus
Saxea corda movens, condit et aedificat.
Doctus ut Amphion Thebanae condictor arcis,
Saca movente sono, suaviter aedificat.'

Musical terms, from the names of the different voices over rhythmic and harmonic notions to dynamics, were, from 1705 on, increasingly drawn into the moral and intellectual goal. Toward the middle of the century, the morals derived from the central themes of the publications show an increasing understanding for and interest in individual feeling and sensitivity. In the year 1712, when the term 'piano' was selected as theme, the vignette shows appropriately a harpsichord with three keyboards and the texts praise the advantage of soft, sensitive music with an eloquence that could equally well be put into the service of the clavichord—the instrument that was to become a favourite with the oncoming generation of amateurs. The title 'Evolutio emblematica' over the Latin text and its free German translation on the other hand characterizes the historical origin of the presentation as such, the *ars emblamatica*.

The German text reads:

Ein starkes Zettergschrey/und überzwängte Saiten/
der Music gwüsser mord/der Ohren ball und zwang:
In sanfter Mässignung bestehn die Lieblichkeiten/
So Seel und Sinnen ziehn; Ja ist die Seel im Gsang.
Der Künstler/ so die Thön im Wechsel weist zuspielen/
sanft seines Herzens-Truck in seine Weisen gibt/
Der kann des Herzens-Beut und Ohren-Lust erzielen:
Der laute schreyer Zahn die Music nur betrübt.

Thus the *Neujahrsblätter* of the Zürich *Collegia musica* in the eighteenth century present in short the most important spiritual and artistic development of the century: the passage from the allegorical tradition of thought and presentation to the beginners of enlightened, secular thinking and a realistic tradition of presentation.

NOTES

1 Grove's *Dictionary of Music and Musicians*, vol. IX, 1954, 'Zürich', p. 430.

2 *Katalog der Allgemeinen Musikgesellschaft Zürich. (Katalog der gedruckten und hand-schriftlichen Musikalien des 17. bis 19. Jahrhunderts im Besitze der Allgemeinen Musik-gesellschaft Zürich)*. Redigiert von Dr. Georg Walter. Zürich, 1960.

3 H. H. Bluntschli: *Memorabilia tigurina oder Merkwürdigkeiten der Stadt und Landschafft Zürich in alphabetischer Ordnung*. Zürich, 1742. 'Music-Saal', p. 298.

4 Anthonius Werdmüller: *Memorabilia tigurina oder Merkwürdigkeiten der Stadt und Landschaft Zürich*. Zürich, 1780. 'Music-Säle', p. 393.

5 Karl Nef: *Die Collegia musica in der deutschen reformierten Schweiz*. St Gallen, 1897, p. 64.

GEORGE J. BUELOW

AN EVALUATION OF
JOHANN MATTHESON'S OPERA,
CLEOPATRA (HAMBURG, 1704)

The sixty-year development of opera in the city-state of Hamburg, between 1678 and 1738, is a key chapter in the history of Baroque opera. This wealthy Hanseatic city built the first public opera house outside Italy, and in this theatre an operatic tradition evolved that was neither purely French nor Italian, but rather an amalgam of forms and styles that originated in French, Italian, German, and Dutch music of the seventeenth century.

The history of opera in Hamburg has been well-documented, most notably by Friedrich Chrysander and Hellmuth Christian Wolff.[1] The music, however, as is true of much Baroque opera, is almost totally unknown. The names of German composers contributing to the Hamburg theatre included Johann Theile, Johann Wolfgang Franck, Johann Philipp Förtsch, Johann Georg Conradi, Johann Kusser, Reinhard Keiser, Johann Mattheson, Georg Philipp Telemann, and George Frideric Handel. However, with the exception of the last named, the music of all these composers has been forgotten as well as largely lost.

One of the most distinguished names in this list is that of Johann Mattheson. He was born in that city in 1681 and died there in 1764. Mattheson published more than two dozen books and pamphlets, which inquire into almost every conceivable aspect of musical thought and practice of the first half of the eighteenth century, a depository of information yet to be fully explored and assimilated by historians of the musical Baroque.[2]

Mattheson was more than just the encyclopaedist of German music theory and history; he possessed a fine voice and began a career as opera singer in Hamburg at the age of nine. For that same opera house he wrote a series of five operas,[3] completing the first in his eighteenth year. Throughout most of his life, until deafness discouraged creative activity, he composed; in addition to the operas, his catalogue of works includes twenty-seven oratorios, numerous cantatas, and a variety of keyboard and instrumental pieces.

Little of this music was printed in Mattheson's lifetime, and none of his many oratorios and operas has been preserved in a printed edition. The great majority of Mattheson's musical manuscripts, including his opera scores, as well as his entire library of books and music, was destroyed by fire during the Second World War. Mattheson the composer, it seemed, had died a second time with the death of the Hamburg Staatsbibliothek.

More recently, however, this writer found Mattheson's most famous opera, *Cleopatra*, in the collection of the Music Division of the Library of Congress. To suggest that the score was rediscovered would not be entirely true, for this copy of the opera was listed by Sonneck in his catalogue of operas in the Library of Congress, although this fact has been overlooked in all previous Mattheson research. Actually, it was Sonneck's wisdom in commissioning various copyists to duplicate scores of important opera manuscripts in major German libraries for deposit in the Music Division that apparently preserved the only existing copy of Mattheson's *Cleopatra*, and the only copy of any opera by this composer.[4]

In his *Grundlage einer Ehrenpforte* (Hamburg, 1740),[5] Mattheson reports the following gossip concerning a performance of this opera:

'On December 5 [1704] . . . when my third opera, *Cleopatra*, was performed and [George Frideric] Handel sat at the harpsichord, the following misunderstanding arose, as is not new with young people who with all their power and little thought, strive for honour. As composer I conducted and at the same time played the rôle of Antonius, who more than a half hour before the end of the opera kills himself. Now, I was accustomed previously, after this action, to go to the orchestra pit and to accompany the rest of the work myself, which without question any composer can do more successfully than anyone else. This time, however, I was prevented from doing so [by Handel]. As a result of a quarrel over this, we engaged in a duel in the open market before a crowd of onlookers, which for both of us could have been most unfortunate, when God's intervention had not been so compassionate so that my sword was broken by striking a large metal button on the coat of my opponent. No particular harm had been done.'

Handel, who had come to Hamburg from Halle in 1703, was a violinist in the opera orchestra, probably employed through the recommendation of Mattheson. The notoriety of this duel, however, is the least important aspect of Mattheson's account. Of far greater merit is the significance Mattheson's opera *Cleopatra* would seem to hold as a probable influence in the early career of Handel. Also, the discovery of a major operatic work by Mattheson permits one to end what previously had been fruitless speculation about the relationship between Mattheson the creative musician and the theorist. Not least important, the preservation of this score makes available for study a rare example of Hamburg opera from the turn of the eighteenth century.[5a]

The three-act opera follows closely the tragedy of Anthony and Cleopatra as we know it in Shakespeare's version. The libretto[6] by the young Hamburg theologian Friedrich Christian Feustking, is richly imaginative and particularly successful in developing the tragic story of the central characters of Anthony and Cleopatra. The poet gave Mattheson many opportunities for music of extraordinary intensity and moving affections, including the suicides of both Anthony and Cleopatra, which Mattheson composed to music worthy of his greatest contemporaries, Keiser and Handel. The three acts consist largely of an alternation of recitative and arias, and there are but three entrances for chorus in the entire work. Sixty per cent of the seventy arias and solo ensembles have a *continuo* accompaniment alone, and the remaining 40 per cent have an orchestral accompaniment that is either unspecified (and we may assume was performed by the orchestra at large), or is designated for unison strings, four-part string ensemble, or strings combined with recorders or oboes. A few arias have a more limited instrumental accompaniment such as an oboe duet or violin solo with the *continuo*, but none of the arias includes parts for either horn or trumpet.

The few existing discussions of Mattheson the composer generally assume that his music was insignificant or that he imitated the style of his contemporary, Reinhard Keiser. However, a comparison of *Cleopatra* with several scores of Keiser written at approximately the same time as Mattheson's, for example, *Adonis* (Hamburg, 1697), *Janus* (Hamburg, 1698), *La Forza della virtù* (Hamburg, 1700), and *Nebucadnezar* (Hamburg,

1704), reveals only a general similarity rooted in the traditions of Hamburg operatic style. Especially the element of melody distinguishes the one composer from the other: Mattheson's melodies are usually smoother, more step-wise in motion, and therefore less angular than Keiser's; Mattheson achieves a style of melodic simplicity, although creating music of great effective expressiveness. He takes more care than Keiser in maintaining poetic metre, and generally he avoids long melismatic passages, which are particularly characteristic of Keiser's arias.

Although written thirty-five years later, Mattheson's thoughts regarding melody in his *Vollkommener Capellmeister*[7] compare essentially with his youthful operatic style. Here Mattheson preached that melody must be simple, *cantabile*, affective, and at all costs 'natural'. He urged composers to imitate French melodic style, but he stood squarely opposed to Rameau's idea that melody grew out of harmony. In seven rules, Mattheson drew up the following prescription for good melodic writing:

1. That there must be something in all melodies that is familiar to almost everyone.
2. Everything unnatural, far-fetched, and dull in character must be avoided.
3. For the most part, one must follow Nature to some extent in practice.
4. One sets aside technical dexterity [*grosse Kunst*] or greatly disguises it.
5. In this [writing melody], the French should be imitated more than the Italians.
6. A melody must have certain limitations of range that everyone can manage.
7. Conciseness will be preferable to prolixity.

Mattheson's score proves these points on every page. The general tunefulness of the arias, their frequently strophic, folk-like structure, and above all their avoidance of any kind of vocal virtuosity clearly support his doctrine of melody. Concerning the importance of French style in relation to melody, one notices that the opera has not only a number of French ballet dances and dance scenes, but that the overall impression of the music is indisputably more French than Italian in general character. The parts are generally contained within moderate ranges, and the fact that Mattheson himself sang the major rôle of Antonius underscores the relative simplicity of vocal technique required for that part. Simplicity, however, must not be construed to mean lack of dramatic effectiveness, for it is in this element that Mattheson's genius stands out and makes this opera a work of impressive beauty and theatrical effectiveness.

The complete aria printed at the end of this article (Ex. 6) will illustrate a number of these points. This aria, sung by Cleopatra, occurs at the first dramatic climax of the first act: Antonius has fled from Cleopatra (following the defeat of the Egyptian forces by the Romans at the battle of Actium), and he has sworn to abandon Cleopatra for ever. Cleopatra arrives, listens to his resolve, and then sings this symbolic farewell to her lover. The seductiveness of Cleopatra's music is intended to persuade Antonius to change his mind. Clearly, when one describes this example as a *continuo* aria with a simple *da capo* form, one has said nothing of the beauty of the music. The key words in the text are 'matter Geist' (exhausted spirit) and 'tausend, tausend Seuffzer schicken' (thousands and thousands of sighs [will my exhausted spirit] send after you). The aria underscores Mattheson's conviction that music is a *redende Kunst*, and the rhetoric of the simple aria impresses one in its union with the total musical elegance that suggests neither the music of Keiser nor of contemporary Italian composers. The gradual decline of Cleopatra's 'gute Nacht', the rising fourths separated by rests, all express her cleverly feigned resignation. The melody as a whole relies on the interval of the fourth as its generative motive, and the opening 'gute Nacht' returns to our inner ear constantly as Cleopatra continues with the remainder of the text (bars 5, 6, 8, 9, 12 contain the more apparent references to this motive).

Also important as a characteristic style of Mattheson's opera, and characteristic of this aria, is the *continuo* bass part that grows out of an established melodic pattern in an almost *ostinato* form. The *ostinato* character, however, is suggested, not realized; and Mattheson uses the device in a large percentage of the arias, duets, and trios accompanied by the *continuo* part. Mattheson is one of the first among composers of opera to achieve this ideal Baroque style in which the bass as well as the melody are often equal in their character of melodic independence and strength. This aspect of Baroque style remains to be traced in detail: certainly Venetian opera displays a prominence of *basso ostinato* patterns. Yet German Baroque opera before Mattheson that is extant, including Keiser's scores, does not have this prevalence of melodic polarity.

Mattheson's many pseudo-*ostinato* basses have a variety of affective results that the composer expresses in a variety of simple ways: Ex. 1,

Cleopatra (Act III, Scene 7)

Ru - he sanfft, ru-he sanfft ge - lieb-ter Geist, ge - lieb-ter Geist, ei - le zu der Ster-nen Büh-nen, ei - - - le zu der Ster-nen Büh - nen. *etc.*

a powerful ascending melodic line, which in other instances is used as a descending melody; Ex. 2, the insistent return to one structurally important interval within the bass, the seventh in this example; Ex. 3, the use of catchy dance rhythms, such as the *siciliana* in this example; Ex. 4, the powerful effect of a bass composed entirely of dotted rhythms.

Also striking in Mattheson's score is the emphasis on many folk-like arias, some in strophic form with several verses, or in other instances in simple binary form based on a dance, such as the minuet in Ex. 5. The folk element was a tradition of Hamburg opera, and Mattheson employs it to special advantage in comic scenes. In Act II, for example, a ballet of chimney-sweeps, a popular North German symbol in folk literature, intrudes upon Cleopatra. The dancers enter as one sings 'Spazzar camino,

2

Antonius (Act I, Scene 1)

Den muss ich bil-lig se-lig schät-zen, der stets in stil-ler

Ein-sam-keit ent-fernt von Herr-sucht, Zanck und Neid, die Mü - de

See - le kan er-get - zen *etc.*

Spazzar camino', a popular Italian street cry. The scene concludes with Dercetaeus, Antonius's servant, singing a ribald song in *Plattdeutsch.*[8]

The study of Mattheson's *Cleopatra* proves that the young composer applied tonalities in a manner consistent with his theory of key affects published in *Das neu eröffnete Orchester* (Hamburg, 1713). Even though the opera was written nine years earlier, the score agrees almost without exception with the descriptions of keys found in the first of Mattheson's great treatises. Since these comments have not been published previously in their entirety in English, the author would like to offer his own translation:

1. C major . . . has a rather rude and bold character, but would not be unsuited to rejoicing and other situations where one otherwise gives full scope to joy. Notwithstanding, a qualified composer can

3

Cleopatra (Act II, Scene 10)

reshape it into something quite charming, especially when he chooses well the accompanying instruments, making it suitable also for application to tender situations.

2. C minor . . . is an extremely sweet as well as also sad key: however, because the first quality will prevail far too much and since one can become easily tired of this sweetness, therefore, nothing is lost when one gives the same a little more animation through a somewhat merry equal-bearing [*ebenträchtiges?*] tempo. Otherwise, some may easily become drowsy through its mildness. Should it, however,

4

Candace (Act II, Scene 4)

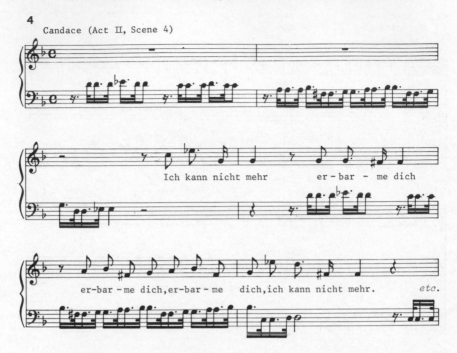

Ich kann nicht mehr   er - bar - me dich

er-bar - me dich, er-bar - me   dich, ich kann nicht mehr.   *etc.*

be a piece that is supposed to promote sleep, then one can omit this comment and soon arrive at this goal in a natural way.

3. . . . . D major is by its nature somewhat sharp and headstrong; [it is] most suitable for alarms, for merry and warlike things, and those giving animation. Yet, no one will deny that this harsh key can also give pleasing and unusual introduction to delicate works when a flute replaces the *clarino*, a violin replaces the timpani.

4. D minor. When one . . . carefully examines this key, one will discover that it contains something devout, tranquil, together also with something grand and satisfying. Therefore, it is capable of promoting devotion in church music, but peace of mind in *communi vita*, although this does not hinder one from setting also something amusing with this key, though not particularly dancelike, but rather flowing.

5. E flat major includes much pathos, and will have nothing voluntarily to do with other than serious and at the same time sad works. Also it is as if it were bitterly hostile to all sensuality.

6. E major expresses incomparably well a despairing or wholly fatal sadness; it is most suited to the helpless or hopeless conditions of

5

Proculejus (Act I, Scene 8)

Aria en minuet

Sich den Män – ner zu ver – trau – en heisst auf leich-tes

Trieb-sand bau – en Wort und Wer – cke sind zum Schein.

Keh – ren sie uns nur den Rük – ken muss ge – geb – ne

etc.

extreme love, and it has in certain circumstances something so piercing, separating, painful, and penetrating that it may be compared to nothing short of a total severing of the body from the soul.

7. E minor . . . can only with difficulty be joined to something merry, no matter how one employs it, because it usually is very pensive, profound, grieved, and sad, indeed, so much so that one even hopes at the same time for consolation. Something quick may be composed with it, but that is not the same as something merry.

8. F major . . . is capable of expressing the most beautiful sentiments in the world, be they generosity, constancy, love, or something else contained high on the scale of virtues [*Tugend-Register*], and can do this with a most natural manner and incomparable facility so that absolutely no force is necessary. Indeed, the niceness and suitability of this key cannot be better described than by comparing it to a handsome person who, in everything he does, no matter how unimportant, behaves perfectly and who, as the French say, has *bonne grace*.

9. F minor . . . appears to represent tenderness and calm, as well as a profundity and weightiness not far from despair, a fatal mental

anxiety; and it is exceedingly moving. It expresses a black, helpless melancholy beautifully and at times will provoke the listener to horror or a shudder.

10. F# minor, though it also leads to great sorrow is, however, more languishing and amorous than lethal; this key in other respects has something in it that is unrestrained, strange, and misanthropic.

11. G major . . . contains much that is suggestive and rhetorical; it shines not a little in this regard and is suitable to serious as well as gay things.

12. G minor is almost the most beautiful key, because it not only mixes, in its relationship to the previous [key], the rather serious with a lively sweetness, but introduces an extraordinary gracefulness and agreeableness, through which, being so thoroughly flexible, it is suited for the tender as well as the refreshing, for yearning as well as the diverting; in short, both for moderate complaints and tempered joyfulness.

13. A major . . . is very affecting, even though at the same time brilliant, and is more inclined to complaining and sad passions rather than to divertissements. It is especially suitable for violin music.

14. . . . The nature of A minor is somewhat plaintive, decorous, and resigned, inviting sleep, but by no means unpleasant thereby. Otherwise, it is especially suited to keyboard and instrumental music.

15. B flat major is very diverting and magnificent; it retains also readily something modest, and it can at the same time pass for magnificent and dainty.

16. B major seems . . . to have in itself an offensive, harsh, and unpleasant as well as somewhat desperate character.

17. B minor is bizarre, morose, and melancholic; for these reasons it seldom makes an appearance.

The number of occurrences of any one of these keys in the non-recitative sections of *Cleopatra* substantiates Mattheson's faith in his own doctrine. The frequency of appearance corresponds to his enthusiasm for certain keys over others. The following tables gives the tonalities found in the opera in the order used in *Das Neueröffnete Orchester*, together with the number of times each is used for a solo or ensemble aria:

C	10
c	5

D	4
d	6
E flat	0
E	1
e	4
F	9
f	1
f♯	1
G	7
g	12
A	2
a	7
B flat	7
B	0
b	1

* 'c' means 'C minor', 'd' 'D minor', etc., Ed.

Of the seventeen tonalities Mattheson defines, fifteen occur in the opera. Of the two he chose not to use, B major he has said was 'offensive, harsh, and unpleasant', and E flat 'is as if it were bitterly hostile to all sensuality', a predominate aspect of the opera.

Meaningful, too, are the arias written in a key appearing only once in the entire score. E major, which 'expresses incomparably well a despairing or wholly fatal sadness . . . it may be compared to nothing short of a fatal severing of the body from the soul', occurs only in Act III, Scene 5, for Antonius's aria, 'Itzt will ich bey dir sein', which immediately precedes his suicide after being deceived to believe Cleopatra was dead. F minor occurs only in Act II, Scene 3, when Candace, Cleopatra's sister, sings an aria, 'Ach mein Hertz', anticipating the moment when her lover Juba, a Mauretanian prince, will be brought before her as a prisoner of the Egyptians, bound in chains. Mattheson's description for F minor, 'fatal mental anxiety and is exceedingly moving', perfectly underscores the affect of this aria. F♯ minor, which he characterizes as leading 'to great sorrow, is however more languishing and amorous than lethal', occurs only in Antonius's aria in Act III, Scene 2, 'Cleopatra dein' Glieder Schnee/die Anmuth deiner Wangen ist eine reine Wollust See und hielte mich gefangen', in which he swears to die to save Cleopatra from the Romans led by Caesar Augustus. Also, B minor, which is 'bizarre, morose, and melancholic', is reserved for a single moment, the trio of Ptolomy (Cleopatra's brother), Candace, and Antonius (Act III, Scene 4), 'Augen weint für bittre Thränen', as brother, sister, and lover sing in despair upon receiving the first (untrue) report of Cleopatra's death.

Equally interesting are the two keys Mattheson chose most often, G minor, which he called 'almost the most beautiful key', and C major, a key he felt had a rather flexible nature and several possibilities of effective expression.

The general harmonic plan of the opera suggests that despite Mattheson's concern for individual key relations to the libretto, nevertheless, he planned a tonal unity of considerable strength:

Act I: B flat major– – – – – F major

Act II: g minor – – – – – – C major

Act III: G major – – – – – B flat major

The tonal unity of the outer acts is supported by the inner relationships: the first act concludes in the dominant of B flat major; the second act opens in the relative minor of B flat and closes in its subdominant C major; Act three moves from the dominant of the preceding act, or G major, and returns finally to the B flat major of the first act.

Paul Henry Lang, in his book on Handel, is the first writer to appreciate Mattheson's significant influence upon the musical development of Handel: 'From his early youth Mattheson was an enthusiastic champion of new music, which of course meant opera and dramatic, concerted church music, as opposed to the Lutheran musical tradition; and at the time of their association [Handel with Mattheson] in Hamburg his experience in this modern music was very considerable.'[9]

The availability of Mattheson's opera, *Cleopatra*, the very work in which Handel took part as a performer, makes possible a deeper understanding of at least one source of Handel's style. On more than one occasion, Handel indicated his respect for Mattheson's music. The closing chorus of *Cleopatra*, 'So wird nach den Thränen güssen folgen müssen ein beliebter Freudenschein', reappears almost exactly in the closing scene of Handel's opera, *Agrippina* (Venice, 1709).[10] The same music is found again as part of the ballet music to Handel's *Rodrigo* (Florence, 1707).[11] Mattheson reports in his *Critica Musica*[12] that Handel used an aria from Mattheson's opera, *Porsenna* (Hamburg, 1702), 'Diese Wangen will ich Küssen', for the aria 'Sotto il lauro, che hai su'l crine', in *Agrippina*, and later in *Muzio Scaevola* (London, 1721), to the text 'A chi vive di speranza'.

These adaptations of Mattheson's music by Handel are important as evidence to contradict Chrysander's belief that Handel learned nothing from his experience in Hamburg.[13] However, of far greater significance, the score of *Cleopatra* suggests that style elements such as melodic simplicity, tunefulness, the *da capo* aria, and the rôle of the bass theme

6

Aria - Cleopatra (Act I, Scene 3)

Adagio

Gu - te Nacht! gu - te Nacht! gu - te, gu - te

Nacht. Wird mich dein ent-fer - nung

drük-ken wird sie drük-ken soll dir doch soll dir

* *Thorough-bass realization by the author.*

D*

Da capo

in arias, and the overall importance of key considerations both to the general structure of an opera as well as for specific affects in arias, were learned by Handel not in Italy but rather from his friend and mentor, Johann Mattheson.

NOTES

1 Chrysander's articles concerning the history of Baroque opera from 1678 to 1706 appeared in the *Allgemeine musikalische Zeitung* in the following issues: 1877, pp. 369 ff.; 1878, pp. 289 ff.; 1879, pp. 385 ff.; 1879, pp. 433 ff.; 1880, pp. 17 ff.; Wolff's book, *Die Barockoper in Hamburg* (Wolfenbüttel, 1957), includes a very valuable volume of opera excerpts, many of which are from sources also lost in the destruction of the Hamburg Staatsbibliothek.

2 The most important study of Johann Mattheson as theorist and journalist in English is Beekman C. Cannon's *Johann Mattheson, Spectator in Music* (New Haven, 1947). For a briefer though richly informative discussion of Mattheson see also Hans Turnow's article in MGG 8, col. 1795–1815.

3 *Plejades* (1699), *Porsenna* (1702), *Cleopatra* (1704), *Boris Godunow* (1710), and *Henrico IV* (1711).

4 The following tantalizing report, in Heinz Becker's review of Wolff's study of Hamburg opera cited above, appeared in *Die Musikforschung* 13 (1960), p. 212: 'Wie erst vor kurzem bekannt wurde, sollen jedoch die während des Krieges ausgelagerten Musikbestände der Staats- und Universitätsbibliothek Hamburg jetzt an die Deutsche Staatsbibliothek in Berlin gelangt und in der dortigen Handschriftenabteilung aufgestellt worden sein. Darunter befinden sich Matthesons *Henrico IV*, *Cleopatra*, *Boris Godunow*, und Telemanns *Emma und Eginhard*.' My inquiry to the Berlin Staatsbibliothek regarding these manuscripts brought the following response from Dr. Hans-Erich Teitge, Abteilungsdirektor, Handschriftenabteilung und Literaturarchiv: 'Der Nachlass Mattheson ist nur in Einzelteilen unter diesen Handschriften, grössere Kompositionen befinden sich nicht dabei. Die zitierte Bemerkung von Heinz Becker entspricht, soweit wir sehen können, nicht den Tatsachen'.

5 Johann Mattheson, *Grundlage einer Ehrenpforte* (Hamburg, 1740); new ed. Max. Schneider (Berlin, 1910), pp. 94–5.

5a A complete edition by this author of Mattheson's *Cleopatra* will be published by *Das Erbe deutscher Musik*.

6 The complete title page of the libretto reads: *Die betrogene Staats-Liebe/ oder die unglückselige Cleopatra, Königin von Egypten/in einem Singe-Spiel auf dem Hamburgischen Schau-Platz vorgestellet* (Hamburg, 1704).

7 Johann Mattheson, *Der vollkommene Capellmeister* (Hamburg, 1739); facs. ed. M. Reimann (Kassel, 1954), p. 140.

8 A portion of the music for this scene, including Dercetaeus's aria, appears in Wolff, *Barockoper in Hamburg*, II, pp. 132–9. Several other excerpts from the same opera are given on pp. 118–28 of the same volume.

9 Paul Henry Lang, *George Frideric Handel* (New York, 1966), p. 33.

10 See Wolff, *Barockoper in Hamburg*, II, p. 128, for the music of both versions.

11 Friedrich Chrysander (ed.) *Georg Friedrich Händels Werke*, vol. 56, *Rodrigo;* repr. Gregg Press (Ridgewood, N.J., 1965), p. 6.

12 Johann Mattheson, *Critica Musica* (Hamburg, 1722–25); facs. ed. (Amsterdam, 1964), p. 71.

13 Friedrich Chrysander, *G. F. Händel*, I, p. 144.

WALTER E. BUSZIN

THE CHORALE IN THE BAROQUE ERA AND J. S. BACH'S CONTRIBUTION TO IT

———

In the Baroque era the hymn is regarded as being relatively unimportant. The era is measured chiefly by many by its larger forms, by its impressive orchestral music, its oratorios, its cantatas and other works of larger dimensions. By comparison, the hymn is to many a small form written for people who prefer more simple types of music based chiefly on sacred texts. Some are convinced that these texts should be artless and simple, rather than complex and intricate. The adroit poet deprecates such poetry because he finds it uncultivated, while the first-rate musician berates it because to him it expresses sentiments of too ordinary a level.

While it is true that there is much second-rate poetry and music, a spirit of discretion should always be applied. Even if neither poem nor music passes muster as being first class, both should be measured according to their intrinsic worth. It is possible for a first-rate composer to use inferior texts (*e.g.* Mozart and Schubert) or that an inferior poet bases his work on exalted and sublime thoughts (*cf.* the products of many hymnists).

The Baroque era is no exception. Its composers are not great simply because they are products of a great era and its poets do not excel because they rub shoulders with men of genius. Each work must be judged on its own merit and skill; none can be regarded on the basis of a counterfeit reputation. The text of a hymn must be genuine and sincere, not pretentious or false. Many people who write religious verse are easily misled by their own work because they overvalue it. Many a poet writes poetry for religious purposes and its real worth does not even come up to the level of most of the sentimental works of Christina Rosetti (1830–94), or, to name a hymn of the Baroque era, James Thomson's *A Hymn* (1730). While the author called his poem *A Hymn*, his product enjoys no reputation as a hymn. Though the poet has addressed it to God, it is not sufficiently religious to be a genuine hymn. The poem contains too much of the spirit of the Enlightenment and lacks the *Volkssprache* and *Volksgeist* of a religious hymn.

Many hymns of earlier eras are more 'hymn-like' than those of the eighteenth century. In the era of Pietism, which preceded the era of the Enlightenment, many hymns were too pietistic and lacked the objectivity which must characterize the classical spirit of genuine hymns. More of the objective spirit found commonly in classical hymnody may be found in Greek and Latin hymns of antiquity. The hymns of the Middle Ages are such classical hymns, though they deteriorated almost steadily as the Middle Ages advanced. Greek hymnody had the same experience; so did Latin hymnody as it advanced towards the Middle Ages. It is not difficult to produce a few examples, all found in the *English Hymnal* (Oxford University Press, London, 1933 edition): Number 77, 'Lord Jesus, think on Me' (Μνώεο, Χριστέ), Number 318, 'Let All Mortal Flesh Keep Silence' (Σιγησάτω πᾶεα σάρξ βροτελα and Number 310, 'From Glory to Glory Advancing' ('Απὸ σοξης εἰς σοξαν πορευόμενοι); (the latter two are from the Liturgy of St. James, which dates from the very beginning of the Christian Century); from the ninth century we have by St. Joseph the Hymnographer 1871 (d. 883): 'Let Our Choir New Anthems Raise' (Τῶν ἴξρῶν ξθλο φόρων).

As stated above, the older hymns are the best. The same applies to the Latin hymns: St. Ambrose (340–397): 'Veni, Redemptor Gentium'; 'At the Cross Her Station Keeping', ascribed to Jacopone da Todi (d. 1306): 'Stabat Mater Dolorosa'.

We must also consider the hymn's religious and Christian nature. The Baroque era was by no means thoroughly Christian. Indeed, much of it was pagan (*cf.* Frederick the Great) and some of it was religiously indifferent. The era of Pietism was religious, even Christian, but this too presented difficulties, since Pietism often pretended to be what it was not. Due to its lack of genuine integrity, much that happened in Pietism reflected sadly on the Baroque and led Pietism and Baroque pomp to the age of so-called enlightenment, to sophistication, and to rationalism.

Experiences of this kind were encountered by J. S. Bach, an orthodox Lutheran before and during his Arnstadt days. He chafed during his brief stay in Mühlhausen, was harrowed and temporarily imprisoned in

Weimar, was embarrassed because of Calvinism in Cöthen, so that he wrote to friends: 'Hüte dich vor dem Kalvinismus', and again, because of his Lutheran orthodoxy, was persecuted by rationalists in Leipzig. Taking into account the many difficulties of his life, which began when he was but a boy of nine and became an orphan, Bach lived through a very difficult time until he reached his life's end at the age of 65. His spiritual and theological difficulties were not the least among the many he experienced.

In 1728 Bach had serious difficulties with Gottlieb Gaudlitz, the youngest sub-deacon of the Nicolaikirche in Leipzig. It had been customary till then for the organist to select the hymns. Gaudlitz, however, took it upon himself to deprive the organist of this duty and to select the hymns for the day himself. This angered Bach, who saw in his privilege to select the hymns of the day, a serious obligation, since it afforded him an opportunity to maintain healthy standards in hymn-singing among the members of the congregation. What is more, Bach had soon become aware of the fact that sub-deacon Gaudlitz, who later became head-pastor of St. Thomas Church, was an outspoken rationalist with very little regard, if any, for the older classic chorales of the *Leipziger Gesangbuch* of 1729; Gaudlitz preferred the rationalistic chorales of his day. Bach saw in this step an attempt to attract people to rationalism and to drag them down to the depths of dangerous doctrinal and theological standards. Bach fought against this tendency and insisted on his own right and duty to select the hymns for the day. Nevertheless, he lost the battle because he could not win against the tendencies of his day. This was by no means the first battle he had lost. He had lost out to the pietists—to the ills of pietism (there were also other reasons, for some of which Bach might be blamed); but now he lost out for an even more important reason; the pietists had, after all, still been Christians who placed their hope for eternal salvation in Christ, whereas the rationalists put it instead in their own reason, intelligence and strength. Bach's conflict with Gaudlitz was probably his most viable battle with rationalism.

Bach was not always alone in waging his battles. Birnbaum and Mizler helped him overcome Johann Adolf Scheibe, the rationalistic author of *Der critische Mussicus* and the originator of modern musical criticism. Among Bach's staunchest friends and defenders, moreover, was, Johann Matthias Gesner (1691–1761): an expert linguist, a man of encyclopaedic learning, and the Conrector of the Gymnasium in Weimar, he played a leading rôle in improving the educational standards of Bruns-wick-Lüneburg. Gesner was also an able organizer and understood how to remedy matters which under his predecessor, Johann Heinrich Ernesti the Elder, had declined. Gesner's activities exerted a wholesome influence in Germany for more than half a century.

It is possible that Gesner was responsible for attracting Lorenz Christoph Mizler (1711–78), a former pupil of J. S. Bach (1731–34), to Leipzig. In 1734 Mizler wrote a master's thesis based on the topic: *Quod Musica ars sit pars eruditionis philosophiae*; in 1738 he organized the *Societät der musikalischen Wissenschaften* and invited noteworthy musicians of his day (Telemann, Handel, C. H. Graun) to join this society. Much to Mizler's displeasure, Bach at first refused to join, fearing, perhaps that the Society would not prove to be worthwhile and would involve him in time-consuming activities. Possibly Bach consented to join, after his return from Berlin, when he learned that various notables had joined. In any case, Bach was elected to membership in 1747. His portrait was painted by Elias Gottlieb Hausmann, the illustrious painter of the Dresden Court. This painting probably became the most famous Bach portrait; it shows him holding a triple canon in six parts which was later (in 1754; after Bach's death) published in the *Musicalische Bibliothek* and is republished in *Bach*, *A Biography* by C. S. Terry (Oxford University Press, p. 255) and elsewhere. Since it was customary for each candidate for membership in Mizler's *Societät* to submit proof of the candidate's ability, Bach sent in: 'Einige canonische Veränderungen über das Weihnachtslied: Vom Himmel hoch, da komm ich her, vor die Orgel mit 2 Clavieren und dem Pedal'. The opus was engraved and published by Balthasar Schmidt of Nuremberg. This composition reflects Bach's delight in the chorales of his Lutheran Church and was among his favourites. Bach's work far outlived Mizler's society, which finally enrolled only nineteen members after nearly half-a-century of existence. Only five additional members were elected to the Society after Bach.

Even Bach's fame as a top-ranking composer did not increase his following, as may be seen from the sixty-nine hymnarias he prepared for Georg Christian Schemelli's (*c.* 1670–1739) *Musikalische Gesangbuch*, written and intended to be a Lutheran antidote to the pietistic hymnal published in Halle in 1704 by the theologian and hymnologist J. A. Freylinghausen (1670–1739); Freylinghausen became a personal vicar of Pastor Aug. Hermann Francke (1663–1727), and also his son-in-law.

Bach participated in this undertaking by preparing the figured basses in Schemelli's *Gesangbuch*. Only one of these bears the signature of Bach; two others ('Dir, dir Jehova, will ich singen' and 'Komm süsser Tod') are ascribed to Bach by men like Arnold Schering, Fred Hamel, and others. The songs of the Schemelli collection are intriguing, but they are arias rather than hymns. They reflect that Bach was not popular as a composer of hymns in his day; some are indeed more popular today than they were in the eighteenth century. Despite Bach's cooperation, the volume did not meet with success and today only Bach's contributions are well known. Thus we have additional proof that the music of J. S. Bach did not enjoy widespread popularity in his day. His hymns were so aria-like that they were never really popular, and the same applies to his settings of the Passions, the majority of his cantatas, and a veritable host of other works, all of which did not enjoy general fame until after Mendelssohn-Bartholdy's performance of the *St. Matthew Passion* in 1829. From then on the situation gradually began to change, at least with people of higher musical understanding.

This does not mean that Bach had only a few friends and supporters. After all, among his admirers were his numerous pupils, his own highly talented sons, Johann M. Gesner, King Frederick the Great, Johann Gottfried Walther, Prince Leopold of Cöthen, Pastor Christian Weiss of the Thomaskirche, Georg Philipp Telemann, the various men who prepared librettos for Bach's choral works, Mizler and Pastor Salomon Deyling (1677–1755), the latter the Pastor and Superintendent at Leipzig and professor at its university. The fact that Deyling was promoted to these positions proves that even after Bach's death, orthodox Lutheranism was still alive. Deyling was called to his posts in Leipzig in 1721, before Bach was appointed to Leipzig, and it was Deyling who required that Bach subscribe to the *Formula of Concord* of the Lutheran Church at the time the new cantor of Leipzig was confirmed in his office and sworn into his new duties. While Bach and Deyling were good friends throughout their joint stay in Leipzig, Bach repeatedly had serious difficulties with Johann Aug. Ernesti from the time Ernesti became Bach's superior in 1734. This may be explained easily when one considers that Ernesti was twenty-two years younger than Bach and a dyed-in-the-wool rationalist, while Deyling, eight years older than Bach, was of one mind and spirit with the Leipzig cantor.

An examination of the texts of Bach's choral work proves that he was usually their true servant, though Bach's Schemelli texts are, more or less, an exception to this rule. We mean the cantata texts, based on the hymns of his *church hymnal* rather than the aria texts of his Schemelli *Choralbuch*. Bach evidently experienced the chorales of his *Kirchengesang-buch* more personally than the arias he prepared as solo pieces. An excellent example is Bach's Chorale-motet *Jesu, meine Freude* whose text has earmarks of his Schemelli chorales. Among his six chorale-motets, this motet is in a class by itself. Five of its movements are each for five voices. Despite its length, it adheres quite rigidly to E minor. Eight of its movements occur in this key. Throughout the basic chorale is never used to strive for what the Germans call *Effekthascherei*—a striving for effects. A romantic approach to the motet is out of place, reflects bad taste, and gives a false impression of what Bach strives for. Bach's motet on *Jesu, meine Freude* resembles Buxtehude's on this same chorale, but Bach's expresses more breadth and depth, and is, perhaps, more theo-logical in concept. Whereas Buxtehude restricts himself to the chorale-text itself and does not deviate from it, Bach draws in related and pertinent passages of Holy Writ and links them with passages from the Epistles of St. Paul; he thus widens the scope. The motet is said to be the one Bach composed as an expression of Lutheran faith. It was, at one time usually sung *a cappella*, thus following the precepts of Justus Thibant of the nineteenth century, who also insisted that the music of Palestrina be sung without accompaniment so as to bring out its inner effects with deeper feeling. Today, however, we have moved away from such *Effekthascherei* and perform the work in a more straightforward and objective manner, eschewing emotionalism and sentimentalism. For this reason, too, we today prefer to sing this chorale motet with instrumental accompaniment. Taking the profound theological content of the motet into serious consideration, we can readily see why Archbishop Nathan Söderblom of Uppsala in Sweden referred to J. S. Bach as 'the Fifth Evangelist'. While the very melody of the chorale, written by Johann Crüger (1653), is fascinating and famous, yet those who feel the profound spirit and appeal of this noteworthy hymn find it best when matched to its glorious text.

So it is with most Bach chorales; each has a noteworthy text; its melody, though engaging and fascinating, is actually secondary. Usually those who undervalue the melodies of these hymns also underrate their text. If the melodies lack immediate appeal, it is better that one learn first to comprehend the more profound theological content of the text in order to appreciate their full value as hymns.

We see here that a hymn text and its tune must match if they are to be successful. An inferior text will cause a good melody to decline while an inferior melody will quickly push a good text into the shade. This applies to sacred verse as well as to secular.

It is remarkable that a composer like J. S. Bach rarely wrote inferior music for texts of superior value. One may not enjoy his music as much at certain times as on other occasions, but his music never becomes trivial or bad. For our present purposes, the chorale melody 'Jesu, meine Freude' is a perfect example. We bear in mind the impeccable superiority of Bach's work when we consider the music of later eighteenth-century composers. We might similarly extol the merits of Morales and Palestrina except that they were from quite another era. Great composers of the eighteenth century like Handel, Mozart, Telemann, the sons of J. S. Bach, and others lacked either the genius of J. S. Bach, or they lacked his integrity and Christian faith. Handel, for example, was a man of high integrity, but he repeated music others had written before; J. S. Bach, too, repeated music: but when he repeated, he usually used material he himself had written before; or he gave credit to composers when the music was not of his own creation. Bach was no plagiarist; his own personal integrity would not permit him to claim credit for himself when others deserved the credit.

This does not mean either that J. S. Bach was the only composer of his century whose hymns were outstanding and noteworthy. There was Martin Luther, whom Bach admired and imitated on various occasions; Bach did not take himself seriously as a poet and to him we ascribe no poetry, though he cooperated with librettists occasionally when they wrote the texts for his Passions and cantatas.

Among the German writers of hymn texts of Bach's time who were among the best known authors of hymn texts in the eighteenth century were: Bartholomäus Crasselius (Krasselt), Johann Freylinghausen, Johann Daniel Herrnschmidt, Salomo Franck, Erdmann Neumeister, Benjamin Scholck, Valentin Löscher, Georg Philipp Telemann, Johann Balthasar König, Johann Gottfried Herrmann, Johann Andreas Rothe, Karl Heinrich von Bogatzky, Johann Jakob Rambach, Philipp Friedrich Hiller, Joachim Neander, Gerhard Tersteegen, Nikolaus Ludwig Graf von Zinzendorf, Christian Gregor, Christian Fürchtegott Gellert, Mathias Claudius and Johann Abraham Peter Schulz. As one scans this list one does not find in it one author on the level of Martin Luther, Paul Gerhardt, Philipp Nicolai, Paul Eber, Johannes Herman,

Nikolaus Selnecker and a few other eminent hymnographers. This proves the truth of the statement made before: The Baroque era was not an age for truly great hymnody; its hymn texts were ordinary, at times sentimental and pompous.

The situation was not a bit better in England, where Handel spent most of his life. Though a native German, Handel is usually identified with the English people. His fame has all but obliterated the names of many famous contemporaries. This applies particularly to authors and composers of hymns (*e.g.* Isaac Watts, Charles Wesley, John Wesley, Philip Doddridge—a noteworthy author of hymn texts whose name is not even mentioned in Webster's *New World Dictionary of the American Languages*, College Edition, Cleveland and New York, 1951—S. Webbe, and other English hymnists of the Baroque era).

Since the Baroque era covered a century and a half, we are hardly surprised to hear that there were many and great differences in the texts and melodies of the hymns. The changes concerned not only the structure of the hymn, but also the character and style of their melodies, the purpose and occasion for which the hymn and its melody were written, the differences in ability of the composer or author, the cultural standards of the land, the theological differences involved, *etc.* If the people were members of a certain denomination, their convictions were likely to coincide; if not, they differed. There is no doubt that in considering the situation *in toto*, we must return again to Bach, whose church works were exegetical treatment of his texts. This, however, does not permit us to go so far as did Albert Schweitzer with regard to the symbolism of these texts and to reduce them to a mere system; nor does it permit us to say what Bach did not say *expressis verbis*. (The same applies to other authors and composers, too.)

On the other hand, there is no doubt that J. S. Bach is often a slave of his texts. This tradition he had inherited from the past; but it linked up perfectly with his theological convictions, and enabled him to remain consistent with the convictions of his heart and faith.

Bach's hymns have enjoyed widespread fame from the eighteenth century to the present. But they are often not true to the sixteenth-century (or even earlier) original. This is due in large part to the aims of Martin Opitz (1597–1639) who, though by no means a great poet, nevertheless exerted a great influence, notably through his book *Von der deutschen Poeterey* (1624) in which he repeated the theses he had set forth previously. He sought to improve original texts, to simplify chorales by depriving them of their original metrical character and by converting them instead into isorhythmic verse. To this day, Bach's reputation rests upon his influence as a metrical reformer. Opitz was succeeded in his isometric endeavours by the Pietists, who flourished from the latter part of the seventeenth century to the middle of the eighteenth. Though pietistically inclined people have always been among the strongest advocates of isometric hymnody, today there is, in Germany as well as in the USA, a clear movement to the return to original rhythmical hymnody.

Bach isometrified many chorales. He lived towards the end of the Pietistic era and at the beginning of the era of Enlightenment which, in the field of isometric developments, continued what the Pietists had perpetuated. That Bach was rhythmically and not isorhythmically minded may be seen from some rhythmical chorales he prepared (*e.g.* the well-known chorales: 'Aus tiefer Not schrei ich zu Dir', 'Aus meines Herzens Grunde', 'Freu dich sehr, o meine Seele', 'Nun lasst uns Gott dem Herren', 'Nun lob, mein Seel, den Herren', 'Erschienen ist der herrlich Tag', *etc.*). Bach seems to have added almost countless ornamental notes to his harmonizations of chorales (passing notes, appoggiaturas, mordents, trills, *etc.*). Bach was by no means the first to use musical ornamentation; in fact, his use of musical ornaments is in close relation to the instrumental music, rather than the *a cappella* style, of his age. It is known today that the chorale harmonizations of Bach's cantatas and Passions were sung with orchestral accompaniment and not *a cappella*. This was in keeping with the spirit of his time and age. His motets were sung in their entirety with accompaniment, and were thus in the same class as cantatas, oratorios, masses, and other types of accompanied choral music. This practice had been followed as early as the time of Monteverdi, Palestrina and his contemporaries. The *a cappella* ideal, therefore, advanced by the Romantic school, was, as we have said above, out of keeping with the standards and practices of the whole age.

We thus see that in the Baroque era the problem of the chorale is complex and fraught with difficulties of every description. This is due to many causes, but especially because the chorale was a product of an era by no means homogeneous, consistent, or uniform, but filled with differences of pose, style, and theology. In all this, it is Bach who has survived the quarrels, the pettiness, and the religious arguments to emerge for posterity in all his towering, all-faith-embracing greatness.

JACQUES CHAILLEY

JOSEPH HAYDN AND THE FREEMASONS

Haydn's connection with the Freemasons seems to have been generally considered an event of minor significance. 'While Haydn felt in tune with the humanitarian precepts of his fellow Masons, he may have been too deeply rooted in the Catholic faith and liturgy to concern himself seriously with the Masonic religious ideas.'[1] Thus writes Karl Geiringer in his masterly book on Haydn, remarks which express the prevailing attitude. One might ask, however, if there are not grounds for revising it. It is known that the antagonism between Freemasonry and the Catholic church did not at that time have the same aspect as in our days. As their constitution of 1723 stated, the Freemasons intended to remain deeply religious while allowing their members liberty to adhere to the denomination of their choice. The bible was for them one of the 'Books of Sacred Law'. The successive condemnations of Pope Clement XII in 1738 and later by Pope Benedict XIV in 1751 had not yet been circulated through the German speaking countries and were not yet in force there.[2] Thus, in spite of such condemnations, the Lodges included numerous members of the clergy, at times high ranking ones. Haydn's Catholic faith did not prevent his sincere adherence to Freemasonry. His piety was probably never more affirmed than when composing the *Creation* and yet this is one of his works most profoundly imbued with Masonic ideas. This aspect of Haydn's output would require a study in depth which we cannot attempt at this occasion. Our aim is only, without using new documents, to draw attention to some connections and coincidences which seem to justify a study of this kind.

117

The first coincidence appears without difficulty if one assembles in chronological order—instead of mentioning them in different chapters— the events which led to Haydn's entry into the masonic order. Let us enumerate the facts. In December 1782 Mozart, influenced by Haydn's 'Russian' Quartets, starts composing a series of Quartets which he was to dedicate to Haydn. (However, there is no proof that he had at this moment decided on the dedication.) At that time the two musicians hardly knew each other.[3] Mozart's work on these Quartets in which no trace of Masonic influence is yet noticeable, proceeds without haste. The first three mature for a whole year, from December 1782 to the end of 1783. Then a year passes before the advent of No. 4.[4] At this moment—the Autumn of 1784—Haydn visits Vienna for a somewhat longer stay than customary and becomes Mozart's friend. He meets him frequently at chamber music sessions where he very often plays the second violin while Mozart takes over the viola.[5] Haydn's presence and the string quartet 'aura' that surrounds him provide a strong impetus for Mozart. The creative schedule for the Quartets suddenly changes; the three last are composed in less than three months, and only a few days lie between No. 5 and No. 6.

This is also the period when Mozart joins the Masons. The ceremony takes place on December 14th, one month after the completion of the fourth Quartet in B flat. This event marks him deeply. The two Quartets No. 5 and 6, in A and C, the first works written after his initiation and under the direct impact of the ceremony, feel strongly the effects of it: they are both imbued with Masonic meaning.

During this very same period Haydn in his turn decided to join the Masonic Order. From now on we shall see events running on with a remarkable parallelism between Haydn and Mozart. The latter had been initiated, it was said, on December 14th, in the Lodge '*zur Wohltätigkeit*'. In the days which followed he was not long, as we know from his signature on the attendance books,[6] in making a special habit of visiting the Lodge '*zur Wahren Eintracht*', presided over by Von Born, who had made of it a true Academy of superior minds. It is to this Lodge that, on December 29th, a fortnight after Mozart's initiation, Haydn sent his application for membership, in the form of a letter to the master of ceremonies, von Weber, Court secretary.[7] On January 10th a Lodge resolution put Haydn's name on the inter-Lodge consultation list preliminary to the decision properly speaking. On the 13th, this Lodge, and not his own which had made the request, received Mozart into the second grade, that of Companion. Two days later, on the 15th, Haydn visits Mozart and hears the first three quartets of the set.[8] Written before their composer's initiation, they are not touched by Masonic ideas, but since the day before Mozart was fully involved in the elaboration of the Quartet in C, and in contrast it very strongly has the Masonic imprint: he must certainly have discussed it with the older man whose application he certainly would have known about. Eight days later, on the 24th, Haydn's application was put to the vote and accepted. The date of admission was at first fixed for the 28th of the same month, but, on being summoned to Eszterháza, Haydn had to ask for a postponement of the ceremony, which was put back to February 11th. On February 2nd Haydn wrote to Count Anton Apponyi a warm letter of thanks.[9]

Haydn found himself prepared for this proceeding. Contrary to Mozart, who from his youth was familiar with Masonic circles, Haydn had for a long time been a stranger to them. Not before 1780 did names of well-known Freemasons, such as the publisher Artaria, appear in his biography, and even then they played but secondary parts. His stay in Vienna must have plunged him abruptly into this milieu. Jacob mentions among his acquaintances of this time, apart of course from Mozart himself, von Sonnenfels, Ignaz von Born, Michael Denis, Alxinger, Blumauer, Schikaneder, Greiner, Puchberg, Tost.[10] Von Kees and Van Swieten, in whose house he performed with Mozart, were Masons, and it is well known that Haydn particularly enjoyed his visits to the salon of Madame von Genzinger, whose husband was a Mason.

And so Haydn's initiation ceremony was fixed for Friday, February 11th.[11] That very day, Mozart's father Leopold arrives in Vienna and settles down at his son's home. Was this new coincidence planned? One does not know, but one is aware that less than a month later Leopold was to follow Haydn's example and become the second one to be converted by his son. When sending Nannerl a few days later a report on his trip, Leopold seemed to be in an unusual state of euphoria; he described with delight Friday's recital where Wolfgang performed his Piano Concerto, but does not say a word regarding the initiation that day although mentioning directly the evening music on Saturday. This evening music is a celebrated one: at this occasion Haydn, after hearing the last three quartets of 'his' set, said to Leopold the famous words: 'I tell you before God as an honest man that your son is the greatest composer known to me.' Leopold reports on this scene with justifiable pleasure. What he did not say (did he know it?) is that the scene followed the initiation ceremony of Haydn which was almost certainly caused by his son. The two artists, who besides Leopold and Wolfgang, formed the quartet, Anton and Bartholomäus Tinti, were also members of the Lodge *Zur wahren Eintracht*. One may assume that Haydn, Wolfgang and these two (for Leopold, not yet initiated, could not take part) arrived at Mozart's home directly after the ceremony[11] and the radiance surrounding this day is reflected in Haydn's famous declaration.[12]

Seven months later Mozart was to dedicate to his new Masonic brother the set of six Quartets, the history of which is linked to these events. One should read the dedication (with its use of the brotherly 'thou') in its historic context;[13] one discovers in it a meaning quite different from that usually found in it.

This combination of facts and dates is, as we see, not without interest, and makes well-known facts appear in a different light. Haydn's entry into the Masonic order was not, as Mozart's, the result of a long development, but of a rapid interaction of circumstances whereby Mozart's example played a decisive part. The composition of the Quartets which Mozart was subsequently to dedicate to him, was a determining factor, and the dedication supplies indirect proof for this. As to the famous verdict Leopold reports, the conditions under which it was uttered (conditions not mentioned in Leopold's letter) makes us consider this verdict not only as proof of a very real artistic admiration, but also as expression of personal feelings resulting from the events of this exceptional week and from Haydn's gratitude to the man who had shown him the way.

Was Haydn's initiation in 1785 merely a single blaze without sequels? Many have thought so—observing that his name appears but rarely in the registers of attendance and was even eliminated in 1787 from the list of members of his Lodge.[14] Doubtlessly Haydn appears to have been much less active a Mason than Mozart. His work destined for Masonic ritual comprises merely a few chants of little significance,[15] but still their mere existence may prove his loyalty. Moreover one begins to understand now that it was not only in such works that Freemasonry played a part in Haydn's musical creation. It seems certain that Haydn, though not attaching to his initiation the philosophical and moral values seen by Mozart, and though remaining as loyal to the Catholic church as he was before the initiation—which may not have been the case with Mozart— was faithful to the Freemasons too. This point of view is indispensable for understanding part of his work which is of considerable significance since it includes a composition as important as the *Creation*.

As to the elimination of his name in 1787, it is easy to explain by his being mostly absent from Vienna. In the dedication of the Quartets dated September 1785, Mozart observes that Haydn's visit in February was but an occasional one and that he had not returned for seven months. 'Thou thyself, dear friend, during thy last sojourn in this capital. . . .' This sentence reflects the importance Mozart attached to the visit, and, this, as we have seen, not only for musical reasons. Moreover another, quite material, reason may have caused the elimination of Haydn's name: he was very careful in matters of money and it is quite possible that he simply neglected paying his dues to a society which he could hardly ever visit, not being a resident of Vienna.

One has often noted the difference in the rapidity of reaction between vivacious Mozart and deliberate Haydn. Here we have a new instance for this fact. While Mozart's initiation exerted only a few days later its influence on his work, it took four years until a similar reaction occurred with Haydn. Once more one may attribute this to his distance from Vienna; it seems that one has to wait for the last months of his service for Nicolas I Esterházy to trace in his music the equivalent of the Masonic crisis which Mozart's music exhibits since the end of 1784. And this time again it appears to coincide with a new phase of intimacy with Mozart. One knows that at the end of 1789 Haydn was in Vienna and spent New Year's Eve with Mozart attending the private dress rehearsal of *Così fan tutte* with another Mason, Michael Puchberg, as Mozart's only guests.[16]

It is only toward 1789–90 that one may observe in Haydn that searching for a musical symbolism based on Masonic ideas which was at times to change his idiom and which Mozart had revealed since the beginning of 1785 in works not directly destined for Masonic use. It seems certain, however, that Haydn had at a very early stage learned—maybe with Mozart's help—to understand the secret allusions. In this way one may probably understand his famous reply regarding the 'dissonant' introduction to the Quartet in C: 'If Mozart wrote it this way, he must have had good reasons.'[17] This has a strange resemblance to what he wrote to Marianne von Genzinger regarding his own Sonata in E flat. (C. Landon No. 59; Pässler No. 49): 'It has a deep significance that I will analyse for your Grace when the time comes.'[18] The reply to Kozeluch has always been interpreted as a sort of blanket endorsement of his friend's genius; even if Haydn had such faith in Mozart, his remark was in this case caused by quite a different line of thought.

At least two Haydn works seem, to an extent still to be determined, to point to preoccupation with esoteric music, probably of Masonic significance: the Quartets opus 54 and the piano Sonata in E flat (C. Landon No. 59; Päsler No. 49) mentioned above. Regarding the Quartets Geiringer[19] noted their unusual form, 'full of attractive little surprises'. Among these one observes the tonal plan of No. 1 which modulates from E flat to G major. Our surprise increases when we become aware these were later to be the two guiding poles of symbolic value in the tonal plan of *Die Zauberflöte*.[20] These Quartets are dedicated to Johann Tost who was a Freemason;[21] he was to marry Anna de Jerlischek. The latter had at the same time commissioned and paid for the Sonata No. 59 (49), again a work in E flat. Haydn had really intended the work for his special friend, Marianne von Genzinger,[22] who likewise was the wife of a Freemason. Geiringer has recognized in this Sonata a completely new concept, especially so in the solemn *Adagio* on which Haydn made the mysterious remark cited above.

In the same year, the death of Nicolas I Esterházy on September 28, 1790, provided Haydn with the freedom to come to Vienna. He did not stay there very long, and left on December 15th for England. One knows, however, that the short time in Vienna sufficed for reestablishing contact with Mozart and taking leave from him. At this very moment—provided our deductions are exact[23] which differ from the customary dates given—Mozart began to think of his great Masonic work, *Die Zauberflöte*. Did he talk about it to his friend? We do not know. However, when Haydn returned from London in July 1792[24] Mozart was no longer among the living, but his *Zauberflöte* was enjoying a triumphant success. Haydn, on the other hand, brought from his trip two great experiences which were to motivate the *Creation*: the oratorios by Handel and his visit to the astronomer Herschel. The latter was especially important as it directed his deep religious feeling toward the Masonic reverence for the 'Great Architect of the Universe'; and it was in this spirit that the text was conceived by van Swieten. The project only took definite shape on Haydn's return for his second visit to London, but it is noteworthy that from 1793 on rumours persisted that Haydn was at work on 'a sequel to the *Zauberflöte*',[25] in other words, on a great Masonic work.

For a long time it was recognized that Masonic inspiration prevails in the text to the *Creation*. On this account, Haydn had to suffer attacks, all the more violent as the new Emperor, Francis II, had, to a far greater extent than his predecessors, entered into an open fight against the Freemasons.* According to all biographers it was merely the text of the oratorio which revealed Masonic aspects. Haydn, it is claimed, did not pay enough attention to it, and no Masonic meaning is to be found in the music.[26] A study of the score does not allow for such an attitude.[27] Moreover the minute details which van Swieten—as later Paul Claudel—indicated to the composer so as to have even the less important intentions of the librettist conveyed in music, make such negligence on Haydn's part seem impossible. One must also consider the well-known reticence of the clergy who became more and more inimical to the Order, and, on the other hand, the great favour which the *Creation* always enjoyed among high-class Masons of the nineteenth century.[28] Masonic tendencies seem at first sight to be less in evidence in the *Seasons* than in the *Creation*, but it is not impossible that they will be traced there, too, and likewise in many other Haydn works which we had no chance to examine from this point of view.

The real study dealing with the Masonic impact on Haydn's music has still to be written. Anyway it did not seem unnecessary to prove at least that such a study ought to be undertaken. It would provide a new chapter in the treatment of Haydn's output which has reached so high a level, thanks to the efforts of many musicologists, and especially the great scholar to whom this volume is dedicated.

* Freemasonry was officially banned in Austria on January 2, 1795, and remained illegal until the Monarchy fell in 1918. Ed.

NOTES

1 Karl Geiringer, *Haydn. A Creative Life in Music*, 3rd ed. Berkeley, 1968, p. 92.

2 J. Kuéss-Scheichelbauer, *200 Jahre Freimaurerei in Oesterreich*, Wien, 1959; J. Palou, *La Franc-Maçonnerie*, Paris, Payot 1966.

3 J. and B. Massin, *Mozart*, Paris, 1959, p. 426, remark that before 1784 one never finds the names of Haydn and Mozart cited together in any source.

4 We use here the numbering in chronological order which has No. 4 precede No. 3, contrary to the edition subsequently established by Mozart.

5 Massin, p. 427.

6 Otto Erich Deutsch, *Mozart und die Wiener Loge*, Vienna 1952.

7 I specially wish to thank H. C. Robbins Landon, who was kind enough to inform me of the text of several documents mentioned here and still unedited. Extracts from some of them have been reproduced by Otto Erich Deutsch, in an article in *Neue Freie Presse*, March 1932, entitled 'Haydn bleibt Lehrling', also by Carl Maria Brand in his book *Die Messen von Joseph Haydn*, Würzburg, 1941.

8 Otto Erich Deutsche, *Mozart, die Dokumente seines Lebens*, Bärenreiter, 1961, p. 209. This calender is rather interesting as it shows that the number of rehearsals considered normal at that time deviates from what is customary today.

9 H. E. Jacob, *Haydn*, French ed., Paris, 1950, p. 148, interprets this letter as a request for candidateship, but this is incompatible with the order of dates.

10 Jacob, p. 147–9.

11 Massin, p. 431, notes the 10th as Friday. As the dates are indicated in the documents sometimes by the date and sometimes by the weekday, such an error may have consequences for the right dating.

12 Geiringer, p. 93.

13 Text often published, *cf. e.g.*, O. E. Deutsch *Mozart. Die Dokumente seines Lebens*, p. 220.

14 Geiringer, p. 83.

15 Hoboken, vol. II (in preparation).

16 Massin, p. 511.

17 Geiringer, p. 83.

18 Geiringer, p. 98.

19 Geiringer, pp. 312–13.

20 J. Chailley, *La Flûte Enchantée, opéra maçonnique*, Paris, R. Laffont, 1968, p. 171.

21 Jacob, p. 147.

22 Geiringer, p. 305, f.n. 2.

23 J. Chailley, *La Flûte Enchantée, op. cit.*, pp. 44–5.

24 Had Haydn's two visits to England left room for Masonic contacts? The research, H. C. Robbins Landon says, has been pursued and found negative. Such a research could also be done about Haydn's connections with Paris, especially regarding the commission of the so-called 'Paris Symphonies' which concern the 'Concerts de la Loge Olympique' open to everybody, but clearly of Masonic intention. Likewise one would have to investigate the exceptional honours granted to Haydn by the Institut de France and the official performance of *The Creation* in 1802, famous on account of the attempt against the First Consul's life at this occasion.

25 Jacob, p. 208.

26 Jacob, p. 240.

27 We have pointed out one of the principal Masonic features of the score in the brief analysis we presented for educational purposes on the journal *L'Education Musicale* of May 1963, and in a paper for the Société Française de Musicologie in December 17, 1964, an outline of which was published in the *Revue de Musicologie*, December 1964, pp. 290–1.

28 Zelter, *e.g.*, Goethe's musical adviser, was one of the work's most ardent supporters (Jacob, p. 239). Wieland wrote a poem in its praise (Geiringer p. 185), *etc.*

MARTIN CHUSID

SOME OBSERVATIONS ON LITURGY, TEXT AND STRUCTURE IN HAYDN'S LATE MASSES

The most significant bodies of vocal music written during the latter part of the eighteenth century and first decade of the nineteenth are the mature operas of Mozart (1780 ff.) and those items of Haydn's sacred music dating from his last years of composition. Significantly, both composers were accomplished masters of the instrumental idioms of their day, and each placed the new, dramatic-symphonic style of the late eighteenth century at the service of vocal texts. However, unlike Mozart who wrote his best orchestral and vocal compositions during the same period of his life, Haydn composed his most important vocal works after he had composed the 'London' symphonies that marked the end of his long career as a symphonist.

As an explanation for this phenomenon, Robbins Landon has offered the provocative thought that by 1795 Haydn had brought the symphonic form as he knew it to its most highly developed state, and in searching for new means of expression returned to the large scale Orchestral Mass which he had cultivated earlier.

It is clear from his correspondence and London notebooks that in the course of his visits to England (1791–92 and 1794–95), Haydn had been deeply impressed with performances of sacred music, especially Handel's oratorios, and was much stimulated in that direction compositionally. Fortunately, during the following years (1795 ff.) his duties for Nicolaus II, fourth of the Esterházy princes under whom he served, were relatively light. In fact, his only regular compositional task was to provide a new mass for performance on the name day of Nicolaus' wife, Princess Marie Hermenegild, an admirer and benefactress of the ageing composer. As a result, he was able to devote the greatest share of his remaining energies to vocal music, and, among other works, completed his two well-known oratorios and the last six masses.[1]

These masses differ markedly from those of his earlier masses still extant, and Landon's thesis that 'the late Haydn masses are in their fundamental construction symphonies for voices and orchestra using the mass text'[2] forms the point of departure for this study.

As is well known, Haydn's masses were written for performance as part of the actual celebration of the High Mass. Consequently, certain portions of the setting were heard successively, that is without a break (*e.g.* the Kyrie and Gloria), whereas others were separated by fairly extensive sections of the Accentus and Concentus, especially preceding and following the Credo. A glance at a scheme for the typical *Missa Cantata*, Figure 1, will make this clear.

FIGURE 1

SCHEME OF A TYPICAL 'MISSA CANTATA' ACCORDING TO THE ROMAN RITE[3]

ACCENTUS: (recited or chanted by the priest)	CONCENTUS: (sung by the choir)	
	PROPER	ORDINARY
1. .... INTROIT		
2.		KYRIE
3.		GLORIA
4. COLLECT(S)		
5. EPISTLE		
6. .... GRADUAL		
.... ALLELUIA		
7. GOSPEL		
8.		CREDO
9. .... OFFERTORY		
.... (MOTET)		
10. PREFACE		
11.		SANCTUS[4]
12.		BENEDICTUS

Because of the passages separating the items of the Ordinary, and because of the manner in which Haydn has subdivided these items, it is here suggested that each of the six late masses may be viewed as consisting of a cycle of three larger structures whose grouping subsumes, without altering, the traditional sections of the Ordinary.[5]

The first such structure consists of the Kyrie and Gloria, the second is equivalent to the Credo, and the third is comprised of the Sanctus, Benedictus and Agnus Dei. Only the last of what may be termed 'vocal' symphonies is interrupted by additional liturgical activity, and these activities (*i.e.* the silent Elevation of the Blessed Sacrament following the Sanctus, and the rapid chanting of the Pater Noster between the Benedictus and Agnus Dei) are not comparable in scope or performance time to those liturgical items separating the three vocal symphonies one from another.

Even more than their positioning within the service, Haydn's balancing of tempos, metres and keys for the subdivisions of the Mass Ordinary suggests the appropriateness of an analogy with his instrumental symphonies. See the diagram of the *Mass in the Time of War*, Figure 2, and the Appendix of similar diagrams for the other five late masses.

Notice that each of the vocal symphonies consists of a cycle of movements. Here there are four in number; in the other late masses there are usually four and never less than three. The first and last of these movements are in the same key, and with a single exception they are fast.[6] The first movement may have a slow introduction,[7] and the last movement is usually in a quicker tempo than the first. Each of the vocal symphonies has at least one slow or moderate movement, and it is always in a contrasting key or mode. As is to be expected in sacred compositions, there is no counterpart to the minuets or scherzos of the instrumental symphony. However, one of their principal functions, that of providing a contrast with an earlier, more solemn movement, is assumed by the more consistently cheerful sections such as the openings of the Gloria or the Et Resurrexit.

FIGURE 2

Mass in C (*Mass in the Time of War, Paukenmesse*) (1796)

Vocal Symphony, No. 1

Mvt.	Text	Tempo and No. of bars	Metre	Key
I.	KYRIE:	Largo (10 bars)–	C	C maj.–c min. V
		Allegro moderato (83 bars)	C	C maj.
II.	GLORIA:	Vivace (124 bars)	3/4	C maj.
III.	Qui tollis:	Adagio (71 bars)	¢	A maj.–a min.
IV.	Quoniam tu solus:	Allegro–Più stretto (102 bars)	3/4	C maj.

Vocal Symphony, No. 2

I.	CREDO:	Allegro (33 bars)	C	C maj.
II.	Et incarnatus est:	Adagio (60 bars)	3/4	C min.
III.	Et resurrexit:	Allegro (91 bars)	3/4	C maj.*
IV.	Et vitam venturi:	Vivace (128 bars)	¢	C maj.

Vocal Symphony, No. 3

I.	SANCTUS:	Adagio (13 bars)–	C	C maj.–V
	Pleni sunt coeli:	Allegro con spirito (25 bars)	C	C maj.†
II.	BENEDICTUS:	Andante (111 bars)	6/8	C min.–C maj.
III.	AGNUS DEI.‡	Adagio (39 bars)	3/4	F maj.–C maj. V
IV.	Dona nobis pacem:	Allegro con spirito–		
		Più presto (125 bars)	3/4	C maj.

* During final six bars there is a modulation to A minor V.
† Opening six bars in minor.
‡ Discussed below.

It may be observed that the longest of the three symphonies is usually the first, the Kyrie-Gloria, and the shortest is the second, the Credo. Furthermore, in deference to the continuity required by the texts, those movements within any complete item of the Ordinary (*i.e.* the Gloria, Credo or Agnus Dei) are usually linked or related in some fashion.[8]

At this point it should be stressed that here, as in other analogies, there is a point at which differences exceed similarities and should not be minimized. The use of voices and the greater importance of the organ, for example, sometimes lead Haydn to scoring procedures that differ from those in his instrumental symphonies. I believe, for instance, that Peter Pirie's comment about the Kyrie of the earlier *Mariazellermesse* (1782) applies to many movements in Haydn's later masses as well: '. . . the way the chorus usurps the function of the strings in cementing the texture and providing a solid foundation for the harmony—leaves the strings free to ornament in a highly individual fashion'.[9]

Furthermore, in his choice of specific melodic contours, as well as numerous details of dynamic contrast, harmony, and scoring, Haydn frequently reveals a remarkably traditional interest in word painting. When setting texts with words such as *resurrexit, coelum, ascendum* or *altissimus,* he favours rising lines or higher registers.[10] Conversely, falling lines or lower tessituras occur often to texts including *descendit, terra* and *sepultus est. Sepultus est, mortuorum* and *invisibilium* are usually set at soft dynamic levels, whereas words like *gloria, glorificamus, conglorificatur* tend to call for louder settings, sometimes with melodic ideas and scoring in fanfare style. Other instances are numerous.

There was another important consideration for Haydn when writing these masses. His choice of formal procedures or specific structural designs was often influenced if not determined by the shape of the text (*i.e.* the number of words or lines to be set, inherent repetitions or recurrences of the same word[s] and the treatment of similar textual ideas).

The Agnus Dei, for example, consists of an alternation of the phrase 'Agnus dei, qui tollis peccata mundi' with the words 'Miserere nobis' (twice), and a final plea 'Dona nobis pacem'.[11] Clearly some type of rondo-like approach would be appropriate here, and in five of the six Agnus movements of the late masses an alternation of melodic elements corresponds exactly with that of the text. The result, from a melodic point of view, is an ordering of sections sometimes found in his instrumental slow movements (*i.e.* A B A B A).[12]

However, there is a most important difference between Haydn's vocal and instrumental approaches here. Because both text and thematic material furnish strong unifying elements, Haydn feels freer harmonically than in his instrumental music and the refrains to the text 'Agnus Dei, qui tollis peccata mundi' recur less often in the tonic key. For example, the Agnus from the *Mass in the Time of War* has the following correlation of themes, keys and text:

Theme	Key	Text
A	F maj.	Agnus dei, qui tollis peccata mundi
B	F maj.–C min.	Miserere nobis
A	C min.–G min. V	Agnus dei, qui tollis peccata mundi
B	G min.–V	Miserere nobis
A	C maj.–V	Agnus dei, qui tollis peccata mundi, dona nobis pacem

E

It is clear from such slow movements as those cited above and the similarly rondo-like *Qui tollis* movements from the *Mass in the Time of War* and *Nelson Mass* that Haydn was led to the repetition scheme of the music by the text itself.

Logically enough, Haydn tends to use forms that resemble his instrumental structures most often in those mass movements with the shortest texts such as the Benedictus. Note, for example, the resemblance to concerto first movement form in the structure of the Benedictus from the *Nelson Mass* or the close resemblance to sonata rondo in the Benedictus from the *Creation Mass*.

The Agnus discussed earlier reveals other important differences between Haydn's vocal and instrumental approach. The individual thematic sections of the vocal movements are shorter and tend to be less independent than those of his instrumental music.[13] Furthermore, as mentioned above, in the masses there is a greater degree of continuity and interrelationship between the individual movements of a vocal symphony than is customary in Haydn's instrumental symphonies. This manifests itself here in the fact that the Agnus ends on the dominant of C major, a key that is itself dominant to the original key of the movement, F major. Haydn's modulatory scheme is obviously designed to prepare the key of the following and final movement, the Dona Nobis in C major. An additional tie between the two movements is provided by the famous timpani part of the Agnus. The second timpani passage occurs in the last bars of the Agnus, and the final *forte* stroke falls in the first measure of the Dona Nobis. This stroke provides the initial impact of a strong rhythmic pattern that proves to be structurally of great importance in that movement. Clearly the fact that the words 'Dona nobis pacem' belong to the Agnus text has led Haydn to link the movements.[14]

Another observation may be made. In a few instances, Haydn recalls previous mass movements within an individual vocal symphony by restating musical passages or themes. In two such instances there is a textual justification—the similar settings of the Osannas that conclude both the Sanctus and Benedictus of the *Nelson Mass* and *Harmoniemesse* (see Appendix). As far as I can determine such interrelationships are found only within vocal symphonies of any particular mass, not between movements of different vocal symphonies.

Do differences of procedure such as those discussed above invalidate the analogy between vocal and instrumental symphony? I think not. These differences reflect, I believe, Haydn's natural concern for the text he was setting, and for the still primary importance of the traditional divisions of the ordinary of the mass. The crucial point is that in the performance of these masses as part of the Catholic service, there are extended natural interruptions of the music of the Ordinary, and these were not overlooked by Haydn. By the symphony-like grouping of major subdivisions, I believe that he has minimized the effect of these interruptions in an eminently logical and musical manner. Just as Verdi's fine Requiem Mass reflects that composer's lifetime preoccupation with opera, so Hadyn's late masses show the unmistakable imprint of a masterful symphonist.

A final question: Would performances of these masses in the concert hall benefit from short intermissions before and after the Credo?

APPENDIX

Mass in B♭ (*Heiligmesse, Missa Sti. Bernardi*) (completed 1797?)

Vocal Symphony, No. 1

Mvt.	Text	Tempo and No. of bars	Metre	Key
I. KYRIE:		Adagio (12 bars)–	3/4	B♭ maj.V
		Allegro moderato (146 bars)	3/4	B♭ maj.
II. GLORIA:		Vivace (66 bars)	C	B♭ maj.
III.	Gratias:	Allegretto-Più allegro (152 bars)	3/4	G min.*
IV.	Quoniam:	Vivace (82 bars)	C	B♭ maj.

* After opening bars, main keys are B♭ maj, E♭ maj. and C min. G minor is prominent for last 24 bars only.

Vocal Symphony, No. 2

I. CREDO:		Allegro (59 bars)	₵	B♭ maj.
II.	Et incarnatus est:	Adagio (60 bars)	3/4	E♭ maj.
III.	Et resurrexit:	Allegro (102 bars)	3/4	C min.–G min. V
IV.	Et vitam venturi:	Vivace assai (111 bars)	3/4	B♭ maj.

Vocal Symphony, No. 3

I. SANCTUS:		Adagio (10 bars)–	₵	B♭ maj.–C min. V
	Pleni:	Allegro (35 bars)	3/4	C min.–B♭ maj.
II. BENEDICTUS:		Moderato (116 bars)	2/4	E♭ maj.
III. AGNUS DEI:		Adagio (46 bars)	3/4	B♭ min.–V
IV.	Dona nobis:	Allegro (106 bars)	3/4	B♭ maj.

Mass in D minor (*Missa in Angustiis, Nelson Mass, Imperial Mass*) (1798)

Vocal Symphony, No. 1

Mvt.	Text	Tempo and No. of bars	Metre	Key
I.	KYRIE:	Allegro moderato (160 bars)	3/4	D min.
II.	GLORIA:	Allegro (105 bars)	C	D maj.
III.	Qui tollis:	Adagio (65 bars)	3/4	Bb maj.–D min. V
IV.	Quoniam:*	Allegro (82 bars)	C	D maj.

* Includes thematic material from the Gloria.

Vocal Symphony, No. 2

I.	CREDO:	Allegro con spirito (83 bars)	¢	D maj.
II.	Et incarnatus est.	Largo (54 bars)	3/4	G maj.
III.	Et resurrexit:	Vivace (108 bars)	C	D maj.*

* During the opening bars (1–6) there is a modulation from B min. to the tonic, D maj.

Vocal Symphony, No. 3

I.	SANCTUS:	Adagio– (10 bars)	C	D maj.–D min. V
	Pleni:	Allegro (44 bars)	3/4	D maj.
II.	BENEDICTUS:	Allegretto (135 bars)	2/4	D min.–V
	Osanna:*	Allegro (26 bars)	3/4	D maj.
III.	AGNUS DEI:	Adagio (41 bars)	3/4	G maj.–B min. V
IV.	Dona nobis:	Vivace (77 bars)	C	D maj.

* Consists of same material as the *Osanna* concluding the *Pleni*.

Mass in Bb (*Theresienmesse*) (1799)

Vocal Symphony, No. 1

Mvt.	Text	Tempo and No. of bars	Metre	Key
I.	KYRIE:	Adagio– (28 bars)	¢	Bb maj. V
		Allegro-Adagio* (76 bars)	C–¢	Bb maj.
II.	GLORIA:	Allegro (111 bars)	3/4	Bb maj.–C min.V
III.	Gratias:	Moderato (137 bars)	¢	C maj.–G min.
IV.	Quoniam:	Vivace (90 bars)	C	Bb maj.

* Same material as initial Adagio.

Vocal Symphony, No. 2

I.	CREDO:	Allegro (48 bars)	C	Bb maj.
II.	Et incarnatus:	Adagio (48 bars)	3/4	Bb min.
III.	Et resurrexit:	Allegro (63 bars)	C	G min.–Bb min.*
IV.	Et vitam venturi:	Allegro (62 bars)	6/8	Bb maj.

* *Et resurrexit* overlaps with *Et vitam venturi* at final cadence.

Vocal Symphony, No. 3

Mvt.	Text	Tempo ond No. of bars	Metre	Key
I.	SANCTUS:	Andante– (21 bars)	3/4	B♭ maj.–F maj.
	Pleni:	Allegro (41 bars)	3/4	F maj.–B♭ maj.
II.	BENEDICTUS:	Moderato (141 bars)	₵	G maj.
III.	AGNUS DEI:	Adagio (44 bars)	₵	G min.–V
IV.	Dona nobis:	Allegro (158 bars)	3/4	B♭ maj.

Mass in B♭ (*Schöpfungsmesse*) (1801)

Vocal Symphony, No. 1

Mvt.	Text	Tempo and No. of bars	Metre	Key
I.	KYRIE:	Adagio– (28 bars)	3/4	B♭ maj.–B♭ min. V
		Allegro moderato (111 bars)	6/8	B♭ maj.
II.	GLORIA:	Allegro (160 bars)	₵	B♭ maj.*
III.	Miserere:	Adagio (63 bars)	3/4	E♭ maj.
IV.	Quoniam:	Molto vivace-Presto (119 bars)	C	B♭ maj.

* Final nine bars in E♭ maj. and overlap with Miserere.

Vocal Symphony, No. 2

I.	CREDO:	Vivace (59 bars)	C	B♭ maj.
II.	Et incarnatus:	Adagio (41 bars)	3/4	G maj.–G min. V
III.	Et resurrexit:	Allegro– (78 bars)	C	B♭ maj.–B♭ min. V
	Et vitam venturi:	Più allegro (45 bars)	C	B♭ maj.

Vocal Symphony, No. 3

I.	SANCTUS:	Adagio– (18 bars)	C	B♭ maj.–F min. V
	Pleni:	Allegro (29 bars)	C	F min.– B♭ maj.
II.	BENEDICTUS:	Allegretto (123 bars)	6/8	E♭ maj.
III.	AGNUS DEI:	Adagio (47 bars)	3/4	G maj.–V*
IV.	Dona nobis:	Allegro moderato (123 bars)	₵	B♭ maj.

* Last phrase in G min.

Mass in B♭. (*Harmoniemesse*) (1802)

Vocal Symphony, No. 1

Mvt.	Text	Tempo and No. of bars	Metre	Key
I.	KYRIE:	Poco Adagio (130 bars)	3/4	B♭ maj.
II.	GLORIA:	Vivace assai (70 bars)	C	B♭ maj.
II.	Gratias:	Allegretto (178 bars)	3/8	E♭ maj.–G min.
V.	Quoniam:	Allegro spiritoso (93 bars)	C	B♭ maj.

Vocal Symphony, No. 2

Mvt.	Text	Tempo and No. of bars	Metre	Key
I.	CREDO:	Vivace (79 bars)	C	B♭ maj.
II.	Et. incarnatus:	Adagio (61 bars)	3/4	E♭ maj.
III.	Et resurrexit:	Vivace (70 bars)	C	C min.–G min. V
IV.	Et vitam venturi:	Vivace (63 bars)	6/8	B♭ maj.

Vocal Symphony, No. 3

I.	SANCTUS:	Adagio– (28 bars)	3/4	B♭ maj.
	Pleni:	Allegro (38 bars)	3/4	B♭ maj.
II.	BENEDICTUS:	Molto allegro–(105 bars)	C	F maj.
	Osanna:*	Allegro (33 bars)	3/4	B♭ maj.
III.	AGNUS DEI:	Adagio (43 bars)	3/4	G maj.–G min. V
IV.	Dona nobis:	Allegro con spirito (168 bars)	₵	B♭ maj.

* Same material as *Osanna* concluding the *Pleni*.

NOTES

1 The sacred music dating from Haydn's last years includes the:

Te Deum in C major for chorus and orchestra, written about 1800 for the Empress Maria Theresa, second wife of Francis II.

The Seven Last Words for chorus, soloists and orchestra, arranged in the mid 1790's to a vocal text by Gottfried van Swieten.

The Creation, oratorio for chorus, soloists and orchestra, completed 1798, with an English text compiled by Lidley, German translation by van Swieten.

The Seasons, oratorio for chorus, soloists and orchestra completed 1801, text adapted by van Swieten from an English poem by James Thomson.

Masses:

1. *Mass in the Time of War* (*Paukenmesse*) in C major (1796).
2. *Heiligmesse* in B♭ major (completed 1797), dedicated to the memory of the monk Bernardus of Offida.
3. *Nelson Mass* in D minor (1798).
4. *Theresienmesse* in B♭ major (1799).
5. *Creation Mass* (*Schöpfungsmesse*) in B♭ major (1801).
6. *Harmoniemesse* in B♭ major (1802).

2 *The Symphonies of Joseph Haydn* (London, 1955), p. 596.

3 Adapted from the University of California Syllabus QA, *Scheme of a Typical Missa Cantata* by Austin H. Thomson. Rev. by David D. Boyden (Berkeley and Los Angeles, 1946).

4 The Elevation of the Blessed Sacrament follows the Sanctus.

5 It should be noted that other commentators have in the past referred to portions of Haydn's masses as symphonies. See, for example, Anne Tatnall's strong master's thesis, *The Use of Symphonic Forms in the Six Late Masses of Joseph Haydn* (Smith College, 1963), pp. 55 and 60.

6 The single exception is the Kyrie of the *Harmoniemesse* which remains in a slow tempo throughout.

7 As in his last instrumental symphonies, the majority of opening movements of the vocal symphonies does so. Only the first movements of the Credo symphonies and the Kyrie of the *Nelson Mass* do not.

8 Some of the techniques for providing continuity are discussed below.

9 Review of Reihe XXIII, Band 2: Messen nos. 5–8, *Haydn Yearbook II* (1963–64), p. 94.

10 Instruments, with ranges wider than those of voices, sometimes underline such passages in striking fashion. See, for example, the violins ascent of two octaves and a fourth while the voices rise a ninth to the text 'Et ascendit in coelum' from the Et Resurrexit of the *Harmoniemesse*.

11 Sometimes Haydn omits the phrase 'Dona nobis pacem' from the Agnus movement since it always provides the text for the next, and final, movement. See, for example, the Agnus Dei of the *Theresienmesse* and the *Harmoniemesse*.

12 For example, the Andante of Symphony no. 90 in C.

13 With repeats taken, the first A section in the Andante of Symphony no. 90 is 32 bars long in binary form. That of the Agnus Dei under discussion is only nine bars. The Andante's B section consists of a forty-four bar rounded binary. The B theme of the Agnus has only six bars.

14 See also the unusual modulatory scheme of the Agnus Dei and the joint between the Agnus and Dona Nobis of the *Harmoniemesse*.

LOUISE E. CUYLER

TONAL EXPLOITATION IN THE LATER QUARTETS OF HAYDN

The writing of string quartets occupied Joseph Haydn intermittently for nearly half a century. No other major composer has found this medium so amenable and so congenial. As might be expected, some of this master's boldest, most individual music lies within the bars of one or another of his seventy-odd compositions for the four stringed instruments.

Haydn's development as a composer was not a spectacular growth; on the contrary, the gauge of his progress, as it lies implicit in the pages of his first twenty or so quartets, is not even consistently bright in its augury. His primary problem lay in devising textures within which four instruments of similar timbre could move freely and effectively. Even in the late 1760's, this problem remained partially unsolved. For neither the polarized sound of the Baroque trio sonata, nor the top-dominated texture of various kinds of solo pieces was especially suited to the string quartet, although both textures are encountered frequently in the works of preclassical composers. Haydn's success in establishing an amiable rapport among the four string instruments was his first signal contribution to music. Evidence of an easy, genial collaboration is found more and more frequently during the quartets of opus 9 and opus 17. The six 'Russian' quartets of opus 33, however, confirm Haydn's complete mastery of the most elegant of ensemble mediums. For twenty-two years after 1781, when these spirited works for Archduke Paul of Russia were composed, the string quartet form was a superb servant of its near-progenitor.

While the task of combining the four stringed instruments effectively remained a troublesome one, Haydn was content to use the conventional harmonic language of his time. Within the syntax of this language, a sense of tonality—implicit always, but generally explicit as well—was the most important factor in pitch organization. As it was plotted most frequently, the tonal scheme for preclassical instrumental movements was dualistic. Typically, a dichotomy of keys was set up during the primary portion of a movement; resolution of the laudable tension created by this dichotomy became, thereafter, the impelling force for extension and termination of the piece. Multi-movemented compositions (suites, sonatas, and the like) were sometimes unified by choice of the same primary key for each constituent movement. More frequently, however, a single movement—perhaps one in slower tempo—was placed in some related key; the choice for this was made almost exclusively from within a highly restricted group comprising the dominant, sub-dominant, and the relative or parallel major or minor keys. Clearly tonality employed in such undynamic fashion was but an organizing element, a mere tool of design. For many years, Haydn concurred in such a realization. Since this is true, however, Haydn's conversion, about 1780, to the role of joyful innovator is the more refreshing to perceive. His bold juxtaposition of contrasting key levels, his stark unison passages and insinuating modulatory procedures, both of these abounding in purposeful enharmonicism—all were employed confidently and de-liberately in the later quartets. Haydn's obvious relish for sheer sound is a delightfully sensual aspect of this composer's taste that emanates from numerous passages in his zesty, original works written during the two closing decades of the eighteenth century. The purpose of the remainder of this paper is to examine the circumstances that induced some of Haydn's most venturesome experiments with tonality, and to illustrate citations with passages from the later string quartets.

As did most of his peers, Haydn showed surprising reluctance to disturb the near-cliché of intermovemental key relationship. The reason is not difficult to deduce: since the various movements comprising the string quartet of the Classical period were likely to be independent, even autonomous pieces, their principal unity lay in a cohesive key scheme. Not until his twenty-second quartet[1] (opus 9, No. 4, in D minor) did Haydn stray at all from the highly restricted group of keys, to centre a third movement (*Adagio cantabile*) in B flat major. This choice, which is certainly not startling, could be identified as the 'mirror' of the more traditional key of F major, or as the submediant level. The principles implicit in both these terms were to become important to Haydn as his

E*   137

schemes for key relationship became more sophisticated. Yet among all Haydn's seventy quartets, only nine, including opus 9, No. 4, just cited, deviate from the closely circumscribed group for the tonal location of the contrasting movement. And in every one of these instances, the deviant key relies on the principle of third relationship for its rationale. What saved the idea of relationship by thirds from becoming yet another cliché was Haydn's assimilation—perhaps unconscious—of three supplementary principles for pitch organization. These were clearly instrumental in expanding the perimeter of key relationship.

The first of these precepts was the principle of bimodality. This term, which needs to be clarified for the discussion to come, premises the inclusion, within one supramode, of all the pitch elements of the diatonic major and minor modes of the eighteenth century. A bimodal realization of a particular key becomes, in such an expanded concept, a mode comprised of ten pitches, achieved through an implicit flexibility of inflection for the third, sixth, and seventh scale degrees. Realized bimodally, the key of C, for example, has the basic pitch resource of C, D, E flat or E natural, F, G, A flat or A natural, and B flat or B natural. Most often, the flexibility available through the variant inflections became a means of greater expressiveness in the linear structure. By Haydn's maturity, however, the significance of the flexible notes had expanded to influence schemes for key relationship.

A second principle that apparently aided Haydn in enlarging his scope of key choice was the idea of 'mirror' relationship among keys. Although the composer never used this term in his own writings, his acceptance of the mirror doctrine is implicit frequently in his music. For Haydn, the mirror principle apparently suggested that he consider the central tonic note as a fulcrum. By benefit of this, any pitch occurring in the diatonic system above or below the tonic might be reflected in another system generated in the opposite direction. If the principle of bimodality were combined with a system of mirror relationships, the potential mediant keys available within the bimodal key of C would be as follows:

A flat Major   A minor   C—Bimodal   E flat Major   E minor
(Fulcrum)

Significantly, the association of these two principles provided the basis for key selection in the deviant movements of four of the nine quartets having interest in their intermovemental key plans. These quartets—opus 42, opus 50, No. 4, opus 76, No. 6, and opus 77, No. 1—will be discussed presently.

A third factor influencing a few of Haydn's key schemes was revolutionary indeed for the late eighteenth century. This was the idea that any diatonic triad of a bimodal system might be altered chromatically to become the tonal location for a single deviant movement. The result of such a choice was the immediate highlighting of the deviant movement, so that it became the veritable apex of a multimovemented composition. Only three quartets—opus 74, No. 3, opus 76, No. 5, and opus 77, No. 2—benefit from the structure of such an advanced concept.

THE QUARTETS WITH SIGNIFICANT INTERMOVEMENTAL KEY RELATIONSHIP

The forty-third quartet (opus 42) is important in revealing that Haydn adopted the principle of bimodality with caution. The first movement (*Andante ed innocentemente*) is in D minor, and the second movement (*Menuetto*) is in D major. (Such clear juxtaposition of minor and major modes does not alone, it must be emphasized, constitute true bimodality.) When the third movement (*Adagio e cantabile*) in B flat major occurs, it places the keys of D major and B flat major in immediate succession. The relationship between these two does rest in implicit bimodality, since B flat is the submediant key of D minor. The Finale (*Presto*) then returns to D minor. The tonal scheme of the entire quartet manifests an 'arch' or 'bow' shape in its key relationships:

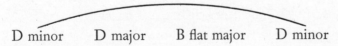

D minor   D major   B flat major   D minor

The forty-seventh quartet (opus 50, No. 4) resembles opus 42, since it shows both aspects (major and minor modes) of the central key (F sharp), but juxtaposes the mediant key of the minor mode to F sharp major. This constitutes another cautious assumption of bimodal key relationship. In this quartet, the first movement (*Allegro spiritoso*) commences in F sharp minor, but moves to F sharp major for a coda section of some length (thirty-eight bars). The movement that follows (*Andante*) is in A major. Accentuating the brilliant sound of the intersection of these two major triads on roots a minor third apart is the subsequent use of

F sharp major for the third movement (*Menuetto*). The Finale (*Fuga-Allegro moderato*) then returns to F sharp minor. A still more interesting arch form is seen to exist among the keys of this movement:

F sharp minor   F sharp major   A major   F sharp major   F sharp minor

In his eightieth quartet (opus 76, No. 6) Haydn confidently assumes both bimodality and complete enharmonicism. The first movement (*Allegretto*) is a set of variations, in E flat major. The second movement (*Fantasia-Adagio*) begins boldly in B major, the only concession to the abruptness of the key change being a visual one: no key signature is used, although the customary five sharps are found when the initial material returns at bar 60. It should be noted, however, that the remoteness of the key of B major is more apparent than real, since its enharmonic equivalent—C flat major—is the submediant key to E flat bimodally conceived. This *Fantasia* is, in fact, related to the surrounding movements in the same essential fashion as were the deviant movements of opus 42 and opus 50, No. 4. The difference is that here bimodality is implicit, not expressed. After the *Fantasia*, which is an extraordinary movement in its own right, the *Menuetto* and Finale (*Allegro spiritoso*) resume the primary key of E flat major.

The key scheme of Haydn's eighty-first quartet (opus 77, No. 1) parallels that of its immediate predecessor, except that no enharmonicism is involved:

G major   E flat major   G major   G major

Only three of all Haydn's quartets make use of a chromatically altered triad for the key centre of a deviant movement. The first of these is opus 74, No. 3, often subtitled the 'Reiterquartett' because of the galloping motive of the introduction. Its key scheme among movements is the boldest found in any of Haydn's quartets. The first movement (*Allegro*), the third (*Menuetto*) and the fourth (*Allegro con brio*) are all cast in the key of G, with the mode of each shifting from minor to major, or vice versa. Set in the midst of these, the second movement (*Largo assai*) is placed in E major-minor to project like a high-set jewel among the more sombre surrounding movements. The relationship of the key of E major to the prevailing key of G might be termed the 'submediant-made-major', to emphasize the striking chromatic alteration. The key scheme of this quartet epitomizes dichotomy of mode, which is, in our definition, a condition quite different from true bimodality. The key sequence: G minor—G major, E major—E minor—E major, G major—G minor—G major, and G minor—G major.

The quartet opus 76, No. 5 uses a 'mediant-made-major' as the key of the second movement (*Largo cantabile e mesto*). This relationship is less arresting than that heard in opus 74, No. 3 because duality of mode is absent. The *Largo* movement itself is, however, one of Haydn's most expressive and tightly built slow movements. The intermovemental key scheme includes D major, F sharp major, D major, and D major.

The final example of Haydn's choice of a central key chromatically altered is found in the last completed quartet—opus 77, No. 2. Here a third movement (*Andante*) is cast in D major, among three surrounding movements in F major, thus constituting another instance of the sub-mediant-made-major.

The two movements published in 1806 as opus 103 were the old master's final works for string quartet. Since the two (*Andante grazioso*, and *Menuetto*) were intended as middle movements, any deductions concerning the intended key scheme of the entire work must remain mere speculation. Even the two movements that exist, however, manifest the same duality of mode, liking for third relationship, and free use of enharmonicism that have been observed in many earlier works. The key plan of the two movements is B flat major—C sharp minor—B flat major, and D minor—D major.

INTRAMOVEMENTAL KEY RELATIONSHIPS

Scarcely a quartet after those of opus 33 fails to show, within the bounds of at least one movement, Haydn's delight in the unpredictable. Although the instances are numerous, only a few of them can be cited within the limits of this paper. Emphasis will be placed, in the discussion that follows, on identifying the contexts within which Haydn was most likely to seek refreshment through unconventional deployment of key.

TONAL EXPLOITATION WITHIN SONATA-TYPE MOVEMENTS

The conventions for a sonata-*allegro* movement of the later eighteenth century prescribed that the exposition show duality of key, the midsection

1

Quartet Op.50,No.2, First Movt.,bars 57-93

freedom, multiplicity, or instability of key, and the recapitulation concentration within the primary key. Clearly Haydn's tonal coups were most vivid when used in an exposition section, slightly less so in a recapitulation, since the effect of the gesture often lay in flouting a stereotype.

A rather early example may be observed in the first movement of the forty-fifth quartet (opus 50, No. 2). The first area, in C major, starts a conventional modulation to the dominant between bars 32 and 42, after which the second subject in G major is introduced. This subject, after moving along in genial fashion for twenty bars, takes an unexpected turn at bar 64, where E flat in the first violin (the enharmonic of D sharp five bars earlier) turns the key toward C minor. This interruption commences a digression of twelve bars, during which the additional tonal levels of A flat major and F minor are suggested, before the key of G, now realized bimodally, returns at bar 77. The remaining thirty bars of the exposition section are occupied in re-affirming this dominant key level.

The first movement of the fifty-eighth quartet (opus 54, No. 2) has a fine example of bold juxtaposition of keys occurring within the very first portion of the movement. The principle theme, in C major, is stated in a period comprising two five-bar phrases, separated from each other by a general pause. After another general pause in bar 12, the key of A flat major (minor mode submediant to C) is assumed without connective material, as the tonal location for recall of the head motive. The phrase, begun in this vivid fashion, is extended, still in A flat, through to bar 22. Here the note F sharp in the first violin produces the so-called German augmented sixth chord, by means of which a strong cadence in the initial key of C major is achieved, in bar 25. The two bars that follow this cadence (these still belong to the first area of the movement) illustrate Haydn's fondness for pointed 'cross-relations', when the first and second violins have the notes F sharp and F natural in near-juxtaposition. The whole passage may be seen in Ex. 2 below.

The second movement of the sixty-first quartet (opus 55, No. 2) bears a close resemblance to the movement just discussed. This is marked *Allegro* (following the variation-chain of the first movement), and is cast in sonata-*allegro* design. A vigorous first theme in the key of F minor achieves a full cadence in that key at bar 16. After a general pause, the key of G flat major is assumed without modulation, and is the tonal location for a passage that commences as a chromatic sequence to the opening statement. Here is a rare instance, for Haydn, of juxtaposing

Quartet Op.54,No.2,First Movt.,bars 1-27

Vivace

keys a minor second apart.[2] The departure from G flat is as unexpected as was its assumption when, in bar 26, G natural is introduced during chromatic movement in the cello—as a means, it turns out, of achieving the key of A flat, the second principal tonality of the movement.

3

Quartet Op.55,No.2, Second Movt., bars 14-26

Among other movements showing striking tonal digressions during the exposition section are the sixty-fourth quartet, opus 64, No. 2, first movement; and the famous 'Emperor' quartet (opus 76, No. 3). The first movement of this splendid work is often overlooked in the preoccupation of so many listeners with the lovely variations on the Austrian (or Prussian, or Anglican!) hymn of the second movement.

In the remarkable first movement of the 'Emperor' quartet, a studied tonal scheme, allied with a highly individual head motive, becomes the means of implying a tripartite design in the exposition section. This head motive, in the key of C, opens the movement. At bar 13, the same head motive is introduced in G (this key being unprepared through modulation) to mark the beginning of the second area of the work. At bar 33, the head motive, in E flat major, marks the beginning of the third major section of the work. It should be observed that the three sections just described are more or less similar in length, a fact that is important in dispelling the conventional bipartite, bitonal cast of the eighteenth-century sonata-*allegro* exposition section. After four bars, E flat major returns to the fold of G major through the convention of the German augmented-sixth chord: at bar 36 (see below), the note D flat in the second violin is, by inference, C sharp, the structure so created moving, then, to the customary six-four position of the G major triad. The remaining eight bars of the exposition section merely affirm G, the second principal key level of the design.

4

"Emperor" Quartet, First Movt., bars 31-37

TONAL EXPLOITATION THROUGH FREE PROGRESSION OR MODULATION

Some of Haydn's finest tonal effects are derived from the extraordinary means employed for achieving a new key. Among these, the free assumption of a fresh key without modulatory preparation, a number of instances of which have already been cited, is perhaps the most dramatic. And, in the late quartets especially, the effect of the new key is often heightened when a general pause is posed just before it. The frequent use of the general pause in a variety of situations is, in fact, a conspicuous device throughout the later quartets.

Several other situations that often induce exploitation of key change are discussed below.

FRUSTRATION OF CONVENTIONAL PROGRESSION OF THE DOMINANT

The so-called deceptive cadence is the germ of all the later, more devious means of circumventing the expected resolution of a dominant chord to its tonic. The simple deceptive cadence, the classical expression of which is the movement of a dominant chord to the submediant, may be found in almost any composition of the Classical period. It came, in fact, to constitute yet another cliché of the time. Haydn experimented with a number of alternative 'deceptive' resolutions, several of which may be observed in the last few quartets.

In the second movement (*Largo*) of opus 76, No. 5, the mirror principle appears to have suggested the vivid assumption of the key of E major at bar 41. In the preceding portion of the movement, a first area in F sharp major is succeeded, conventionally enough, by a second area in C sharp major. This second key level is maintained, without disruption except for a change to minor mode, from bar 18 to the pause on the dominant triad (G sharp B sharp D sharp) at bar 40. The progression of this dominant triad to E major may be explained as a deceptive resolution that incorporates the dual principles of mirror relationship and bimodality.

A = VI of	C# —Bimodal	E = III of
the minor mode, the usual destination of a deceptive resolution.		the minor mode, the 'mirrored' destination of a deceptive resolution, used in this movement

In the second movement (*Fantasia*) of opus 76, No. 6, a still more devious process of avoiding a prepared cadence may be observed, between

5

Quartet Op.76,No5, Second Movt.,bars 39-50

bars 42 and 48. During this passage, a prepared pause on the dominant of C sharp minor is frustrated at bar 46 with a diminished-seventh chord. This is followed by yet another diminished-seventh, then by the dominant seventh chord of the key of A flat, the tonal location of the next section.

6

Quartet Op.76,No.6, Second Movt.,bars 42-48

MODULATION BY UNISON OR BY FREE LINEAR MOVEMENT

The second movement of the quartet opus 76, No. 6—already cited several times—has splendid examples of modulation by free linear motion. Many of the changes of key in this multitonal movement are accomplished by chromatic alteration applied progressively to a single linear part. Examples occur in bars 16 to 19, which accomplish a change from C sharp minor to E major; bars 27 to 30, which move from G major to B flat major; and bars 56 to 59 which mark a return to B major, the primary key.

The first movement of opus 74, No. 1 has a clear example of modulation by a passage of octave unison. The exposition section of this C major movement closes, as expected, with a strong cadence in G major—the dominant key. Following this, two measures with the successive notes G, A flat, F sharp, G, taken at octave unison, lead to the key of E flat, which, as the submediant of the key of G minor, is the first tonal location of the development section.

Another passage that uses the octave unison for modulatory purpose occurs in the second movement of opus 76, No. 5. This passage, which may be seen in Ex. 5 above, occurs in bars 46, 47, and 48. The effect is especially vivid, since a chromatic bass line, and quasi-sequence are also involved in the highly unorthodox sound.

A supreme example of complete tonal freedom is the *Fantasia* of opus 76, No. 6, many details of which have already been described. The structure of the movement as a whole is based upon free deployment of the head motive as stated in the first two bars, through a series of tonal levels that are related only remotely. The vital head motive is seen below:

7

Head motive of "Fantasia" of Op.76,No.6

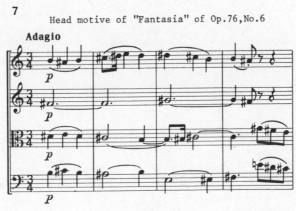

The plan of tonal dispersion for the sections initiated by this head motive is as follows: B major, E major, B flat major, A flat major, B major, E major, B major. A surprising additional factor is the interpolation of a strong inference of the key of C sharp minor—first between the B major and E major portions; then again between those in B flat major and A flat major. The persistent head motive is, it goes without saying, the cohesive factor that makes so diverse a key system tenable within the bounds of late eighteenth-century style.

Careful study of Haydn's incomparable string quartets makes amply clear that this virile composer explored, especially during his days as music's senior citizen, resources that were not fully realized until a century after his death. Veritably, Haydn forged the basic tonal language for all of the nineteenth century.

NOTES

1 The numbering is that found in the Eulenburg Edition of Haydn's quartets.

[It is now known that Haydn did not compose eighty-three string Quartets but about seventy. Ed.]

2 The same relationship of keys is used in the opening of Beethoven's quartet opus 95.

WINTON DEAN

VOCAL EMBELLISHMENT
IN A HANDEL ARIA

Amadigi di Gaula, Handel's fifth London opera, was produced at the
King's Theatre in the Haymarket on May 25, 1715. It is one of three
surviving Handel operas of which the autograph has vanished without
trace,[1] though early manuscript copies are fairly numerous. The only
autograph material for *Amadigi*, apart from a sketch for the overture, is a
single aria among the miscellaneous fragments in the Fitzwilliam Museum,
Cambridge (30 H 6, pp. 41–3). This is neither a sketch nor a portion of
the original score, as Handel's heading 'Aria dell'Opera d'Amadigi'
sufficiently indicates. A. H. Mann in his Catalogue[2] conjectured that
Handel wrote it out 'for the soloist to study the song from', and remarked
that 'the vocal part is more florid than that printed'. This statement is
reasonable as far as it goes, but the manuscript has puzzling features and
others that throw light on Handel's artistic intentions and methods of
work.

The aria is 'O caro mio tesor', a love song addressed by the heroine
Oriana to Amadigi in Act I. The part was written for the soprano (later
contralto) Anastasia Robinson, a young singer about twenty years old
who had made her debut the previous year. A comparison between the
Fitzwilliam manuscript and the aria as it appears in the Chrysander score
and the early copies reveals many differences, which may be summarized
as follows.

(i) The Fitzwilliam manuscript has an accompaniment for figured
bass only, whereas in Chrysander there are parts for two violins (doubled
by oboes) and viola.

(ii) The opening *ritornello* (bars 1–8) is omitted, and the *ritornello* after the first part of the aria reduced from eight bars to four by the suppression of bars 52–55. The bar numbers cited here apply to the full (Chrysander) version.

(iii) The tempo mark is *Larghetto*, not *Largo e staccato*.

(iv) The principal rhythm of the accompaniment is phrased

♩. ♪♩. ♪ not ♩. ⅞ ♪♩. ⅞ ♪

(v) There are many minor differences in note-values; for example

where the bass note is repeated Handel sometimes writes ♩ instead

of ♩. ♪

(vi) The vocal line, as Mann noted, is more elaborate. This is discussed in more detail below.

(vii) There are a number of changes in the bars (bass 13, 22, 24, 28–29, 42–43, 48–49, 62, 64–65, 67, 71–73, 75–76). In the first part of the aria these are mostly different inversions of the same chords; in the second part they range further afield.

If we assume that the Chrysander score is essentially correct (and the early manuscripts support it), it is obvious that Handel was not copying. He was writing out the aria from memory. Even if the change of tempo was deliberate, the numerous altered note values (v) are a clear indication of this (see Ex. 1 and 3). A point of some interest for performance practice is that in Chrysander all four instrumental parts have the principal rhythm (iv) in its double-dotted form (more strictly a dot followed by a pause of articulation), whereas the voice has dotted crotchets followed by quavers, like both parts in the Fitzwilliam manuscript. At first glance this looks like an ingenious type of syncopation, especially as the notation is consistent throughout. But a performance of the music as written, with every alternate chord entering a quarter of a beat after the voice, would not be satisfactory. The discrepancy can be reconciled if the voice conforms to the instrumental rhythm (Ex. 1c), omitting the pauses, which would produce a singularly jerky delivery for a love song.

There is much to be said for Mann's suggestion that Handel intended the Fitzwilliam copy for a singer. Points (i) and (ii) are consistent with this, though, as we shall see, (vii) presents certain difficulties. Moreover most of the variants under (iv) are undoubtedly vocal embellishments.

1

A. Chrysander

O ca - ro mio te - sor, deh! pre - sto tor - ni a me

B. Fitzwilliam

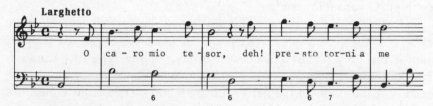

O ca - ro mio te - sor, deh! pre - sto tor - ni a me

C. (Upper parts omitted)

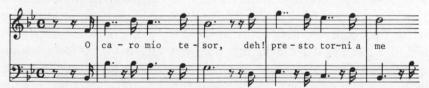

O ca - ro mio te - sor, deh! pre - sto tor - ni a me

As such they are very valuable. Handel's autograph scores contain plenty of decorative writing for the voice, chiefly in the form of coloratura; occasionally he indicates appoggiaturas and cadential trills; but he never writes out the optional ornamentation regularly added at this period, especially in *da capos*, because this was the province of the individual singer. A part so embellished by Handel suggests exceptional circumstances, such as a projected performance by an artist with little experience of the Italian operatic style.

The closest parallel to the Fitzwilliam 'O caro mio tesor' appears to be a Smith copy of five arias from *Ottone* in the Bodleian Library (MS. Don. c. 69).[3] Four of these arias have embellishments added by Handel. All five belong to the soprano part of Teofane, composed for Francesca Cuzzoni and sung by her in the seasons of 1723 and 1726. In the Bodleian copy they are transposed down a fourth or a fifth for contralto, perhaps for the hurried revival in April 1727. During part of that month Cuzzoni and Faustina were incapacitated by illness, and the existence of scores of *Ottone* and *Floridante* (revived for two performances a fortnight later) with both the leading soprano rôles transposed for altos suggests that Handel had to take drastic measures. It seems possible that he added the ornaments in the Bodleian copy for the benefit of an inexperienced singer who had to learn the part in a hurry (in his only subsequent revival of *Ottone*, in 1733, Teofane was sung by the soprano Anna Strada). Can some such explanation account for the Fitzwilliam copy of 'O caro mio tesor'?

Before considering the possibilities it may be as well to look more closely at the manuscript. Together with the *Ottone* songs it supplies almost the only positive evidence we have of the type of decoration Handel thought suitable in his operatic arias. (A number of eighteenth-century manuscripts in the Barrett Lennard and Gerald Coke collections and elsewhere contain ornamentation, but not in Handel's autograph.) It has several interesting features. In the first place, both parts of the aria are affected, though the embellishments in the first part must be presumed to apply to the *da capo*, which of course is not written out. This agrees with Tosi's opinion about the decoration of *da capo* arias: 'In the second [part] they expect, that to this purity some artful Graces be added, by which the Judicious may hear, that the Ability of the Singer is greater; and, in repeating the Air, he that does not vary it for the better, is no great Master.'[4] Of the *Ottone* arias, two are ornamented throughout, one in the first part only, one has a single ornament on the first phrase of the voice, and one is untouched; this suggests that Handel left the job incomplete. The decorations, though for lower voice, are rather more florid than those in 'O caro mio tesor'. Secondly in neither manuscript are there any cadenzas. This should not be taken as evidence that Handel never tolerated them. In some arias they are clearly implied; but Burney's remark about 'Rival ti sono' in *Faramondo*, that 'in the course of the song [Caffarelli] is left *ad libitum* several times, a compliment which Handel never paid to an ordinary singer',[5] probably indicates the general trend. Cadenzas were certainly not obligatory; the Fitzwilliam version of

VOCAL EMBELLISHMENT IN A HANDEL ARIA

'O caro mio tesor' even simplifies the closing vocal cadence of the second part. Thirdly Handel's embellishments do not confuse or deface the vocal line, though they occasionally modify it in detail for expressive purposes. They occur most frequently in the approach to cadences and in melismatic passages, and they are carefully graded: little or no ornament when the material is first sung (in the *da capo*), considerably more when it is repeated or varied.

The first twelve bars of the voice part (10–21) are untouched. The cadential figures in bars 22, 24 and 30 are lightly decorated, those in bars 28 and 37–38 receive more elaborate treatment. Towards the end of the first part, with the ideas now familiar, the ornament becomes more ambitious. When the triplet figure first heard in bars 26–28 is repeated in bars 40–42[6] Handel recasts it in a flowing quaver movement and intensifies the approach to the cadence by changing the rising seventh in bar 43 to a ninth, as in bar 29. This however anticipates and devalues the quaver figure in bars 46–48, which is replaced by a charming rhythmic variation adorned with trills. And having twice employed the rising ninth before cadences Handel reverts to the seventh in bar 49. Ex. 2 shows all the ornamentation in the first part of the aria, with the Chrysander vocal line for comparison; the bass is the same except where indicated.

The opening of the second part (59–64) also remains unadorned. In bars 65 and 68 (and later 77) we find the same type of simple ornament as at corresponding points in the first part, though bar 65 has a new bass. A change in the vocal line of bar 70 (G for D on the third beat) might be considered an improvement rather than a decoration. But the most interesting modification occurs towards the end (bar 71 ff.), where not only the vocal line but the harmonic movement is radically altered, and with it the whole approach to the D minor cadence (Ex. 3).

This goes beyond mere embellishment and brings us back to point

3

Chrysander

Es - ser lon-tan da te, che bra-mo o - gn'or   mi -

- rar il tuo sem - bian - te,   che bra-mo o - gn'or mi-

- rar il tuo sem - bian - te.

Fitzwilliam

Es - ser lon-tan da te, che bra-mo o - gn'or mi -

- rar il tuo sem - bian - te, che bra-mo o - gn'or mi -

- rar il tuo sem - bian - te.

(vii). What exactly was Handel doing? It is obvious here that the voice and bass of the Fitzwilliam version would require considerable alteration of the upper parts in the Chrysander score if they were to be used together. This is by no means the only discrepancy: the changed bass in bars 28–29, 42–43, 48–49 and 63–65 would produce consecutive octaves or other anomalies when associated with the upper parts. Although Handel was no pedant in such matters he would scarcely have tolerated such a crop of them, even without the evidence of bars 71–73. Any singer who tried out the ornamented version with Chrysander's instrumental parts would be in for a rude surprise.

It is difficult to resist the conclusion that in writing out the aria Handel was not only using his memory but to some extent recomposing the music. This is consistent with what we know of his method of composition, in which there was always a strong element of improvisation. Much of his reworking of old material seems to have arisen from just this type of situation: he begins by quoting more or less exactly, and as his pen runs over the paper his inventive power leaps into activity, like the engine of a car running down hill, until reproduction turns into new creation. The *Amadigi* aria does not take this process very far; indeed it may have been unconscious. But as we know from other contexts, the Habermann borrowings in *Jepththa* for example,[7] Handel found it difficult even to copy another man's music without making adjustments and improvements.

For what singer, and on what occasion, did he prepare the Fitzwilliam copy? In many respects the original Oriana, Anastasia Robinson, who was young and inexperienced and had no Italian training except what she picked up from Pier Giuseppe Sandoni in London, would seem to fill the bill. Another possibility is the unknown substitute who replaced her after the first performance in 1715. But it seems unlikely that Handel, so soon after composing the opera, would give either artist a version materially different from that of the full score, unless he intended to modify this; and there is no evidence from the copies that he did so. It is just possible, though unlikely, that the Chrysander version is the later of the two, dating perhaps from the 1716 or 1717 revival, and that the lost autograph conformed to the Fitzwilliam version. A more tenable solution is that Handel wrote out the latter for some singer who was to be accompanied only by continuo, perhaps at a concert. This might have happened at any period, before or after his last revival of *Amadigi* in 1717, or even when his memory of the original detail had begun to fade. The heading 'Aria dell'Opera d'Amadigi' might be taken to support a date after the production of the opera. We shall probably never know the answer. But the manuscript deserves to be published; the vocal line could then serve as a model for singers and conductors who wish to recreate the correct style of embellishment in Handel's operas.

NOTES

1 The others are *Almira* and *Admeto*.

2 *Catalogue of Music in the Fitzwilliam Museum, Cambridge,* by J. A. Fuller-Maitland and A. H. Mann (London, 1893), p. 171.

3 Described by James S. and Martin V. Hall in *Handel's Graces* (*Händel-Jahrbuch* 1957, pp. 25–42). I am indebted to Dr. James S. Hall for the loan of a film of the manuscript.

4 Pier Francesco Tosi, *Observations on the Florid Song,* translated by J. E. Galliard (London, 1743).

5 *A General History of Music* (London, 1935), II. 819.

6 It is interesting to find that Handel originally copied the triplet on the first beat of bar 40, followed by a crotchet rest, exactly as in bar 26. The variation evidently occurred to him as he wrote.

7 See Winton Dean, *Handel's Dramatic Oratorios and Masques* (London, 1959), p. 624.

ROBERT DONINGTON

AMORE TRADITORE:
A PROBLEM CANTATA

PART ONE: THEORY

Famous because it is so very fine, *Amore traditore* (BWV 203) is a solo cantata on anonymous Italian words, for bass voice with a continuo accompaniment which in the last aria becomes a part for *cembalo obbligato*.

The problems of *Amore traditore* arise in two areas which are closely connected. One is the authorship of the music (and of the words, but I am not discussing that). The other is the performance and especially the realization of the music, which may influence our opinion of its value, and thus indirectly of the likelihood of its being by a great composer.

I am aware of two surviving copies of *Amore traditore*.[1] One copy is Berlin (West), Staatsbibliothek, Preußischer Kulturbesitz, Musikabteilung, Mus. ms. Bach P 1159/I, pp. 1–15. This is the copy used and mentioned by Wilhelm Rust for the old Bachgesellschaft edition, where he estimated it, perhaps a little optimistically, as having originated 'positively in the beginning of the previous [*i.e.* the eighteenth] century'.[2] Kast dates it quite differently, from the first half of the nineteenth century.[3] Schmieder, usually so reliable, omits to mention it. The copyist is unknown, but Rust states that the manuscript was in the possession of Hauser. The title is: 'Cantate/a Voce sola e Cembalo obligato/di/Giov. Seb. Bach.'

The other copy is now part of a composite bundle, Berlin, same library, Mus. ms. Bach P 467. The folios containing *Amore traditore* are ascribed to the first half of the nineteenth century by Schmieder,[4] and to the middle of the nineteenth century by Kast:[5] a fair agreement in view of the difficulty and uncertainty of dating manuscripts on internal evidence alone. Schmieder states that the manuscript was in the possession of Fischhof. The copyist is unknown. The title is: '*Cantata*/a Voce Sola e Cembalo obligato/comp: da/Giovanne Seb. Bach.'

The differences between these two surviving manuscripts of *Amore traditore,* though not crucial, are of some interest. There is in either manuscript a fair number of small, obvious and easily corrected mistakes. Some of these are the same in both manuscripts, others are different. The last two bars of the first aria are more obscurely corrupt in both manuscripts; the corruptions (which were excellently emended by Rust) are the same. In addition, the last bar but one of this aria in P 1159/I has some bass notes wrongly copied again from the previous bar; the correct bass notes are also copied in, but the incorrect notes have not been scratched or crossed out (perhaps this was postponed till the ink dried, but then forgotten). Rust correctly ignored the miscopied notes. This miscopying does not occur in P 467. In the second aria, P 467, though not P 1159/I, has one bar missing and several bars incompletely copied.

There are numerous differences, without much musical significance, in the details of the notation. Some, but not all of these are merely what one might expect from the different dates of copying. Some slurs and ties are applied inconsistently in both copies, but differently in each. There are sometimes dots in one copy, but rests in the other copy; and notes (especially at the ends of phrases) different in length, though no more so than might occur anyhow in performance.

There are many differences in the notated accidentals. Of these differences, some are mistakes or merely notational variants, but at least two appear to be meant differently. There is little reliance, in either manuscript, on the bar-line convention, either in maintaining or in cancelling the force of accidentals; but this may be merely an older feature carried over from prior sources, and therefore cannot be counted on to help with the dating of either manuscript. (See Ex. 2a below.)

Signs for ornaments appear in either copy, but differently; performers, of course, would make their own choice in any case.

The vocal melody diverges very slightly, in one place apparently with intention. The text also differs very slightly in the choice of words to be repeated. Neither scribe can have been an Italian, since gross mistakes and failures in accent of marks occur in both manuscripts; but the Italian of P 1159/I is if anything more often wrong, and worse wrong, than the

F

Italian of P 467. There are also unimportant differences in capitalization. The text has been corrected in the Bachgesellschaft edition.

One real oddity is that in the bass of the first aria, just two figures appear, and in the bass of the recitative, just one; but they are at the same places (bars 9 and 10 of the aria, bar 5 of the recitative). In the early manuscript, P 1159/I, however, it is absolutely clear that the first two figures, and reasonably clear that the third figure, have been added subsequently. The manuscript itself is in a particularly bold and heavy hand; but the figures in the aria are so faint and spidery that they can only just be seen. Moreover, notes seem to have been added subsequently to at least two chords in P 1159/I (bars 18 and 20), thereby aligning them more closely with P 467. It appears possible that a partial attempt at collating the two manuscripts may have been made by some subsequent investigator.

Finally, there are a very few passages in which the actual chords are different. In one passage, P 467 gives the tone-cluster G, A, B, where P 1159/I leaves out the B; Rust's emendation, correctly, gives D (see Ex. 1j). In two passages, either choice of harmony is acceptable, and in one of these (see Ex. 1 d–f), the later variant is distinctly interesting, not to say powerful.

In sum, these differences are perhaps sufficient to suggest, though not to prove, that the surviving manuscripts were copied not from one lost source, but from two. Some identical mistakes, at least, would have to be assumed to have been present already in both these supposed prior sources; and both would have to be presumed to bear the attribution to J. S. Bach, since this appears in both of the actually surviving manuscripts, and there is nothing to make us suspect any falsification at this stage. On the contrary, we have some valuable confirmation from another quarter, not much later than the death of J. S. Bach.

In Breitkopf's *Verzeichniss musicalischer Werke* (Leipzig, 1764, p. 32), *Amore traditore* is listed, under 'Cantaten mit einer Singstimme und dem concertirenden Clavier', where it is attributed to 'Bach, *G. S.*'. It is also listed, with its incipit, in the thematic *Catalogo delle arie, duetti, madrigali e cantate, con stromenti diversi e con cembalo solo, che si trovano in manoscritto nella officina musica di Breitkopf in Lipsia*, Parte IVta. 1765 (p. 29), under 'Cantate a voce con cembalo'; and here it is attributed to 'Bach'.

Breitkopf was himself well aware of the fallibility of attributions, and took all the care he could, in spite of which he was bound to make mistakes. We know that he did so; yet he must have had some solid grounds for his attribution of *Amore traditore* to 'Bach', and it carries some considerable weight in the balance, coming, as it does, fairly near the music in both time and place.

I do not know of any conflicting attributions for *Amore traditore* in any source material. The external evidence therefore points unconflictingly to J. S. Bach. It is the internal evidence of the music itself on which judgments have differed.

Spitta took his stand on 'Breitkopf's Catalogue for the New Year, 1764', and he did not doubt J. S. Bach's authorship. On the contrary, he gave it as his firm judgment that 'the breadth of form exhibited in the work points to the time of his [J. S. Bach's] fullest maturity'.[6]

In 1910, however, there appeared the first part of Schreyer's influential *Beiträge zur Bach-Kritik*. In this book, Schreyer, himself a respected music teacher and author of a harmony treatise, brought standards of correct harmony to bear which, in the opinion of Dadelsen, owed more to the prevailing theories of Riemann than to the characteristics observable in J. S. Bach's undisputed music. Dadelsen regards Schreyer's conclusions as largely untenable, while respecting him for the example he set in trying to find objective standards by which to test our attributions.[7] In Schreyer's book, there occurs a celebrated discussion of *Amore traditore*.[8]

Schreyer (p. 24) took Spitta's word for it that 'an autograph is lacking', but brushed aside Spitta's reliance on Breitkopf's attribution. Schreyer used (p. 22) as the basis of his own discussion the Bachgesellschaft edition. Rust gave fair warning in his preface that he had made many undisclosed emendations; yet Schreyer, for all the severity of the judgment he was about to pass, saw no necessity to investigate the manuscript sources for himself. The consequence was that out of the three music examples, taken from the Bachgesellschaft edition, by which Schreyer supported his case, one shows a substantial difference from P 1159/I (the basis of the Bachgesellschaft edition), and the other two show differences of less substance. Three out of three of Schreyer's music examples are in some degree incorrect representations of the sources.

This is the more unfortunate in that it was from his discussion of *Amore traditore* that Schreyer evolved (p. 24) two principles: first, that in the absence of an autograph, J. S. Bach's name on a copy gives no certainty; second, that crude and numerous faults of composition make J. S. Bach's authorship of a work attributed to him highly improbable.

These are useful principles, so far as they go. However, not even an autograph, except perhaps when signed, can itself give certainty (Bach copied other men's music), and moreover, even Bach autographs are occasionally doubted or disproved; while with most other Baroque composers, to wait for an autograph before accepting an attribution would be completely unrealistic. Again, we cannot count even on a good composer (especially when so prolific as J. S. Bach) never having written a bad passage or a bad piece; whereas we can count on a minor composer never having written (because he cannot) a major masterpiece. I offer, therefore, two further principles complementary to Schreyer's:

(*a*) Early attributions are evidence; unconflicting early attributions are stronger evidence.

(*b*) Consistent masterfulness in a style fundamentally suggestive of J. S. Bach makes J. S. Bach's authorship of a work attributed to him highly probable.

It is, in effect, on these two principles that Spitta was acting when he gave weight to Breitkopf's attribution, and when he formed a judgment in favour of J. S. Bach's maturest style. What had Schreyer to advance against that considered judgment?

Schreyer held 'more important than the lack of the autograph the circumstance that in the accompaniment of this [second] aria the Contra A comes three times and even the Contra G once, notes which are never met with in Bach's keyboard compositions'. An objective detail, we are to suppose; but Schreyer's interpretation (that what Bach had not done elsewhere he could not have done here) is no less subjective than Spitta's broader judgment. It could as well be argued that Bach wanted an exceptional range for an exceptional accompaniment; and it is certainly an objective fact that the standard harpsichord then went down to Contra F.

Schreyer's objective detail, on the other hand, turns out to be an objective mistake. In the *obbligato cembalo* parts of J. S. Bach's gamba sonatas, there are eight occurrences of Contra A, and two occurrences of Contra G.[9] As in *Amore traditore*, the solo to be accompanied is itself low in tessitura. The objective fact is that these low notes on the harpsichord *are* a part of J. S. Bach's style where a musical need for them arises.

The same unavoidable (I do not say undesirable) element of subjective judgment enters into Schreyer's interpretation of more strictly musical details. Schreyer faults (without illustrating) certain 'forbidden' parallels between solo and accompaniment. But parallels in such a situation were commonplaces not censured at the time unless they sounded bad, which these do not. Not only do they not sound bad; they are normal elements in the 'dividing bass' technique so widely cultivated throughout the whole Baroque period. They are not faults, and can have seemed so to Schreyer only because he was unaware of the 'dividing bass' technique. (See Ex. 1 g–h.)

Schreyer also illustrated (without discussing) further 'forbidden' parallels within the *cembalo obbligato* part itself. Two of these are not in the source anyhow, but result from an editorial addition made by Rust (see Ex. 1 a–b). None of them are faults. Eugen Schmitz, who strongly though laconically upheld J. S. Bach's authorship of *Amore traditore*, dismissed the faults alleged by Schreyer as trivial breaches of the rules.[10] But these parallels within the accompaniment, like the parallels between solo and accompaniment, are not breaches of the rules at all; they are normal occurrences, not only allowed but encouraged in the 'full-voiced accompaniment' as taught by Heinichen, Mattheson and other reputable authorities of J. S. Bach's period. Schreyer must also have been unaware of this 'full-voiced' technique of accompaniment.

Again, Schreyer faulted certain thick, low chords which presumably sounded quite horrible to him when he tried them over on his piano. But these are no faults of composition when performed on the instrument for which they were composed. Whittaker saw the point here when he described these chords as 'ringing magnificently on a harpsichord, but thick and muddy on a pianoforte'.[11] These, too, are normal 'full-voiced accompaniment', which at certain points in this *cembalo* part makes an effective contrast to the predominantly open texture. And there are other clashing harmonies of outstanding boldness and fitness for the harpsichord. To Schreyer they seemed crudities. To us they may no more seem so than some of those censured in Blow by Dr Burney; on the contrary, we may think the craftsmanship of *Amore traditore* as splendid as its inspiration. So much may depend upon a change of standpoint.

In 1912, Schering, in an otherwise quite critical article, backed Schreyer in the following strong but unsupported words: ' "Amore traditore" is certainly a piece of valuable music, but not by Bach'.[12] No fresh work of consequence having, apparently, been done since on the subject, that damning *Echtheit des Werkes angezweifelt* still hangs over *Amore traditore* in Schmieder. The second edition of Neumann had *Echtheitszweifel bei Schreyer I und Schering (BJ 1912)*; the third edition has only *Echtheit angezweifelt*.[13] But for Cantata 209, the only other surviving Italian cantata attributed to J. S. Bach, Neumann has *Echtheitszweifel (Schreyer II) wenig begründet* in the second edition, and in the third edition, does not even retain this much doubt.[14] Blume thinks the grounds for doubting *Amore traditore* insufficient.[15]

Since there has never been any other reasoned objection but Schreyer's to J. S. Bach's authorship of *Amore traditore*, this too, I suggest, need no longer be regarded as a doubtful work. What grounds, external or internal, have we really got for doubting it? What grounds for rejecting its consistent masterfulness in a style fundamentally suggestive of J. S. Bach? The actual evidence is all favourable to J. S. Bach.

Ex. 1: Second aria, (*a*) bar 30 as it stands in the manuscript (P1159/I)—with consecutive octaves between the bass and an inner part, normal in the 'full-voiced' accompaniment as taught by Heinichen *etc.*, but faulted by Schreyer; (*b*) bar 30 as printed by Schreyer following the Bach-gesellschaft edition, with further consecutive octaves, not in the manuscript, between the top parts in either hand; (*c*) bar 31 as in P 1159/I, bold major seventh further clashing with the voice, normal and excellent in performance, but faulted by Schreyer; (*d*) bar 114 as in P 1159/I; (*e*) bar 114 as in Schreyer following the Bachgesellschaft edition, with one note of additional thickening added by Rust, though this is still all perfectly acceptable accompaniment in the 'full-voiced' style, but faulted by Schreyer; (*f*) bar 114 as in P 467, with interesting variants in the bass, the harmony and the part-writing or doubling—the B sharp is an obvious mistake, probably for G sharp, possibly (still more attractive but less likely) for B natural; (*g*) bar 21, as in both MSS, and (*h*) bar 43 (where both MSS read, incorrectly as the sequence and the parallel passages show, *d'* for *c'* in the fifth note of the right hand, but Rust in the Bachgesellschaft edition made the correct emendation as shown here), characteristic passing unisons in the normal technique of bass 'divisions'; (*i*) bar 102 (the tie in the accompaniment and the sharp in the voice part are missing in P 1159/I but correctly supplied by Rust; both are present in P 467; both MSS have the phrasing slur in the voice part, omitted by Rust); (*j*) bar 109 (faulty in both MSS, though differently, but correctly emended, with the aid of the sequence, by Rust, and so shown here); (*k*) bar 111 (as in both MSS and correctly printed by Rust), further characteristic clashes between voice and accompaniment, looking harsh, but sounding excellent in performance:

AMORE TRADITORE: A PROBLEM CANTATA

PART TWO: PRACTICE

In preparing for a performance of *Amore traditore*, it was not the much-discussed second aria that gave me most trouble. The *cembalo obbligato* of that aria is in every respect a magnificent composition, sounding (like the best Baroque accompaniments whether composed or realized) complete in itself, yet fulfilling its accompanying function masterfully. It has a breath-taking assurance and boldness of counterpoint, a very long sweep to its phrases, a very poetical feeling through all its brilliance: and it has these qualities in a measure only given to the greatest of composers. It clashes quite powerfully with its solo part in some bars, but so logically on either side that the mind accepts the clashing with excitement and delight (see Ex. 1). A powerful performance, to match, is indeed needed from both harpsichordist and singer; but there are no special problems. Nor are there special problems over the brief recitative in the middle. But the first aria, on a (barely) figured bass, is a problem child indeed.

There is no way of getting to know the problems of a Baroque work quite like having to realize its *continuo*. Sometimes it goes quickly; at other times with labour and difficulty and many a slow revision; and this aria could hardly be more difficult. The solo is mellifluous in the main, but it gets into some convolutions of extraordinary chromatic complexity, which tax the singer hard though rewardingly. To support these vocal convolutions, the bass twists and turns through augmented seconds and diminished thirds and multiple cross-relationships—with just two figures in the whole movement to guide or rather tantalize the accompanist.

In such a situation, the best policy is often to bear in mind what an accompanist realizing the part at sight could be expected to make of it, and do just that. In Purcell, for example, whenever I have contrived a tortuous realization to follow each chromatic shift of the solo parts, the effect has tended to be bad in performance; and whenever I have simply done the obvious thing suggested by the bass and the (scanty) figures on the harpsichord stand, disregarding the ensuing clashes, the effect has tended to be good in performance. Do what the man with nothing but the figured bass in front of him will do is no bad rule for many difficult *continuo* situations. But in *Amore traditore*, there seems to be no such consistently simple solution which will fit the music. There is nothing for it but to go right in with a harmonization as chromatic and contrapuntal as the given parts.

How like Bach, the experienced *continuo* player will be inclined to say; and that was certainly my impression as I strove on towards a realization fit for these extraordinary passages, and for others where the parts themselves are smooth enough, but their relationship is intransigent. Unrealized, they possibly look like crudities; more or less adequately realized, they certainly sound like J. S. Bach. I feel as sure in practice as I do in theory that *Amore traditore* is by J. S. Bach.

Ex. 2: First aria, with my realizations, (*a*) bar 11, as in both MSS (except that P 1159/I, but not P 467, lacks the flat before the first B, carrying the force of an immediately previous B flat across the bar-line, while P 467, but not P 1159/I, has C natural miswritten for the second B, and one word is left out in P 1159/I), and (*b*) bar 43—passages which look harsh as between solo and bass, but sound well; (*c*) bars 20–21, as in both MSS (except that P 467 dots the bass G sharp in place of the rest), and (*d*) bars 28–34, as in both MSS. (except for small notational details, one word of text, some ties and a slur missing in P 1159/I, and, in bar 29, the rest being half as long again and the third note half the length in P 467)—passages difficult to realize, but looking and sounding obvious enough once adequately realized. See Ex. 2 on pages 170–1.

But this cantata of many surprises had still a problem saved up for me, as a gambist if not as a musicologist.

The first aria, and still more the recitative, are best served by the usual eighteenth-century combination of harpsichord with melodic bass: a cello or a gamba or possibly even a bassoon. In the first aria, both voice and bass parts are particularly strong melodies, and need a mutually balancing sonority; in the recitative, sustained support is needed beneath the harpsichord's customary arpeggiation. But what is to be done when we arrive at the second aria with its 'Clavicembalo solo'?[16]

If we take *solo* in its literal meaning of 'alone', and allow the melodic bass instrument to fall silent, the piece ends with less sonority than it began with, and this makes something of an anticlimax. If we dispense with a melodic bass instrument throughout, we cannot be wrong, and to many this will seem the best option. But there is another option which, from the inherent flexibility of Baroque performing conditions, I think is open to us. This is to retain the melodic bass instrument throughout.

In casting around for helpful comparisons, I recalled the title on Berlin,

Deutsche Staatsbibliothek, Mus. ms. Bach St 162, some few pages of which (though not this title) are in J. S. Bach's autograph: 'Six Sonatas for concerted Cembalo and Solo Violin, with Bass for accompanying Viola da Gamba at pleasure'. In no source is the harpsichord *obbligato* part called *solo*; but it is no more nor less so than the harpsichord *obbligato* part in the second aria of *Amore traditore*. It seems a fair comparison.

Now I have performed some of J. S. Bach's violin sonatas with gamba doubling the bass line of the harpsichord, and not been pleased at all: the delicate three-part balance seems worsened, not improved. So too in

Amore traditore: merely doubling the left hand of the harpsichord *obbligato* was, I felt, ruled out because it sounded bad.

But suppose the gamba, instead of doubling, extracted a continuo bass line of its own, in the main a more elemental version of the harpsichord left hand? Again, there are possible comparisons. There is, for example, a fine solo cantata, *Pastorella vaga bella*, for which conflicting attributions occur in the sources: Handel (very possible for the style) and Telemann (favoured by two ascriptions against one, but the two were written by the same copyist).[17] Here also there are aria, recitative, aria. The recitative stands on a well-figured bass. The first aria stands on an unfigured bass, evidently for a melodic bass instrument, since there is in addition a largely written-out harpsichord part on an elaborated ('dividing') form of the same bass; the right hand has nice figuration (mainly on broken chords) but sometimes gives place to ordinary figured bass. The second aria is similar except for not 'dividing' the bass much, and for being if anything still more melodious in the right hand. The general effect is that of an exceptionally fine but not otherwise untypical accompaniment.

I prepared a *continuo* bass on these lines for the second aria of *Amore traditore*, as an experiment, and played this on the gamba very happily.

Ex. 3: (*a*) *Pastorella vaga bella*, first aria, bars 19–31, as in Copenhagen, Kongelige Bibliotek, MS. mu 6509.2831 (except that in the seventh and eighth bars cited, the bass reads as in Leipzig, Musikbibliothek der Stadt, MS. S x 6); (*b*) *Amore traditore*, second aria, bars 1–11, as in both MSS (except for slurs missing in P 1159/I, and one note replaced by rest, one lacuna and two wrong clefs in P 467), with 'extracted' *continuo* bass as suggested by myself.

Chi in a - mo - re ha ne-mi-ca la sor - te

e fol - li-a se non la-scia d'a - mar chi

etc.

And that puts me in mind of another happy occasion which also depended on its musicological preparations. This was the Haydn opera during the 1967 national meeting of the American Musicological Society. It was one of those unusual performances, at the same time scholarly and musicianly, which speak worlds for somebody behind the scenes. After the performance, Karl Geiringer took a brief bow from the audience, and I have never seen a man look happier. There was something in the quality of the clapping which told us what they think of him at Santa Barbara.

NOTES

1 I should like to express my especially grateful thanks to Dr. Heinz Ramge, Director of the Music Division, Staatsbibliothek, Preußischer Kulturbesitz, W. Berlin, and Dr. Karl-Heinz Köhler, Director of the Music Division, Deutsche Staatsbibliothek, E. Berlin, for their help, so promptly, skilfully and courteously given.

2 Wilhelm Rust, Preface to his ed. of J. S. Bach, *Werke*, XI, 2 (Leipzig [1862]), p. ix.

3 Paul Kast, *Die Bach-Handschriften der Berliner Staatsbibliothek* (Trossingen, 1958), p. 64.

4 Wolfgang Schmieder, *Thematisch-systematisches Verzeichnis der musikalischen Werke von Johann Sebastian Bach* (Leipzig, 1950), p. 268.

5 Kast, *Die Bach-Handschriften*, p. 33.

6 Philipp Spitta, *Johann Sebastian Bach* (Leipzig, 1873–80); Engl. trans. C. Bell and J. A. Fuller-Maitland (London, 1884–85); (New York reprint, 1951), II, p. 638.

7 George von Dadelsen, 'Schreyer, Johannes', *MGG*, XII (1965), cols. 77–8.

8 Johannes Schreyer, *Beiträge zur Bach-Kritik* (Dresden, 1910), pp. 22–4.

9 Gamba Sonata in G major (BWV 1027): Contra A once in the second movement, four times in the third movement, and once in the fourth movement. Gamba Sonata in D major (BWV 1028): Contra A twice in the last movement. Gamba Sonata in G minor (BWV 1029): Contra G twice in the last movement.

10 Eugen Schmitz, *Geschichte der weltlichen Solokantate* (Leipzig, 1914); 2nd ed. (Leipzig, 1955), p. 283, n. 1.

11 W. Gilles Whittaker, *The Cantatas of Johann Sebastian Bach* (London, 1959), II, p. 721.

12 Arnold Schering, 'Beiträge zur Bachkritik', *Bach-Jahrbuch, 9. Jahrgang, 1912* (Leipzig, 1913), p. 132.

13 Werner Neumann, *Handbuch der Kantaten Johann Sebastian Bachs,* 2nd ed. (Leipzig, 1947), p. 172; 3rd ed. (Leipzig, 1967), p. 207.

14 Neumann, *Handbuch,* 2nd ed., p. 179; 3rd ed., p. 217.

15 Friedrich Blume, 'Bach, Johann Sebastian', MGG, I (1949–51), col. 1010.

16 Designation in Berlin, Staatsbibliothek, Preußischer Kulturbesitz, Mus. ms. Bach P 467, but not in P 1159/I.

17 Werner Menke (*Das Vokalwerk Georg Philipp Telemann's,* Kassel, 1942, p. 125) regards Telemann as the probable author, on grounds of style. Max Seiffert prepared an edition of this cantata (*Organum,* II, 18) from a manuscript now in Leipzig, Musikbibliothek der Stadt, MS. S x 6, where it is entitled 'CANTATA/Pastorella vagha bella/ à Soprano/e/Cembalo Concertato/dell Sig: Hendel'. The other two sources of this cantata, with attributions to Telemann, were very kindly communicated by Dr. Menke: Darmstadt, Hessische Landes- und Hochschulbibliothek, Mus. ms. 1046/13; and Copenhagen, Kongelige Bibliotek, MS. mu 6509.2831.

VINCENT DUCKLES

JOHANN ADAM HILLER'S 'CRITICAL PROSPECTUS FOR A MUSIC LIBRARY'

The eighteenth century is generally recognized as the starting point for modern musical scholarship, as it was the starting point for so many of the disciplines that make up the constellation of learning as we know it today. First to come to mind as one reviews the beginnings of what is now called musicology, is the work of the pioneer music historians of the eighteenth century: Martini, Hawkins, Burney, La Borde, and Forkel. No less significant is the contribution of the music lexicographers: Brossard, Walther, Rousseau, and Gerber, or those men who founded the first critical journals in the music field: Mattheson, Mizler, Marpurg, and Scheibe. Along with these names one might mention a host of scholars who helped to establish such comparatively recent studies as that of acoustics and aesthetics.

If these developments can be termed 'scientific' it is because they all find a place within that omnibus German word 'Wissenschaft', a term loosely identified with specialized and systematic learning, but much broader in its connotations than anything suggested by the English 'science'. Actually, the eighteenth century was not a scientific age in the sense that we apply the term to research in the natural sciences. Its great gifts lay in the direction of the organizing and humanizing of knowledge. Pure scholarship works on the unexplored frontiers of learning; humanistic scholarship makes those frontiers habitable for the cultivated layman, and it was as humanists that the eighteenth-century men of letters exerted their greatest influence. Their objective was to bring enlightenment to that species of humanity known variously as the *Liebhaber*, the *dilettante*, the *man of taste*. We have lost the appropriate terms for this individual in our modern vocabulary. For us the amateur or dilettante suggests the dabbler. In the eighteenth century, on the contrary, he was prone to be a man of culture with wide intellectual interests, interests that cut across the traditional disciplines and enabled him to arrive at insights that often escaped the professional. More than one observer has called attention to the rôle of the amateur in defining and extending the scope of musical learning at this period. Ernst Ludwig Gerber writes:

'Fortunately, among the lovers and venerators of music are to be found from time to time men of broad cultivation who take precious pains to concern themselves with matters that have been neglected by the professionals. Who can fail to mention in this connection the names of Mizler, Ebeling, Eschenburg, Schubart, Rellstab, von Eschstruth, and Cramer? And who were those to whom we owe the greatest debt as specialized music historians, a Mattheson, Marpurg, or Hiller, or, most recently, the worthy Abbot Gerbert of St. Blaise—did they not all function as amateurs in their work?'[1]

Among the four professional historians whom Gerber singles out as representatives of the amateur spirit, the name of Johann Adam Hiller is perhaps the least expected in such a context. We think of him as 'the father of the German *Singspiel*' or, in another connection, as a successful teacher of singing and writer of vocal methods or, further, as conductor and impresario, one of the founders of the *Gewandhaus* concerts in Leipzig. Less attention has been given to his work as a journalist and editor, exemplified, above all, in the pages of his *Wöchentliche Nachrichten und Anmerkungen, die Musik betreffend*, issued in Leipzig from 1766 to 1770.

Hiller's periodical owes much in format and point of view to the earlier eighteenth-century journals edited by Mattheson, Marpurg, and Scheibe in Berlin and Hamburg; but there is a new element in its makeup. That element is sufficiently marked for Lothar Hoffmann-Erbrecht to claim with considerable justice that the *Wöchentliche Nachrichten* was 'die erste Musikzeitschrift im modernen Sinne'.[2] What gives the journal its 'modern' quality is the kind of reader for whom it was intended. It was directed not to the *Gelehrter*, the professional musician, the music theorist, but to the cultivated layman. Its tone is direct and unpatronizing and it conveys the assumption that its readers are men of wide cultural interests.

There is much in Hiller's periodical that is worthy of more careful study by music historians, but that part which claims our attention at the moment is a series of bibliographical articles running from July 4, 1768, to October 3rd of the same year. The series bears the heading, 'Kritischer Entwurf einer musikalischen Bibliothek', and it consists of a narrative discussion and appraisal of those publications that the editor regards as important for the library of a cultivated musical amateur. The list is obviously intended for German readers since only a few foreign titles are included. The editor's commentary is directed both to literature on music and to musical scores. I shall confine myself to a discussion of the books alone, since a survey of the scores would require more space than is appropriate for the present paper.

Hiller's model library comprises some sixty titles, classified according to a simple scheme. His first section is devoted to some current bibliographies of books on music. This is followed by sections on music history, criticism, and theory, the latter subdivided into general works, works on composition, thoroughbass, instrumental tutors, and works on the construction and tuning of instruments. The full list is given below in the order in which the editor presented it. Some of his citations were incomplete, and these have been completed. Most of the titles are well known to students of eighteenth-century music, but their distribution and emphasis, together with the editor's fresh and revealing commentary, makes Hiller's *Kritischer Entwurf* a document of more than ordinary interest.

Bibliographies of writings on music

1. Jacob Adlung—*Anleitung zu der musikalischen Gelahrtheit* (1758)
2. Johann Christoph Stockhausen—*Kritischer Entwurf einer auserlesenen Bibliothek für den Liebhaber der Philosophie und schönen Wissenschaften* (1752). [A second edition appeared in 1758, a fourth in 1771.]
3. Johann Lorenz Albrecht—*Gründliche Einleitung in die Anfangslehren der Tonkunst* (1761).

In another twenty-five years Hiller could have cited Forkel's *Allgemeine Literatur der Musik* (1792) as the last word in comprehensive classified bibliographies of music literature. In 1768 the resources were not rich. Of the above three works, the Adlung was by far the most important. It ranks as the first critical bibliography of its kind. Hiller's estimate of its value is clearly indicated in the fact that he, himself, prepared the second edition of the work for publication in 1763. His only criticisms were directed toward its somewhat artificial and schoolmasterish organization, and the author's stilted use of language. Grace and clarity of expression occupied a high place in Hiller's system of literary values.[3] The Stockhausen work is a general bibliography of books on philosophy and the liberal arts, with a special section devoted to music, while the Albrecht is a ten-page list of titles arranged alphabetically by author and appended to a beginner's introduction to music.

Books related to music history:

4. Friedrich Wilhelm Marpurg—*Kritische Einleitung in die Geschichte und Lehrsätze der alten und neuen Musik* (1759).
5. Wolfgang Caspar Printz—*Historische Beschreibung der edelen Sing und Kling-Kunst* (1690).
6. Johann Adolph Scheibe—*Abhandlung vom Alter und Ursprung der Musik* (1754).
7. Johann Gottfried Walther—*Musikalisches Lexicon* (1732).
8. Johann Mattheson—*Grundlage einer Ehrenpforte* (1740).
9. Friedrich Welhelm Marpurg—*Historisch-kritische Beiträge zur Aufnahme der Musik* (1754–1778).

Special studies of Ancient music:

10. Marcus Meibom—*Antiquae Musicae autores septem* (1652).
11. Athanasius Kircher—*Musurgia universalis* (1602).
12. Pierre-Jean Burette—[A series of monographs on the music and dance of the Greeks, published in the *Mémoires de l'Académie des Inscriptions*, Paris, 1726–48].

Further French writings on music history:

13. Bonnet-Bourdelot—*Histoire de la musique, et de ses effets* (1715).
14. Charles Henri de Blainville—*Histoire générale, critique et philologique de la musique* (1767).
15. Jean Jacques Rousseau—*Dictionnaire de musique* (1768).

Hiller's list of historical writings and his commentary on them indicates the need, already felt by the mid-eighteenth century, for a comprehensive work on music history. The first volume of Martini's *Storia della musica* had been published by 1760 or shortly thereafter, but it had little to offer the readers of Hiller's journal. Great admiration is expressed for Marpurg's *Kritische Einleitung* (4), but its coverage did not extend beyond the music of the Ancients and Hiller laments the fact that 'like so many of this author's projects it was unlikely to be completed'. The Printz work (5) is acknowledged as out of date and scarce and more like a set of academic lecture notes than a work of literature. Scheibe (6) does not pretend to offer more than speculation about the origins of music. This leaves two lexicographical works, Walther (7) and Mattheson (8), that are rich in historical information whatever they may lack in chronological organization. Marpurg's *Historisch-kritische Beiträge* (9) is also commended for the historical matter it contains.

Meibom (10) and Kircher (11) are both early and inaccessible books but they held the key to the eighteenth century's understanding of the music of the ancient Greeks. Burette's work (12) was recognized throughout Europe as the first critical and scientific investigation of this obscure region of historical study.

Mention of Burette leads Hiller to consider the work of three other French writers on music. The Bonnet-Bourdelot (13), which he construes as two separate works, is dismissed as disorganized, incomplete, of little substance and therefore useful only to the French. Rousseau (15) is acknowledged as very deficient as an historical work, but all the more rich in 'Raisonnements'.

Works on musical criticism:

16. Lorenz Mizler—*Neu eröffnete musikalische Bibliothek* (1739–1754).
17. Johann Adolph Scheibe—*Critischer Musikus* (1737–1740).
18. Johann Mattheson—*Critica Musica* (1722–1725).
19. Friedrich Wilhelm Marpurg—*Historisch-kritische Beyträge zur Aufnahme der Musik* (1754–1778).
20. Friedrich Wilhelm Marpurg—*Kritische Briefe über die Tonkunst* (1760–1764).

Musical criticism in Hiller's view is closely allied to history. It is an easy step from the proto histories of his own day to the critical journals that were among the major contributions of the German Enlightenment. Mattheson's *Critica Musica* (18) was the first of its kind, but it was soon followed by similar periodicals undertaken by Scheibe, Mizler, and Marpurg. Hiller makes the important observation that the influence of these journals had much to do with the fact that music had come to be regarded as a learned discipline. He also draws attention to the musical criticism to be found in general periodicals such as the *Allgemeine deutsche Bibliothek* and the *Leipziger gelehrten Zeitung*.

Works on music theory:

(1) Comprehensive systematic works:

1. Johann Mattheson—*Das neu eröffnete Orchester* (1713).
2. Hartong—*Musicus theoretico-practicus* (1749).

According to Hiller, no complete, systematic approach to music theory has yet been written. He does however cite two small books either of which could serve as a prospectus for such a universal, fundamental introduction. One is Mattheson's first treatise on music (21), the other a treatise published in Nürnberg in 1749 by a musician named Hartong who wrote under the pseudonym of P. C. Humanus. Hiller has a high opinion of this work, claiming that it contains more within its small dimensions than many a large folio volume.

Theory (2): Mathematical foundations

    23. Friedrich Wilhelm Marpurg—*Anfangsgründe der theoretischen Musik* (1757).
    24. Georg Andreas Sorge—*Ausführliche und deutliche Anweisung zur Rational-rechnung* (1749).

For the remaining sections on music theory, Hiller admits a high degree of selectivity in his choice of titles. The world is full of theory books, many of them badly written and covering much the same ground. For those who have an interest in the mathematical foundations of music, he recommends hours spent experimenting with a *monochord* with the assistance of the books by Marpurg and Sorge (23 and 24 above).

Theory (3): Composition

    25. Johann Joseph Fux—*Gradus ad Parnassum, oder Anführung zur regelmässigen musikalischen Composition.* (Trans. by Mizler, 1742.)
    26. Friedrich Wilhelm Marpurg—*Abhandlung von der Fuge* (1753–54)
    27. Johann David Heinichen—*Der General-Bass in der Composition* (1728).
    28. Johann Mattheson—*Kern melodischer Wissenschafft* (1737).
    29. Johann Mattheson—*Der vollkommene Capellmeister* (1739).
    30. Georg Andreas Sorge—*Vorgemach der musicalischen Composition* (1745–47).
    31. Georg Andreas Sorge—*Compendium Harmonicum, oder Kurzer Begrif der Lehre von der Harmonie* (1760).
    32. Meinrad Spiess—*Tractatus Musicus Compositorio-practicus* (1746).
    33. Joseph Riepel—*Anfangsgründe zur musicalischen Setzkunst* (1752–68).
    34. Friedrich Wilhelm Marpurg—*Handbuch bey dem Generalbasse und der Komposition* (1757–62).
    35. Alembert, Jean Le Rond d'—*Élémens de musique, théorique et pratique, suivant les principes de M. Rameau* (as translated by Marpurg under the title: *Systematische Einleitung in die musikalische Setzkunst* (1957).

Theory (4): Performance (Thorough bass)

    36. Leonhard Reinhard—*Kurzer und deutlicher Unterricht von dem General-Bass* (1750).
    37. David Kellner—*Treulicher Unterricht im General-Bass* (1737 and later editions).

38. Georg Simon Löhlein—*Clavier-Schule, oder Kurze und gründliche Anweisung zur Melodie und Harmonie* (1765). Cited by Hiller as 'eine Generalbassschhule'.
39. Johann Mattheson—*Grosse General-Bass-Schule* (1731).
40. Johann Mattheson—*Kleine General-Bass-Schule* (1735).
41. Friedrich Wilhelm Marpurg—*Die Kunst das Clavier zu spielen. Zweiter Th, worinnen die Lehre vom Accompagnement abgehandelt wird* (1761).
42. Carl Philipp Emanuel Bach—*Versuch über die wahre Art das Clavier zu spielen. Zweyter Theil, in welchem die Lehre von dem Accompagnement und der freyen Fantasie abgehandelt wird* (1759–62).

Theory (5): General keyboard performance

43. Carl Philipp Emanuel Bach—*Versuch über die wahre Art das Clavier zu spielen. Erster Theil* (chapters treating problems of fingering, ornamentation, performance).
44. Friedrich Wilhelm Marpurg—*Anleitung zum Clavierspielen* (1754).
45. Hartong—*Musicus theoretico-practicus*, II. *Die methodische Clavier-Anweisung* (1749).
46. Christian Gottlieb Tübel—*Kurzer Unterricht von der Music, nebst den dazu gehörigen LXXVII Piecen, für die jenigen welche das Clavecin spielen, nebst eine kurze Nachricht von Contrapunct* (1766).
47. M. J. F. Wiedeburg—*Der sich selbst informirende Clavierspieler* (1765–75).

The last two titles mentioned above, the Tübel (46) and Wiedeburg (47), are cited as examples of the kinds of works to be avoided at all costs. The Tübel work is described as deficient and full of errors in its presentation, with misleading or false explanations written in what is often a bad German. The Wiedeburg, on the other hand, is verbose and oversimplified, moving one to sympathy because so much effort has been expended to so little purpose.

Theory (6): Vocal practice

48. Johann Lorenz Albrecht—*Gründliche Einleitung in die Anfangslehren der Tonkunst* (1761).
49. Friedrich Wilhelm Marpurg—*Anleitung zur Musik überhaupt und zur Singkunst besonders* (1763).
50. Johann Samuel Petri—*Anleitung zur practischen Musik, vor neuangehende Sänger und Instrumentspieler* (1767).
51. Pietro Francesco Tosi—*Anleitung zur Singkunst. Aus dem italiänischen . . . von Johann Friedrich Agricola* (1757).

Theory (7): Violin, flute, and lute performance

52. Leopold Mozart—*Versuch einer gründlichen Violinschule* (1756).
53. Johann Joachim Quantz—*Versuch einer Anweisung die Flöte traversiere zu spielen* (1752).

54. Ernst Gottlieb Baron—*Historisch-theoretisch und practische Untersuchung des Instruments der Lauten* (1727).

Theory (8): Musical-literary relationships

55. Christian Gottfried Krause—*Von der musikalischen Poesie* (1752).
56. François Jean Chastellux—*Essai sur l'union de la poesie et de la musique* (1765).

Theory (9): Keyboard instruments, construction and tuning

57. Jacob Adlung—*Musica mechanica organoedi* (1768).
58. Georg Andreas Sorge—*Ausführliche und deutliche Anweisung zur Rational-Rechnung* (1749). Also cited as No. 24.
59. Barthold Fritz—*Anweisung, wie man Klaviere, Clavecins, und Orgeln, nach einer mechanischen Art, in allen zwölf Tönen gleich rein stimmen könne* (1757).
60. Georg Andreas Sorge—*Zuverlässige Anweisung Claviere und Orgeln behörig zu temperiren und zu stimmen . . . auf Veranlassung herrn Barthold Fritzens* (1758). Sorge's reply and critique of Fritz's work, No. 59 above.

Thus we have Johann Adam Hiller's sketch of the composition of an eighteenth-century music lover's library. It is a 'modern' library in the sense that at least thirty-five of the sixty titles cited were written after 1750, and nineteen of these after 1760. The works which posterity has recognized as having enduring importance (C. P. E. Bach, Quantz, Leopold Mozart) are given their expected prominence, but light is also directed towards some lesser known items, as for example the treatises by Hartong and Krause. Marpurg emerges as one of the leading figures in mid-eighteenth-century musical thought, at least in Hiller's view. But the most important aspect of Hiller's *Kritischer Entwurf* is that it gives us a bearing on the content of the German musical mind of the late eighteenth century, a mentality to which both amateur and professional musicians contributed significant elements, and which in the succeeding generations was to support the structure of modern musical scholarship.

NOTES

1 Zum Glücke fanden sich unter den Liebhabern und Verehrern der Musik hin und wieder Männer von ausgebreiteter Gelehrsamkeit, welche durch ihre schätzbaren Bemühungen dasjenige zu ersetzen suchten, was bisher in diesem Fache gefehlet hatte. Wem fallen hier nicht die Namen eines Mizler, Ebeling, Eschenburg, Schubart, Rellstab, von Eschstruth und Cramer bei? Und wer waren selbst diejenigen, denen wir das mehrste in dem Fache der Geschichte, sogar vollständige Werke, zu danken haben, ein Mattheson, Marpurg, Hiller, und neuerlichst, der um die Musikgeschichte so sehr verdiente und verehrungs-

würdige gefürstete Abt. Gerbert zu St. Blas? Arbeiteten sie nicht alle als Liebhaber an ihren Werken?

Ernst Ludwig Gerber: 'Gedanken über das Studium der Geschichte der Musik in Deutschland', in *Musikalische Real-Zeitung*, Speier, 1789, pp. 186 ff.

2 See the article 'Hiller, Johann Adam' in *MGG*, vol. 6, col. 409–19.

3 'Die Gabe von der Musik gut zu schreiben ist noch so alt nicht. Bey vielen Büchern, die heut zu Tage noch sehr brauchbar sind, wünscht man immer, dass sie besser geschrieben seyn möchten.'

Wöchentliche Nachrichten. Zweytes Stück (Leipzig, den 11ten Julius 1768), p. 10.

GEORG FEDER

SIMILARITIES IN THE WORKS
OF HAYDN

———

The conscious use of earlier compositions, so frequent in the cantatas, oratorios, and masses of Bach or in Gluck's operas, seldom occurs in Haydn. The proportionately few examples appearing in his instrumental music are mentioned by Anthony van Hoboken in the first volume of his Haydn Catologue. In the vocal music it is known of the 'Benedictus' in the *Mariazellermesse* that an aria of the Cavaliere Ernesto in the opera *Il mondo della luna* is the source of it; of the 'Et incarnatus' of the *Heilig-messe* that it is built on the canon *Gott im Herzen*; of the sacred chorus *'Insanae et vanae curae'* that it harks back to the chorus 'Svanisce in un momento' from *Il Ritorno di Tobia*. A lesser known example is evidenced in the use of the finale from the opera *Orlando Paladino* used again for a congratulatory chorus 'Su cantiamo', which Haydn wrote on an unknown occasion in London, and for the chorus of the amorini in his last opera *L'anima del filosofo*. In these and similar instances Haydn has, quite intentionally, taken up an earlier manuscript and reworked the piece.

The situation is perhaps different with the *Presto* section in B flat major with which both the duet between Clarice and Ecclitico in *Il mondo della luna*, composed in 1777, and that between Armida and Rinaldo close: the similarity of the main idea as well as the middle sections with their imitation and their culminating in a fermata is striking. Nevertheless, it is not necessary to assume that Haydn, in composing *Armida* in 1783, knowingly took the older opera as a model. It is also possible that the source of inspiration which nourished the corresponding section of the earlier work again broke out at a quite analogous point of the new work and spent itself in a similar, even more expanded and artistically realized music.

Did Haydn really choose the same theme 'with premeditation' for the *Scherzando* in the piano Sonata in C sharp minor (Hob. XVI: 36) and for the first movement of the G major Sonata (Hob. XVI: 39) of the same series? The master so asserts in his letter of February 25, 1780, to his publisher. Parallel instances lead us to presume that such relationships crept in involuntarily. He could have sent an apology similar to that given to his publisher also to the King of Naples; for two Notturni for *lire organizzate* begin in the principal movement with the same idea, which, it is true, continues in different ways.

Much less striking is the connection that exists between the beginning of the second movement (*Adagio ma non troppo*, 3/4, C major) of the second Concerto for lira (Hob. VIIh: 2) and the vocal entry, especially that of Eva, in the duet 'Holde Gattin' in the *Creation*. Nevertheless, the two motives have the same thought as their basis. Only in the lira Concerto it is simple and direct, whereas in the *Creation*, through the extension of the first note of the melody, it is transformed and made more expressive. With such an example it becomes clear that the reminiscence is more than a repetition.

But similarities need not be sought in the main themes only. More frequently they are found in less obvious places, for example in bars 31–35 of the Finale of the early piano Sonata Hob. XVII: D1 and in bars 46–50 of the finale of the Sonata Hob. XVI: 10 written at about the same time. Both passages are joined together not only by the same figuration, the same rhythm, the same tempo, but also by a very similar modulation with similar steps in the bass. In each piece they have even the same function: a temporary modulation in the development section of the finale shortly before the return to the recapitulation. Nevertheless one is not a slavish imitation of the other.

Or compare the episode in the *Allegro* (4/4, G major) of the baryton Trio No. 123, bars 10–11, with the quite similar one in the *Presto* Finale (2/4, also G major) of No. 125, bars 13–16. Haydn was inexhaustible in the invention of playful sections like this, which 'see-saw' between tonic and dominant and are supported by a pedal point on the dominant. Such pronounced repetitions as in the case in question are seldom found. Mostly Haydn injected new life into this favourite idea. For example, in the C major aria of Silvia (*Andante*) in *l'Isola disabitata*, in bars 25–28 ('fra un dolce deliro') there is a passage that represents a variation of bars 10–13 ('in sui memoriam') of the fourth *Hymnus de Venerabili* (*Largo*, E flat major, but B flat major at this point); even the echo-like return is the same in both works. But while the original thought is related to the above mentioned playful episodes, Haydn has later given it a more song-like form not only by changing some of the notes of the melody but, above all, with the walking bass through which other inversions of the triad arise. The type has brought forth a new variant.

The examination of such similarities serves as a most fruitful starting point in understanding the work of the master and becoming acquainted with his style. The phenomena which permit comparison, can be of a very different kind. Just as different is the basis of their correspondence (reminiscence, imitation, craftsman's routine), and correspondingly different also is the composer's actual manner in creating (unconscious, conscious, partly conscious). Only the intuition of the attentive listener who has become acquainted with many comparable moments and who discovers such similarities spontaneously, can give the answer to the questions, how far the actual similarity extends, what is its nature, and to what degree of consciousness it corresponds. Naturally such examination dare not rely on evidence garnered in a more visual than musical way. It is essential to comprehend the actual musical phenomenon in its totality and to place it in reference to another phenomenon grasped in the same manner.

Let us take for example the final theme of the 'Military' Symphony completed in London in 1794. It already occurs almost exactly in the rondo-finale of Symphony 61, composed in 1776, not as principal theme, but somewhat hidden as a second couplet, bars 101–108. The similarity extends not only to the succession of notes, but also to the tonality (G major), the tempo (*Prestissimo* and *Presto*), the metre (6/8), the dynamics (*p*) and the periodic form (a four bar antecedent with half-

2

cadence and a four-bar consequent with full cadence, with repetition of the whole period).

Also the great similarity that exists between the Trio of the Minuet of the baryton Trio No. 102 and the same movement of the baryton Trio No. 91, especially in the second part (after the double bar) relates to the whole complex:

3

a)(Hob.xi:91)

b)(Hob. xi:102)

The one in Trio No. 91 has evidently served as model for that of No. 102, or, expressing it in another way: they both stem from the same prototype hidden in the composer's mind.

Another 'agreement' is melodically downright weak, but in the texture and character strong enough to prove it to be a reminiscence: the canonic stretto in the Terzetto of *Armida* as it appears in bars 105–111. Its predecessor is evidently to be found in bars 135–139 of the first movement of Symphony 75 composed several years earlier. In both cases there is a little canon in D major, 4/4, *Presto* and *Allegro* respectively, in the compass of a major sixth; the upper voice begins at the fifth, and the lower voice follows accompanied by parallel thirds, at the distance of one bar with the tonic. Both end with a half cadence which is followed by a section built on a pedal point in A. However in the opera the original *piano* is brightened by *sforʒati* and the effect increased still more by the additional *stretto* in the sixth bar.

In all these cases a new realization of the same idea is achieved. In some examples the later setting is at a higher level than the earlier one. In the 'Military' Symphony this is shown especially by the continuation of the quoted section, in the baryton Trio No. 102 by the more artificially developed period itself. It would be wrong, however, always to see progress in a new use of an old idea. Some of the different shapings of the same material occurring within a larger or smaller space of time are of equal value. If we have presumed correctly about the chronology, the following example indicates even a retrogression. It concerns the identical principal motive that forms the basis of the Finale of the G major baryton Trio No. 124 and of the Finale of the D minor string Quartet out of the so-called opus 9 (Hob. III: 22) composed in 1770 at the latest:

4

While in the string quartet the first motive is supplemented by a second, rather contrasting one, the theme of the baryton Trio prolongs the first motive only by a sequence. That is a lower level of form. It corresponds almost exactly to the transitory bars 11–13 of the Finale in the Quartet where the motive is similarly extended by a sequence. The baryton Trio seems to have originated a few years later than the string Quartet. Thus Haydn took up an idea previously worked out in a more refined form— which is easy to understand in view of the mass production of baryton works he had to achieve; he made use of the old idea in a less demanding, though by no means unattractive, manner. So easy-going, yet highly skilful an employment of an old idea gives us a chance to study Haydn's amazing routine. The master did of course not go through the music of the string Quartet or make efforts to reconstruct the earlier theme.

Quite involuntarily he reproduced the same idea and let it this time move on a path which had partly been prepared before.

Perhaps a subsidiary motive in the first movement (bars 62 ff.) of the Paris Symphony 'La Reine', composed 1785–86, may supply an answer, though not the only possible one, as to how reminiscences of this kind occur. This subsidiary motive is a reminiscence of the first eight bars in the 'Farewell' Symphony composed 1772, transposed half a note down (from F sharp minor to F minor). Possibly the lower part in the fifth and sixth measure of the theme (bars 16–17) was responsible for the resumption of the idea:

In bar 24 the broken chords become the upper voice and in bars 26 and 28–30 they are further expanded. In bar 42 a new transformation of these broken chords is given a syncopated accompaniment with the support of a murky bass. Most likely these three elements—broken triads, syncopation, murky bass—made Haydn remember the beginning of his 'Farewell' Symphony where these features occur together, though with a pounding figure in the bass instead of the murky mass. One might even say that bar 16 had already awakened this association and gradually led to the other features. As a matter of fact in bar 62 the pounding figure in the bass replaces the murky bass, the tonality turns toward the minor mode, and the variant of the older idea sounds in *fortissimo*:

Though the syncopated accompaniment is missing here, both passages are much alike in character (3/4 metre, *Allegro assai* and *Vivace*, closely related harmonic progressions, etc.).

Also in the Symphony *Il distratto* we find a certain reminiscence of the theme from the 'Farewell' Symphony, this time in the development of the first movement (bars 109–122) which develops a passage from the exposition (bars 41–51). The theme from the 'Farewell' Symphony does not appear here in its original form, but as a variant to be found in bars 38–43. No certain date has been established for the Symphony *Il distratto*; the music accompanying a play on which the Symphony is based, must have been composed or at least have been available in 1774. Perhaps even earlier? One could thus easily explain the origin of the theme in the 'Farewell' Symphony by assuming that it originated from the insignificant passage in the exposition of *Il distratto*. The composer may have recognized the potentialities of this passage in the development section and after thus trying it out made it the main subject in the 'Farewell' Symphony. This seems possible, but it cannot be proved. Anyway the example reveals how Haydn's musical thought extended over several compositions. His art in reworking, developing, varying an idea reached beyond a single work.

The text for a vocal work may also serve as bridge for recollection, as the following example may prove. The music conjuring up the magic forest in the third act of *Armida* describes impressions of nature in a manner resembling that in the *Creation*. As in the oratorio, the words of the singer—Rinaldo in this case—follow the descriptive music. There sounds, for instance, in bars 18–21 a soft music which is based on the B flat major chord and slowly ascends and descents in triads; against this background a ruffled figure moves. The following text explains the picture: all round high trees rise into the air and nothing else is to be seen. ('Altro non miro che verdi piante intorno erger l'altera fronte'.)

The soft stationary sound suggests the quiet forest, the firmly rooted trees; the slowly ascending and descending motion the glance of the spectator; the ruffled figure the light motion of the leaves. This lovely picture of nature is suggested already at the close of the slow movement (bars 123–125) of Symphony No. 68 composed in the 1770's. There we find the same stationary sound (in E flat major instead of B flat major) and the same figure in the first violin. There is also great similarity in tempo (*Largo* ₵ and *Adagio* 2/4 respectively), dynamics (*sempre p* and *p* respectively) and instrumentation (the slow motion of the woodwinds, the long-held deep note of the horn, the sound repetitions of the second violin and viola, the slowly throbbing double bass). We do not know whether Haydn, when first composing this music, had a forest scene in mind. In any case, this musical 'picture' reappeared when the right occasion presented itself.

The musical connection between a vocal and an instrumental passage may, as this example shows, throw some light on the problem of expression in 'absolute music'. Another example is supplied by the cello Concerto in C major of the 1760's (Hob. VIIb: 1) rediscovered in 1961. In its first movement there is a passage (bars 19–20) which is clearly derived from the Esterházy Cantata *Destatevi* of 1763, *viz*. from the C major duet 'Grand'eroe' (*cf*. bars 1–3 or the entry of the vocal parts). In view of the Cantata's text it would seem to be more than just a phrase to describe the respective measures in the cello Concerto as 'heroic'.

7

(Hob.VIIb :1,Moderato C)

(Destatevi)

By observing such concurrences we seem to approach the immemorial question why a musical phenomenon should produce a certain expression. Let us take as example the beginning of 'Consummatum est' in the *Seven Last Words* (1786). It is nothing but a cadence in unison g^2-e flat^2-c^2-d^2-g^1 which one finds already in the large chorus 'Svanisce in un momento' which Haydn inserted in 1784 in his oratorio *Il ritorno di Tobia* (bars 147–149, there in D minor istead of G minor). At the beginning of the movement and at the words 'Consummatum est' the cadential formula is suffused with significant expression and becomes a symbol.

This example is also interesting from another point of view. It opens up a view into the relationship existing between the individual work of art and the store of vocabulary, formulae and stereotypes common in a certain era or school. Similarities of such kind are due to certain devices of craftsmanship mastered through experience, or even to quotations from common musical property.

Mention might be made at this point of the signal played by four horns with which Symphony No. 31 of 1765 begins. Rhythmically somewhat varied and transposed from D major to C major this signal appears as a surprising coda in the Minuet (bars 32–36) of Symphony No. 48 'Maria Theresa', this time played unison by the whole orchestra. The value of such a passage is not provided by the signal itself, rather by its surprising appearance at this place. The element of surprise again occurs when this signal is heard in the 5th movement of the bizarre symphony *Il distratto*, where, intoned in unison by the *tutti*, it breaks into the delicate *Adagio* (bars 29–31). Rhythmically the upbeats are somewhat different, but the tonal progressions are clearly c^1-e^1-c^1-g -c^1, followed by the blaring sequel which appeared in a related manner already in Symphony No. 31. In a clearly symbolic way this signal is used in the *dramma eroico Armida*. Rinaldo's belligerent first aria begins and ends with a variant of this signal played at first in unison by the whole orchestra (bars 1–6, bars 127–end). In the Finale this fanfare is sounded by the trumpet alone, without accompaniment, as a realistic signal of departure (bars 52–56). A variant played again in unison by the orchestra concludes the opera and thus ties it to the beginning. Haydn uses the trumpet signal to great effect in the coda of the *Allegretto* in the 'Military' Symphony. The original shape of 1765 is still clearly noticeable. In all these cases a certain historic military signal doubtlessly served as the basis. A different situation prevailed with the trumpet calls in the Agnus of the *Missa in tempore belli* (1796) and in the Benedictus of the 'Nelson' Mass (1798); their symbolic meaning resembles that of the other examples we mentioned, but the musical shape has freed itself from the realistic model.

Similar circumstances had their effect on other quotations from areas which originally lay outside the realm of art music. In specific cases their origin may even be proved. But in most cases when we are inclined to assume a connection of Haydn's work with folk music, the present state of research allows merely for conjectures. We do not plan further to deal with this problem here and would rather return to aspects inherent in art music.

Art music is, as it were, a language which is transmitted from generation to generation, which changes, becomes richer or poorer, and combines well-known features in ever-new constellations. It has its own inner history and represents a sort of continuity, with occasional occurrence of discontinuity, of new ideas and pictures. The smaller and less significant the phenomena which we recognize as occurring repeatedly, are the more they prove to be traditional elements of language.

The following variant of the main theme of the first movement of the London piano Sonata (Hob. XVI: 52) in E flat major (1794) is certainly more than commonplace though it consists only of a sequence of three chords. In the exposition it is in B flat major, in the recapitulation (bar 104) in E flat major. Two years later Haydn writes in his *Danklied zu Gott*, bars 61–63 the same three chords, here again as a variant of the beginning:

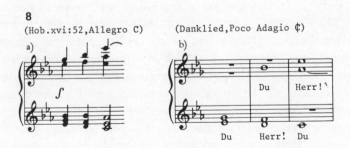

In both cases the expression is energetic, even full of pathos.

On the other hand another sequence of three chords often used by Haydn is not connected with a certain mood. It belongs rather to the language elements mentioned above and represents a craftsman's device he acquired.

9

(Hob.I:101,4.Satz)

T3   S6   T6

Examples for this typical 'three-step' pattern are to be found in the Symphonies No. 101 (theme of Finale), No. 80 (2nd movement, bar 36), No. 74 (1st movement, bars 29–30), in the Finale of the string quartet opus 76–5 (bars 109–110); in the Credo of the 'Nelson' Mass (bars 161–162); in the opera *L'isola disabitata* (Silvia's aria in G major, bars 22–23), but also in comparatively early works such as *Applausus* (No. 8b, bar 29) and the baryton Trio No. 97 (1st movement, bar 62).

In observing similarities of this kind, we find that a very wide area of investigation opens to us; for they appear so often that they may be deemed typical for the composer. This refers to certain cadential-formulas, sequences, ornaments, accompanying figures, modulations, *etc.* As they all belong to comparatively subordinate layers of the composition, the analyst will as a rule pay not much attention to them—unjustly so, for they are part of the foundations of the composer's style. However, also more highly organized forms such as themes and movements may be compared and often they prove to have a typical character. Likewise the same fundamental idea may be at work in symphonic devices such as the technique to extend a motive, to shape a retransition, to carry the development to a climax, etc. Even the formal structures of whole movements follow certain ideas.

The last mentioned is nothing new in the academic study of form which starts *a priori* from certain schematic concepts. As a matter of fact, however, formal concordances constitute the ultimate realization of the law of primordial shape and metamorphose, a law governing all the layers of a musical work. Therefore the study of forms should accumulate its knowledge *a posteriori* by being part of a general musical morphology.

Such a morphology deduces from similarity of details a type, and from the type the birth of the variants. In the case of Haydn a morphological observation reveals to us not only the immense variety of the metamorphoses he achieves but also illuminates the workings of a truly creative mind full of original ideas.

HELLMUT FEDERHOFER and RENATE FEDERHOFER

EIGHTEENTH-CENTURY LITANIAE LAURETANAE FROM THE REPERTORY OF THE VIENNESE PROVINCE OF THE FRANCISCAN ORDER

While numerous studies[1] about the liturgy of the Franciscan order are in existence, only little research has been done on the order's cultivation of polyphonic music, especially that of the seventeenth and eighteenth centuries.[2] In order to fill this gap the musical archives have to be catalogued systematically. For this reason the pioneering work undertaken by P. Theodor Tabernigg OFM,[3] Graz, is of the greatest significance in that he is going through the libraries and musical holdings of the entire Franciscan province of Vienna, cataloguing them and assembling them in the town of Graz under the designation 'Zentralbibliothek der Wiener Franziskanerprovinz in Graz'.[4] The Franciscans—never tied to a *stabilitas loci*—frequently went within the province from one monastery to the other, this being the case even for monks in charge of church music. The work of centralization carried out so far does not yet allow an exhaustive survey of the musical monuments which have survived in the Viennese province. However, several samples examined and viewed in the light of results established by F. Grasemann with the Mass and Requiem compositions of the Franciscan monastery of Maria Enzersdorf near Vienna, make us assume a far reaching originality and uniformity of the Viennese repertory with some peculiarities in its performing practice.

The Franciscan province founded in 1451 by St. Johannes Capistran (1386–1456) and dedicated to St Bernardin of Siena counted among its members a number of excellent musicians, among whom the most famous or, at least, best known in our time, is Blasius Amon (*c.* 1560–90), possibly a pupil of Andrea Gabrieli. The register of deaths in this province compiled from older sources and completed in 1962 lists nearly 200 names of patres and fratres, alternately described as composers, *regens chori,* organists, singers or instrument makers.[5]

Among the holdings of the Graz Central Library one finds the hand-written volume[6] of litanies which forms the subject of this study, a project the authors felt encouraged to carry out since up to now little research was undertaken on the polyphonic litany of the seventeenth and eighteenth centuries[7] and on its cultivation within the Franciscan order.

The MS. bound in brown marbled leather volume in folio of 32 cm × 21, 8 cm, comes from the Franciscan monastery of St Pölten, Lowre Austria. It comprises 62 sheets with the original page numbering 1–124. The original title on the unnumbered flyleaf reads: *XVIII/Lytaniae/ B.V.M./pro/Festis minus principalibus.* The backtitle and the heading of the first Litany reads "*Organo*". The remaining Litanies have no heading. The sheets are ruled with 12 lines.

As the original title denotes, the MS, which has so far not been given a call number, comprises eighteen Litanies supplied with Roman numerals which were written in 1771 with an ink appearing brown today by P. Borgias Federlechner. This is evidenced by the remark on p. 122: *Conscripsit/P. Borgias Federlechner p.t. organista /*1771. On pp. 123–4 there is an index with the *incipit* of all pieces. For the majority of the Litanies, Federlechner added at the end of the respective piece the name of the author. We find his own for No. 1 (with the date 1768), No. 4, No. 7 (with the date 1769) and No. 12 (with the date 1771). The name of P. Engelbertus Katzer[8] appears at the Litanies No. 2, 3, 5, 6, 9, 10, 11, while Litany No. 18 bears the name of P. Adrianus Damian. The remaining six works, i.e. No. 8 and Nos. 13–17 are anonymous. Only for Federlechner's Litanies is a date indicated, this being evidently the year when the work was composed.

Apparently the date does not refer to the copying since the hand-writing makes a uniform impression and seems to have taken place within a short time.

Of the three composers named in the volume only Adrianus Damian was known so far. F. Grasemann[9] refers to him as a noteworthy composer of five Requiem compositions owned by the Monastery of Maria Enzersdorf and gives a biography which may be supplemented now by the correct place of birth, the baptismal name and the name of his parents.

Damian was born as son of Hans Michael and Maria Damian on March 10, 1708, at Neuhofen an der Krems/Upper Austria (not at Neuhofen, Parish Mauer near Melk/Lower Austria, as also the register of deaths of the province indicates erroneously) and was baptized with the name of Georg Joseph.[10] His investment to the Franciscan order took place on July 5, 1725, his profession on June 5, 1726 (which may be a writer's error as, according to canonic law, the profession should have taken place a full year after investment, thus on July 5, 1726).[11] He took the name of Adrianus in the order and was given ordination in Vienna on September 18, 1728, April 2, 1729 and March 10, 1731. In 1738 he is known to have served as organist in the Franciscan monastery of Pupping in the Inn Valley (Upper Austria), for which he contributed an organ book still preserved which comprises 16 Requiem compositions.[12] According to the death register of the province he was for 25 years in the order, for 19 years a priest, and he died as '*praeclarus organista et cantandorum in nostro choro compositor eximius*' on April 1, 1750 at the Franciscan monastery of Maria Lanzendorf near Vienna.

Also for the two other composers biographical facts have been unearthed.

Katzer was born in Vienna on November 18, 1719, as son of Christoph and Magdalena Katzer and was baptized with the name of Joseph Carl.[13] On September 11, 1736, he entered the order and a year later made his profession under the name of Engelbertus.[14] When in 1740 a chapter meeting of the Franciscan province took place at Stockerau, Lower Austria, he was described as '*cler., stud. Moral., Organista*'. He died as 'vortrefflicher organist' (excellent organist) in the Franciscan monastery of Feldsberg/Lower Austria (today Valtice/ČSSR) on December 5, 1779.[15]

Federlechner was born on May 8, 1742 as son of Wolfgang and Theresia Federlechner in Kefermarkt/Upper Austria and was baptized Franz Anton.[16] At the age of 19 he was invested on September 1, 1761, and a year later, on September 1, 1762, he made his profession as Fr. Borgias.[17] His activity as catechist at the Normal School in Vienna and as preacher at the early services is attested by entries for the chapter meeting of 1779 and those of provincial chapters in 1780, 1781 and 1782 in which he participated. He died in Vienna as 'ausgezeichneter organist' (excellent organist) on October 11, 1803, after belonging to the order for 42 years.[18]

It could not be ascertained so far where and by whom these Franciscan composers received their theoretical and practical training. It need not have been confined to the monastery, though the order soon after its inception had founded schools for the musical training of young clerics and had always maintained an affirmative attitude toward a musical expansion of the service.[19] However, it is noteworthy that even when included in the book of novices at Graz, Federlechner was, for instance, described as 'organista'[20] and Katzer even as 'bonus organista'.[21] Further musical training may have been given to them in the respective monastery under the guidance of the *regens chori* or the organist, especially if the mentor was also active as a composer.

All eighteen Litanies are written on two lines, the leading vocal part in soprano clef and a figured bass. The same kind of notation was observed by F. Grasemann in six Organ Books containing nearly ninety mass compositions in the archives of the monastery of Maria Enzersdorf.[22] In accordance with the ruling of the order's founder, Franciscus of Assisi (1182–1226) to maintain poverty, figural music was reserved for special occasions only. As late as 1698 the following ruling was given: 'Cantus choralis sive Gregorianus observetur, et figuralis non facile admittatur, nisi in praesentia Sac. Caes. vel Regiae Majestatis, Serenissimorum Archiducum, Dominorum Cardinalium et Principum, aut ad Praelatorum principalium obsequium. In festis quoque S.P.N./Sancti Patris Nostri/Francisci et Portiunculae, ubi Fratres ad Confessiones excipiendas simul et Missam in Choro cantandam non sufficiunt, et aliqui Musici saeculares ex devotione se offerunt, poterit subsidium musices adhiberi.'[23] This may account for the modest scoring provided at a time when the church music was mainly distinguished by rich instrumental accompaniment.

A characteristic feature of the Franciscan Mass distinguishes it from the customary Mass formula: 'eine in das Ordinarium zwischen Credo und Sanctus einkomponierte marianische Antiphon' (it interpolates in the ordinary a Marian antiphon between Credo and Sanctus).[24] This is the hymn *Stella Coeli*, a traditional rhymed prayer in medieval prose form, also called '*Pestgebet*'[25] which is to be found from the seventeenth century to the end of the eighteenth in Franciscan Masses. In a similar way, texts are added to the *Lauretanae* which as in the Mass—refer exclusively to the most blessed Virgin Mary. Each of the eighteen Litanies, whose text also formed the basis for Mozart's *Lauretanae* K. 109 (74e) and K. 195 (186d) is followed by several invocations. To the *Agnus Dei* forming the conclusion of the Litany formula, the Franciscans add the following verses:

Tota pulchra es Maria et macula originalis non est in te.[26]
Tu gloria Jerusalem, tu laetitia Isreal, tu honorificentia populi nostri.[27]

They form *inter alia* the first and third antiphon in the Vesper *Immaculatae Conceptionis Beatae Mariae Virginis* (December 8th).[28]
There follow three other invocations:

Tu advocata peccatorum o Maria,
Virgo prudentissima, ora pro nobis,
Virgo clementissima, ora pro nobis

and the oration:

Intercede pro nobis ad Dominum Jesum Christum.

The conclusion is formed by the so-called Angelic Salutation, taken partly from the Gospel of St Luke:

Ave Maria, gratia plena, Dominus tecum: benedicta tu in
mulieribus, et benedictus fructus tui.[29]
Sancta Maria, Mater Dei, ora pro nobis peccatoribus nunc et
in hora mortis nostrae, Amen.

These final words were 'Zuerst von den Franziskanern gebetet und dann erst während des 16. Jahrhunderts Gemeingut des Katholischen Volkes [geworden]' (first prayed by the Franciscans; only in the sixteenth century did they become common property of all Catholics).[30] Moreover, it may be termed typically 'Franciscan' that a section of this added invocation was taken from the proprium of December 8th, for 'Am bekanntesten ist die Entschiedenheit, mit welcher der Orden für die unbefleckte Empfängnis Mariens eintrat' (best known is the determination with which the order declared itself for the Immaculate Conception of the Virgin Mary).[31] On the other hand, the enlargement of the text may be also explained from the liturgical point of view. In the Viennese province, one formerly used to pray or sing a Litany after the vesper of the daily office; on Saturdays, or on days dedicated to the Virgin, the *Lauretana* was intoned. Immediately afterwards there resounded, as symbol of the veneration for the Virgin, the *Tota pulchra es*[32] which even in our time is prayed after the Vespers on the respective days. Through the polyphonic setting, the text is given special significance and its content is expressed with suitable solemnity.

The Litany formula itself is given a clear and concise structure. After the customary introductory sections[33] the unique position of the Virgin is treated systematically with emphasis on the economy of salvation, the Virgin's position in the heavenly hierarchy and her special privileges following therefrom.

Like the cantata-litanies of the late Venetians and the Neapolitans in the seventeenth and eighteenth centuries which also served as models for W. A. Mozart's Litanies, the present compositions are determined by the law of contrast as to structure, choice of tempo and key. At the same time, a well balanced form is achieved which fits the character of the text as a prayer formula. Apart from the addition of the Marian texts *Tota pulchra es* and *Ave Maria* which are always separated from the Litany as musical units in their own right, the Litany itself may consist of one to eight portions. W. A. Mozart has in his two *Lauretanae* five separate movements, *Kyrie—Sancta Maria—Salus infirmorum—Regina Angelorum—Agnus Dei*, a structure likewise used by his own father, by Michael Haydn and F. X. Pösinger.[34] Katzer's Litany No. 10 comes nearest to this form though, contrary to Mozart, it combines *Regina Angelorum* and *Agnus Dei* into a single movement. In the other works great variety prevails in the division of the text. In Federlechner's Litany No. 7 and in Damian's Litany No. 18 the entire text formula is composed as one unit. Only the added texts constitute—as in all other litanies—separate sections without, however, changing their key—F major in both works. On the other hand there are eight sections in Litanies No. 13 and 14 which about doubles their size. No. 7 comprises 84 bars, No. 18—89; No. 13—164 and No.14—162, while No. 8 consisting of seven movements encompasses 201 bars, this including, however, a few small organ solos. A division into four sections is most frequent, the allotment of the text not being bound by a specific rule. The clearest tendency toward treatment in a separate section may be observed in the *Salus infirmorum* which comprises the four invocations to the patrons and the *Regina Angelorum* consisting of the eight invocations of the *corona sanctorum*.

It cannot be considered a matter of course that most of the works bear the name of the composer. On the contrary, when a more complete survey of the Franciscans' musical contributions will be available, we will probably find the majority of these works to be anonymous. This is not due to negligence; rather to the Order's special emphasis on humility and modesty. The same spirit is apparent in the simple setting of the Litanies similar to that of the Masses. One might at first be inclined to believe that the organ book merely served as a compressed score comprising the vocal part carrying the melody and a figured bass while further vocal and instrumental parts supplementing it were lost. This is, however, clearly contradicted by the nature of the compositions. The text of all eighteen Litanies is completely included in the soprano part. Further parts could only function as filling voices, but would have no opportunity for expansion as the soprano and bass move not infrequently in thirds and even in unison. For this reason it would be unjustified to assume a four-part choral setting as F. Grasemann assumed[35]—probably erroneously —for the Franciscan Masses notated in a similar way. The careful marking of alternation between *solo* and *tutti* found in all Litanies refers merely to the execution of the vocal part by solo or chorus. Such alternations were caused by the need for sound contrasts and not determined by the textual structure; they vary from one Litany to the other. The text '*Intercede pro nobis*' is the only one always appearing as a *tutti*, even in the not-infrequent cases when it is treated in an independent movement. A different treatment of *soli* and *tutti* is not to be found. On the other hand, nothing points to missing instrumental parts; there is no hint of their appearance or disappearance. The vocal part is but rarely interrupted by pauses lasting longer than a measure. In such a case the organ is usually treated as concertizing instrument and into the vocal line the corresponding one-voice part for the right hand is entered (without changed clef) with a remark like '*Org.: S.:*', or '*Org.:*' or merely '*S.:*'. From all these facts, one may deduce that the musical text we have is complete and merely required the realization of the continuo.

All these works exhibit a remarkable stylistic uniformity. This seems to require an explanation inasmuch as the three composers known by name belong to different generations. P. Damian died in the same year as J. S. Bach. At that time, the youngest of our three composers was only eight years old, while Katzer, who may have been Federlechner's teacher, was thirty-one. Two reasons may be mentioned for the uniformity of these works: 1. the strong tradition maintained within Franciscan music-making which apparently had a particular impact on the musical form in question; 2. the fact that Federlechner wrote his four Litanies at a young age, thus not too distant in time from Katzer's. Damian's work and the six anonymous Litanies fit into this stylistic pattern. Their composition may have taken place shortly before 1750 or around that year.

Even if we leave aside for comparison Mozart's second Loretian Litany K. 195 (186d) of 1774 which strongly embodies the symphonic principle, we notice how strikingly Mozart's more modest and shorter first Litany K. 109(74e) of 1771 differs from the eighteen Litanies under discussion which were penned in the same year. The latter obviously present more old-fashioned features. They frequently reveal a bass line progressing stepwise and there is a lack of the drumming stereotyped bass figures which play quite a sizeable role in Mozart's first work. Moreover in these Litanies the thorough bass, though conceived instrumentally, is not merely a harmonic basis; it displays a strong melodic movement and thus constitutes a true counterpoint to the vocal part. The latter is, according to a late Baroque principle, guided by the bass and dependent on its movement. The predominance of the melody, as revealed in Mozart's Litanies, is not to be found here. The vocal part is shaped in a formulatory way and closely follows the text. One may therefore speak here of declamatory melodics which in even metre confines itself to crotchets, quavers and semiquavers; in triple time to minims, crotchets and quavers. Only in the cadences do we find larger note values. As a result, we have an extraordinary conformity of motion which makes the different pieces resemble each other. The harmonic relations are of utmost simplicity. Modulation confines itself to the closest neighbouring keys. The interior structure depends solely on the text and no clear rules can be discerned in this regard. Longer or shorter textual segments may lead to a cadence concluding a musical section. Thus in Katzer's Litany No. 2 the text from the *Kyrie* up to and including the *Salus infirmorum* is shaped into a single musical section, while in No. 3 by the same composer the section reaches only up to '*unus Deus, miserere nobis*' inclusively. On the other hand, the anonymous Litany No. 13 has its own short movement for the *Kyrie* alone. We are reproducing it here in full because its structure may be considered as typical for those of the other Litanies.

The sections within each movement are often motivically related and follow a uniform musical course in which syncopated dissonances and *Quintschrittsequenz* play a large part. Not even a trace may be noticed of the sonata form which had so great an impact on both the instrumental

and vocal forms of the second half of the eighteenth century. By and large the composition proceeds by following the text, and purely musical concepts of form are but rarely used. Only occasionally do refrain formations exert an influence on the form, as we notice in Federlechner's Litany No. 4 (section *Virgo prudentissima—Stella matutina, ora pro nobis*). The rare use of this technique is easy to understand, for the same theme had to be applied to different textual segments and the textual material does not lend itself to this procedure. It is strange, however, that even the stereotyped contrast between *solo* and *tutti*, occurring in every Litany, does not pay any need to the responsory nature of the text. It would seem obvious to entrust invocations to the *solo* and supplications (*ora pro nobis, miserere nobis*) to the *tutti*. Even Mozart did not do so and apparently this had no bearing on the Litany composition of the time.

A song-like shape is mainly achieved in sections in triple time, *e.g.* in Federlechner's Litany No. 12:

At times the affinity to the minuet and other dance types cannot be overlooked, thus, for instance, the connection with the bourrée in the anonymous Litany No. 16 (section *Regina Angelorum*), Ex. 3. Even the typical repetition sign is not missing here. A specific treatment is given to the section *Virgo prudentissima* in Federlechner's No. 1. Here the text is entrusted to a church-song-like melody mostly progressing in minims, to which the bass supplies a counterpoint in crotchets and later also in minims. The arioso-like *Adagio* type, in which harmonic features assume the strongest role as a vehicle for expression, usually appears in the minor and always has the function of text interpretation. Composers like to use it for the section *Salus infirmorum* and Mozart,

3

treats it in such a manner. As an example, we may quote the respective section in Federlechner's Litany No. 1:

4

The section *Refugium peccatorum* is at times given a similar treatment. However, even in these portions there may be no attempt at text interpretation, and by and large it occurs only rarely. A clouding in minor is to be found with the text '*in hora mortis*' in Litany No. 8:

or for the word '*miserere*'. Coloratura is used rarely and sparingly; thus over '*ora*' in Katzer's Litanies No. 2 and 3, over '*Amen*' in his Litany No. 11, over '*Ave*' in the anonymous Litany No. 17. Of tempo indications we find only *Largo* (Katzer's No. 10 to the section *Sancta Maria* and beginning of the anonymous Litany No. 16); *Adagio* (mainly in the section *Salus infirmorum*); *Moderato* (only at the beginning of Federlechner's Litanies No. 1 and 7 of 1768 and 1769); *Andante*, *Allegro* and

Vivace (only in Federlechner's No. 4 and 13 to the sections *Regina Angelorum* and *Mater Christi* respectively).

Similarly to the Franciscan Masses, the Litanies equip certain sections with short fugal expositions which obscure the real two-part writing maintained in all these cases. There occur up to five entrances so that five-part writing is implied; in fact, however, the entrances are merely distributed between the vocal part and the bass which plays the first entrance in unison or in the octave. Here the stroke usually means *tasto solo* (the figure '1').[36]

It is difficult to answer the question why Federlechner assembled just these eighteen works in a volume. Surely he was guided by a clear sense of style when selecting the pieces. By and large, it may be said that the Franciscan composers, while using well-known accepted formal principles, were able to combine them with their own ideas without, however, transgressing the limits imposed by the rules of the order. Future research may prove that the Franciscans played a part of considerable significance in the cultivation of the eighteenth-century polyphonic Litany of Loreto, a field which has hardly been investigated so far.

In conclusion we should like to point to two other, so far unexplored, collections of eighteenth-century Litanies in the Franciscan monastery of Graz,[37] the second of which comprises no less than fifty *Litaniae Lauretanae cantata*. In both these collections the typical Marian texts of *Tota pulchra es* and *Ave Maria* have been added and set to music.

NOTES

1 H. Hüschen, paragraph 'Franziskaner' in: *MGG* 4, Kassel-Basel, 1955, col. 829–41.

2 P. C. Huigens ofm, 'Blasius Amon, ein Beitrag zur Geschichte der Kirchenmusik in Österreich.' phil.Diss. Vienna, 1914. Partial reproduction in: StMw. 18, 1931, S.3 –22. F. Grasemann 'Die Franziskanermesse des 17. und 18. Jahrhunderts' in StMw. 27, 1966, S.72 –124 (with older literature).

3 We should like to express on this occasion our best thanks to the Rev. P. Theodor Tabernigg, ofm, for his numerous efforts to obtain source material, references as to literature, *etc.*, for us.

4 The holdings of the following monasteries are assembled here: Bad Gleichenberg/Styria; Graz/Styria; Graz-Mariatrost; Maria Enzersdorf near Vienna; Maria Lankowitz/Styria; Maria Lanzendorf near Vienna; St. Pölten/Lower Austria; Tischen/Styria; and Vienna. Likewise the monasteries of Eisenstadt and Frauenkirchen located in the Burgenland belong to it, while the library of Güssing, which has already been catalogued, remains in this monastery. Regarding these different monasteries *cf.* among others '500 Jahre Franziskaner

der österreichischen Ordensprovinz –Festschrift zur Gründung der österreichischen Franziskanerprovinz zum hl.Bernardin von Siena durch den hl.Johannes von Capistran im Jahre 1451'. Wien, 1950.

5 A study on this subject is planned by the authors.

6 The authors are again indebted to the Rev. P. Theodor Tabernigg, OFM, Graz, for having directed their attention to this manuscript.

7 R. Federhofer-Königs, Mozarts 'Lauretanische Litaneien' K 109 (74e) and 195 (186d), in: *Mozart-Jahrbuch* 1967, Salzburg 1968 (with further literature). Moreover two extensive publications by theologians have recently dealt with the subject, *i.e.* J. A. E. van Dodewaard, *Die Lauretanische Litanei*, Mainz, 1959; C. Kammer, *Die Lauretanische Litanei*, Innsbruck, 1960.

8 In the manuscript always spelled 'Kazer'.

9 *loc. cit.*, p. 122.

10 Parsonage of Neuhof an der Krems/Upper Austria. Register of baptisms, Tom B, p.16: 'Die 10. Martii ist getauft worden Georg Joseph, der Ältern Hanns Michael Damian, Maria uxor, patrino Georgio Hözl, Hofgartner zu Gschwendt'.

11 Graz, Archives of the Franciscan Monastery, Album Novitiatus Graecensis, pars I [entrances into the order], p. 226: 'Josephus Damian, Austriacus Neuhoffensis, legitime natus parentibus Michaele et Anna Maria, Confirmatus, Annorum 17 completorum 10. Martii, Studio Rhetor. Vocatur Adrianus'. Signed in person by 'Frater Adrianus Damian'. The profession is attested in the same source, pars II, p. 99.

12 Grasemann, *loc. cit.*, p. 119.

13 As in note 11; pars I, p. 259 f.: 'Josephus Carolus Kätzer, Austriacus Viennensis, natus 18. Novemb. anno 1719, Patre Christophoro, matre Magdalena, Civis, Confirmatus, studio Rhetor et simul bonus organista. Nominatur in Religione P. Engelbertus'. Signed in person: 'F. Engelbertus Katzer'.

14 *loc. cit.*, pars II, p. 131.

15 Graz, Archives of the Franciscan Monastery 'Aus dem Totenbuch unserer Provinz', 'From the Death Register of our Province', as well as kind information by the Rev. P. Theodor Tabernigg, OFM, Graz.

16 As in note 11; pars I, p. 348: 'Franciscus Antonius Föderlechner [!], Austriacus Köffermarcktensis, natus parentibus Wolfgango et Theresia 8. Maii 1742. Confirmatus, Rhetor, Organista, vocatur Fr. Borgias'. Signed in person: 'P. Borgias Federlechner'.

17 *loc. cit.*, pars II, p. 190.

18 As in note 15; as well as kind information by the Rev. P. Theodor Tabernigg, OFM, Graz.

19 As in note 1, Sp. 825 ff.

20 As in note 16.

21 As in note 13.

22 As in note 2.

23 Laid down in: *Statuta, Ordinationes, et Decreta provincialia Ord. Min. Strict. Observ., pro Provincia Austriae, Styriae et Carinthiae*. Vienna, 1698, p. 20, under VII.

24 Grasemann, *loc. cit.*, p. 76.

25 As the members of the order devoted themselves selflessly to nursing the sick during the great plague epidemics, this hymn enjoyed special esteem.

26 C. Marbach, *Carmina Scripturarum scilicet Antiphonas et Responsoria*, Strassburg, 1907 (reprint Hildesheim, 1963), p. 271: *Ex Cantico Canticorum Salomonis*, cap. 4, 7.

27 *loc. cit.*, p. 52; *Ex Libro Judith*, cap. 15, 10.

28 *loc. cit.*, p. 271, and 52.

29 *loc. cit.*, p. 425; *Ex Sancto Jesu Christi Evangelio secundum Lucam*, cap. 1, 28.

30 H. Holzapfel, OFM, *Handbuch der Geschichte des Franziskanerordens,* Freiburg, 1909, p. 228.

31 *loc. cit.,* p. 227.

32 Decreed among others in 'Ordo agendorum et cantandorum in actibus processionalibus pro. F. F. Franciscanis strictioris Observantiae, in alma Provincia Austriae Deo famulantibus Anno M.DC.LVI. accomodatus', Vienna (1702). Leopold Voigt, p. 48: 'Forma Processionis. Archi-Confraternitatis Immac. Concept. B. V. Mariae. Post Vesperas fit exhortatio, post exhortationem cantantur Litaniae et Tota pulchra.'

33 These comprise: *Kyrie, Christe, Kyrie eleison, Christe audi nos, Christi exaudi nos,* and the single invocation to the divine members of the Trinity *Pater de coelis,* etc.

34 Federhofer-Königs, *loc. cit.,* p. 113.

35 Grasemann, *loc. cit.,* p. 80.

36 H. Federhofer, 'Striche in der Bedeutung von "tasto solo" oder der Ziffer "1" bei Unisonostellen in Continuostimmen', in: *Zeitschrift des historischen Vereins f. Schwaben* (= *Neues Augsburger Mozartbuch*), 62/63, 1962, p. 497 ff.; H. Federhofer, 'Eine Salzburger Generalbasslehre (1803)', in: *Festschrift Bruno Stäblein zum 70. Geburtstag.* Kassel, 1967, p. 36 f. Joseph Alois Holzmann mentioned therein, author of the respective manual on thorough bass (b. October 22, 1762 at Hall–d. April 17, 1815, there), served as town organist at Hall and presented numerous compositions, among which the sacred works in particular were given a wide circulation. Among his numerous pupils Johann Baptist Gänsbacher (1778–1844) should be mentioned. Works by him are to be found in the Bavarian State Library of Munich, in the Ferdinandeum of Innsbruck, at Stams and Hall (Tirol). *Cf.* W. Senn, 'Aus dem Kulturleben einer süddeutschen Kleinstadt. Musik, Schule und Theater der Stadt Hall in Tirol in der Zeit vom 15. bis zum 19. Jahrhundert', Innsbruck-Wien-München, 1938, p. 302 ff. The paper factory CJN (recte U) JF (= Carl Ignaz und Josef Falger) was located at Reutte, not at Breitenwang. Kind information from Dr. Walter Senn (Sistrans near Innsbruck) and Dr. Robert Münster (Munich).

37 Old signatures $T^2$13 and $T^2$14.

K. G. FELLERER

THE PROBLEM OF HERITAGE
IN THE MUSICAL LIFE
OF THE PRESENT

———

Musical life is bound to man,[1] to his spiritual, biological and sociological existence.[2] As with man himself and his society, this musical life has its own form and development.[3] It has as little to do with the stylistic development of musical forms and shapes as with those highlights and points of emphasis of musical composition which a stylistic study reveals.[4]

In this reality of music-making, the stylistic differentiation of contemporary art, which in turn is the expression[5] of different personalities, reveals itself.[6] Also the variety of musical expression required by any given task reveals itself: *e.g.* dance music, church music, 'work music', music for recreation and relaxation, music for the concert, with its different aspects (such as social, educational or for mere amusement).[7] We distinguish the music of different social strata, of individuals and groups of people, in their changing intellectual circumstances.[8] But also we may clearly observe the creative selection which the musician and music listener make from the musical 'fund'. For this selection, men search beyond the art of their own particular time and circumstance for a type of music[9] which corresponds to their own kind of expression or which they interpret or refashion according to their own expression.[10]

Whenever the necessity arises to enlarge this musical 'fund' beyond the art of its own age, this endeavour leads to collisions:

(1) With the music of other nations—an example is the importance

213

of Turkish music[11] in the European music of the eighteenth century;

(2) With folk music as expression of different sociological classes: the instrumental music of the seventeenth and eighteenth century offers in its treatment of dances[12] just as many examples as the Scandinavian or Slavonic national music in the nineteenth century.[13]

(3) With the music of the near and remote past, which thus becomes a living heritage.[14]

This last point seems less of a problem of composition technique, of performance practice and stylistic development than a problem of musical life itself. These problems, however, cannot strictly be divided from each other. That which is alive in the musical life of a period bears fruit in its musical composition; and each new composition—new as it may appear—must face its own tradition and the heritage, be it in reaction or continuation. Greatness of art is rooted in tradition and builds upon it.[15]

The Gregorian Chant in church music has remained alive for centuries to our own times, for liturgical, *i.e.* non-musical reasons.[16] Its interpretation was subject to various circumstances in various eras. Apart from its liturgical obligation, Gregorian Chant as a musical heritage continued to live in different epochs and was thus open to creative changes.[17] *Ars antiqua*[18] and *ars nova*[19] are—from the point of view of liturgical music— 'sonic enlargements' (*Klangverbreiterungen*) of Gregorian melodies. Artistically they have a new face, but also a new conception of the *cantus prius factus*. Here, the heritage of medieval liturgical melodies not only remained alive in its tradition but passed over into a new artistic form which, at first, was interpreted only as a new version of the original model. As modern as was this process—which forced the old improvising practice[20] of paraphony, *discantus* and/or *organum* into what was a tight form as far as technique of composition goes—it was not until the beginning of the fourteenth century that it was perceived as a new form, alien to the chants of liturgical music.

The shift in interest from the Gregorian *cantus firmus* to the new musical form of polyphony which no longer seemed a polyphonic version of Gregorian Chant but indeed had a quite separate life of its own—all this mitigated to arouse the suspicion of the church authorities who were worried at the invasion into the church service of an art which had broken its ties from the liturgical melody.[21]

This contrast has remained in Catholic church music throughout the centuries; the heritage of the Gregorian Chant exists along with the 'free' (*i.e.* non Gregorian) compositions,[22] whose style naturally changes continually.

The problem is similar in Protestant church music, mainly in its tie to the German Chorale of the Reformation which has remained a lively heritage[23] up to this day in its original form as a group song and also as *cantus prius factus* in motet and cantata.

In the changing course of 'free' church composition since the seventeenth century, once more a break appears: in *stile moderno* and *stile antico*[24] (*i.e.* the successor of the old classical polyphony); this break once again derives at least in part from non-musical, liturgical reasons—such as prohibiting instruments in quadragesimals[25]—but, on the other hand, the mood of the time had changed and their art could not find fulfilment solely in church music.

The seventeenth and eighteenth centuries tried to find the expression of themselves in the novelty of their own contemporary art. Music was not tied to existing old forms as was architecture, which met the contemporary taste by reclothing old sacred and profane buildings in the Baroque style. It was simpler for music to break with the past, to find new forms which fitted contemporary needs.

This musical life, apart from church and folk music, was solely adjusted to the music of the present, but could transform also foreign musical forms into its own shapes: it experienced a change in the nineteenth century. Romanticism,[26] in its search for the exotic, for the past, and for the artistic expression of other cultures, tried to combine this foreign music—which had its own past—with its own music life. Thus in the beginning of the nineteenth century 'contemporary and tradition' (*Gegenwart und Erbe*) go side by side.[27] The music of the present is influenced by a heritage which has suddenly become active; and on the other hand the problem arises how this old music should continue to live sonically and how to interpret it.[28]

In the newly resuscitated motet and madrigal of the sixteenth century, not the historical authenticity (the combination of voices and instruments; the use of soloists) but the *a cappella* is the ideal and the *a cappella* chorus the chosen bearer of this art.[29] From the sphere of chamber music, the madrigal has been transferred to the world of choruses and concerts. In the nineteenth century, instrumental music was predominant; and to supplement this modern art, the 'vocal ideal' was taken from the past, and the old polyphony received a new character, alien to its historical reality. Also its sociological basis was changed by conditions of the nineteenth century.

The madrigal no longer appears as soloistic 'house music' in court chapels and churches,[30] for virtuosi and amateurs. As a successor to the ornate splendour to the old madrigal, the madrigal chorus, *i.e.* choral *a cappella* arrangements—rare in the sixteenth century—become the rule. So-called 'madrigal choruses' with their choral *a cappella* distorted the actual sound of this art, not to speak of their conception of tempo, pitch, dynamic-agogic rendering and, not least, the structural concept without consideration of diminution.[31] The nineteenth century projected its wishful thinking, its will and desire into the 'heritage', and thought to recognize and re-live that heritage; but actually discovered something new which was not at all inherent in the sonic reality of the heritage during its own period.[32] Something was found which did not correspond with the historical reality but came to life as a new artistic form, a new interpretation.

In the eighteenth century, the relationship to the heritage was similar. The creative evaluation and interpretation of Handel's oratorios, of the Passions and cantatas of Bach produced a different picture of Baroque music than that of historic reality.[33]

The modernization and historical resuscitation of old music as a living heritage in present-day musical life therefore pose new problems, even in a consciously historical conception and execution. Because man, in the intellectual current of his time, determines the musical life, the driving forces with which he seeks to supplement the art of his time. Even a firm scientific perception of historical reality is not essential for his re-creation of old music. Here the span between contemporary man and the art of the past becomes evident. It leads to different solutions and interpretations.'

While in nineteenth-century Germany, a bygone music became alive as a heritage[34]—in the endeavour to extend the expression of the present—classicism continued to be preserved uninterruptedly in the musical tradition. The works of Haydn, Mozart and Beethoven remained living music in the nineteenth century together with the music of its own time.[35] For the first time in history, music of one period remained alive in the following century and preserved, as part of the new era's cultural tradition, its effect and stimulation. This is a different kind of heritage than the one derived after a deliberate creative search. The composition remains, but a change results: (1) in the choice of composition; (2) in its interpretation; and (3) in the performance of such a work which belongs to tradition.

Haydn's oratorios throughout the entire nineteenth century enjoyed a lively existence and, with the revived oratorios of Handel, became the basis for the oratorios of Friedrich Schneider, Spohr and Carl Loewe.[36] His operas, however, fell into complete oblivion; and of the more than 100 symphonies only a small selection remained alive. Mozart's output had a similar fate. Although classicism in direct tradition continued as a living art in the nineteenth century, its performance in contemporary sonic concept differed from historical reality. The sound became bigger, the tempo faster as instrumental technique advanced[37]—Mozart had been adamant against 'bungling' of his own works by speeding the tempo;[38] agogic and dynamic marks were transformed into the taste of Romantic pathos and brought with them new dimensions of expression which were foreign to the work, and thus superimposed on them alien interpretations.[39] Thus it is not far fetched that even in new music of the time the 'heritage' continued to have its effect.[40] Next to new forms of expression, we also find traditional forms in certain cases, and thus an academic and historical-minded style which reaches into our own times.[41]

Along with this attitude came a new and lethargical enjoyment of what was known and familiar.[42] It is not always the new message of the composer that is found interesting, but the technical rendering and interpretation of the familiar work by the performer(s). Man becomes unaccustomed to grappling with the composer's message. He perceives the interpreter's[43] conception and imagines it to be the essence of the work. Thus the work is in the hands of the interpreter who, himself, moulds the work and does not in every case perceive its original spirit; but in revealing himself through the work, he becomes more interesting than the work itself. Because of this subjective interpretation, the heritage itself begins to appear in a new light. On the one hand, the work is evaluated by its interpretation, on the other as an escape from its own reality and the resulting confrontation with the artistic forms of its own time.[44]

The circle which dares to really come to terms with new music, becomes smaller and smaller. Already in the conflict around Wagner and Liszt,[45] this narrowing of the group which promotes new music becomes evident; in the twentieth century, especially after the First World War, the gap between the new music and the heritage in musical life becomes only bigger but the different groups of persons involved become more diffuse.[46]

This situation is a new factor in the musical life of our age, in whose manifold complexities ever new problems of contemporary music and heritage arise.[47] The recess of individual music-making, especially furthered by so-called mechanical music and the consciousness of the distance between wish and fulfilment as far as the purely technical aspect of music-making is concerned, has promoted the search for a simple kind of music. Similarly, in reaction to contemporary music, one searches for a type of music removed from the pathos of the nineteenth century. It would be found in the musical wealth of past centuries which research has rendered more accessible. The Youth movement, with its discovery of the old folk song and *Lied*, had prepared the ground for an understanding of old music even before World War I.[48] The heritage of music has entered in the broadest sense the musical life of our time and has thrown open an abundance of problems which concern first the fundamental position of old music in musical life and secondly its sonic realization.

Ortega y Gasset wrote in 1925 a sensitive study 'The expulsion of man from art'[49] which discusses the alienation of new art in all spheres.[50] The distance from the reality of life and its feelings has led to the speculative, to the abstract in new art. 'In music', as Nietzsche put it, 'passions no longer disport themselves.' Music has become a play of sound and construction, in which the technique of these two aspects is pushed the utmost distance away from the measured 'laws' experienced by man, *e.g.* electronic music. Although not many people have in their inner beings followed this trend, it is still the expression of one feature of our times, which tries to force into artistic expression the objective and collective in the abstract.[51] The inhuman awakens the human, not in the pathos of untrue feelings but in the reality of life.[52] Here is the justification for the reaction which seeks instead of the unintelligible the intelligible, instead of the abstract the real. Romanticism of the nineteenth century, which is so close to us, could not fulfil this desire.

Human society has changed, and with it its thinking and feeling.[53] Although the desire for contrast and the long ties with the past century keep this art alive, new thinking gives it new meaning; and out of time-bound subjectivity we move to the timeless in contemporary objectivity, as exemplified in Bayreuth's new relationship to Wagner's work. But the needs of our time have found in old music a part of what we need and want. This is why the great movement of old music could expand our musical life as it has. This search has also marked the face of the heritage. The historic reality which research has revealed to us is interpreted today as in the past, and therefore subject to the changing mood of our generation. Between the subjectively romantic, and the objectively realistic, interpretation lies the span which binds us to the heritage itself. Man pendulates between objective and subjective, between what Kant termed 'intelligibler Charakter' and vital life; he does this in his social attitudes, in daily life; and he can experience his attitude towards the heritage of music in different ways. He can comprehend intellectually this remote art and recognize in it his own mode of expression. In the cultivation of the heritage 'modernization' and 'historical accuracy' have become the slogans which dominate in particular the way old music is performed. In this duality, the heritage of music has become the present of musical life. For our musical life it is just as important to realize the rôle played today by music of the past as it is to consider the rôle of actual music-making. In the heritage of music, the life tie between man and music becomes evident. That which at the beginning of the twentieth century the 'Wandervögel' (hikers) gained from the old wander songs; that which was experienced in the school communities and in the youth-music-movement;[54] that which was gained from the rediscovery of the harpsi-chord and the recorder[55]—all this could not remain restricted to the heritage but had to induce a new kind of music-making which once again bound man and life together as in historical past. Here forces are being roused which are creating a new situation in musical life and must lead to a reconsideration of our rigid 'music business'.

The heritage, as we have seen, has led to a new attitude in performance, but it has also influenced musical creativity. In the above-mentioned development, whereby the spirit of old music gave shape and direction to new contemporary music, the form and shape of old music also gave stimulation to new compositions. When Stravinsky says that true tradition is not the 'testimony of a closed past', but a living force which stimulates and teaches our present,[56] he confirms his own artistic interpretation of Pergolesi in *Pulcinella*. Although there is a heritage in the actual themes, its interpretation, however, is far remote from its original form and spirit. Not only the heritage of the past, but also the heritage of folk music attain in Stravinsky's work decisive importance in sound, form and rhythm.[57]

There are problems even within the historical practice of performance, just as in the 'modernization' and 'historical accuracy'. On the one hand, the desire to reconstruct the historical reality of the work in question determines the performance practice, while on the other not the absolute art work but the experiencing man becomes the centre.[58] The question arises: with which type of sound can contemporary man experience the historical art work in the way the person of that time experienced it? Or: how can the historical art work be made to react on contemporaries in the same manner as it did then? This type of question throws open anthropological, psychological and sociological aspects. Man of today lives under different spiritual conditions than man of the sixteenth or eighteenth centuries. The class of society for whom Baroque music was written was different from the one who hears Baroque music today. The musical perception, the hearing of sonic structures in the shape and purity of the Baroque period, were different from today, as is evident from the musical, theoretical and aesthetical writings of that epoch.[59] This is true for every music of the past which is alive in our time as a heritage. The history of Fine Arts knows this problem concerning the evaluation of the historical art work, but not concerning its form. For the musical heritage which has come to life again in our time, there is the decisive problem of performance practice. If we had recordings from the Baroque time, many questions about sonic reality which musical research tries to clarify would be solved; and an historical reconstruction corresponding to the sonic conception of the old work would be clearly possible. There is the question, however, whether man of today could experience this sonic effect in the same way as man of that time; whether it would not mean something entirely different; whether the technique of the period—in such strong contrast to today's demand for perfection of intonation—would not wholly take away his appreciation of the work.

Old music has become a living heritage because our time experiences in it traits which it yearns to find. But it requires a verification how far this experience coincides with the meaning of the work in relation to its time; in particular, how the work exists not only as an historically viewed museum piece (*i.e.* heritage) but as something new, and perhaps even alien. Problems arise because heritage means life and is borne by man.

It is different to recognize and experience (1) the desire for understanding historical reality and (2) the experience that this art has for our present life. Both cannot, however, be separated. The very fact that old music could become a living heritage in our time (whose own music is entirely differently oriented) shows that we have artistic material of importance to the questing mind of today. Otherwise we could hardly speak of the life of old music in our time and of its heritage. Research has made accessible the entire music from the Middle Ages to the present, even if many questions remained unanswered. From this abundance of artistic material, creative man has selected part to form a living heritage; selected by man who lives in the present but experiences the art of the past. He is faced with the problem of reconciling present time with past heritage. Music research faces the task of recognizing these numerous problems of music and music-making. In musical life, however, the relationship of present-day man to his heritage solves itself in the obligation of art and in the respect for the creative spirit of present and past which, in terms of actual sound, determine that the artistic experience is one of contemporary man in a contemporary setting.

NOTES

1 M. Weber, *Die rationalen und soziologischen Grundlagen der Musik*. München, 1924; E. H. Meyer, *Musik im Zeitgeschehen*. Berlin, 1952.

2 A. Gehlen, *Der Mensch, seine Natur und seine Stellung in der Welt*. Berlin, 1940; E. R. Jaensch, *Grundformen menschlichen Seins*. Berlin, 1929.

3 A. Silbermann, *Wovon lebt die Musik?* Regensburg, 1957; H. Engel, *Musik und Gesellschaft*. Berlin, 1960.

4 K. Blaukopf, *Musiksoziologie*. Köln and Berlin, 1951.

5 F. v. Hausegger, *Die Musik als Ausdruck*. Wien, 1885; L. Klages, *Grundlegung der Wissenschaft vom Ausdruck*. Leipzig, 1936.

6 A. Wellek, *Typologie der Musikbegabung im deutschen Volke*. München, 1939; P. Lamparter, '*Die Musikalität in ihren Beziehungen zur Grundstruktur der Persönlichkeit*, in: Erg. Bd. 22, *Zeitschr. für Psychologie*. Leipzig, 1932; C. C. Pratt, *The Meaning of Music*. New York–London, 1931.

7 K. G. Fellerer, *Einführung in die Musikwissenschaft*. Hamburg, 1953.

8 A. Silbermann, '*Musikformen und Gesellschaftsformen*', in: Bernsdorf u. Eisermann, *Die Einheit der Sozialwissenschaft*. Stuttgart, 1955.

9 V. Zuckerkandl, *The Sense of Music*. Princeton 1959; W. Wiora, *Die vier Weltalter der Musik*. Stuttgart, 1961.

10 H. Nohl, 'Die mehrseitige Funktion der Kunst', in: *Deutsche Vierteljahr-schrift Literaturwiss. u. Geistesgesch*. II, 1925, 179.

11 G. Farmer, *Turkish Instruments of Music in the 17th Century*. Glasgow, 1937; P. Panoff, 'Das musikalische Erbe der Janitscharen', in: *Atlantis* XX, 1938.

12 P. Nettl, *Tanz und Tanzmusik*. Freiburg, i. Br. 1962; P. Nettl, *The Dance in Classical Music*. New York, 1963.

13 J. Horton, *Scandinavian Music*. London, 1963; R. Newmarch, *The Music of Czechoslovakia*. London, 1942; Fr. Zagiba, *Geschichte der slowakischen Musik*, Pressburg, 1943; J. Keldysch, *Geschichte der russischen Musik*, Leipzig, 1956; Z. Jachimecki, *Die polnische Musik in historischer Entwicklung*, Krakau, 1951.

14 R. Haas, *Aufführungspraxis der Musik*. Potsdam, 1931; A. Schering, *Aufführungspraxis alter Musik*. Leipzig, 1831.

15 A. Einstein, *Grösse in der Musik*. Zürich, 1951.

16 K. G. Fellerer, *Soziologie der Kirchenmusik*. Opladen, 1963.

17 R. Molitor, *Reformchoral*. Leipzig, 1902.

18 G. D. Sasse, *Die Mehrstimmigkeit der ars antiqua in Theorie und Praxis*. Diss, Berlin, 1940; H. Besseler, *Die Musik des Mittelalters und der Renaissance*. Potsdam, 1934.

19 G. Reese, *Music in the Middle Ages*. New York, 1940.

20 E. T. Ferrand, *Die Improvisation in der Musik*. Zürich, 1939.

21 K. G. Fellerer, La 'Constitutio Docta sanctorum patrum', di Giovanni XXII e la musica nuova del suo tempo, in: *L'Ars nova Italiana del Trecento*. Certaldo, 1959.

22 K. G. Fellerer, *Geschichte der kath. Kirchenmusik*. Düsseldorf, 1949 (English: Baltimore, 1961).

23 F. Blume, *Geschichte der evangelischen Kirchemusik*. Kassel, 1965.

24 K. G. Fellerer, *Der Palestrinastil und seine Bedeutung in der vokalen Kirchenmusik des 18. Jh*. Augsburg, 1929.

25 F. Romita, *Jus musicae liturgicae*. Roma, 1947.

26 A. Einstein, *Music in the Romantic Era*, New York, 1947; W. Reich, *Musik in romantischer Schau*. Basel, 1946.

27 W. Ehmann,' Der Thibaut-Behaghel-Kreis', in: *Archiv f. Musikforschung* III, 1938, IV, 1939.

28 R. Hohenemser, *Welche Einflüsse hatte die Wiederbelebung der älteren Musik im 19. Jh. auf die deutschen Komponisten?* Leipzig, 1900.

29 Th. Kroyer, 'Acappella und conserto', in: *Festschrift H. Kretzschmar*, Leipzig, 1918; ditto, 'Zur Acappella-Frage', in: *Archiv. f. Musikwiss.*, II, 1919–20; A. Schering, *Die niederländische Orgelmesse im Zeitalter Josquins*. Leipzig, 1912.

30 M. Ruhnke, *Beiträge zu einer Geschichte der deutschen Hofmusik-Kollegien im 16. Jh.* Berlin, 1963.

31 H. Besseler, 'Umgangsmusik und Darbietungsmusik im 16. Jh.', in: *Archiv f. Musikwiss.* XVI, 1959; E. Elsner, *Untersuchung der instrumentalen Besetzungspraxis der weltlichen Musik i. 16. Jh. in Italien*. Diss, Berlin, 1935.

32 E. Th. A. Hoffman, 'Alte und neue Kirchenmusik (1814)', in: *Schriften zur Musik*. Darmstadt, 1963, 209.

33 F. Volbach, *Die Praxis der Händel-Aufführung*, Bonn, 1899; A. Dolmetsch, *The Interpretation of the Music of the XVII and XVIII Century*. London, 1946; M. Geck, *Die Wiederentdeckung der Matthäuspassion im 19. Jh*. Regensburg, 1967.

34 A Symposium on the question of *Historismus in der Musik*, edited by W. Wiora, is about to appear (Regensburg, 1969).

35 A. Schmitz, *Das romantische Beethovenbild*. Berlin and Bonn, 1927; H. K. G. Fellerer, 'Zum Haydn-Bild im frühen 19. Jh.' in: *A. v. Hoboken-Festschrift*. Mainz, 1962, 73; ditto, 'Mozart-Überlieferungen und Mozart-Bild um 1800', in: *Mozart-Jahrbuch*, 1955, 145.

36 A. Schering, *Geschichte des Oratoriums*. Leipzig, 1911.

37 Th. W. Adorno, 'Neue Tempi' in: *Moments musicales*. Frankfurt M., 1964.

38 W. Fischer, 'Selbstzeugnisse Mozarts für die Aufführungsweise seiner Werke', in: *Mozart-Jahrbuch*, 1955.

39 F. Rothschild, *The Lost Tradition-Musical Performance of Mozart and Beethoven*. London, 1961; H. Engel, 'Probleme der Aufführungspraxis', in: *Mozart-Jahrbuch*, 1955; E. and P. Badura-Skoda, *Mozart-Interpretationen*. Wien, 1957.

40 K. G. Fellerer, 'Musik als Aussage. Das Erbe der Musik im Musikleben der Gegenwert', in: *Musikleben*, VIII, 1955, 300.

41 H. Riemann, *Geschichte der Musik seit Beethoven*. Berlin and Stuttgart, 1901, 559.

42 Th. W. Adorno, *Dissonanzen*, Göttingen, 1958; G. Haydon, *On the Meaning of Music*. Washington, 1948, Z. Lissa, *Fragen der Musikaesthetik*. Berlin, 1954.

43 K. Fabian, *Die Objektivität in der Wiedergabe von Tonkunstwerken*. Diss. Hamburg, 1929; Th. Wohnhaas, *Studien zur musikalischen Interpretationsfrage*. Diss, Erlangen, 1959. *Vergleichenden Interpretationskunde*. Berlin, 1963.

44 R. Hammerstein, 'Musik als Komposition und Interpretation', in: *Deutsche Vierteljahrschr*, XL, 1966; I. Strawinsky, *Musikalische Poetik*. Mainz, 1949.

45 Th. W. Adorno, *Versuch über Wagner*. Berlin u. Frankfurt, 1952.

46 Th. W. Adorno, *Prismen*. Frankfurt, 1955; ditto, *Dissonanzen*. Göttingen, 1958; ditto, *Klangfiguren*. Berlin-Frankfurt, 1959.

47 Th. W. Adorno, *Philosophie der neuen Musik*. Frankfurt, 1958.

48 W. Ehmann, *Erbe und Auftrag musikalischer Erneuerung*. Kassel, 1950; R. Stephani, *Die deutsche musikalische Jugendbewegung*. Diss, Marburg, 1952.

49 *Gesammelte Werke*, II. Stuttgart, 1955, 229.

50 K. G. Fellerer, *Das Problem Neue Musik*, Krefeld, 1967.

51 K. G. Fellerer, *Klang und Struktur in der abendländischen Musik*. Köln and Opladen, 1967.

52 C. Sachs, *The Commonwealth of Art*. New York, 1946.

53 A. Cuvillier, *Manuel de sociologie*. Paris, 1958.

54 F. Jöde, *Unser Musikleben. Absage und Beginn*. Wolfenbüttel, 1926; ditto, *Vom Wesen und Werden der Jugendmusik*. Mainz, 1954.

55 N. Dufourcq, *Le Clavecin*. Paris 1949; R. Russel, *The Harpsichord and Clavichord*. London, 1959; E. H. Hunt, *The Recorder and Its Music*. New York, 1963.

56 *Poetique musicale*. Dijon, 1942.

57 H. Kirchmeyer, *Strawinsky*. Regensburg, 1958.

58 H. Pfrogner, *Musik. Geschichte ihrer Deutung*. Freiburg-München, 1954.

59 R. Dammann, *Der Musikbegriff im deutschen Barock*. Köln, 1967.

ARIETTA VARIATA

In the second half of the eighteenth century it occurred several times that a number of composers wrote variations on the same theme. The comparison of such variations is extremely instructive for a knowledge of the style. A beautiful example of this sort is to be found in the period between 1760 and 1782: C. P. E. Bach, C. G. Neefe, and C. F. C. Fasch composed variations on the same theme, an arietta in Italian style.[1] There are even two works each by Bach and by Fasch on this arietta, appearing in different years. Following is a list of these works:[2]

1. C. P. E. Bach, 'Clavierstück mit Veränderungen', publ. in *Musikalisches Allerley*, 7. Sammlung, parts 51 and 52 (1762), pp. 190–6. 14 Variations (No. 1–11, 13, 14, 17) in A major. Dated by Wotquenne and Miesner: Berlin, 1760.[3] Identified in the following as Bach I.

2. C. F. C. Fasch, 'Clavierstück mit Veränderungen', publ. in *Musikalisches Allerley*, 7. Sammlung, parts 51 and 52 (1762), pp. 194–6.
   Variations 12, 15, 16 contained in the work described in 1, above. Begun in Berlin about 1760. Identified in the following as Fasch I.

3. C. P. E. Bach, 'Einige noch unbekannte Veränderungen von Herrn Capellmeister Bach in Hamburg, über folgende bekannte Ariette', publ. in *Musikalisches Vielerley*, part 29 (1770), pp. 123–5. 5 Variations in A major, originated in Hamburg before 1770. Identified in the following as Bach II.

4. C. G. Neefe, 'Veränderungen über ein bekanntes Arioso', publ. in *6 neue Klaviersonaten nebst Veränderungen* . . . , Leipzig, 1774, pp. 55–62.[4]

12 Variations in A major, begun in Leipzig before 1774.

5. C. C. Fasch, *Ariette pour le clavecin ou fortepiano avec quatorze variations*, Berlin, 1785.[5]

14 Variations in A major, begun in Berlin before 1782. Identified in the following as Fasch II.

While with Fasch I and Neefe we are dealing with early works greatly under the influence of C. P. E. Bach,[6] the Bach cycles and Fasch II belong to the mature productive period of their respective masters. The works under discussion originated at about the time when Mozart's Variations K. 24 (1766) to K. 352 (1781) saw the light, though the latter belong of course to a different stylistic era. Fasch II appeared in the same year as Beethoven's 'Dressler' Variations (WoO 63) or shortly before that.

Let us now briefly consider the five groups of variations. The theme designated in the list of Bach's estate (p. 16, No. 121) as 'Veränderungen auf eine italienische Ariette' (Variations on an Italian Arietta) appears in Bach I and II, Fasch I and Neefe in the same shape.

1 Theme   Bach I u. II, Fasch I, Neefe

da capo

Significant is the remark to be found regarding the piece in the list of Bach's estate: 'The Ariette itself with its Italian variations was, where necessary, Germanized'. Though we do not know the ariette in its original form,[7] we may assume that the term 'Germanized' refers to the Berlin fashion, *i.e.* the Lombardic rhythm connected with suspensions of a fourth and small motives, appoggiaturas and alternation of duplets with triplets (see bars 7–8). Our statement results mainly from a comparison with the theme appearing in Fasch II.

2

Theme Fasch II (*from edition of* Landshoff)

Here, the Berlin manner of the 1760's and 1770's has given way to a new, once more Italian, *cantabile* idiom. The 'Germanized' Arietta, in assuming features of the somewhat affected *galant* style, has now turned toward the song-like, more widely-contoured melodic language of the late eighteenth century. Significantly enough, the 2–4 has changed to 4–4. In lieu of the two-part, scaffold-like thorough bass, a differentiated setting with more abundant harmonies has been achieved, in which one may observe the imitation of the bass at the outset in bars 1–2. Merely the triplets followed by duplets in bars 9 and 10 remind us somewhat of the former Berlin manner. Even without knowing the original theme one may claim anyway that the theme, as appearing in Fasch II, is at least not 'Germanized' in Bach's way. Though the fundamental structure has remained unchanged in both shapes, the two versions reveal even from a formal point of view noteworthy differences probably due to Fasch's artistic handling of the problem. Not only are the first four bars enlarged in Fasch II to an eight-bar period; Fasch II also replaces the former *da capo* by a new period of four bars (13–16) which, though motivically deriving from the beginning of the theme, achieves through the downward motion of the melody a stronger cadential effect contrasting with the first eight bars.

Without planning to present within this study a complete analysis of the variations, we should like to make a few remarks regarding the type of the variation technique and the problem of the cyclical form. As to Bach I and II, brief remarks will suffice since the author already discussed the works in a former study.[8] In Bach I, one finds a combination of the types of melodic variation and thorough-bass variation with constant harmonies[9] which means that—as Mattheson observes—the 'fundamental motions' (*'Grund-Gänge'*) of the bass and frequently also of the upper voice are retained.[10] This is the type of variation which was designated in the early and middle eighteenth century as 'alla maniera italiana', and for this reason these variations are clearly marked in the list of Bach's estate as 'Italian variations'.[11] As a characteristic example of a thorough-bass variation we present the first four bars of Variation 11 in Bach I:

Two of Fasch's variations included in the Bach cycle (Nos. 15, 16) are noteworthy because, similarly to Bach's Variation 17, they free themselves of the thematic bass, especially so in the second part. This applies, *e.g.* to bar 5 of Variation 15, where the root form of the dominant seventh cord is replaced by the four-two chord. Here we meet the variation type with constant harmony which likewise belongs to the group of variations 'alla maniera italiana'.

That such dissociation from the thorough-bass variation (and from the thorough-bass too) corresponds to the trend of the time, is revealed by the variations in Bach II. In these pieces, composed about ten years after the first set, the harmony, and at times also the melodic principal notes, constitute constant elements.

227

A cycle formation achieved by the different variations is hardly notice-able in Bach I, Fasch I and Bach II. This was prevented by the very fact of the feuilletonistic publication of the variations. That the virtuoso

4

Fasch I, Var.15, bar 5

elements—what Mattheson called *Faustfertigkeit* ('ready with the fists') —are piled up towards the end of the series of variations, is due to the performing practice of such works.

5

a) Bach I, Var.17, bars 5–6

b) Bach II, Var.5, bars 1–2

Because of the loose sequence of variations, even those interspersed in minor (Bach I and Fasch I: Variation 2, 5, 8, 13, 18; Bach II: Variation 2, 4), though providing temporary contrast, do not achieve a cyclical form for the entire set.

Neefe's variations correspond to the artistic development Bach under-went in the late 'sixties and the 'seventies. The thorough-bass type of variation has generally disappeared; harmony and form are constant elements; in addition there are also true melodic variations such as No. 2.

6

Neefe, Var.2,bars 1-2

A new feature is provided by Neefe when he (like Haydn in the A major Variations, Hob. XVII: 2) shapes over a harmonic bass a melody which has hardly any connection with the theme's upper part:

7

Neefe, Var.6,bars 1-2

Yet more important than the potentialities resulting from the variation-type with constant harmony is Neefe's aim to increase the expressive power and individual character of different variations by concentrating on certain motives maintaned through a whole variation and by dynamic contrasts as well.

8

Neefe, Var.8,bars 5-8

A feature of this kind, boldly developed, is to be found in Variation 8 of C. P. E. Bach's *Folia* Variations[12] composed 1778. From examples of this kind one learns that the figurative *Klangfuss* (literally 'sound-based')

variations of the middle of the century were transformed by Bach and Neefe into a more subjective and expressive type.[13] That a direct line leads from Neefe to young Beethoven need hardly be stressed. If one compares Neefe's second variation with No. 5 of Beethoven's 'Dressler' Variations (WoO 63), one notices that in both pieces the variational elements appear in a clearly motivic concentration; the *arpeggio* figure is more important to the composer than the melody of the theme.

9

a) Neefe, Var.1, bars 1-2

b) Beethoven, Dressler-Var.5, bar 1

Contrary to Bach I and II, Neefe uses also changes in metre and tempo which, on the other hand, are also to be found in Bach's supplementary variations to the song 'Ich schlief, da träumte mir', apparently composed about 1770.[14] Neefe's Variation 10 headed 'Pastorale' and 'Un poco lento' is in 6/8 time; Variation 11 is a *passepied*-like piece in 3/8 time comprising a *Maggiore* and a *Minore* section; the final Variation 12 is an 'Alla Polacca' in 3/4 time. These pieces connected with certain dance types (and by no means to be considered as precursors of Romantic variations) help to organize the variation-cycle. There is also Variation 4 in minor to be played 'sempre piano'. Thus Neefe's cycle reveals the alternation of 'exuberant' and 'tenderly singing' moods stipulated by J. F. Daube in *Der musikalische Dilettant* of 1773.[15] The conscious formation of a somewhat coherent cycle with the *Polacca* as finale results also from the linking of several variations into a group, Theme with Variation

1–3 (♪ - ♪ - ♪♪♪) ; Variation in minor 4; Variation 5–9

(♪♪ - ♪♪♪ - ♪♪♪♪) Variation 10–12 (*Pastorale, Passepied, Polacca*).

In conclusion, the Fasch variations composed shortly before 1782 (Fasch II), are still to be considered. This is their new feature: in lieu of the rhythmic unity within the variation observed in the works discussed so far, a differentiation is now to be noticed, apparent even in the version of the theme. Instead of the former continuity there appears in some variations a discontinuity due not only to dynamic, but also to rhythmic contrasts. The beginning of Variation 9 and 12 may serve as examples:

10

a)Fasch II, Var.9, bars 1-2

b)Fasch II, Var.12, bars 1-2

A new kind of differentiation within the individual variations is also due to Fasch's composing the repeats, *e.g.* in Variation 5 where the second eight bars of the second section (*i.e.* the repeat of this section) appears in the minor key.

11

a)Fasch II, Var.5, bars 10-

b)ibid, bars 18-

In Variation 8 the repeat of the first section, written out, offers an intensification in part writing, dynamics and harmony compared to the first bars:

12

a)Fasch II, Var.8, bars 1-2

b)ibid, bars 9-10

The variation technique is now liberated from any schematism. Fasch was apparently conscious of these innovations, for he remarked to the lexicographer Gerber that 'he was the first to bring to the variations, nowadays so popular, more variety in characterization'.[16] However, these innovations do not proceed in the direction of the melodic variations with constant harmony as are found in works by the older Neefe, young Beethoven and Mozart. This is apparent in the following example taken not from one of the last variations of the cycle, but from No. 1.

13

Fasch II, Var.1, bars 1-4

Bar 1 presents a very free approximation of the theme; in bar 2, the melody is spun out whereby neither the melody nor the harmony of the theme is maintained; bar 3 starts once more with the motive of the preceding bars and with the third and fourth crotchets leads back to the theme.

Contrary to Bach and Neefe, Fasch II has no variation in the minor.

There are also no alternations in metre. In order nevertheless to differentiate certain variations and variation-groups, Fasch introduces changes in tempo: Theme, Variation 1, 3, 6–9, 11–13 *Allegretto*; Variation 2 *più mosso*; Variation 4, 5, 10, 14 *Allegro*. Moreover, a certain division (though only a loose one) results from the appearance of the head of the theme at the beginning of Variation 5, 8, 13 (rhythmical):

14
a) Fasch II, Var.5, bar 1   b) Var.8, bar 1

c) Var.13, bar 1

However, the main aim toward a cyclic cohesion of the series appears more clearly in Variation 14, which shows truly virtuoso features and providies a striking conclusion completely free of the theme. As in some other variations of this set, here too the repeat of the second section is spelled out. Bars 21–24 if compared to bars 13–16 present a great final climax.

15
a) Fasch, Var.14, bars 13–16

b) ibid, bars 21-24

The variation cycles by Bach, Neefe and Fasch discussed above show that the development of the variation in North and Central Germany during the later part of the eighteenth century pursues a path of its own. Imagination and sense of colour may be mentioned as essential aesthetic principles of this stylistic trend. Except for a few instances variety and diversity of colouring are stressed to a greater extent than strict cyclic cohesion. It should be noted, moreover, that in lieu of a scaffold-like variation type we find more and more a variation developed motivically; in Fasch II there is a trend toward contrast within individual variations. I believe that such features reveal tendencies which led, at just this time within sonata form, to motivic work and thematic dialectics. It would seem worthwhile to investigate such connections in depth. However, the tonal-functional development so decisive for the sonata did not apply— or at best did so to a very small extent—to cycles composed about 1760–80 and consisting of individual variations built on analogous harmonies.

NOTES

1 The variations quoted in Hoboken's Haydn catalogue under group XVII a No. 1 may belong to the same group, but the piece was not accessible to me.

2 On Bach's variations, see K. von Fischer 'C. Ph. E. Bachs Variationenwerke', in: *Revue Belge de Musicologie*, VI (1952), 190 ff.

3 A. Wotquenne. *Thematisches Verzeichnis der Werke Ph. E. Bachs*. Leipzig, 1905, under No. 118, 2; H. Miesner, 'Ph. E. Bachs musikalischer Nachlass', *Bach Jahrbuch*, 1938, 1939, 1940–48; p. 16, No. 121 of the original list.

4 Cf. J. Leux, *Chr. G. Neefe als Instrumentalkomponist*. Leipzig, 1925, pp. 158 ff.

5 For the present study, refer to new edition by L. Landshoff, Nagels Musik-Archiv, No. 38, Hanover, 1929.

6 In Fasch I, even a close co-operation with Bach is evident. Such is also the case with the Cantata 'Die mit Tränen säen' from the year 1756, to which Bach contributed a recitative. See the article 'Fasch', list of works, in MGG 3, column 1860.

7 Leux, 158, names Hasse, Handel and Graun as possible composers of the theme.

8 *Cf.* p. 225

9 Regarding terminology *cf.* K. von Fischer, article 'variation' in MGG 13, column 1276.

10 J. Mattheson, *Der vollkommene Capellmeister*, facs. reprint of the edition of 1739, p. 232.

11 *Cf.* note 2.

12 *Cf.* example 19 on p. 206 of the study quoted in note 2. Reprint of *Folia* Variations by C. F. Peters (ed. Herrmann).

13 The expression 'Klangfuss' is to be found in Marpurgs 'Anleitung zum Clavierspielen'. Berlin, 1755, p. 43.

14 *Cf.* the study mentioned in note 2. Bach's Variation 4 is a 'Polacca', Variation 6 a 'Ciciliano' (*sic!*) and Variation 8 a 'Tempo di Minuetto'.

15 *Cf.* K. von Fischer, 'Zur Theorie der Variation' in *Festschrift J. Schmidt-Görg*. Bonn, 1957, p. 157.

16 *Cf.* E. L. Gerber, *Neues historisch-biographisches Lexikon der Tonkünstler*. Leipzig, 1812–14, vol. II, p. 87, as well as the preface to the new edition of these variations quoted in note 5. The German original reads: 'dass er der erste gewesen sey, welcher in die gegenwärtig beliebten Variationen mehrere Mannichfaltigkeit der Charaktere gebracht habe'.

EDITH VOGL GARRETT

GEORG BENDA, THE PIONEER
OF THE MELODRAMA

The musical scene of eighteenth-century Berlin furnishes us with an example of an entire family from Bohemia which for religious reasons became absorbed into the ranks of German musicians: the Benda family might be called the Bach family of Bohemia.

The first was Johann Georg (Jan Jiří) Benda (1685–1757). His wife also came from a family of musicians, the Brixis.[1] Benda combined the occupation of weaver and local musician in the villages of Staré and Nové Benátky in Bohemia. His four sons and one daughter all distinguished themselves in the musical profession and in at least two instances passed their talent on to a third generation.

The most important figure was the third son Georg (Jiří Antonín)[2] (1722–95) who made a European reputation as the most successful composer of the modern melodrama, i.e. recitation accompanied by orchestral music.

Georg Benda spent his youth in Bohemia. He received his first musical education from his father and at the Latin school of the Piarists in Kosmonosy.[3] Especially important was his stay in the Jesuit College in Jičín (1739–42) where—like Gluck years earlier at the Jesuit College in Komotau—the future composer underwent a thorough education which included not only music but the traditional rhetoric and also school dramas. This comprehensive training was invaluable later when Benda dealt with the manifold elements involved in the new artform of the melodrama. From the Jesuit rhetorics, young Benda acquired the ability to feel the rhythm of the spoken word. He recognized the importance of clear and expressive recitation and became familiar with the possibilities offered by exciting dramatic monologues. His sensitive memory harboured a lifelong impression of the tragic spirit maintained by the dramatics of antiquity in their monologues. In essence, these monologues were already melodramas. One might observe that Italian opera in pre-Scarlatti days, and the French from Lully onwards, had likewise emphasized clarity of diction as a means of expression, virtually independent of abstract music.

Georg Benda's oldest brother Franz[4] was from 1740 on *Konzertmeister* to King Frederick the Great of Prussia. Georg followed his brother in 1742 to Berlin as violinist of the Berlin Theatre orchestra. He also played the harpsichord and rehearsed arias with singers, which gave him an occasion to familiarize himself with the quasi-Neapolitan style of the opera represented at the Prussian Court, especially cultivated in Graun's works. Stylistically the latter's *recitativi accompagnati* are significant predecessors in the evolution of Benda's later melodramas.

In 1750, he was appointed *Konzertmeister* at the Court of Gotha, a Thuringian province with a rich cultural atmosphere and heritage. The Masonic order had spread in Northern and Central Germany. Benda absorbed many of its concepts, in addition to the philosophical ideas of Voltaire and Rousseau. Rousseau, incidentally, with his *Pygmalion* of 1762–65, is considered the originator of the melodrama.

A chain of unexpected events furnished Benda an opportunity to create something great and new for dramatic art. In 1774, the Duke of Weimar's castle, including the theatre, was destroyed by fire. The actors suddenly found themselves without employment, and the Duchess of Weimar wrote to the Duke of Gotha, asking his assistance for the homeless company. An invitation to the Ducal Palace Theatre of Gotha was gratefully accepted. Among the company were Johann Christian Brandes and his wife Charlotte, a famous actress.[5] It was for Charlotte Brandes, whom he greatly admired, that Benda wrote his melodramas *Ariadne auf Naxos*[6] and *Medea*.[7]

Mozart wrote on November 12, 1778, from Mannheim to his father:[8]

'The Seyler company are here, whom no doubt you already know by reputation; Herr von Dalberg is their manager. He refuses to let me go until I have composed a duodrama for him, and indeed it did not take me long to make up my mind, for I have always wanted to write a drama of this kind.[9] I cannot remember whether I told you anything about this type of drama the first time I was here? On that occasion I saw a piece of this kind performed twice and was absolutely delighted. Indeed, nothing has ever surprised me so much, for I had always imagined that such a piece would be quite ineffective! You know, of course, that there is no singing in it, only recitation to which the music is like a sort of *obbligato* accompaniment to a recitative. Now and then words are spoken while the music goes on, and this produces the finest effect. The piece I saw was Benda's *Medea*. He has composed another one *Ariadne auf Naxos* and both are really excellent.[10] You know that of all the Lutheran Kapellmeisters Benda has always been my favourite and I like those two works so much that I carry them about with me. Well imagine my joy at having to compose just the kind of work I have so much desired. . . .!'

In Gotha, before 1774, Benda had little opportunity to get to know music-dramatical works on stage, but at least he studied their scores. From preserved lists it appears that he focused his attention mostly on the works of Graun and Hasse. The latter with his great dramatic sense for the recitative, aria and scenes was important for Benda's development. In the years 1765–67 in the Gotha Court Theatre Italian *intermezzi* were played: musically, they could not have had much influence upon Benda because they were very naïve and awkward pieces put together from well-known *opere buffe*.

During his Italian journey (1765–66), he became well acquainted with the Italian *opera buffa* which helped him in the style of his German *Singspiel*; Traëtta's operatic output also influenced Benda's later works.[11]

The unique combination of word and music represented in Benda's melodramas is derived chiefly from the *durchkomponierte* ('through-composed') recitatives as found in the works of Graun, Hasse and later Schweitzer's *Alceste*. The difference is that in the melodrama, the climax of the spoken line is not rigidly determined by the musical accompaniment but may be manipulated variously in each performance at the discretion of the protagonist. The texts which Benda used for his melodramas were dramatic scenes which had to be set to music. It was necessary to find the most effective expression in the shortest possible form which would serve the purpose of the traditional 'numbers' and still fulfil the dramatic demands. He decided to alternate between short sentences of spoken words and small musical descriptions. Thus he discovered a new structural and expressive means.[12] A good example is offered by the episode in *Ariadne auf Naxos* when Theseus hears for the second time the march of the Greeks urging him to return to his homeland. He remembers the time of love which he spent with Ariadne on the island of Naxos.[13]

Aller Widerstand ist vergebens! Man wird mich mit Gewalt aus ihren Armen reissen! Veškerý odpor je marný! Stejně by mne vyrvali z jejího objetí!

In the first bar the music relates Theseus' loving memories in the tender melody of the oboe (which Benda often used to express lyrical moods). In the next two bars, the *cantilena* of the oboe and second violins changes into a sharply torn melody by the first violins, flute and oboe. The dramatic tension is increased by rapidly changing dynamics and irregular accents leading to the outburst: 'Aller Widerstand ist vergebens' (all resistance is in vain). Theseus decides to leave.

The relationship between words and music took new forms and these forms in turn created new possibilities for both drama and music. Except for the overture, which is derived stylistically from the French *ouverture*, the very nature of the melodrama does not allow any of the conventional forms because there is neither time nor room for any such development. We can notice certain 'Erinnerungsmotive' which became the fashion also in the French opera seria.[14]

Rousseau's *Pygmalion* meant for Benda mainly the impetus of a first inspiration.[15] He used for his own *Pygmalion* Rousseau's libretto in a German translation. The author of a melodrama text (J. C. Brandes' *Ariadne auf Naxos*, F. W. Gotter's *Medea*) could work with greater freedom than an opera librettist. His text no longer remained in bondage to abstract vocal forms such as the *da capo* aria, which had become an obstacle to dramatic effect. The necessity to differentiate the aria text from that of the recitative likewise vanished. Furthermore, the words in the melodrama needed not to be in verse form. The expressive part of the text was given more freedom and the author could employ all kinds of rhythms which are contained in the spoken word, especially in monologues. The quick change of words and music in itself offered the possibility of using the rhythm of the spoken word for the musical melody.

The orchestra, as Benda said, holds the paint brush to express these sentiments which animate the declamation of the actor. *Ariadne* contains most of such examples. The text of Brandes in itself is suggestive, but the composer had to forgo many usual devices and forms because of the shortness of phrases. Therefore the music had to concentrate upon the detail to paint particular moods and where the text demanded it, even describes phenomena like the murmuring of the forest, sea storms, the rising sun, etc. He uses very subtle effects, such as in the *Andante quasi allegretto*[16] after the words of the frightened Ariadne 'Wie schlägt mein Herz!' (How my heart is beating). We hear the heart beat in the *pizzicato* motive of the first violins and the steady syncopated rhythm of the second violins. (See Ex. 2.) Did Mozart remember it when he used the same device for Belmonte's first aria in *Entführung* and for Zerlina's second aria in *Don Giovanni*?

Benda's contributions to the genre of melodrama *Ariadne auf Naxos*, *Medea*, *Pygmalion*, *Almansor und Nadine* (*Philon und Theone*) share certain stylistic characteristics. The same melodic and harmonic formulas,

instrumental colourings and expressive delineation of mood are found in all these works. Obviously the composer had worked out a vocabulary of devices that sufficed for his purposes. The average listener who today hears any of these works, is charmed by the idiom. He perceives a mixture of rococco delicacy and grace, naïve self-confidence, and skilful instrumentation that exploits every means of tone colouring possible for the modest forces employed. Sudden eruptions of force suggest Gluck among Benda's contemporaries and at times anticipate the ruggedness of Beethoven in tempestuousness. The sudden variations in dynamics, the dramatic string tremoli surely stem from the Mannheim orchestral innovations. Georg Benda positively revelled in expressing pathos; which is hardly to be wondered at, since this is the era that gave birth to 'Empfindsamkeit'.

The impact of the melodrama upon Mozart's output is well known (*Zaïde*, *Zauberflöte*). The dungeon scene in Beethoven's *Fidelio*, the Wolf's Glen in Weber's *Freischütz*, Zumsteeg's ballads, many of Schubert's dramatic songs and ballads, numerous neo-romantic melodramas, Richard Strauss' 'Enoch Arden', etc. would not have been written, had it not been for the pioneering spirit of Georg Benda. His melodramas with their new ideas and style played, together with Gluck's reform, the most important part in the music-dramatic development of his time.

NOTES

1 Otakar Kamper: *Frant. Xaver Brixi*, Prague, 1926, pp. 47–8.

2 The most extensive study on Georg Benda so far by Vladimír Helfert: *Jiří Benda, příspěvek k problému české hudební emigrace* (Georg Benda, a contribution to the problem of the Czech musicians' emigration), I, II, Brno (Brünn), 1929, 1934.

3 Dlabáč: *Künstlerlexikon*, Prague, 1815, tells of Benda's older cousin Viktorin Brixi who wrote in the same school music to schooldramas, perhaps the first inspiration to Benda's Melodramas.

4 Franz Benda: *Selbstbiographie* (was translated by Paul Nettl in: *Forgotten Musicians*, New York, 1951, pp. 204–45.

5 Joh. Christ. Brandes tells in his *Lebensgeschichte* (Berlin, 1799–1800), II, p. 59, that Charlotte studied in Berlin with Professor Ramler and cultivated a recitation which was 'almost like singing'.

6 'My here (in Gotha) newly acquired friend Georg Benda was given by me the melodrama *Ariadne auf Naxos* soon after my arrival. It found his approval and he offered (since Schweitzer's music for it had remained incomplete) to compose it' (Brandes: *Meine Lebensgeschichte*, II, p. 172).

7 *Medea* was composed to the text by Friedrich Wilhelm Gotter, member of Goethe's Wetzlar round table. Gotter's very dramatic *Medea* ranks artistically far above Brandes' *Ariadne*.

8 Translation of letter No. 339 by Emily Anderson, MacMillan, 1966.

9 Mozart was to compose the music for *Semiramis*, a drama by Otto Heinrich v. Gemmingen.

10 *Ariadne auf Naxos* had its first performance on January 27, 1775, and *Medea* on May 1, 1775.

11 Benda wrote only one Italian opera *Xinto riconosciuto* which was commissioned and which did not please him, as he explains in a letter 'Ueber das einfache Recitativ'.

12 Benda calls his *Ariadne* a 'Drama mit musikalischen Zwischensätzen' (Drama with musical interludes).

13 P. 26 printed score: *Ariadne auf Naxos/ein Duodrama/von Georg Benda*/Leipzig, 1781.

14 See Grétry: *Richard-Coeur-de-Lion*, also Italian *opere serie* of Scarlatti and Jommelli.

15 According to the diary of the actor Conrad Ekhof in Hodermann's *Geschichte des Gothaischen Hoftheaters*, 1775–79, p. 150, the Seyler Company had Rousseau's melodrama with the music of Anton Schweitzer (the score is lost, unfortunately) in their repertoire. We have, however no proof that Benda ever saw a performance of Rousseau's work.

16 P. 27 in Alfred Einstein, *Georg Benda 'Ariadne auf Naxos', Ein Duodrama mit musikalischen Zwischensätzen (1775). Nach der Partitur von 1781 im Klavierauszug herausgegeben.*' Leipzig, 1920.

JOHN GILLESPIE

THE KEYBOARD SONATAS OF
FÉLIX MÁXIMO LÓPEZ
AN APPRECIATION

Within the last few decades, performers and audiences alike have developed an increasing interest in eighteenth-century Spanish music for harpsichord and piano. Until about the end of the first quarter of this present century, any mention of Spanish keyboard music usually referred to the vivacious sonatas written by Domenico Scarlatti (1685–1757). Although Scarlatti had been born in Naples, his harpsichord works were largely composed in the various Spanish cities where the royal court stayed, for during the last twenty-eight years of his life he lived in Spain under the patronage of Queen María Bárbara. Thus it happened that most of the more than 500 Scarlatti pieces destined for the harpsichord were created in Spain, not his native Italy. Scarlatti's complete harpsichord works (eleven volumes edited by A. Longo in 1906 and 1910 for G. Ricordi of Milan) have been available for some time, and his music has been assiduously studied and analysed by Ralph Kirkpatrick (*Domenico Scarlatti*: Princeton University Press, 1953).

In this century, we have come to recognize that the renowned Scarlatti is only one of several composers who created a tradition of keyboard composition in eighteenth-century Spain. When Joaquín Nin (1879–1949), the eminent Spanish music historian and composer, brought out two collections of keyboard sonatas by Spanish composers (*Seize Sonates Anciennes d'Auteurs Espagnols*, 1925 and *Dix-sept Sonates et Pièces Anciennes d'Auteurs Espagnols*, 1929, both published by Max Eschig), he introduced keyboard musicians and audiences to the works of hithertofore little-known Spanish composers: Mateo Albéniz (*c.* 1760–1831), Padre Rafael Anglés (1730–1816), Cantallos (b. *c.* 1760), Padre Narciso Casanovas (1747–99), Mateo Ferrer (1788–1864), Freixanet (b. *c.* 1730), Padre José Gallés (1761–1836), Padre Felipe Rodriguez (1759–1814), Padre Vicente Rodriguez (*c.* 1685–1761), Blas Serrano (b. *c.* 1770), and Padre Antonio Soler (1729–83). The Nin collections revealed that these composers all wrote delightful keyboard sonatas strongly influenced by the Scarlatti tradition.

By far the greater number of sonatas in the Nin collections were written by Padre Antonio Soler, a priest of the order of Saint Jerome, who had lived and worked within the confines of El Escorial, a monastery located some thirty miles from Madrid. After the Nin collections were published, Soler's name appeared with growing frequency on harpsichord and piano programmes in Spain and other countries. Spanish dancers, like the versatile Antonio, arranged groups of Soler sonatas into dance suites which they used with the utmost success. In 1957 the Union Editorial Española, Spain's most distinguished publishing house, began to publish the sonatas under the editorship of Padre Samuel Rubio, and to date around a hundred sonatas have been printed.* Soler's name now appears in practically every important music encyclopedia, and music scholars generally agree that Scarlatti and Soler are the foremost representatives of eighteenth-century Spanish keyboard music. However, in addition to their works, music by various other composers represented in the Nin publications now often appears in recordings of Spanish keyboard musi c Another composer, Manuel Blasco de Nebra (d. 1787), published in his lifetime *Seis Sonatas Para Clave, Y Fuerte Piano* and in 1963 Robert Parris edited a modern edition of this work for Union Musical Española.

Despite this interest and activity in the field of eighteenth-century Spanish keyboard music, much of it still remains unpublished. Many composers—Padre José Gallés, for example—wrote numerous sonatas, yet only a few have to date been published. What is even more regretful is that some of these eighteenth-century composers are almost entirely ignored, even by the Spanish, although their music is often readily accessible in manuscript.

A manuscript in the Biblioteca Nacional de Madrid titled *Libro de música de clavicímbalo del S.ʳ D.ⁿ Francisco de Tejada, 1721* contains

---

* A parallel edition, edited by Frederick Marvin, is appearing in London (Mills Music) Ed·

eighty-eight pieces, and though most are anonymous dances with extremely simple texture, they impart a definite charm and persuasiveness.

Another manuscript in the Biblioteca Nacional de Madrid is dated more than forty years after the Tejada collection. Its title page reads *Joan Roig y Posas Comercian en Barcelona 1764*. Here again the pieces are largely anonymous, but it is important to note that during the forty-year span between the two manuscripts the writing style has changed considerably. The music in this collection reveals a preclassical influence in the expressiveness of its melodic lines and in the obvious attempts at development sections. Ten minuets in the manuscript were written by D. Joaquín Montero, an organist at the parochial church of San Pedro el Real in Seville during the second half of the eighteenth century.

A third manuscript valuable to the study of Spanish keyboard literature is kept at the Biblioteca Musical de la Diputació in Barcelona. Entitled *Sonatas de Varios Autores*, this early nineteenth-century manuscript includes works by known composers such as the Italian Baldassare Galuppi (1706–85) and the Catalan Carlos Baguer (1768–1808), as well as others whose names are not so easily identifiable.

One composer unfortunately overlooked in modern editions of eighteenth-century Spanish music is Félix Máximo López (1742–1821), whose name is not listed in most standard reference works and whose music has not been issued in twentieth-century editions. This oversight should be corrected, for Máximo López enjoyed an excellent reputation in his own day and his music well merits a hearing in our time.

The few facts we have concerning Máximo López come from the *Catálogo Musical de la Biblioteca Nacional de Madrid* (1946), compiled by Higinio Anglés and José Subirá; the *Historia de la Música Española e Hispanoamericana* (1953) by José Subirá; and the *Enciclopedia Universel Ilustrada* (1930).

According to the *Catálogo*, Félix Máximo López was born in Madrid in 1742 and baptised on November 23 of that year. On October 13, 1787 he was named third organist to the Royal Chapel, and on May 6, 1808 he became first organist. He possessed a fine talent for improvising at the organ and keyboard and an equal gift for composing. The *Enciclopedia* states that he published many of his works: eight duets for two violins in 1794; villancicos in 1796 and 1798, and miscellaneous compositions for organ and guitar.

The best examples of Máximo López's keyboard writings—including

sonatas, versos, pasos, and fugues and caprichos for organ—may be seen
in several manuscripts at the Biblioteca Nacional. The Biblioteca also has
the manuscript of an organ method written by Máximo López: *Escuela
orgánica supuestos los principios. Contiene una coleccíon de Pensamientos
cortos, para la Elevación, y otra de sonatas, para el Ofertorio . . . 1799.*
Another manuscript by Máximo López reads *Escuela de acompañar al
órgano o al clave* (the word *clave* is translated as harpsichord).

In the same library there are two Máximo López manuscripts of music
for either harpsichord or piano. One contains several sets of variations;
the other manuscript consists of fifteen (or possibly sixteen) two-, three-,
four-, and five-movement sonatas, and some single pieces. This latter
manuscript—catalogued M.1234 (= G. 5.ª = 17). Procedencia: Fondo
Barbieri—deserves close inspection. Entitled *Música de Clave de D.^{n}
Félix Máximo López, Organista D.L.R.C.D.S.M.C.* (de la Real Capilla
de Su Majestad Católica), the collection perhaps dates from the last decades of the eighteenth century. If Máximo López or the copyist had made
it after 1808, either one would probably have mentioned in the title the
fact that Máximo López was then first organist to the Royal Chapel.

The title of this manuscript indicates that the music is intended for the
harpsichord (*clave*) even though the piano was at that time widely used
elsewhere in Europe. Certainly the harpsichord remained a favourite
instrument with the Spanish long after the invention of the piano, an
attachment sometimes attributed to the fact that the harpsichord shares
a kinship with the Spaniards' beloved guitar. Spanish harpsichords were
being built as early as the seventeenth century, as witnessed by the none-
too-clear description of a harpsichord (with one keyboard and three
independent eight-foot registers) designed by a Dr Bartolomeo Gio-
bernardi (see his *Tratado de la Música*: MS 8931, Biblioteca Nacional de
Madrid) for the court of Felipe IV (reigned 1621–65). Later, the learned
Dr Charles Burney (1726–1814), in describing a visit in Bologna with
Farinelli, the Italian castrato singer who spent so many years at the court
of Spain, wrote:

' . . . he has a great number of harpsichords made in different countries.
. . . The next in favour is a harpsichord given him by the late Queen of
Spain . . . this harpsichord, which was made in Spain, has more tone than
any of the others. His third favourite is one made likewise in Spain, under
his direction.'

When María Bárbara, the Queen of Spain and patroness of Domenico

Scarlatti, died in 1758, an inventory of her personal property listed twelve keyboard instruments—seven harpsichords, three pianos, and two pianos that had been converted into harpsichords. Considering the immense popularity of the piano in France, Germany, Austria, and elsewhere at that time and the fact that the Máximo López sonatas seem definitely styled for piano technique and use expressive markings commonly associated with the piano, it is very likely that he intended them for either piano or harpsichord—whichever instrument was available for performance.

The manuscript contains fourteen sets of pieces that are specifically called sonatas, another set without a title, and a trio of pieces in *F, F*, and *C* respectively, which might—this is the writer's personal conjecture—constitute a sonata if rearranged tonally. In addition, there are two isolated pieces at the beginning of the manuscript: a pleasing *Pieʒa de clave* in *D* and a *Capricho* in *E*—which seem to stand apart from the rest of the manuscript. The sonatas are listed below and for convenience I have added numbers.

1. *Sonata in D Minor*
   Moderato (D minor).
   No tempo indication (F major).
   Vivo non molto (D minor).
2. *Sonata in G Major*
   Allegro (G major).
   No tempo indication (G minor).
   Allegro Vivace (G major).
3. *Sonata in A Major*
   Poco aire (A major).
   Allegro Subito (A major).
   Andante (D major).
   Vivace (A major).
4. *Sonata in G Minor*
   Allegro (G minor).
   Ayroso (E♭ major).
   Vivace non molto (G minor).
5. *Sonata de quatro manos* (C major)
   Preludio: Largo (C major).
   Allegro Moderato (C major).
   Tempo di Minuetto (C major).
6. *Sonata 2ª de quatro manos* (C major)
   Allegro Moderato (C major).
   Andante (F major).
   Rondo (C major).

7. *Sonata in E♭ Major*
   Allegro (E♭ major).
   Tempo di Minuetto (E♭ major).
   Largo (B♭ major).
   Finale: Allegro non molto (E♭ major).
8. *Sonata in F major* (movements 2 and 3 are inversed in the MS)
   Andante (F major).
   Stracto de la Polaca en Variaciones: Allegro Moderato (C major).
   Rondo: Allegretto (F major).
9. *Sonata in D major* (title is missing in the original)
   Grave (D major).
   Allegro Vivo (D major).
   Minuetto (D major).
10. *Sonata in C Major*
    Allegro (C major).
    Tempo di Minuetto (C major).
11. *Sonata in G Major*
    Rondo: Andante (G major).
    Allegretto (G major). Mistitled: should read Minuetto.
    Vivo (G major).
12. *Sonata in C Major*
    Allegro non molto (C major).
    Largo non molto (F major).
    Minuetto (C major).
    Final: Vivace non molto (C major).
13. *Sonata in G Major*
    Allegro (G major).
    Andante (C major).
    Tempo di Minuetto en Canon (G major).
14. *Sonata in C Major*
    Grave (C major).
    Allegro Vivo (C major).
    Andante (F major).
    Tempo di Minuetto (C major).
    Final: Vivo (C major).
15. *Sonata in F Major*
    Allegro (F major).
    Largo non molto (B♭ major).
    Tempo di Minuetto (F major).
16. *Sonata in D Major*
    Andante Largo (D major).
    Minuetto: Allegro (D major).

Upon analysis, these compositions reveal the influence of both the *sonata da camera* and the *divertimento*. Keyboard composers in eighteenth-century Spain usually wrote one-movement pieces in binary form and called them sonatas. Soler produced mostly one-movement sonatas (although at least nine four-movement Soler sonatas exist), and Manuel Blasco de Nebra composed six two-movement sonatas. However, Máximo López seems to have been the only Spanish composer of this era who consistently created poly-movement keyboard works. In this manuscript, the *sonata da camera* tradition is evident in the number of movements: of the sixteen sonatas two have two movements, ten have three movements, three have four movements, and one contains five movements. The *divertimento* character is affirmed by the light texture, the fact that thirteen sonatas are in a major key, and the emphasis placed on the minuet. Nine of the sixteen sonatas include either a minuet or a *Tempo di Minuetto*, and of these nine sonatas, six conclude with one of these minuet-style movements.

Máximo López undoubtedly heard and assimilated music from various sources: on the Spanish stage, opera and *tonadilla*; at the royal court, the instrumental music of Karl Friedrich Abel (1723–87), Johann Christian Bach (1735–82), Luigi Boccherini (1743–1805), Franz Joseph Haydn (1732–1809), Karl Ditters von Dittersdorf (1739–99), Karl Stamitz (1745–1801), Johann Anton Stamitz (1717–57), and others; and on every side, the keyboard music of Domenico Scarlatti and his Spanish emulators.

Many of these influences emerge in Máximo López's music. His sonata movements are typically binary, more than reminiscent of Scarlatti and Soler, and yet a fair number resemble preclassical monothematic sonata movements. A Máximo López monothematic sonata is based on (1) the exposition of one principal theme with a secondary idea (derived from the first) that modulates to the dominant or relative major, (2) a development (or divertimento) section in which imitations of the principal and secondary ideas eventually modulate to the main key, and (3) a re-exposition that presents the material from the exposition.

Máximo López's music emanates a Spanish feeling, but it is not as strong as that in the music of Soler or Mateo Albéniz or Padre José Gallés. Like Soler, Máximo López creates a Spanish mood by using broken chords, repeated notes, and note flourishes about one note. Unlike Soler—and Scarlatti—he seldom uses Spanish dance rhythms or melodic patterns. (This is not atypical, for the music of Juan Crisóstomo de Arriaga [1806–26] is for the most part not Spanish in its effect or characteristics.)

Much of the interest generated by Máximo López's music derives from his experiments with the elements of form, for he obviously enjoyed deviating from commonly accepted procedures. For instance, one of his sonata movements will begin as though following standard binary form, but immediately after the double bar, the music bears no relation to previous material; then, an almost exact recall of the first-section material gives the piece an ABA design. Occasionally the second section of a Máximo López sonata movement nearly duplicates the material (*and* number of bars) of the first section, with the necessary modulations in the second to achieve the principal key. Sometimes his manuscript for a *Tempo di Minuetto* gives the impression of containing two trios, but the key remains unchanged throughout and what develops is a *menuet en rondeau*. In *Sonata 14* he employs a startling device: its last movement—*Final: Vivo*—is a rondo; when the sixteen-bar theme returns for the last time, it stops abruptly after two bars and the piece terminates with a few chords.

Máximo López's melodic practices are closely associated with Baroque ideas. He often uses repeated (or echoed) phrases, sometimes constructing an entire section around such phrase pairs, and he emphasizes sequential melodic figures in the sonatas.

There are other noteworthy characteristics of his writing. His liking for octave passages—broken and parallel—recalls Soler's predilection for this device. In his slow movements, Máximo López uses brief cadenza-like sections. (Haydn and Mozart occasionally used these in their keyboard works.) For melodic purposes and passage work, he employs triplet figures. Dynamic and performance indications, unusual in keyboard music before the late eighteenth century, occur sporadically throughout Máximo López's manuscript, the most frequent indications being *For* (forte) and *Po* (piano). When a passage in one clef is to be divided between the hands, he uses the letter *m* to indicate the assisting hand. Interpretive indications are sometimes in Spanish and sometimes in Italian.

Because he was an organist, Máximo López would have been expected to be competent in contrapuntal writing. That he possessed a definite skill in this area is well documented in the *Tempo di Minuetto en Canon* from *Sonata 13*, where the left hand follows the right hand in strict canon at the octave.

Another writing characteristic evident in this Máximo López manuscript is his rather timid range of keys. He uses eight keys for the sixteen sonatas and only one of these ventures beyond one or two accidentals. Two are in minor keys, D and G; there is one in the key of Eb, and one in A; the keys of F and D are each used twice and G major dominates three sonatas. However, five sonatas are in the key of C major, including the two large sonatas for four hands! There is no clear explanation for this except that Máximo López may have designed these sonatas especially for performers with limited facility.

Admittedly the sixteen sonatas in this collection do not have equal value. Several reveal awkward modulations, and occasionally a tedious movement results from overuse of devices such as repeated phrases and sequence. Yet the positive qualities inherent in most of the sonatas more than outbalance any defects.

Sonata No. 2 combines variety and an obviously skilful technique. The intitial *Allegro* in binary form contrasts with the finale, which has a real development section, and these two are separated by an attractive central movement. *Sonata No. 3* is even better: a short introductory *Poco aire* leads *subito* into an *Allegro* in sonata form with one subject; the resilient *Andante* uses a typical Andalucian flourish as the basis for its melodic line; and the *Vivace* finale is a vibrant rondo built on a dance-like theme containing seventeen bars.

Sonata No. 8, the rearranged sonata in the above list, is very pleasing. The F-major *Andante* is a rondo with three episodes, and the rondo theme is unusual in that it includes two fermata. The third episode is in F minor. What strikes the observer is that each episode preserves its individuality while at the same time acknowledging that it was inspired by some element of the rondo theme. The *Polaca* (or Polonaise) maintains a dignity throughout the five variations designed around the ternary theme. The last variation is marked *en Volero* (en Bolero?). The *Rondo: Allegretto*, which precedes the *Polaca* in the manuscript, has a Classic-type theme that consistently uses Alberti bass patterns. This theme is reinforced in octaves when repeated. The third and fourth episodes— the latter in B♭ major—offer the performer the most virtuoso passages thus far encountered in Máximo López's works.

Many of these sonatas have outstanding individual movements. We have already mentioned the adroit *Tempo di Minuetto en Canon* from *Sonata 13* and the surprise ending to the *Finale* from *Sonata 14*. The *Andante* (third movement) of *Sonata 14* is also interesting: a two-part theme full of rhythmic devices is succeeded by two variations that engagingly exploit the theme's melodic and rhythmic possibilities. The *Tempo di Minuetto* from *Sonata 15* is an enchanting, brief *menuet en rondeau*, and the *Andante Largo* from the final sonata is another very convincing rondo type.

The finest sonatas in the manuscript are the two written for four hands, both in the key of C major. Each sonata testifies to the composer's skill in handling the idiom. He evenly divides the difficult parts among the players and judiciously distributes the melodic lines in a similar manner. The preclassical sonata design proves that Máximo López was more than casually acquainted with this newly emerging style. His rhythmic element, not always strong in some of the solo sonatas, becomes definite and vigorous in these four-hand sonatas.

The first of these (*No. 5*) opens with a stately *Preludio: Largo*, which serves as an introduction. The following *Allegro Moderato* has two themes, a fairly expansive development, and a normal recapitulation—but no coda. The third movement, marked *Tempo di Minuetto*, is actually a rondo in C major with the second and third episodes in A minor and C minor respectively. The minuet spirit remains constant throughout this movement.

The other four-hand sonata (*No. 6*) contains Máximo López's finest writing in sonata form. The first movement—*Allegro Moderato*—has an extremely simple principal theme built on a sequential pattern, but as this theme rises nearly two octaves, it creates tension and excitement. The following series of melodic motives, none expansive enough to constitute an authentic second theme, modulate to a codetta-like passage in G. A development section concentrates on melodic motives from the first section, and the recapitulation unexpectedly introduces new material after the principal theme.

The second movement—*Andante* in F major—is a short rondo with two interludes, the first predominantly in C major, the second in B♭ major. Although the third movement is marked *Rondo*, the intended tempo must surely have been *Allegro*. The *primo* part states the rondo theme—a melody recalling the exuberance of the young Mozart—and the *secondo* joins in for a more intensified thematic statement. The very brief first episode begins in C and terminates with a cadence in G major. Like the first, the second episode is strictly unmelodic, concentrating on modulations with broken-chord passages. The final episode is almost a little composition by itself: it begins in C minor, modulates to a passage in E♭ major, and then returns to C minor to await the ultimate return of the rondo theme.

The sonatas of Félix Máximo López are worthy of a modern edition, for these works add another important segment to the slowly emerging background of Spanish keyboard music and possess substantial musical qualities which should recommend them to both listener and performer.

THEODOR GÖLLNER

J. S. BACH AND THE TRADITION
OF KEYBOARD TRANSCRIPTIONS

The aesthetic theory which emphasizes originality as a criterion of creativity considers the epigone as a counterpart to genius, that is the mere craftsman, who depends on others for his inspiration and exercises only those skills which can be acquired through rigid training. This attitude, however, represents a relatively modern point of view, which though well supported by the music of the last two centuries does not at all coincide with the musical reality of earlier periods, including the eighteenth century. From the Middle Ages to the time of Bach's death, the history of music is full of adaptations and arrangements in the form of *contrafacta*, parodies, intabulations and the like. Indeed the Parody Mass of the Renaissance, which makes use of pre-existent motets and chansons, was the leading musical form of a whole period. The practice of substituting texts in different languages or sacred for secular words was widespread for many centuries. And the countless settings of *cantus firmus* melodies furnish convincing evidence of the close relationship between given musical material and the individual musician's own creative activity.

Among Bach's compositions the *cantus firmus* settings build a large group which is represented in his organ music as well as in the cantatas, in the instrumental as well as in the vocal medium. Another group of significant size is formed by arrangements of various kinds. Besides the numerous examples of *contrafacta* or parodies, where Bach adapts his own works to new texts, there are various transcriptions of instrumental works for keyboard. As long as Bach took his own compositions as the basis for these transcriptions, musical scholars and critics have never seriously objected to the procedure. But in the case of pieces which were

253

originally the creation of other composers the reaction has generally been one of amazement and lack of understanding.[1] Why should a great composer simply take over existing works of his contemporaries? Albert Schweitzer expressed this attitude in the following words[2]: 'It is really quite inconceivable that Bach, now in the epoch of his first mastery . . ., should need to lean upon the ideas—often commonplace—of others. That his Weimar friend Johann Gottfried Walther should have delighted in making transcriptions and cultivated the practice assiduously, is not astonishing, his was not at all a creative mind.' According to Schweitzer this can only be explained by the fact that Bach frequently 'went to external stimuli and examples for his own creations'. This provides us at best, however, with a kind of vague psychological explanation.

At least for the keyboard transcriptions, sufficient evidence can be gathered to show that Bach's activity in this field was part of a long and deeply rooted tradition. When Walther and Bach arranged orchestra concertos for keyboard instruments during their common years at Weimar, they were simply following an old organist's custom of transcribing ensemble music for a solo instrument. This practice, known as intabulation, was widely spread during the fifteenth and sixteenth centuries and forms the historical background for Bach's keyboard arrangements.

To be sure, the situation in the early eighteenth century is not easily comparable to the sixteenth century, when the bulk not only of keyboard but also of lute music consisted of adaptations of vocal polyphony. These pieces, moreover, had to be transcribed from the vocal choir or part book notation into a special instrumental script, the so-called tablature, which is a 'finger notation', related to the mechanics of playing. 'In tabulaturam transferre', transcription into tablature, was one of the most common practices among sixteenth-century organists.[3] In Bach's time, on the other hand, this practice by no means represents the main field of keyboard music. Its point of departure is not vocal polyphony but the instrumental concerto and its notation is not in tablature but the normal keyboard staff. Yet the procedure is essentially the same in both cases: the organist or harpsichord player takes pre-existent ensemble music and adapts it to his own instrument. It is therefore surprising that the connection between Bach's keyboard arrangements and the long tradition of intabulation practices seems to have been overlooked.

From the first appearance of keyboard transcriptions in the earliest known source of keyboard music, the so-called Robertsbridge Codex of the fourteenth century, to the time of Bach there was never a serious disruption in the chain of adaptations of ensemble music for the keyboard. There were, of course, periods when the organists' activity in this field was more obvious than in others. The vast majority of intabulations can still be found in the fifteenth and sixteenth centuries. During this time the keyboard player, often himself unfamiliar with the sophisticated structure of polyphony, strove to reach the level of an acknowledged artist by first adapting already existent pieces of vocal ensemble music, then imitating them and finally developing his own independent keyboard style on the basis of what he had learned from the masters of vocal polyphony. A few documents have been preserved which show how the organist went about this task by coordinating the different parts of the choir book in a special kind of score, that enabled him to read the polyphonic texture and relate it to the hands at the keyboard.[4] There is evidence that as early as the fifteenth century keyboard players began to alter the underlying principle of mensural notation, *i.e.* the relativity of note values, by introducing the conception of the modern bar with its absolute note values.[5] From its very beginnings keyboard music showed a natural tendency towards rhythmic uniformity in which the actual tones played coincided with the beat of the basic time unit. Thus sustained notes in the vocal model were often rendered as repeated notes in the keyboard version.[6] From the time of the Buxheim Organ Book to the end of the sixteenth century we can differentiate between various stages in the technique of intabulation. These range from almost literal adaptations of vocal models, which preserve the vocal texture with all its individual voice lines, to versions so elaborate that it is almost impossible to recognize the original prototype.[7] In contrast to the wide variety and immense number of intabulations characteristic of the sixteenth century, there appears to have been relatively little activity in this field during the seventeenth century. The reason for this change is obvious: by this time, keyboard music had not only assumed an important rôle within the field of instrumental music but was beginning to challenge the supremacy of vocal polyphony. There are, moreover, indications that a significant change had already taken place during the last decades of the sixteenth century. The Venetian organist Claudio Merulo, for instance, uses his own 'canzoni da sonar a quattro', *i.e.* instrumental music for 4-part ensemble, and not vocal pieces as the basis for his organ canzonas.[8] Italian instrumental canzonas appear frequently in German keyboard tablatures of the early seventeenth century,[9] and the process of intabulation, the transformation from a 'partitura' to an 'intavolatura', which also employs diminution of the original parts, is demonstrated by G. Diruta on instrumental canzonas of G. Gabrieli and A. Mortaro.[10] Though at this time the instrumental ensemble seems to have had priority, sixteenth-century motets were still being intabulated as late as the middle of the seventeenth century. In 1656 Orlando di Lasso's motet *Ego sum panis* appears in one of the Lüneburg organ tablatures,[11] attributed to the Hamburg organist H. Scheidemann. Scheidemann also arranged a number of other motets by Lasso, Hassler and H. Praetorius, usually adding typical keyboard colorations to the original.[12] Arrangements of this sort, which scarcely differ from sixteenth-century practices are also preserved among the works of Scheidemann's contemporary, Delphin Strungk.[13] Some particularly popular pieces seem to have enjoyed an extremely long and tenacious existence in the form of intabulations. J. Arcadelt's madrigal *Ancidetemi pur*, for example, still appears in seventeenth-century keyboard arrangements by his compatriots A. Mayone (1603), G. M. Trabaci (1615), G. Frescobaldi (1627) and even as late as 1687 in G. Strozzi's *Capricci da sonare cembali et organi*.[14]

But aside from this retrospective activity it is contemporary orchestral music which leaves its lasting mark on keyboard literature of the seventeenth century. In 1689 J. H. d'Anglebert, musician at the court of Louis XIV, published his clavecin transcriptions of some of Lully's compositions for orchestra.[15] Among these pieces, which include dances, a chaconne and a passacaglia, is one of the most prominent types of orchestral music of that period, namely the French overture.[16] Here we encounter this species for the first time as a keyboard piece rather than in its normal operatic environment. Significantly it is again the keyboard arrangement modelled after an already existent prototype that precedes later independent works for keyboard such as Bach's introductory movements to some of his partitas for harpsichord (*Clavier-Übung* I, 1726–31) or his famous 'Overture nach Französischer Art' (*Clavier-Übung* II, 1735).

Bach's Italian Concerto, the 'Concerto nach Italienischem Gust', which forms the first half of the *Clavier-Übung* II, is also the result of a continuous effort in adapting a leading genre of orchestral music to the keyboard instrument. Bach had already employed typical features of the Italian *concerto grosso* in the preludes to his English Suites,[17] but preceding these independent compositions for harpsichord are the numerous keyboard transcriptions of existing orchestral concerti by other composers, which Bach had made during his Weimar years. As the Italian concerto was the most advanced and fashionable musical genre of its time and was particularly favoured at the ducal court of Weimar, it is not surprising that Bach, the organist, should have fallen back on an old tradition of the profession by arranging this music for the keyboard. His Weimar friend and kinsman, J. G. Walther, transcribed fourteen concertos for the organ,[18] mostly the works of Italian composers, whereas Bach's arrangements of this species number six for the organ[19] and sixteen for the harpsichord.[20]

It is not the purpose of the present study to compare and analyse the original versions of these concertos and their transformation into keyboard music or to show how Bach's transcriptions are superior to those of Walther. To some extent this has already been done,[21] and it would be even more rewarding to consider the subject in the light of the earlier intabulation practices which have been outlined above. It is true that 'Bach did not mechanically transfer the string parts to the keyboard instrument. Wherever it seemed necessary, he gave greater flexibility to the bass line, filled the middle parts, enriched the polyphonic texture, and ornamented the melodic lines, in order to adapt the sustained tone of strings to the transient sound of the clavier.'[22] But in so doing he continued a genuine keyboard tradition, which is rooted in the intabulation practices of the past. In a way the intabulator of the Renaissance treated his vocal prototypes in a manner similar to Bach's adaptation of instrumental models. The keyboard player was always concerned with the continuity of sound in relation to the action of the keys. He did not like rhythmic holes. The flow of musical sound must not be interrupted, and whenever individual chords could be connected, they were taken out of their polyphonic context and treated as separate entities which could be joined together by means of certain keyboard figurations and passages. Thus, the intabulator of an early fifteenth-century *frottola* by B. Tromboncino[23] tends to 'build bridges' between separate chords, thereby unifying the rhythmic structure of his model, just as Bach does at the beginning of the last movement of Vivaldi's violin Concerto, opus 3, Nr. 12.[24]

In both cases, the original has been altered considerably in the arrangement. The horizontal voice lines of the vocal setting have given way to vertical chord structure, which is held together by fast moving figurations. The connecting function of the keyboard formulae is particularly evident in the appearance of sixteenth notes in the second half of bar 2 of the 'Tromboncino' setting. With the help of these notes, the passing character of the C-chord vanishes, and it becomes an autonomous unit, which has to be connected to the following G-chord. This chord in turn receives similar treatment through the addition of quavers which run through a whole octave and continue into the next C-chord. Here,

B. Tromboncino

Non piu mor - te al mio mo - ri - re   Che per te pur

Non piu morte

Non piu mor-

Non piu morte

A. Antico

a bridge is built not only between separate chords but also between two verses of the text (*Non piu morte al mio morire/Che per te pur troppo moro*). The physiognomy of the original has lost as much as the keyboard version has gained by the continuous flow of smaller note values.

If we compare Bach's keyboard version to Vivaldi's original, the most obvious alteration lies in the addition of semiquaver passages in the bass. While these contribute to the virtuoso possibilities of the keyboard, they also fulfil a function similar to the smaller note values in the earlier intabulation. Vivaldi's Concerto opens with a sharply defined and well balanced thematic unit, which consists of one full bar in quavers and two contrasting chords in crotchets. The same gesture is repeated after a crotchet rest. Bach not only eliminates the imposing quality of this opening with his semiquaver notes but also makes us conscious of the underlying chordal structure, which the keyboard passage emphasizes. Indeed, this passage bridges the decisive gap between the statement of the opening gesture and its repetition, connecting the C- with the G-chord and this in turn with the following C-chord. It thus fulfils a function similar to

the connecting keyboard formulae in the intabulation of the 'Tromboncino' *frottola*.

The example brings out one of the most important and long-lived traits in the tradition of keyboard arrangements: these adaptations tend not only to emphasize the chordal structure as opposed to the horizontal lines of the original, but they also add weight to these chords by connecting and embellishing them through a continuous action of the keys. Since this process is basically the same in the intabulations of the sixteenth century as it is in Bach's adaptations of instrumental ensemble music, we feel justified in our attempt to look at these two practices not as separate fields of specialized knowledge but as integral parts of one and the same phenomenon. Bach as an organist was also an *'intabulator'* in the old sense. In this capacity he gave keyboard music new impulses, especially in the hitherto unexplored realm of the solo concerto for organ and harpsichord.

NOTES

1 *Cf.* the comprehensive list of Bach's transcriptions and arrangements in the recent publication of N. Carrell, Bach the Borrower, London, 1967.

2 A. Schweitzer, *J. S. Bach*, English translation by E. Newman, vol. I, Leipzig, 1911, 195.

3 *Cf.* C. Paesler, Das Fundamentbuch von Hans von Constanz, in: VfMw V, 1889, 33.

4 *Cf.* Th. Göllner, 'Notationsfragmente aus einer Organistenwerkstatt des 15. Jahrhunderts', in: AfMw XXIV, 1967, 170 ff.

5 *Cf.* also Th. Göllner, 'Eine Spielanweisung für Tasteninstrumente aus dem 15. Jahrhundert', in: *Essays in Musicology*, A Birthday Offering for Willi Apel, Bloomington, Indiana, 1968, 72 f.

6 H. R. Zöbeley, 'Die Musik des Buxheimer Orgelbuchs', in: *Münchner Veröffentlichungen zur Musikgeschichte*, Bd. 10, Tutzing 1964, 28 ff.

7 H. R. Zöbeley, *Buxheimer Orgelbuch*, 114 ff; *cf.* also J. Ward, 'The Use of Borrowed Material in 16th-Century Instrumental Music', in: JAMS V, 1952, 88 ff.

8 *Cf.* Cl. Merulo, *Canzonen* (1592), ed. by P. Pidoux, Kassel 1941; Cl. Merulo, *Sei Canzoni da sonar a quattro*, ed. by B. Disertori, Milano, 1950 (from the MS. 1128 of the Biblioteca Capitolare in Verona.

9 B. Schmid, *Tabulaturbuch . . .*, Strassburg 1607; J. Woltz, *Nova Musices Organicae Tabulatura*, Basel, 1617; also in the Munich MS., Bayerische Staatsbibliothek, Mus. 1581.

10 G. Gabrieli, *Canzone detta la Spiritata*; A. Mortaro, *Canzone detta l'Albergona*; *cf.* G. Diruta, *Seconda Parte del Transilvano*, Venetia, 1609, 14 ff., 18 ff., resp.

11 Ratsbibliothek, KN 210, fol. 57v–58, see Facs. in MGG VIII, Taf. 64.

12 *Cf.* G. Fock, Art. Scheidemann, in: MGG XI, 1623 f.

13 Lüneburg, Ratsbibliothek, KN 209; *cf.* D. Härtwig, Art. Strungk, in: MGG XII, 1618; W. Apel, *Geschichte der Orgel- und Klaviermusik bis 1700*, Kassel, *etc.*, 1967, 367 f.; see also M. Reimann, *Pasticcios und Parodien in norddeutschen Klavier-Tabulaturen*, in: Mf VIII, 1955, 265 ff.

14 *Cf.* W. Apel, *Geschichte der Orgel- und Klaviermusik*, 420, 424, 430, 440, 667, 679.

15 *Pièces de clavecin*, Paris 1689; modern edition by M. Roesgen-Champion, in: *Publications de la Société française de Musicologie*, Tome VIII, Paris, 1934.

16 Overture to Lully's opera *Cadmus et Hermione*.

17 *Cf.* K. Geiringer, *J. S. Bach, The Culmination of an Era*, New York, 1966, 294.

18 *Cf.* M. Seiffert (ed.), Joh. Gottfried Walther, *Gesammelte Werke für Orgel*, DDT XXVI/XXVII, Leipzig, 1906; selection of six concertos edited by W. Auler, Kassel, 1953.

19 BWV 592–597; *cf.* K. Geiringer, *The Bach Family*, London, 1954, 246 f.; same author, *Joh. Seb. Bach*, New York, 1966, 221 ff.

20 BWV 972–987; *cf.* K. Geiringer, *The Bach Family*, 262 f.; same author, *Joh. Seb. Bach*, 264 f.; as to other keyboard adaptations, particularly those from the *Hortus Musicus*, by J. A. Reinken, *cf.* also N. Carrell, *Bach the Borrower*, London, 1967, 244 ff.

21 *Cf.* Ph. Spitta, *J. S. Bach*, English Translation by C. Bell and J. A. Fuller-Maitland, vol. I, London, 1883, 411 ff.; P. Graf Waldersee, 'Antonio Vivaldis Violinconcerte unter besonderer Berücksichtigung der von Johann Sebastian Bach bearbeiteten', in: VfMw I, 1885, 356 ff.

22 K. Geiringer, *The Bach Family*, 262 f.

23 K. Jeppesen, *Die italienische Orgelmusik am Anfang des Cinquecento*, vol. I, Copenhagen 1961, 17*; edited from *Andrea Antico, Frottole intabulate da sonare organi. Libro Primo. Roma 1517*, fol. 29r/v; in the above example the note values are reduced by one half for comparative purposes.

24 Example after A. Vivaldi, *Concerto for Violin and String Orchestra*, opus 3, Mr. 12, ed. by H. Husmann (Eulenburg), 10; for the present purpose transposed from E to C; Joh. Seb. Bach, *16 Konzerte zu 2 Händen*, ed. by A. Schering (Peters), 44.

DOUGLASS GREEN

PROGRESSIVE AND CONSERVATIVE TENDENCIES IN THE VIOLONCELLO CONCERTOS OF LEONARDO LEO

From the time of his first appearance as a composer in 1712 until his death, Leonardo Leo (1694–1744) produced a steady stream of operas, church music and cantatas, but only a small amount of instrumental music. Aside from the opera and oratorio overtures, he wrote for instruments only various pieces for harpsichord, the Concerto for four violins, and six Concertos for cello with two violins and basso continuo. The autograph score of the cello Concertos are in the library of the Conservatorio San Pietro a Maiella in Naples. They are not numbered but five of them are dated.

September 1737

Concerto in D major
   Andante grazioso, C
   Con bra[v]ura, ₵
   Larghetto, con poco moto, 3/4
   Fuga, ₵
   Allegro di molto, 3/8

Concerto in A major ('first A major')
   Andantino grazioso, 3/4
   Allegro, C
   Larghetto a mezza voce, 3/4
   [Allegro], 3/8

October 1737

   Sinfonia Concertata in C Minor
     Andante grazioso, C
     Mol [to] presto [fugue], ₵
     Larghetto, 6/8
     All [egro], 3/8

August 1738

Concerto in A major
   ('second A Major')
   Andante piacevole, 3/4
   Allegro, C
   Larghetto, e [gustoso?], 6/8
   Allegro, 12/8

Concerto in D minor
   Andante grazioso, C
   Col Spirito, ₵
   Amoroso, 12/8
   Allegro, 3/8

Undated

   Concerto in F minor
     Andante grazioso, C
     Allegro, C
     Largo e gustoso, 6/8
     Allegro, 12/8

The autograph of each concerto bears the title 'Concerto di Violoncello con violini per solo servizio di Sua Eccellenza il Signore Duca di Madalone'. Domenico Marzio Caraffa was the Duke of Maddaloni (as the name of the present town is spelled) from 1716 to 1760.[1] He was an amateur of the cello and, as Pergolesi's patron from 1734 to 1736,[2] presumably brought about the composition of Pergolesi's *Sinfonia* for cello and basso continuo. The exact nature of his relationship with Leo is not known. The Marchese di Villarosa, writing about 100 years later, states that Leo, in addition to singing, harpsichord, and counterpoint, learned cello while a pupil at the Conservatorio della Pietà dei Turchini.[3] Fétis goes on to declare that Leo 'joua du violoncelle en virtuose et fut un des premiers qui mirent cet instrument en vogue en Italie'.[4] Just where Fétis obtained this bit of information is unclear. It is possible, of course, that Leo wrote the concertos to play at the court of the Duke. More probably they were intended for the Duke himself. The technical difficulty of the solo cello parts is not so great as to preclude performance by a gifted amateur. Whatever the answer, in view of the titles of the concertos and the fact that Leo was primarily interested in opera and sacred music, there can be no doubt that the concertos were a commission from the Duke and probably his idea.

Leo's cello concertos, like virtually every solo concerto from the earliest to around 1760 and often after, call for an orchestra consisting solely of strings with improvising keyboard instrument. While outside

Naples the custom was to write for string orchestra in four parts—two violins, viola, and bass—Neapolitan composers after Scarlatti generally preferred three parts only, omitting the viola. Although Pergolesi's violin Concerto does include the viola, the two flute Concertos attributed to him do not. Similarly, Porpora's Concerto for violoncello in G major uses the viola, but Eitner mentions that there are in Karlsruhe two concertos for transverse flute by Porpora which are accompanied by an orchestra consisting only of two violins and bass.[5] Durante's Concerto for *cembalo* omits the viola part, and, according to Schering, the original version of Hasse's twelve flute Concertos was written for two violins and bass only, the printed viola part being added at a later time.[6] If the presence in the Naples conservatory of the anonymous cello Concerto in C major can be taken as indicative of its origin, it provides a further example of a Neapolitan concerto in which there is no provision made for the viola.

Whether or not the viola was actually employed in performance is, however, another question and one which is not liable to a definitive answer. The presence of violas in the Neapolitan opera orchestra is certain, as all the *sinfonia* scores testify. It may be, then, that in actual performance the viola was intended to double the bass part, either in unison or an octave higher, depending on the range and context.

It is well known that the solo instrument in the Baroque concerto customarily played during the tutti sections. The same is true of Pergolesi's concertos for violin and for flute, as the separate parts testify, and of Durante's concerto for *cembalo*. Leo apparently did not intend the solo cello to join with the orchestra in the *tutti* sections. Rather than leaving the staff blank or writing simply 'col basso', he has carefully inserted rests into the cello's staff during these sections.[7]

Five of Leo's cello concertos, like his Concerto for four violins, are in four movements: *Andante-Allegro-Larghetto-Allegro*. In the D major concerto, one of the two earliest, Leo has added a fifth movement, a fugue, before the finale.

The four movement scheme was not common at this time in Italian concertos, though it appeared often enough in sonatas. Still, it was far from unknown. Instances of four movement concertos by Neapolitans are the D major flute Concerto attributed to Pergolesi (the other flute Concerto and his violin Concerto are in three movements) and the cello Concerto of Porpora. The affective tempo indications in Leo's concertos ('andante grazioso', 'amoroso', etc.) were not uncommon in the instrumental music of the Neapolitan school at that time. Durante's concertos for strings contain many similar markings, including 'affetuoso' and even a 'canone amabile'.

On hearing these concertos, one feature particularly strikes the listener —about half of the writing is in a two-part texture which depends on the filling-in of the harmonies by the harpsichord. Of course, such a texture was common enough in all Baroque music, but Leo's two-part writing is different from that found in the typical Baroque concerto. The concertos of Torelli, Albinoni, Vivaldi, and other northern Italians, as well as those of the Neapolitan school of Pergolesi, Durante, Porpora, and Hasse abound in two-part writing. But in these cases, the two-part texture is mostly restricted to the solo sections in which the solo instrument is accompanied only by the *basso continuo* or perhaps by one or more of the other instruments in a single line. The tuttis are generally in three or four parts. In Leo's concertos the situation is almost reversed. The majority of the tuttis are written in two parts while the solo sections often have a three- or four-part texture: a two- or three-part accompaniment to the melodic line of the solo cello.

The second movement of the C minor *Sinfonia Concertata* and the fourth movement of the D major Concerto are fugues. These, along with the triple fugue in the Concerto for four violins, are the only movements which bear a close relationship to the great choruses of Leo's masses, psalms, and oratorios. Leo's sacred works almost always avoid the sensuous melody. Rather, they are dignified, contrapuntal, and intellectual, in some cases perhaps tending toward dryness and ponderousness. The attitude toward religious music displayed by Leo was different enough from that of his contemporary Durante to cause the younger generation of Neapolitan musicians to split into two camps, calling themselves the 'Leisti' or the 'Durantisti' depending on whether they favoured the severe or the sentimental in church music. The existence of these two camps has tempted some historians into the trap of placing each composer in a neat category, Leo on the intellectual side, Durante on the emotional.

This fact, in addition to the general accessibility and greater familiarity of Leo's church music (which was quite well known and some of it rather frequently performed in England during the nineteenth century) have combined to create the impression that he was essentially a backward-looking composer, distinguished by his intellectuality and capable of writing music of massive strength, but lacking the warmer, appealing qualities of Pergolesi or Durante.

The fugal movements are not without interest, however, particularly that of the C minor *Sinfonia Concertata*. Just as J. S. Bach combined in certain of his fugues the *ritornello* principle with the fugal (*e.g.*, organ fugues in E minor, BWV 548, and C minor, BWV 537) so Leo in this movement contrasts the *tutti* with the solo within the fugal framework. It is like the fugal section of the French overture opening Bach's B minor Suite for flute and strings, written about fifteen years earlier. Both these works are so constructed that the various sections have double meanings. From the fugal point of view, each movement is made up of a number of expositions separated by episodes. From the concerto point of view, there are *tutti* sections separated by solo sections. But in neither case is the movement worked out in so simple a plan as to associate each tutti with a subject entry and each solo section with an episode, as in Torelli's violin Concerto in C minor.

An attractive characteristic of these concertos is the appealing quality of the themes of the fast second movements. The opening theme of the second movement of the F minor Concerto, for instance, begins:

The appearance of the sweetly singing melodies, the 'dolce stil novo' of eighteenth-century music derived from *bel canto* and applied to instruments, has often been discussed. Aside from the fugal movements and the finales, the cello concertos of Leo are based as completely on this melodic style as any luscious aria of Durante or Pergolesi. Leo had in the cello an instrument capable of a gorgeous singing tone, admirably suited to the rendering of flowing melodies, and he does not hesitate to make full use of these qualities.

His predecessors in the field of cello writing did not use a melodic style which could make the most of the *cantabile* possibilities of the cello's tone. Jacchini's cramped melodies do not allow the cello to sing freely. Vivaldi's fast movements provide brilliant passage work for the cello and figuration of great power and intensity, but almost no opportunity for a *cantabile*. This opportunity is provided, to be sure, in the slow movements but by no means regularly or for long periods. Some of the slow movements consist entirely of figuration. Others begin with a songlike theme but soon pass over into figuration. Only occasionally in Vivaldi is there a complete movement devoted to a melody in a singing style (*e.g.*, Fanna III, No. 4) and this is invariably a slow movement. But in Pergolesi's *Sinfonia* for violoncello and *basso continuo* one does find the second movement, an *allegro*, written in a manner calculated to make the most of the cello's ability to play sweetly. Leo was surely aware of the activities of his younger contemporary and could well have been acquainted with this particular piece, it apparently having been written for the same Duke of Maddaloni for whom Leo composed his concertos. But it does not follow that Pergolesi was an influence on Leo. Sixteen years younger than he, in many ways inferior to him as a composer[8] and not particularly successful during his lifetime, Pergolesi was probably not considered by Leo to be one from whom to learn the art of composition. Moreover, the melodic style used in the cello concertos had already fully matured in Leo's vocal music, as an examination of any of the arias from his operas, oratorios, or cantatas will show. (See, for instance, the aria 'Ahi che la pena mia' reproduced in Nef's *Outline of Music History*.)[9]

The slow third movements in the last four of the six cello concertos are of the *siciliano* type. Leo's application of this style to the solo cello is singularly appropriate, and he sets the languid melodies in the cello's most advantageous range, the bulk of the melody lying in the fifth between *c'* and *g'*—a range which, for sheer tonal beauty, is surely the cello's finest.

The first two concertos, that in D major and the first A major, do not contain *siciliani*. Their third movements are both in 3/4 and marked *larghetto*. In the D major Concerto, the orchestral prelude of the third movement presents a melody beginning with a long sustained note

(see Ex. 2). This melody will be repeated with slight variations at the entry of the cello. Here Leo is arranging for the solo cello to enter on a long note held through moving figures in the accompaniment, a device much used in the Baroque opera aria and providing opportunity for the practice of *messa di voce*. In the F minor Concerto the same device opens the slow movement and, in this case, the dynamics are expressly indicated.

E. J. Dent has maintained that the musical progress made by the generation after Scarlatti in Naples was technical rather than along the lines of poetic expressiveness.[10] This statement may well be true in opera and church music, but it cannot be applied to the instrumental music. Both Durante and Leo endowed their concertos with a noble sentiment utterly lacking in the instrumental works of the elder Scarlatti. Leo had already imbued the slow movements of his opera overtures with a genuine expression rarely indulged in by his contemporaries. In these concertos he went even further, and the slow movements of the D major Concerto and the first A major can be compared in depth of feeling to the sensitive style of C. P. E. Bach.

Leo's concern with the emotional impact of music is not limited to the expression of a simple pensive mood as a discussion of one of the fast movements will show. It is in the second movement, *Col Spirito*, of the

3
a) **Col spirito** *(first subject)*

b) *(second subject)*

D minor Concerto that Leo perhaps most completely abandons the Baroque spirit and strikes out toward the Classic, for in the range and placing of its contrasts the movement has a strong dramatic quality. Like a number of Mozart's themes, the opening subject comprises a vigorous idea (bars 1–3) immediately opposed by a lyric one in double stops (see Ex. 3a).

Ex. 3b shows the second subject which, in spite of its initial bars, is in the relative major key. The solo cello plays in parallel sixths with the first violins, striking features being the syncopations and *forte* intrusions into a generally calm mood. Following this is a closing tutti theme marked *forte* and *staccato* which, with its augmented and diminished intervals, adds still another element of contrast. By calculating the differing character of each of his several ideas, and balancing and contrasting them with each other, Leo is able to produce a dramatic movement without having the advantage of a real development section. At the return of the second theme in the recapitulation, its character is changed (see Ex. 4). Now no longer in the major mode but in the tonic key of D minor, it is given an added poignancy. Both parts are played by the violins, freeing the solo ̇cello for the underlying sustained *d'*, which in turn releases the basses for delicate punctuation. The rhythm is smoothed out, there are no *forte* interruptions

4 (second subject, recapitulation)

to disturb the peaceful atmosphere, only a gentle chromatic rise in the cello lifting the two-bar phrase to a new higher level. Here is an example of transformation of a theme in the recapitulation quite close to the manner of Mozart.

From the structural point of view the first movements of Leo's concertos are early examples of what can be called the concerto-sonata form—that is, an application of the sonata form to the tutti-solo principle of the concerto. The first movement of the classic concerto consists of six sections:

R1 *Ritornello*; tonic key
S1 Solo similar to a sonata form exposition
R2 *Ritornello*; in, or beginning in, dominant or relative major key
S2 Solo either made up of new material or constructed along the lines of a sonata form development
R3–S3 Recapitulation beginning like R1 and forming a kind of synthesis of R1 and S1; in tonic key
R4 *Ritornello*, interrupted by cadenza; tonic key

Though the structure of the individual sections varies from concerto to concerto, the same six sections are to be found as the basis for the first movements in virtually all the concertos of the classic composers. Much older than Mozart, this scheme served as the basis for many concerto first movements of C. P. E. Bach and for some of Johann Christian Bach, written in the 1740's and 1750's. Yet it is not at all common to find this pattern in an Italian concerto. Concerto first movements of Leo's fellow Neapolitans Porpora, Pergolesi, and Durante do not tend toward this application of the sonata form idea to the concerto, still less, those of Hasse, Tartini, Nardini, or even the *galant* keyboard concertos of Padre Martini to whom J. C. Bach acknowledged his indebtedness.[11]

It is a matter of some interest, then, to note the structural similarity of the first movements of four of Leo's six concertos to the general plan of the concerto-sonata form. The sonata form was appearing spasmodically in various Italian instrumental works during the 1720's and 1730's. Leo's overtures, like those of Vinci, Sarri, Feo and the others were, during the 1720's, shaped in a variety of ways. But after 1730 he became more and more deliberate in his use of sonata form and after 1735 it appears exclusively in the first movements of his overtures.[12] Leo is the only Neapolitan composer to show such a preoccupation with this particular way of shaping a movement. Given his predilection for sonata form, it is perhaps not so surprising that Leo should have hit upon the very structure which much later in the century was to play such an important rôle in concerto writing. It cannot be maintained that Leo influenced later composers for no evidence has been forthcoming that his concertos were known outside his immediate circle. They were not published nor have any manuscript copies turned up other than a nineteenth-century copy in the Archivio Musicale Noseda at the Conservatorio G. Verdi in Milan.

There is a number of other formal innovations in these concertos which have not been discussed here. These cannot be considered contributions to the development of instrumental music for they stand as isolated phenomena: ideas which have been, as it were, offered but not accepted, never followed through and gathered up into the mainstream of music. Such are the particular combinations of sonata form and Baroque concerto elements exhibited in the movements other than the first.

Stylistically, Leo took part in the new *allegro cantante* in the fast movements of these concertos, particularly the second movements, thus helping to pave the way toward the establishment of the melodic style of the Classic era. In so doing he was a pioneer in the treatment of the cello as a means of great poetic expression. Singing melodies in the instrument's most advantageous range like those he poured forth in these concertos are hardly to be met with in the cello works of his predecessors. The discovery of Leo's concertos by performers would help close the gap in the usual cellist's repertoire between Bach and Vivaldi on the one hand and Boccherini and Haydn on the other.

The merit of Leo's concertos lies in the balance of heart and brain which he put into their creation. All the passion and sentiment characteristic of the music of southern Italy is here, but in Leo's hands it is controlled and moulded with the detachment of the intellect to achieve high artistic ends. An artist of Leo's calibre—living, performing, composing, and teaching at a time when too many Neapolitan composers tended toward the superficial, the immediately appealing, or the brilliant but empty—must have exerted a healthy influence, raising the standards of his art without loosening his hold on the appreciation of the general public.

NOTES

1 Alfred von Reumont, *Die Carafa von Maddaloni*, Deckersche Geheime Ober-Hofbuchdruckerei, Berlin, 1851, II, 309.

2 Giuseppe Radiciotti, *G. B. Pergolesi, Vita, Opere, ed Influenza su L'Arte*. Rome, 1910.

3 Marchese di Villarosa, *Memorie dei Compositori di Musica del Regno di Napoli*, Stamperia Reale, Naples, 1840, p. 106.

4 F. J. Fétis, *Biographie Universelle des Musiciens*, 6th edition, Paris, 1878, vol. 5, p. 275.

5 Robert Eitner, *Biographisch-Bibliographisches Quellen-Lexicon*, Leipzig, 1903, vol. 8, p. 23.

6 Arnold Schering, 'Revisionsbericht' in *Denkmäler deutscher Tonkunst*, Leipzig, 1892–1931. Erste Folge, Bd. 29–30, p. xxiii.

7 In his edition of Hasse's Concerto in B minor for flute, Schering indicates (*ibid.*), that the flute should rest during the tuttis.

8 See E. J. Dent's comparison of the aria 'Grandi e ver' from Leo's *Olimpiade* with the corresponding aria in Pergolesi's *Olimpiade* in 'Leonardo Leo', *Sammelbände der Internationalen Musikgesellschaft*, Leipzig, 1906–07, p. 555.

9 Karl Nef, *Outline of Music History*, trans. by Carl Pfatteicher, Columbia University Press, N.Y., p. 211.

10 E. J. Dent, 'Leonardo Leo', *Proceedings of the Musical Association*, vol. 32, 1905–06, Novello, London, 1906, p. 63.

11 Karl Geiringer, *The Bach Family*, Oxford University Press, N.Y., 1954, p. 412.

12 When speaking of works composed in the 1730's and 1740's, I mean by 'sonata form' a plan corresponding more to what is now called 'sonatina form', *i.e.* an exposition and recapitulation of four sections each (first subject, transition, second subject, closing subject) but with little or no development section. There is an isolated instance in the concertos of what can be considered a genuine development section. This occurs in the finale of the C minor *Sinfonia Concertata* and is twenty-three bars long.

GERHARD HERZ

BWV 131

BACH'S FIRST CANTATA

———

Cantata 15: *Denn du wirst meine Seele nicht in der Hölle lassen* figured as Bach's first extant cantata until William Scheide identified it in 1959[1] as one of 18 cantatas composed by Bach's Meiningen cousin, Johann Ludwig Bach. Johann Sebastian copied them for performances of his own in 1726 at the time of his first profound disillusionment in his Leipzig position. With the mystery of Cantata 15 solved, any one of Bach's Mühlhausen cantatas could claim to be the first among his 194 surviving church cantatas.[2] The following *calendar of events in Mühlhausen* will place them into context:

1. 1706—December 2: Johann Georg Ahle, organist at St Blasius' Church, dies.
2. 1707—April 24 (Easter): Bach applies for the position and plays before the Council.
3.   May 27: The Council agrees on Bach's selection.
4.   May 30: The parish of St Blasius bears the full fury of a disastrous fire that destroys one-fourth of the town (360 houses).
5.   June 14: Bach returns from Arnstadt to state his conditions.
6.   June 15: The certificate of appointment is signed, sealed, and accepted by Bach 'by a handshake to show his agreement'. Three of the Councilmen are absent, stating that the recent fire had left them even without pen and ink.
7.   June 29: Bach requests his dismissal in Arnstädt, hands in the keys to his organ and assigns his salary for the Crucis quarter (June 15–September 14) to his cousin Johann Ernst.[3]

8. 1707—Undated Arnstadt document: Bach 'received his dismissal in July ... 1707.'

Items 6–8 indicate that Bach became organist at St Blasius' in Mühlhausen as early as June 15 and no later than July 1707.

9. August 10: Bach's uncle on his mother's side, Tobias Lämmerhirt, dies childless.

10. September 18: His testament is opened. The four children of Bach's mother receive each 50 Gulden which meant to Bach the equivalent of seven months salary.

11. October 17: Bach, now not only socially but also economically secure, marries in nearby Dornheim his cousin Maria Barbara of Arnstadt. Joh. Lorenz Stauber officiates 'without charge'.

12. 1708—February 4: Performance at St Mary's Church of the *Ratswahl* Cantata (BWB 71).

13. June 5: Wedding of Joh. Lorenz Stauber to Regina Wedemann, an aunt of Bach's bride.

How do the Mühlhausen cantatas fit into this calendar? If Bach, in addition to showing his mastery of the organ, composed and performed also a cantata at Easter 1707 (item 2 above), BWV 4: *Christ lag in Todesbanden* might well have been Bach's Mühlhausen 'Probestück' and thus his earliest extant cantata. This writer has recently posed this question[4] but realizes that, in the form in which *Christ lag* has survived,[5] it is a more mature composition than any one of the other four Mühlhausen cantatas.

Gottes Zeit ist die allerbeste Zeit (BWV 106) has been associated with items 9 and 10. Pirro's interpretation of the *actus tragicus* as a mourning cantata for Bach's uncle has recently received new corroborating evidence:[6] (1) The recorders are notated a whole tone higher which is typical of the woodwind parts in Bach's Mühlhausen cantatas. In his Weimar cantatas they are normally notated a minor third higher.[7] (2) The form of the fugue is, in both Cantatas 106 and 131, still in a state of flux which, however, points clearly towards a fugue-type that characterizes Bach's vocal music from Cantata 71 (of 1708) onwards well into his Weimar time: the permutation fugue.[8]

The date of *Gott ist mein König* (BWV 71)—item 12—is known through the event proper (the inauguration of a new Town Council), the autograph score 'de l'anno 1708' and the title page of the printed text.[9]

Cantata 196 has been assigned by Spitta for cogent reasons to the Stauber wedding (item 13). Spitta's interpretation has remained unquestioned and is still upheld by Frederick Hudson, editor of the *Trauungskantaten* in the NBA (1958).

This leaves only Cantata 131 unassigned or not properly assigned. Terry's supposition that it was composed for the anniversary of the Mühlhausen fire, *i.e.* for May 30, 1708, is stylistically untenable, as shall be shown.[10]

In contrast to Cantata 106, Bach's autograph score of Cantata 131 has survived. It is, in fact, the earliest autograph of a complete major work by Bach that has come down to us.[11] In 1840 it was in the possession of the Viennese collector Alois Fuchs who added a lovingly adorned title page that includes the date 1707.[12] At such an early time stylistic insight could hardly have caused Fuchs to decide on 1707 in favour of 1708. One wonders whether a document now lost or oral tradition may have been responsible for Fuchs' dating. A generation later, the manuscript is found in the hands of the long-time editor in chief of the Bach Gesellschaft, Wilhelm Rust. His edition of Cantata 131 takes over Fuchs' date of 1707,[13] however, without presenting new evidence. Jealousy of Spitta's Bach biography, completed in 1880 when Spitta was not yet 39 years old, caused Rust to resign his editorship in 1881 after the publication of volume 28. The hard feelings he harboured against Spitta (see Rust's foreword to BG 28!) imply that Spitta, when he described Cantata 131 in volume I of his biography (*i.e.* before 1873), had no access to the autograph score since it was in Rust's possession. Had Spitta known the postscript in which Bach signs himself as 'Mühlhausen organist', he would not have misdated this cantata, and consequently neither Cantata 106, as of about 1711.[14]

The watermark in the paper of Cantata 131—the crowned double eagle of the Free and Imperial city of Mühlhausen—is identical with that of Cantata 71 and Bach's other Mühlhausen documents. Also Bach's handwriting shows these cantatas to be neighbours. However, the festive occasion of the *Ratswahl* Cantata prompted Bach to produce a score penned with unusual meticulousness. In contrast, Cantata 131 was written at great speed. Nevertheless its clear writing shows, with two minor exceptions, no corrections. The manuscript is thus a fair copy rather than the composing score. Bar lines are drawn throughout with a ruler. The figuring of the *continuo* part is written out with rare completeness. The same can be said of the many tempo indications and dynamic markings.

Above the three systems that constitute page 1 of the score—there is no title page—Bach gives the title in old-fashioned German and the instrumentation in amusingly faulty Italian:

'Aus der Tieffen ruffe ich Herr zu dir. a una Obboe, una Violino,
doi Violae, Fagotto. C.A.T:B. è Fond.
da Gio: Bast: Bach'

The bassoon part is written throughout on the staff above the soprano rather than above the *continuo*.[15] Both oboe and bassoon are notated in true pitch (*i.e.* in A minor, *Kammerton*), a whole note higher than the other instruments and voices. Except for changing metre and tempo indications, the different sections flow one into another as if the cantata were written in one continuous movement.[16]

Below the completed score, at the bottom of the last (the 15th) page appears something unique, an inscription in Bach's hand that reads:

'Auff begehren Tit: Herrn D: Georg: Christ: Eilmars in die
Music gebracht
von
Joh: Seb: Bach
Org: Molhusin(?)'

Georg Christian Eilmar was pastor at the Church of Mary. He represented, as third generation minister in Mühlhausen, the Lutheran orthodoxy, then embattled with the Pietists whose leader was the minister of Bach's church, Johann Adolph Frohne.[17] Eilmar was the author of a book[18] which Mattheson still used to back up his attack on the rigid Pietist stand in matters of church music.

The deceased organist, J. G. Ahle, had been an avowed Pietist, like his pastor Frohne, and as such an enemy of the church cantata. Pastor Eilmar must have looked with profound satisfaction at the election of J. S. Bach, a member of the renowned orthodox Lutheran family of the Bachs, as new organist of his rival's church. The postscript below Cantata 131 shows Eilmar, about 20 years Bach's senior, as instigator of this cantata. It was thus an orthodox Lutheran minister who caused Bach to write his first church cantata. Dürr places Cantata 131 because of stylistic characteristics before Cantatas 106, 71 and 196, *i.e.* before September 1707.[19]

Hence:

> 'at the request of Herrn Dr. Georg Christ. Eilmar
> set to music by/Joh. Seb. Bach,
> organist at Mühlhausen'

might mean the following: shortly after the devastating fire, Eilmar offered the use of *his* church (St Mary's), the traditional location of the annual *Ratwahl* cantata, for a special service.[20] According to his writings[21] and his inclination as orthodox Lutheran, Eilmar promoted the place of the cantata in the service. By furnishing Bach with the most suitable text for such a mourning service—the *De Profundis* (Psalm 130)—he gave the young organist, who had just arrived in town, an opportunity to react as creative musician to the disaster that was still in everyone's mind in the summer of 1707. About a half year later Bach would collaborate again with Eilmar in the *Ratswahl* Cantata. Their friendship outlasted the composer's short stay at Mühlhausen; for Bach asked Eilmar to be Godfather at the birth of his first child, Catharina Dorothea, who was christened on December 29, 1708, in Weimar.

It is, moreover, likely that Bach compiled the texts of his earliest cantatas in collaboration with Eilmar, whose theological influence may be suspected from Bach's preference for Old Testament texts, especially those taken from Psalms. Of the 36 vocal movements in his first 6 cantatas (BWV 131, 106, 71, 196, 4, and 150) almost one-half, or 17, make use of Psalm verses, 12 of hymn stanzas—of which total, however, 7 comprise the text of Cantata 4—4 of scriptural quotations from the Old and only 3 from the New Testament. Five are composed to newly written texts.

Of these cantatas only No. 71 lacks an introductory *Sinfonia*.[22] Independent instrumental opening movements which also occur in six of Bach's Weimar Cantatas—mostly in the earlier ones—thus typify Bach's youthful cantata style. About half of these have two viola parts carrying on the tradition of the five-part texture seventeenth-century composers preferred.

Cantata 131 is based on the complete text of the 130th Psalm, thereby achieving an unusual textual continuity. In movements 2 and 4 two stanzas of Bartholomäus Ringwaldt's Lenten hymn of 1588: *Herr Jesu Christ, du höchstes Gut* are superimposed, with their hymn tune of 1593, on the psalm text. The innate contrast of the *De Profundis* that of sin and hope for redemption, is softened by the two hymn stanzas.

These represent the New Testament's assurance that the sins of the faithful shall be 'washed away'.

The first task that confronted Bach was the organization of the eight verses of Psalm 130 into a definite number of musical movements. Bach decided on five:

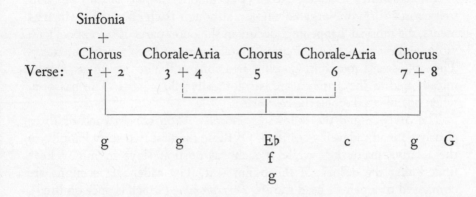

The majority of Bach's early cantatas are conceived symmetrically with a chorus in the centre, one at the end and one at the beginning (following the introductory *Sinfonia*).

Rather than fusing a movement into a unified musical whole, as became his ideal later on, Bach is guided in his Mühlhausen and earliest Weimar cantatas by the word. Absorbing himself into his scriptural text, Bach considers it line by line to detect any change of meaning. He does not even shy away from isolating a single word such as the dramatic 'aber' in the first chorus of Cantata 21 (bar 38). Having organized his textual material and thus created a blueprint for his composition, Bach sets it, idea by idea, as a series of separate musical sections that vary in speed, metre, key, and style according to the implications of the text. The young Bach subscribed to the dictum: 'In the beginning was the word,' and becomes a master in the description of textual detail. In the motif-creating power of the word he follows the tradition of the seventeenth-century motet. When seven years later, in 1714, he falls under the spell of the operatic aria, the word becomes of necessity the 'handmaiden' of music. Yet Bach's habit of seizing upon one word and letting it inspire his musical thought may well have its root in his youthful text-serving approach to composition.

FIRST MOVEMENT (binary)

A: *Sinfonia* (binary) *Adagio* (above the *continuo* called: *Lente*);
3/4; G minor
B: *Vivace* C; G minor

Among Bach's cantatas, No. 131 is unique insofar as *Sinfonia* and first chorus form one organic whole. Although Bach employs six instruments, the musical 'happening' occurs in the outer parts of solo oboe, solo violin and *continuo*, a combination characteristic of Bach's early cantatas.[23] The style seems rooted in Corelli's trio sonatas.[24] The two violas, rhythmically tied to the *continuo*, are harmonically filling parts. The bassoon, when not silent, doubles the *continuo*.

The *Sinfonia* and the following choral portion consist each of three clearly defined cadencing sections. Of these the first two stray happily to the relative major key while the choral portion stays in minor keys underlining the despair of the psalm text. The cadencing sections are composed of a pair of head motifs, *Fortspinnung* (which is once omitted), and closing cadence. The downward plunge of the opening motif

a_1:  [25] again unique with Bach, seems

inspired by the psalm's opening words: 'Out of the depth.' The second

motif a_2 is but an embellished variant of a_1:

that inverts the downward swoop of a fifth, characteristic of a_1, by an upward leap of a fourth. In the choral portion, a_2 is sung unadorned:

and thereby made more singable and more closely related to a_1.

The jarring major second, produced by the overlapping of the motif, set to the second text clause: 'rufe[26] ich, Herr, zu dir,' (in bars 28, 30, 39–41, 43–44, 50–51) is not an inevitable outgrowth of what precedes it musically. Otherwise it would already have appeared in the *Fortspinnung* of the opening orchestral section. Its entrance at the words: 'ruf' ich, Herr, zu dir' indicates that the effect was text-inspired. In bars 39–41 the realistic picture of voices crying in anguish out of the depth reaches its dissonant climax. Above the chromatically rising *continuo*, the voices climb by whole-tone steps in overlapping imitations thereby spanning the tritone from B flat to E.

Contrary to his later practice, the young Bach keeps the instruments out of the way of imitations or harmonically complex passages such as this one. He uses the orchestra either antiphonally to strengthen or to echo cadences. In bar 36 the vocal bass descends to the lowest note in the

whole cantata on the word 'Tie-fe':

Since in Bach's Mühlhausen time this C ('*Chorton*')[27] sounded a whole note higher we should perform this cantata nowadays in A rather than in G minor.

The *Vivace* that leaps out of the final cadence furnishes the earliest vocal instance of Bach's sense of contrast. Bach interprets the text of the second psalm verse as consisting of two parts. 'Herr, höre meine Stimme' is treated as a syllabic shout repeated four times. Between the last two shouts Bach inserts a monodic statement that has all the qualifications of a fugal subject, set to the remainder of the text: 'lass deine Ohren merken auf die Stimme meines Flehens.' Instead of the expected fugal development, however, each solo statement is cut short by the remaining shouts of the chorus. That these show *Stimmtausch* (among all voices but the bass) indicates the young composer's early and as yet inconclusive concern with 'total counterpoint'.

After the fourth chordal shout, the fugue gets finally under way. Its subject is syllabic except for the graphic portrayal of 'Flehen' (supplication). This word inspired Bach not only to the movement's one long, wailing, broken-up melisma which leaps up a diminished seventh, but also to the later echo effects. The rather tentative fugue has paired themes[28] of which the first one does not turn out to be the true fugal subject. It is rather a herald that ushers in the second, the true fugal subject, with seven identical notes. As if this ambiguity were not enough, the two first fugal statements enter, not at the fifth, but at the octave.[29] From the third statement on, the 'herald' subject shows its short-lived nature. As it fades away (in bar 78) the true subject is joined, half a bar later in imitation at the octave, by the remainder of the subject. The same canonic double exposure recurs between alto and bass in bars 83–85. After these four fugal statements, of which none follows the grammar of fugal writing, the fifth offers yet further surprises. The (solo) soprano enters without its twin subject. Instead, it inserts two sequences before completing itself, or rather trying to complete itself: for three delicious pairs of echoes—instruments alternating with the voices—prolong its completion. After a repeat of the last four measures Bach continues with yet another echo, a three bar coda in which he seems to take reluctant leave of the sobbing motif he had used as a fitting farewell to the word 'Flehen'.[30] This movement which refused to begin like a fugue also refuses to end like one. Of its forty-one bars only eighteen 'behave' according to fugal terms.

SECOND MOVEMENT (Bar form)

Chorale-Aria   *Andante*; C; G minor
Quartet texture: Oboe, Soprano (*c.f.*: d'—d″), Bass (D—eb′),
        Continuo

With precocious skill, Bach unifies his musical material. The ceaseless motion of quavers in the *continuo* flows from one movement into the next, though now slowed to *Andante*. With similar continuity, the bass voice takes up the echo motif of the previous movement. The oboe, making it idiomatically its own, gives it a new soothing yet plaintive expression. Above all, the soloistic, personal element enters with the bass voice and the oboe as its sympathetic instrumental companion. Did Bach sense an aesthetic conflict between this personal musical prayer and the psalm text, generally more appropriate to choral treatment?

The superimposition of a chorale—complete, unadorned, and in long note values—certainly objectifies the insistent pleading of the solo voice. Here Bach applies for the first time the German Organ Chorale of the seventeenth century to the cantata, and that at a time that witnessed the waning of the influence of Pachelbel, the master of polyphonic integration of the chorale into the musical texture.[31] Bach's adoption of the chorale in this, his second cantata movement, places him still more dramatically outside the trend of *his* time that moved from artistic chorale elaborations to a shallower homophonic concept of the chorale (*cf.* Telemann). With the incorporation of chorales into Cantatas 131, 71, 106, and 4 Bach became the last master who carried on the Scheidt, Böhm, and Pachelbel tradition that his 'progressive' colleagues were to undermine.

The juxtaposition of aria, which in Bach's early cantatas usually hovers between a declamatory and arioso style, with a vocal *cantus firmus*, appears in 75 per cent of his Mühlhausen cantatas but only in 5 per cent of his total cantata output.[32] Combining Bible words with suitable hymn verses goes back to Hammerschmidt, even to Bach's two predecessors in Mühlhausen, father and son Ahle, and to Bach's Arnstadt uncle, Johann Christoph. Setting two dissimilar texts simultaneously to music is a dangerous device. It attests to Bach's courage that he tried to master it to a far greater extent than his predecessors.

In Cantata 131 Bach solves it logically by assigning Psalm Verse 3 to the 2 × 2 lines that make up the two *Stollen* of the *cantus firmus*; then by synchronizing Psalm Verse 4 with the three lines of the chorale's *Abgesang*. The Psalm text: 'If thou, Lord, shouldest mark iniquities, O Lord, who shall stand?' addresses itself to the God of vengeance of the Old Testament. Ringwaldt's Lenten Hymn (Verse 2) and its tune: 'Herr Jesu Christ, du höchstes Gut' that the listeners of Bach's time knew by heart, present the New Testament's way out of such apprehension:

> Have pity on me in such distress,
> Take this burden from my heart,
> Because you have atoned for it
> On the cross with pains of death.

Eilmar might have chosen this hymn text, but the musical solution was Bach's alone.

As the chorale tune is the form-giving element in this as well as the fourth movement, neither movement shows traces of *ritornello* or *da capo*. The *c.f.* in both movements is intoned above the solo voice, whose emotions it holds in check. The interludes between the seven chorale phrases belong in 131/2 to the bass voice which either insists, with declamatory repetitions on its text, or enters into dialogue, or is intertwined with the oboe in melismatic semiquavers (bar 44 ff. or end of movement). The note repetitions found in this movement[33] are typical of Bach's youthful vocal style. They are a carry-over from the century-old *stile recitativo*. Here (in bars 11–14, 27 f., 37–40, 49 f., and 54–56) they intensify the text. In bars 1–2 and 6–7 of the third movement and bars 13 and 27–28 of the fourth, they vivify musically the text: 'I *wait*' and 'my soul waiteth for the Lord'.

In 131/2 it is the word 'bestehen' of the question: 'If thou, Lord, shouldest mark iniquities, O Lord, who shall *stand*?' that draws from Bach—six times—a long melisma. By letting it glide downwards in syncopated steps that tend to end in a twisting figure, Bach seems to imply that the sinful mortal cannot 'stand' firmly before the Lord. In the second part of the movement, set to Psalm Verse 4: 'But there is forgiveness with thee, that thou mayest be feared', the first half drives home the message of 'forgiveness' by its reiteration of the same note. Again a troubling thought—the word 'feared'—is underlined by a long melisma of undulating semiquavers that begin with diminutions of the *continuo* figure repeated three times (bar 44) before drawing the oboe into dialogue.

In spite of much thoughtfulness, Bach's inspiration was hardly burning here at white heat. The melodic and rhythmic inventiveness seems somewhat uninspired, and bars 41 and 44 present even two curious harmonic lapses. The composer's workmanship, however, shows already an unusual, *i.e.* Bachian solidity.

THIRD MOVEMENT

Chorus (binary) A: *Adagio* (short Prelude to) B: *Largo* (Fugue). C; Eb major—F minor—G minor.

Three homophonic blocks of chords open the *Adagio* and modulate from Eb to Bb and finally to C major. This key in turn serves as dominant to the ensuing fugue in F minor. Already in the solemn opening chords Bach insists on keeping oboe and violin independent from the soprano. Throughout the fugue he gives these two instruments and the two violas true *obbligato* parts.

Bach divides the three clauses that make up the one sentence of Psalm Verse 5, by using the first phrase 'Ich harre des Herrn' for the three opening chordal pillars and the two Monteverdian florid melismas (on '*har*re') that keep the Eb, Bb, and C major tutti blocks neatly separated. The moving from major to major chord, a welcome surprise, is but a moment's relief as the ensuing fugue demonstrates. The second phrase: 'meine Seele harret' clings to the principal subject throughout the course of the fugue. The remainder of the text: 'und ich hoffe auf sein Wort' is, along with occasional repeats of 'meine Seele harret', assigned to the contrapuntal voices.

The fugue is based on a subject that begins with the note repetitions so characteristic of the young Bach. Here they declaim in even rhythm of slow quavers, and a minor third above the tonic, the words 'meine Seele'. The key word '*harret*' (waits) caught Bach's imagination. A flowing melisma of chromatically descending crotchets and minims that dip down to the leading note below the tonic before cadencing, represents the stoic 'waiting' for the 'word of the Lord'. Of the two countersubjects, the first is exciting, full of leaps, sequential and portrays with its syllabic word repetition of 'ich hoffe' the hope that the text speaks of. This combination of themes of fatalism and active energy shows the textual and musical perception in depth of the young composer.

The first fugal exposition (bars 6–16) is a solid piece of polyphonic architecture—too solid, in fact, to last.

Ob.	5	6	5	6
Vl.		5	6	5
S.				1
A.			1	2
T.		1	2	3
B.	1	2	3	—

The design[34] shows an independent two-part fugue for oboe and violin superimposed upon the opening of a four-part vocal fugue. The latter follows the permutation principle[35] that Bach was to develop soon more fully, though its pattern, overly symmetrical and harmonically confining (tonic-dominant), would not satisfy him for long. That permutation is applied only to the first fugal exposition is an indication of the extremely early time of origin of this cantata. The two remaining expositions retain the principal fugal subject though changing its melodic course and thus its harmonic destination. Condensed or stretched out, depending on the unforeseeable length of the subject, this destination turns out to be often quite different from what its initial note seems to imply. Countersubjects 2 and 3 of the opening exposition give way to free counterpoints, and the two-part follow-the-leader game of oboe and violin lapses into a free, though frequently imitative, pattern based on the first phrase of its subject, *i.e.* on our old *Leitmotiv*: ♫ ♩. The two violas to which Bach had assigned independent filling parts (in 'hocket' style) follow the dictates of the figured bass. Twice, however, they are drawn into the imitative game between oboe and violin, causing passages of eight- and even nine-part writing. The unusual fugue without episodes that started in F minor ends in G minor, with Picardy third 3 bars later.

283

In the three-bar Handelian coda—*Adagio*—the bassoon takes over the enlivening instrumental work that oboe and violin had engaged in up to this point, and that the oboe seizes upon once more in the last moment for a touching highlight, ending an octave above the sopranos. Throughout this movement the bassoon part was differentiated from the *continuo* by *staccato* treatment. By this modest declaration of independence, Bach prepared the bassoon for its brief moment of eloquence at the solemn (*Adagio*) end of the musical action. Only once more, in the two swift antiphonal surges of the last movement (bars 21–26) will the bassoon be called upon to add to the drama—there, however, as equal partner of oboe and violin.

FOURTH MOVEMENT (*Bar* form)

Chorale-Aria   12/8; C minor
Trio texture: Alto (*c.f.*: g—g′); Tenor (c—ab′); *Continuo*.

Since Bach employs the same hymn tune here he had used in the second movement, no tempo indication is needed. Playing the quavers 50 per cent faster than in 131/2 assures the *c.f.* of its former pace. Bach now had to embed his *c.f.* into music of less apprehensive anxiety. In contrast to the bass voice in the second movement, the tenor in 131/4 moves with greater intervallic freedom and emotional abandon. A true *basso ostinato* opens the movement. Sequential in its melodic profile and gigue-like in rhythm, though flowing more smoothly, the *continuo* starts out like a *Passacaglia*, presenting three statements of a three-measure theme. By what remarkable yet simple sleight-of-hand Bach turns this *ostinato* theme from an insufferable bore, composed of nothing but sequences, into a distinctive melodic and rhythmic entity!

i.e. from:

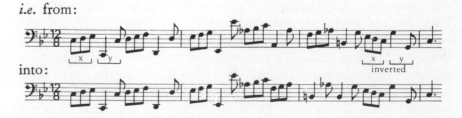

into:

On the last note of the first *ostinato* theme the voice enters, haltingly, with a monotonous seven-note phrase that for 20 out of 21 beats dwells on one note (g); no doubt, to sustain and thereby to illuminate the word '*wartet*' of the opening text-phrase: 'My soul waiteth for the Lord.' This vocal opening stands at the beginning like a motto, a favourite device in Bach's arias though rarely found in arias that are twinned with a *c.f.*

The moment the alto chimes in with the fifth stanza of Ringwaldt's hymn: 'Herr Jesu Christ, du höchstes Gut', it takes over the form-giving function from the *continuo*. The latter gives up the repetitions of its clearly-profiled *Passacaglia* theme in favour of continuous motion. Yet this motion uses, with one three-note exception (bar 20, resp. 42), throughout the *Stollen* the material of the opening *ostinato* theme, *i.e.* x, y and their inversions. Whereas the ceaseless flow of the *continuo* provides only transitory cadences before arriving at a clear cadence at the end of the *Stollen*, the tenor voice, preserving its melodic independence from the *continuo*, tends to create smaller divisions. With the *Abgesang* the procecedure changes subtly. Bach emphasizes the new textline: 'Von einer Morgenwache bis zu der andern' (more than they that watch for the morning), by giving the voice a new and, on the whole, more syllabic melody. In contrast to the *Stollen*, this melody is taken up by the *continuo* in short *stretto* passages (bars 52–53, 54, 69–70, 79–80). This new relationship of *continuo* to tenor is reinforced by frequent common cadences that Bach had avoided before and that now throw the three remaining *c.f.* phrases into sharper relief (three times C minor—B flat major—E flat major— C minor—E flat major, and again three times C minor). During the *Abgesang*, only half of the *continuo* figures derive from the old ostinato theme—and these mostly from bar 59 onwards, when the text of the *Stollen* is repeated. This is further proof of the relative independence of *Abgesang* from *Stollen*.

In 1729 Bach, then twice the age he was when he composed Cantata 131, produced with an instinct of shattering proportions his conceivably most moving superimposition of a *c.f.* upon a chorus. In the opening chorus of the Matthew Passion, Bach intones the German *Agnus Dei*, the chorale: 'O *Lamm* Gottes unschuldig' as the timeless yet immediate answer to the great cries of the two choruses: 'sehet – Wen? – den Bräutigam, seht ihn – Wie? – als wie ein *Lamm*.' While light years separate the two chorale arias of Bach's first cantata from this sublime solution of 1729,[36] the principle, *i.e.* the simultaneous setting of two sacred texts, is nevertheless already established in 1707. Though lacking the aptness of the juxtaposition in 131/2, one might even see in 131/4 a forerunner of the opening chorus of the Matthew Passion—the soul waiting for the Lord (tenor), pacified through the confidence expressed by the *c.f.* (alto) which speaks of the sorrowful sinner who would gladly have his sins washed away in Christ's blood.

FIFTH MOVEMENT (binary)

Chorus A: *Adagio—un poc' allegro—adagio—allegro.*
       B: Fugue.   C; G minor.

As in the two preceding choruses, a predominantly homophonic prelude is followed by a fugue. Again, the prelude adheres to the motet-like principle of interpreting every single textual idea by a different musical setting. In 131/5 four such tempo-changing sections compose Psalm Verse 7. Like 131/3, the final chorus opens (*adagio*) with three mighty syllabic shouts, here of 'Israel'—D major (in first inversion), G minor, D major. The completion of this first text clause: 'hoffe auf den Herrn', marked '*un poc' allegro*', leads from G minor to the relative major and back to the tonic. When the orchestra in this section is not on its own— which it is at beginning, middle, and end—it doubles the opening phrase of the voices. This syllabic *tutti* phrase is, with slight modifications, heard four times. Twice it is followed by a closely-knit imitative melismatic passage on '*hof*fe' and twice by a homophonic echo, marked expressly '*piano*'. These four interludes are accompanied only by the *continuo* (excluding even the bassoon). A final instrumental passage, marked '*pianissimo*', reduces the second echo to a double echo.

For the two remaining text-phrases of Verse 7 Bach renews the time-honoured *adagio–allegro* contrast. In the first: 'denn bei dem Herrn ist die Gnade' the chorus extols three times (!) the 'mercy of the Lord'. In a majestic chordal style and *forte*, this passage moves from C minor (SD) eventually to D major. While the third statement is an extended version of the first, the middle one uses new material. When the first, quasi *a cappella* statement reaches shining G major, stimulated by the word 'Gnade', Bach floods the senses with an instrumental halo, floating a tender oboe melody above the emotional throb of the remaining instruments. The idea of 'mercy' that the text promises here, inspired Bach to the most moving harmonies in the whole cantata. Thereafter Bach is carried away by the thought of 'plenteous redemption' of the final text clause: 'und viel Erlösung bei ihm'. He treats it as an *allegro* whirlwind in 'hocket' style that whips both the voices and the even more agitated independent instruments (oboe, violin, bassoon) into frenzy.

In two breathless imitative waves they move from D major through B flat back to G minor

The concluding fugue, based on the 8th Psalm Verse, begins in bar 27. Did Bach at the age of 22 already employ the number 27 as a symbol of the Trinity, of divine forgiveness?

The cadential motif (ii – V – I) that ushers in this tentative permutation fugue is not its principal subject. Its brevity, its preferred position in the bass and on the dominant, and its lack of physiognomy speak against this. It is rather a fragment, detachable from the second subject,[37] with which it forms a textual rather than musical union: 'und er wird Israel/erlösen' (called 2a and 2b on the following chart). The principal subject (1) is set to the final text clause of Verse 8: 'aus allen seinen Sünden' (from all its iniquities). It is characteristic of Bach's literal identification with his texts that he portrays not so much redemption from sin but rather the heaviness of stripping off *sin*,[38] the keyword of the German phrase. He does so, slowly, and by a chromatically ascending theme that rises with difficulty and appears to be the counterpart of the stepwise descending fugal subject of 131/3. In 131/5 it is twinned with a counter-subject of the *Fortspinnungs*-type (2b) set to the word 'erlösen'. Inspired by the thought of 'redemption', Bach treats it as he was to do a thousand times hence, by joyous chains of florid melismas that rise in sequences of semi-quavers. The juxtaposition of two strongly profiled, contrasted, yet complementary, subjects is typical of concluding movements in Bach's early cantatas. Bach does not, however, help the clear intelligibility of the words—always a problem in choral composition—by introducing his two chief subjects simultaneously from the outset. At the second fugal entrance they are joined by a third subject. Less well defined as to beginning and end, it supplies the welcome concise rhythm of syllabic quavers. While counterpoints 2a and 2b divide the phrase: 'und er wird Israel/erlösen' between themselves, the last counterpoint (3) not only presents it whole but repeats it as if to compensate for the tendency to divide shown by 2a and 2b.

When the over-eager opening motif (2a) appears within the framework of the other three subjects it is heard in the proper key rather than in conflict with its environment (*cf.* bars 57–59). The graph does not indicate that the young composer handles the permutation principle, in spite of all attempted strictness, rather freely. The score alone reveals the frequent abbreviations of the counter-subject (2b) and the many different forms that the third subject (3) assumes. In 131/5 Bach had not yet learned

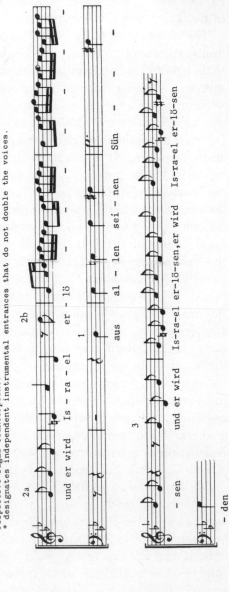

how to organize the counterpoints of a permutation fugue into logical members of a unified whole, i.e. into one successive melody consisting of beginning, *Fortspinnung* and cadence.[39] The jumbling of the counterpoints that begin here with the cadence motif (2a) betrays a lack of sense of continuity typical of a composer still in an experimental stage. Also the order of keys of the twelve fugal statements: G-D-G-D-G-G-C-G-G-D-G-D, all in minor, leaves room for more imaginative treatment.[40] Only the bold final *Adagio* cadence seems to break out of the self-imposed shackles that enclosed Bach in the fugue proper.

After the first fugal exposition (which ought to be sung by solo voices since instrumental support is lacking), the instruments begin (from bar 36 onwards) to double the voices (which therefore ought to be sung *choraliter*). As five instrumental parts—not counting the *continuo*—face four vocal parts, one instrument is always free to add fresh contrapuntal material to the four-part fugue: until bar 52 predominantly the oboe, thereafter the violin. In the final Handelian *adagio* cadence, another characteristic of Bach's early compositions, the composer reverts to the more piercing timbre of the oboe to float a high independent line that begins and ends a sixth above the sopranos and the violin, now doubling.

Only false hero-worship could cause us to call the three fugal movements of this cantata vocally truly effective. It is immaterial whether Bach could not detach himself from the style of the organ, as Spitta believed, or whether he was still grappling with the intricacies of vocal fugal writing, as this writer believes. What matters is Bach's extreme concern with contrapuntal detail, his desire to get maximum usage out of the musical material, once he had chosen it. This, in turn, means: refusal to pad the musical texture for the sake of effect. In this respect Bach differs even at the age of 22 from his contemporaries. Thirty years later, one of them[41] would take Bach to task for darkening the beauty of his compositions by an 'excess of art'. Finally, Bach's first cantata reveals that the composer had already in 1707 arrived at his artistic credo: the vivification of his text through music.

NOTES

1 See *Bach-Jahrbuch*, 1959.

2 In addition to BWV 15, another five cantatas have been wrongly attributed to Bach: cantatas 141 and 160 are by Telemann, 53 and 189 by Melchior Hoffmann and 142 is probably by Kuhnau.

3 Who had substituted for Johann Sebastian during his extended stay at Lübeck one and a half years earlier.

4 Herz, Gerhard, *Bach–Cantata No. 4*, Norton Critical Scores, New York, 1967, 94.

5 The autograph score is lost. The surviving performing parts were copied before Easter, 1724 (April 9), except for the cornetto and three trombone parts that were added a year later, before Easter, 1725 (April 1).

6 Dürr, Alfred, *Studien über die frühen Kantaten J. S. Bachs*, Leipzig, 1951, 49 and 153.

7 By the same reasoning, Cantata 150, with its bassoon part notated a minor third higher than the other parts, qualifies as a Weimer cantata; but one that on account of its pre-Weimar textform (no recitatives!) was probably composed very early during Bach's Weimar period. Dürr, who finds no reason to question its authenticity, dates it 'between 1708 and early 1710' (*op. cit.*, 210).

8 The permutation fugue follows the scheme of the round. Not only the fugal subject (1) but also all its counter-subjects (2, 3, 4, etc.) are consistently retained and constantly exchanged. No episodes interfere with this rotating process. As in a 20th century serial composition, practically every note in a permutation fugue is part of a preconceived, kaleidoscopically unrolling structure such as:

$$1 \quad 2 \quad 3 \quad 4 \quad 1 \quad 2 \quad 3, \quad \text{etc.}$$
$$1 \quad 2 \quad 3 \quad 4 \quad 1 \quad 2, \quad \text{etc.}$$
$$1 \quad 2 \quad 3 \quad 4 \quad 1, \quad \text{etc.}$$
$$1 \quad 2 \quad 3 \quad 4, \quad \text{etc.}$$

9 This one and a now lost cantata, composed for the next Town Council election in 1709, are the only cantatas by Bach printed during his lifetime.

10 See also Dürr, *op. cit.*, 153.

11 It is now owned by the pianist Lilian Kallir-Frank of New York, the wife of pianist Claude Frank. I am indebted to her and her father, Dr. Rudolf Kallir, the previous owner of the manuscript, for permission to acquire a microfilm for my studies.

12 'Componirt zu Mühlhausen im J. 1707.'

13 BG 28, XXI.

14 Spitta, Philipp, *Johann Sebastian Bach*, 3 vols., New York (and London), 1951 (reprinted from the English edition of 1889), I, 442 and 456.

15 This arrangement is retained in BG 28.

16 The same can be observed in Cantata 106, another bit of corroborating evidence for its similarly early dating.

17 While Frohne was apparently a more soft spoken person, easy to get along with, the picture of Eilmar, the orthodox zealot, painted by Spitta (I, 359 ff.) seems overdrawn.

18 *Güldenes Kleinod Evangelischer Kirchen*, 1701. See Mattheson, *Der Musikalische Patriot*, 1728, 151.

19 *Op. cit.*, 153.

20 No cantata performances can be documented for St. Blasius' Church: *Cf.* BWV 106, 71, and 196.

21 In addition to the publication of 1701 (see fn. 18 above): *Entwurf der Andacht bei der Papperoder Brunnensolennité* of 1714.

22 Though the one of Cantata 131 connects with a chorus of the same thematic material.

23 *Cf.* BWV 21.

24 Published between 1681 and 1695.

25 Observe the consistent word-underlay!

26 To suit his purpose, Bach uses both 'rufe' and 'ruf', a licence regarding the scriptural word he shuns in later years.

27 'Choir pitch', *i.e.* the higher pitch of the organs of that time.

28 Like the second movement of the early keyboard Toccata in D minor, BWV 913. *Cf.* Spitta, *op. cit.*, I, 450 and 439.

29 This again has its counterpart in two early keyboard toccatas: the last movement of the one in D minor (BWV 913), and the second movement of the one in G minor (BWV 915). A cantata by G. Bertuch furnishes the sole known parallel among cantata compositions of this time.

30 A year earlier, in his *Capriccio on the Departure of a Beloved Brother*, Bach had used the same motif in order to portray the 'Coaxing of the friends to deter him from his journey'.

31 *Cf.* the music of the generation of Joh. Ph. Krieger, Kuhnau, and Zachow—all Bach's seniors.

32 Besides BWV 131, 106, and 71, in 80a, 60, 158, 49, 58, 156, 159.

33 Also in 131/3 and 4 as well as in 106/3 and 6.

34 *Cf.* Werner Neumann's graphic method of indicating the structure of fugal movements in his *J. S. Bachs Chorfuge*, 3rd ed., Breitkopf und Härtel, Leipzig, 1953.

35 See note 8.

36 The vocal version of the *c.f.* belongs, however, to a later revision of the Matthew Passion.

37 See bars 33/4.

38 *Cf.* BWV 28/2; the motif: 'hat dir dein "Sünd" vergeben', with its identical keyword 'sin'.

39 *Cf.* Dahlhaus, Carl, *Zur Geschichte der Permutationsfuge* in *Bach-Jahrbuch*, 1959, 95 ff.

40 The transcription for organ (BWV 131a), can hardly be blamed on Bach though it attests to the instrumental nature of this fugue. It has come down to us in a copy by Mich. Gotth. Fischer, not by Bach's last pupil Kittel, as was formerly believed. It is included, perhaps wrongly, in BG 38, 217.

41 J. A. Scheibe, in *Der Kritische Musicus*, Leipzig, May 14, 1737.

ANTHONY VAN HOBOKEN

A RARE CONTEMPORARY EDITION
OF HAYDN'S
'HYMN FOR THE EMPEROR'

Haydn's Emperor's Hymn, sung for the first time on February 12, 1797,[1] on the 29th birthday of the Emperor Francis II (later Francis I of Austria) and since then in innumerable editions, with variant texts for the Emperor's spouses, for his successors Ferdinand I and Francis Joseph I, finally adopted as the Austrian National Anthem, soon found its way to England. Charles Burney, MUSD, FRS, translated the text into English and published the song, set for 2 sopranos and bass with piano accompaniment in London, at Broderip and Wilkinson, under the title: 'Hymn for the Emperor/Translated by Dr Burney/Composed by/Doctor Haydn.'[2]

This translation is striking because the verses contain each 10 lines. The original poem by Haschka has only 8 lines. The first two lines are sung to bars 1–4 of the melody, the following two to the repeat of these bars, while the refrain in lines 7–8 with bars 9–12 of the melody is repeated again. The two middle lines 5 and 6 belong to bars 5–8 of the melody, and are sung only once. Because Burney writes four instead of these two lines, bars 5–8 are also repeated in his arrangement. Thus the song loses the proportion which Haydn so carefully considered.

It is not known how Haydn reacted. Burney writes to him on August 19, 1799 from Chelsea College[3] *inter alia*: '. . . . I have given our friend Mr Barthelemon[4] a copy of my translation to transmit to you . . . ', but there is no evidence that Haydn ever received this translation. In his answering letter to Burney of September 14th (a preceding letter had been lost), he discusses the business part of Burney's letter, but does not

292

mention the copy of the Hymn. The work does not appear in the list of Haydn's library[5] and also not in the inventory of the auction of his estate.[6] Neither the further Collected Correspondence, nor Burney's Memoirs[7] or his letters, in so far as they are preserved in the British Museum,[8] give information about the whereabouts of this copy, but also no evidence that Haydn ever objected to it.

It is also not clear why Burney did not send his translation directly to Haydn with whom he was in close contact, but gave it to Barthélémon. Besides the lengthening of the verses by 2 lines, Burney also treated the rest of the text freely. He writes about it—still in the same letter of August 19th—: '. . . in comparing my version with the original, you will perceive that it is rather a paraphrase than a close translation; but the liberties I have taken were in consequence of the supposed treachery of some of his Imperial Majesty's generals and subjects, during the unfortunate campaign of Italy, of 1797, which the English all thought was the consequence, not of Bonaparte's heroism, but of Austrian and Italian treachery.' This concerns lines 5–8 of the second verse of his translation:

> 'Fill the hearts of his Commanders
> With integrity and zeal;
> Be they deaf to lies and slander
> Gainst their Prince and public weal.'

where Haschka simply writes:

> 'Und mit seiner Hoheit Blitzen
> Schalten nur Gerechtigkeit!'
> ('And with His Majesty's lightning
> Only justice rules!')

There exists still another, less known edition of Haydn's song with Burney's translation with which I became acquainted through the kindness of Dr. Alan Tyson, London, who owns the only copy which I ever came across. It was published without title page like the above edition, with the heading:

'HYMN for the Emperor FRANCIS,/Composed by Dr Haydn,/and Sung at the public Theatres at Vienna,/in the manner of GOD SAVE

GREAT GEORGE OUR KING in England. Set as a Duet and Chorus with a Piano Forte Accompaniment by/I. B. CIMADOR.—Price 1s.'

and below the remark:

'Messrs Monzani and Cimador, are particularly Obliged to Dr Burney, for his/English Translation of this Hymn; and his permission to publish it'

giving the name of the publisher below the music of the first page:

'Printed for Monzani and Cimador, Music Sellers, to his Royal Highness the Prince of Wales, No 2 Pall Mall.'

Burney starts in his letter of August 19th the paragraph about the hymn: 'The Divine Hymne, written for your imperial master, in imitation of our loyal song: "God save great George our King" . . .' and this sentence reads almost exactly as the title of this other edition. Also the remark: '. . . and his permission to publish it' could imply that the translation had not been published as yet. The publishing house Monzani and Cimador can be traced only from the beginning of 1800.[9] But if we suppose that Burney sent a printed edition of his translation to Haydn, it would have to be at hand as early as August 1799.

Since both editions are not registered in Stationers' Hall[10] and so far I have not found any announcements of it in the newspapers, the publishing dates cannot be discussed here.

The translation here is also different from the first mentioned edition. For the sake of comparison I give the first verse of the edition Broderip and Wilkinson and the one of Monzani and Cimador:

(Broderip and Wilkinson)

God preserve the Emp'ror Francis
  Sov'reign ever good and great;
Save, o save him from mischances
  In Prosperity and State!
May his Laurels ever blooming
  Be by Patriot Virtue fed;
May his worth the world illumine
  And bring back the Sheep misled!
God preserve our Emp'ror Francis!
  Sov'reign ever good and great.

(Monzani and Cimador)

God preserve our Emp'ror Francis!
  Sov'reign ever good and great!
Save, o save him from mischances
  In felicity and state!
May his days be crown'd with glory,
  And with wreathes his brows entwin'd,
May his name long live in story,
  And his worth illume mankind!
God preserve our Emp'ror Francis!
  Sov'reign ever good and great!

The other verses are in both editions identical with the one exception that the seventh line of the fourth verse at Monzani and Cimador reads: '(Each by supplication trying),' while in the edition Broderip and Wilkinson it says: '(Will by supplication. . . .).'

The text is, moreover, differently put under the melody by Cimador, who has the seventh and eight lines already sung to the melody of the refrain (bars 9–12) and the repetition of these bars sung by the chorus to lines 9–10. For the middle bars 5–8 only lines 5–6 remain so that these need not be sung twice.

Cimador has arranged the song for two voices and piano. In this connection I refer to a passage from Burney's diary of September 5, 1799, '. . . My translation of the hymn, "Long live the Emperor Francis!" was very well sung in duo by Lady Susan Ryder and Miss Crewe; I joining in the chorus.' He does not mention the bass part of the Broderip and Wilkinson edition!

The musical setting shows in both editions several bad errors compared to Haydn's original composition, though Monzani and Cimador adhere more closely to the first edition than Broderip and Wilkinson. Both editions, however, contain the ingenious bass part in bars 10–11 which the later arrangement as *Deutschlandlied* [11] unfortunately omits.

The edition of Broderip and Wilkinson was reprinted many times by other English publishers; I know of no other reprint of the edition by Monzani and Cimador.

NOTES

1   Gott, erhalte den Kaiser!

Verfasset   In Musik gesetzet
von   von
Lorenz Leopold Haschka   Joseph Haydn
Zum ersten Mahle
abgesungen
den. 2. Februar 1797

2 Cf. Otto Erich Deutsch: 'Haydn's Hymn and Burney's Translation in: *The Music Review*, vol. IV, no. 3 (August 1943), p. 157 ff.

3 H. C. Robbins Landon: 'The Collected Correspondence and London Notebooks of Joseph Haydn', London, 1959, p. 164.

4 François-Hippolyte Barthélémon, 1741–1808, French violinist, lived in London and was a friend of Haydn (*cf.* Pohl: Mozart in London, p. 163).

5 British Museum, Add. MS. 32070.

6 Archives of the City of Vienna, no. 60–75.

7 Published by his daughter, Madame d'Arblay, London, 1832.

8 I wish to thank Miss P. N. Cadell, Assistant Keeper of Manuscripts, for this information.

9 Charles Humphries and William C. Smith: 'Music Publishing in the British Isles from the earliest times to the middle of the nineteenth century', p. 236.

10 Information kindly provided by Mr. Stanley J. Osborne, Beadle and Assistant to the Clerk of Stationers' Hall.

11 Das/Lied der Deutschen/von/Hoffman von Fallersleben./–Melodie nach Joseph Haydn's /'Gott erhalte Franz den Kaiser/ Unserm guten Kaiser Franz'/Arrangirt für die Singstimme/ mit Begleitung des Pianoforte oder der Guitarre./ – / (Text Eigenthum der Verleger.)/ 1. September 1841/Hamburg, bei Hoffman und Campe./Stuttgart, bei Paul Nef./Preis 2gGr.

DOLORES MENSTELL HSU

WEBER ON OPERA: A CHALLENGE TO EIGHTEENTH-CENTURY TRADITION

———

Carl Maria von Weber is a transitional figure who stands at the crossroads between Classicism and Romanticism. Born and nurtured in the tradition of the eighteenth century, he remained indebted to, though discontented with, the musical practice of his day. Seeking with difficulty to make his way as a composer and performer in an era of change, he was increasingly drawn to the field of music criticism. His was a resourceful and imaginative mind, working to improve the lot of the musician and to cultivate higher standards of performance. Though comparatively little attention has been given to this aspect of his career, it is in his writings, particularly those dealing with opera, that we find Weber formulating those ideas that challenged the past and paved the way for his future evolution as a composer.

Basically, Weber approached music criticism as a means of fostering a broader appreciation of music among his readers, and through the years from 1809 to about 1820, he addressed himself to almost every phase of the art: opera, instrumental music, composition, performance and analysis. Many of his articles appeared in such influential journals as the *Allgemeine musikalische Zeitung* and the *Zeitung für die elegante Welt;* others he circulated among his friends and colleagues; a few remained unknown until after his death.[1] A dedicated, if not always a dispassionate writer, Weber completed more than 100 articles and reviews that stand as an eloquent testimony to the farsightedness of his personal objectives in music, as well as the accuracy that, for the most part, characterized his estimate of the contemporary musical scene.

In many of his critiques, Weber assumed the position of mentor and focused his attention on what he considered to be the education of prospective audiences. This didactic concept of the function of criticism, combined with his repeated recommendation that music critics be drawn primarily from the ranks of composers, would seem to indicate his awareness of the new relationship that was gradually emerging between the professional musician and an ever-increasing public audience. When writing about an opera, he generally sought to unite brief descriptive analysis of the structure with commentary on such matters as orchestration, treatment of voices and dramatic plausibility. Often, he incorporated pertinent information about the composer, in an attempt to make the music more understandable to his readers. As one of the earliest and most outspoken champions of German opera, he deplored the so-called 'Italian invasion' as an inhibiting factor, if not a corrupting influence, on young composers; and he took every opportunity to promote operas by German musicians on an equal basis with those by Italian and French composers. Though his commitments as a conductor, performer and composer left him little time for other pursuits, Weber was always ready to take up his pen, and he never wavered from the conviction that such a course would ultimately produce a more sympathetic and discriminating public.

Quite apart from his ability as a critic, he possessed considerable skill as a writer. His style is direct and clear, his attitude reasonably impartial, and his purpose always functional. To the German musical scene of the early nineteenth century he brought a keen interest in new music, analytical ability of high order, and an articulate voice which helped guide the musical taste of his day.

Weber's writings on music include critiques of musical scores; reviews of concert performances, most of which were written during his stay at Prague in 1815 and 1816; an impressive number of essays and letters; and finally, a delightful, but fragmentary novel, *Tonkünstlers Leben*, at which he laboured sporadically from 1809 until 1820.[2]

Undoubtedly his most significant work as a critic is the series of 'Notes on Drama and Music' which he wrote while serving as director of opera at Prague and later at Dresden. In both cities, he found his efforts as an operatic conductor hampered by unfavourable conditions of every sort, and in the course of time he turned to writing as a method of improving these conditions. When first named conductor at Prague in 1813, Weber was charged with the responsibility of re-organizing the theatre, an assignment which, among other things, gave him complete freedom in the selection and production of new works. This was a rare opportunity for a 27-year-old conductor, and he set about the task of hiring singers, examining scores and rehearsing new operas with boundless energy. During the three and a half seasons of his tenure at Prague, he presented more than sixty operas, including thirty-one entirely new productions. Mozart, Beethoven, Cherubini, Spontini, Méhul, Grétry, Spohr and Dittersdorf were among the composers represented in his repertory.[3]

Despite all his efforts, however, Weber seemed unable to overcome the general apathy of the public toward opera. A series of incompetent conductors and many seasons of poor performances had reduced the theatre at Prague from a flourishing opera centre to a poorly supported and rather neglected one. In an attempt to improve this situation, Weber conceived the idea of preparing his audiences for new productions by introducing and explaining the operas in articles to be published in the local paper shortly before each performance. Though the project was not well-received by some, the general reaction—to judge from accounts found in Weber's correspondence—was favourable.[4] At any rate, he considered the plan so valuable to his work as a conductor that he continued writing these educational articles at Dresden when he went there in 1817 to head the newly established German opera house. Altogether he wrote twenty-two essays on various operas: six at Prague and sixteen at Dresden. He also prepared an introductory article, entitled 'Notes on Drama and Music', in which he set forth the purpose and scope of the project. This article appeared in the *Prager Zeitung* on October 20, 1815, and two years later, revised and extended, in the Dresden *Abendzeitung*.

The two versions of the 'Notes on Drama and Music', together with the articles that followed, are remarkable in several respects. Quite obviously, they contain factual information concerning matters of repertory, production and personnel, as well as interesting commentary on the structure, the strengths and weaknesses of the operas at hand. These are the opinions of Weber as a conductor, absorbed in every aspect of operatic production—the practical musician turning to criticism as a means of arousing public interest in and support for his work.

But the articles are equally valuable for the light they shed on the evolution that was gradually taking place in Weber's position as an operatic composer. It was during these years that the thought of composing an opera on the *Freischütz* story remained in the back of his mind. He first encountered the legend in 1810 in the first volume of the *Gespenster-*

buch edited by Apel and Laun, but he put the idea of an opera aside until he found a librettist in 1817, and even then he did not complete the score until 1820.[5] If one examines his operas prior to the Prague and Dresden period, the three-act *Silvana* of 1810 and the one-act *Singspiel*, *Abu Hassan* of 1811, for example, and compares them with *Der Freischütz* and *Euryanthe*, one can only be amazed at the strides he made as a composer. It will be remembered that he wrote no operas between the completion of *Abu Hassan* and the beginning of *Der Freischütz*, *i.e.* from 1811 to 1817. This pause was probably not a consciously planned one, for his letters reveal a fairly constant search for suitable libretti. We know, for example, that in 1814 the possibility of a *Tannhäuser* seemed very attractive to him.[6] However, he postponed any decision to begin a new work from year to year. No doubt this situation can be partly explained by the unsettled condition of his life at the time, as well as by his heavy performance schedule, but these facts alone do not fully account for the quiescence, for he remained productive in other forms of composition. It would seem, rather, that this was a period of growth during which his ideas regarding opera underwent certain fundamental changes; a period during which his concept of a distinctly national style of opera gradually made a transition from theory to practice. The 'Notes on Drama and Music' reveal a good deal about this transition and the development that was taking place in Weber's compositional thinking. In fact, from one point of view, the articles seem almost to have served as a kind of workshop in which he gradually formulated his ideas, applied them to the operas he was conducting, and finally attempted to employ them in a work of his own.

Turning first to the introductory articles, we find Weber announcing his series of 'Notes on Drama and Music' as 'an attempt to facilitate the appreciation of operas to be performed for the first time, by means of historical accounts and artistic observations'.[7] His opening paragraphs, however, reflect a cautious, almost defensive approach. He termed the project 'risky' in the sense that there was no precedent for a man in his position to publish such articles in a local newspaper. But he answered the objection in advance by stating that as a conductor he considered it his 'duty to influence the mind and taste of the public'.[8] In this connection, it is interesting to observe the frequency with which such expressions as 'influence the taste' and 'guide the artistic judgement', *etc.*, appear in Weber's writings. Time and again he stressed the function of the artist as a leader or guide, clearly anticipating what was to become one of the major trends in the nineteenth-century concept of the rôle of the artist in society. As early as 1810 he had established a 'Harmonic Society' which was designed to combat what he called the 'mediocrity of pseudo-critics' with skilfully written reviews of new music. For several years, he and four other musicians, among whom were young Meyerbeer and the theorist, Gottfried Weber, published numerous articles in a wide variety of journals.[9] Much of Weber's early criticism dates from this period, and his later, more mature writings, such as the 'Notes,' were, in a sense, an outgrowth of this previous experience.

Not to be overlooked in these introductory articles is the fact that Weber sought to strengthen his position as a critic by opening his comments with two quotations taken from Goethe and Schiller. Both the passages, which neatly underscore his own thoughts concerning the current state of art and aesthetics, are typical of the kind of references he frequently used not only in his critical writings, but also in his notebooks and letters. It is indeed indicative of the increasing literary awareness of the Romantic musician that he should have drawn inspiration from sources such as these:

'Crude men are satisfied with action, the educated want to experience emotion, but only the truly cultivated find contemplation pleasurable.'[10]

'Events have moved in a direction which threatens more and more to separate the man of genius from ideal art. True art must abandon reality and rise courageously above materialism. Art is a daughter of freedom; she will take direction from spiritual need but not from material necessity. At the present time, however, expediency rules and a decadent mankind bends beneath its tyrannical yoke. Profit, to which all powers submit and all talents must pay homage, is the great idol of the day. On these crass scales the spiritual merit of art carries no weight, and robbed of all encouragement it disappears from the noisy market place of our century.'[11]

The introduction to the Prague series consists of a concise statement of policy and little more. Having encountered a public distracted by unsettled political conditions, a public grown indifferent to the quality of theatrical productions, Weber determined to restore something of the former enthusiasm for opera. Writing in the ornate style characteristic of the period he stated:

'In fairer times, the blessings of universal and lasting peace inspired every man to devote his leisure hours to science and the fine arts. The appearance of a new work of art was the topic of the day in every social circle. Free from turbulent worldly pressures, one could quietly pursue the finer things of life. These were considered essential for the sensitive mind; a nourishment for the spirit. But those good days have long since passed and with them, naturally, the indispensable sympathetic interest of the public in the progress of art has also disappeared.

'Over a long period of time, a truly fine work certainly establishes its own merits. It gradually wins public acclaim because through repeated performances it ultimately touches the heart. However, the process is completely different if the mind is prepared in advance for the pleasure that awaits it.'[12]

Weber went on to assure his readers that he did not intend to favour the works of any particular group of composers, that he merely wished to discuss the 'distinctive qualities' of his new productions. There is no statement here concerning his preoccupation with national styles in opera, no indication that he was, as yet, particularly involved with the problem. The ensuing articles do occasionally refer to the matter, but at no time during his stay at Prague did the question loom paramount in his mind. That step in his development had to await the move to Dresden.

As the first director of the German Opera Theatre at Dresden, Weber found himself confronted with many of the same difficulties he had previously experienced at Prague. In addition he was hampered by inadequate financial support and constantly plagued by the intrigues that inevitably developed between the court-sponsored Italian opera and his own unproven and, in many quarters, unwelcome company. The introduction he prepared for the Dresden series of his 'Notes' reflects his concern with these troubles. Using the same format as in the Prague articles, he described his position with his customary grandiloquence.

'By virtue of the benevolent support of their exalted monarch, the residents of Dresden are to experience a splendid enrichment of their cultural life through the founding of a German opera company. It therefore seems advisable, perhaps even necessary for the success of this venture, that the one to whom the care and leadership of the entire affair has been entrusted should seek to point out the ways, means and conditions, through which such an undertaking can be realized. . . .

'It is thus the duty of administrators entrusted with the artistic treasures of the public to tell the people what they should expect and hope for, and to what extent a friendly reception is required of them. Great expectations are easily and quickly aroused, but it is often difficult, because of the nature of things, to satisfy even the most justifiable demands.'[13]

The apologetic tone here results from Weber's frustration with the limited resources placed at his disposal. A small, poorly equipped theatre actually located outside of Dresden, and personnel consisting largely of actors rather than singers were conditions that placed him at a great disadvantage. He continued:

'The musical forms of all other nations have always been more clearly defined than those of the German. By this I mean that the Italian and Frenchmen have created for themselves an operatic form in which they can move about freely and comfortably. Not so the German. It is entirely characteristic of him, in his curiosity and desire for continual improvement, to draw to himself the superior elements of all the others; but he grasps everything more deeply. Where with the others the aim is mostly directed toward sensual enjoyment of the individual moment, *he wants a self-contained work of art in which every part rounds off and unites in the perfect whole.*'[14]

To the conductor falls the task of creating an ensemble capable of realizing this all-important element of unity.

This passage, published on January 29, 1817, contains the first hints of Weber's concept of opera as a unified work of art. Though he could not have foreseen the extent to which his ideas were developed during the course of the nineteenth century, he was obviously aware of their significance, for reference to them becomes increasingly frequent in his writings. It was, for example, precisely at this time that he wrote his notable review of E. T. A. Hoffman's opera, *Undine*, for the *Allgemeine musikalische Zeitung*.[15] He had attended the first performance of the work in Berlin and was deeply impressed by Hoffman's treatment of an entirely new kind of libretto. Quite apart from the technical weaknesses of the score which he was quick to detect, Weber recognized the possibilities of such elements as the use of supernatural beings, the incorporation of folk-like melodies and choruses, and the definite, if restricted use of the *Leitmotiv*. Here, clearly foreshadowing the style of his own *Freischütz*, was a work that elicited still another description of his new approach to opera.

'It goes without saying that I am speaking of the opera which the German wants: a self-contained work of art in which all the parts and contributions of the related and collaborating arts are blended together and thus disappear, and somehow, in disappearing, form a new world.

'For the most part, a few striking numbers determine the success of the whole. Only rarely do these numbers, which are pleasantly stimulating at the moment of hearing, merge at the end, as they actually should, in the great over-all impression. For one must first grow fond of the whole work; then, on more intimate acquaintance, one may enjoy the beauty of the separate parts of which it is composed.'[16]

Weber's ideal was thus an opera in which music, drama, dance, scenery, and costumes would all stand in perfect balance, with no display of special effects to compromise either the musical integrity or the dramatic plausibility. This ideal not only formed the basis of much of his criticism but also accounted for the great care which, as a director, he lavished on every aspect of a production.[17] If, in his own music, he never completely achieved his goal, he at least laid the foundation on which others were able to build.

Ludwig Spohr's *Faust* was another work which Weber recognized as a significant landmark in the search for greater dramatic unity in opera. Though remembered today for his violin music and perhaps his oratorios, Spohr was also widely acclaimed during the first half of the nineteenth century as a conductor and opera composer. An ardent admirer of Mozart and to a large extent a self-educated musician, he introduced many forward-looking devices into his music and lived on to become an early champion of Wagner. After meeting Spohr in 1807, Weber followed his work closely and took great pride in presenting the first performance of *Faust* on September 1, 1816. In writing about the opera for his prospective audience, he stressed those details that showed the composer moving in a new direction. He praised the choice and treatment of subject matter—a dark, 'Romantic' world compelling to the imagination of the listener. Skilful orchestration and rich, chromatic harmonies also helped to enhance the effect. Of special interest to Weber was the fact that Spohr had written a preface to the score in which he described his efforts to depict Faust's character in the music of the overture. The thematic material of each section of the overture was meant to suggest a particular facet of personality. By establishing these motivic ideas in the overture and using them systematically throughout the opera, the composer developed a device capable of creating an element of unity which Weber found lacking in most contemporary operas. He wrote of 'melodies moving like gentle threads through the entire work' binding it together in a unique manner.[18] Though Weber did not use the term *Leitmotiv*, he was, in fact, describing the technique; and that as a composer he was attracted by the possibilities of such a procedure is evident in all of his own later works.

There were other matters, many of them genuinely practical problems of production and performance, to which he addressed himself in the course of his articles. Much of his repertory, both at Prague and at Dresden, consisted of operas by French and Italian composers. Accordingly, the question of translating libretti had to be faced. There is no doubt about Weber's policy in this regard. When producing an opera written in a foreign language, he nearly always used a German translation. That the audience understand the text seemed more important to him than retaining the original language. He often discussed this and made a practice of explaining any unusual textual features to his readers. Sensitive to the possible distortions of meaning and rhythm that could result from translation, it was his custom to consult the original whenever possible and make whatever changes in the text he deemed necessary. Furthermore, nearly all of his articles included some commentary on the libretto itself. He took great care to familiarize his readers with the plots of less well-known operas, and frequently traced the history of various versions of a particular story or play.

The use of interpolated musical numbers was also discussed at some length. The occasion was Weber's production of the French composer Pierre Gaveaux's one-act opera, *L'Echelle de soie* (*Die Strickleiter*, in the German version). It was a common practice in those days to add pieces to an operatic score. Weber, himself, wrote an extensive body of separate numbers to be used in operas and *Singspiele* by other composers. The reasons for such additions were various: to add length to the opera, to satisfy a singer's demand for a more substantial or more brilliant part, or, in the case of a foreign opera, to incorporate familiar tunes. In Weber's production of Gaveaux's opera, it was probably a combination of all three factors that led him to introduce four numbers by other composers to supplement the five pieces written by Gaveaux himself. The article in which he explains this procedure to his readers indicates that Weber regretted the practice in principle, considered it an artistic abuse and often a real disservice to the composer. But nonetheless, it seemed justifiable to him when the selection of new material exhibited good taste and stylistic understanding, and when the addition of such numbers ensured the performance of worthwhile compositions that might otherwise be neglected. In Vienna, he pointed out, the practice was common and frequently successful.

In his notes on Mozart's *Abduction from the Seraglio*, Weber concerned himself almost entirely with stylistic appraisal. The article, written for a Dresden performance in 1818, is short and represents an attempt to share with his readers some of his own enthusiasm for the ingenuous quality he found expressed in the music. As often in his writings, he tries with a few sentences of descriptive material to capture something of the spirit of the work.

'It is interesting to note how the perfect dramatic sense and characterization in declamation which are revealed in *The Abduction*, are occasionally combined with a not yet completely successful solution of the elements of form and design traditional at the time. In the later works, *Figaro, Don Giovanni, The Magic Flute, Titus*, etc., there is absolute conviction, masculine strength, and discretion. As far as my own artistic feeling is concerned, this happy, tenderly sensitive creation is extraordinarily charming. It is aglow with the exuberance of youth. I seem to find in it that which symbolizes youthful happiness to everyone. Never again can one regain those golden days, and when the blemishes are erased, an irretrievable charm also flees. Indeed, I feel confident in expressing the opinion that in *The Abduction*, Mozart's artistic skill reached its maturity, and from then on was only further refined by experience in life. The world was justified in expecting more than one opera like *Figaro* or *Don Giovanni*, but with the best of intentions he could never again have written another *Abduction*.'[19]

Like many of his contemporaries, Weber used the term, 'Romantic' very freely in his writings without making any real attempt to define it in relation to music. He was familiar with some of the critical literature that had surrounded the term for several decades, and he knew a number of the writers active in the movement.[20] Though he never treated the subject of Romanticism in music in a detailed manner, he did refer to it in several articles. Like Hoffmann before him, he placed Mozart and Cherubini within the ranks of Romantic composers. Beethoven, too, despite Weber's earlier negative criticism of his instrumental music, was to be called a Romantic. Hoffmann and Spohr, though admittedly composers of lesser stature, brought Romantic elements to their operas. Weber's criteria in making these judgments were simple: these were the musicians who 'moulded the traditions of the past into the forms of the future', and who, giving free reign to their imaginations, devised new ways of blending all the components of opera together.

Many of the operas Weber staged at Dresden were works of little significance. The production of popular but musically very limited compositions by such all-but-forgotten composers as Friedrich Himmel, Joseph Weigl, Johann Schmidt and Karl Hellwig, for all of whom Weber wrote relatively short introductory notices, illustrate the principal reason why his efforts to promote German opera remained a constant struggle. As eager as he was in his desire to encourage composers to develop a distinctly national opera, the taste of the majority of the public and the pressure of competition from the firmly entrenched Italian opera, tended to discourage young composers from venturing much beyond an imitation of the prevailing style. Meyerbeer, whose early career Weber had watched with great hope, proved to be the source of his deepest disappointment in this respect. After several attempts at German opera, which met with little success, Meyerbeer abandoned the cause, then travelled to Venice in 1815, 'thoroughly Italianized' his style, and found himself on the road to fame. Disheartened by this and many similar experiences, Weber had no choice but to produce what was available and to turn frequently to the production of French opera. As a composer, however, the situation was far less troublesome for him. The years of directing, conducting and writing articles about opera had given him the opportunity to experiment and develop his own approach to a new kind of opera; had, in fact, prepared him to become the founder of German Romantic opera with his composition of *Der Freischütz*.

Weber's 'Notes on Drama and Music' ceased after 1820, as did most of his other literary activity. Although his interest in producing new operas remained undiminished during the final years of his life, his health had deteriorated and his energy was clearly limited. However, despite the relatively short time during which he was active in the field of music criticism, it is indisputable that he established a unique precedent for those nineteenth-century musicians who, in their effort to guide the musical taste of their times, were to develop literary skill of remarkable quality. Moreover, he singlehandedly championed the cause of German opera against the tremendous weight of Italian and French style productions. Although his valiant attempt met with only partial success insofar as public support was concerned, yet as an outspoken leader in an unsettled period of transition, Weber took the first steps in a direction that many later composers were to follow.

NOTES

1 Considerable portions of Weber's writing on music have been published in three editions. Carl Maria von Weber, *Hinterlassene Schriften*, edited by Theodor Hell [Karl Winkler], 3 vols. (Dresden and Leipzig, 1827–28); Max Maria von Weber, *Carl Maria von Weber: Ein Lebensbild*, 3 vols. (Leipzig, 1864–66), the third volume contains a collection of writings that date from 1809 to 1824; Carl Maria von Weber, *Sämtliche Schriften*, edited by Georg Kaiser (Berlin and Leipzig, 1908). Of these Kaiser's edition, hereafter cited as *Sämtliche Schriften*, is the most complete and chronologically accurate. Several abridged editions are also available. Weber's letters, an important source of information about his music criticism, have unfortunately never been published in collected form. In addition to those we know through various small collections and publication in periodicals, there are still hundreds of unpublished letters to be found in archives at Berlin and Dresden. That his correspondence is rich in critical commentary, particularly relating to the subject of opera, may be seen in the 48 letters he wrote to Count Karl von Brühl, manager of the Hoftheater at Berlin. Carl Maria von Weber, *Briefe an den Grafen Karl von Brühl*, edited by Georg Kaiser (Leipzig, 1911).

2 For commentary on Weber's novel see André Coeuroy, 'Weber as Writer', *Musical Quarterly* (1925), 97–115; and Gerald Abraham, 'Weber as Novelist and Critic', *Music Quarterly* (1934), 27–38.

3 Max Maria von Weber, I, 432–33, 441, 469 and 518.

4 See *Sämtliche Schriften*, lxx and xci.

5 Max Maria von Weber, II, 64.

6 Max Maria von Weber, I, 457. The subject was proposed by Clemens Brentano, who offered to write the libretto.

7 *Sämtliche Schriften*, 259. All translations, unless otherwise noted, are mine.

8 *Sämtliche Schriften*, 259–60.

9 The 'Rules of the Harmonic Society', which Weber drafted toward the end of October, 1810, reveal a good deal about the 23-year-old musician as an organizer and critic. His object was to promote good taste in music, to win recognition for young composers and to create a source of qualified, impartial criticism. See *Sämtliche Schriften*, 11–15. His insistence that the society be secret and his stipulation that each member adopt a pseudonym may strike us as curiously naïve, but it was, after all, the age of secret societies. What is more significant is the fact that with his plan for influencing the general taste in music, Weber became a true precursor of Schumann. Although Schumann's 'Davidsbund' existed purely as a child of his imagination while Weber's 'Harmonic Society' was an active and remarkably efficient organization, both men were motivated by the same ideals. And when Schumann lamented the state of music in the Germany of the early 1830's and called for vigorous action to improve the situation—action that resulted in the foundation of his *Neue Zeitschrift für Musik*—he was really echoing an appeal made several decades earlier by Weber.

10 Johann Wolfgang von Goethe, *Wilhelm Meisters Lehrjahre*, Book II, Chapter 3.

11 Friedrich Schiller, *Über die ästhetische Erziehung des Menschen*, 'Politik oder Asthetik', (second letter).

12 *Sämtliche Schriften*, 260.

13 *Sämtliche Schriften*, 276.

14 *Sämtliche Schriften*, 276–7.

15 *Allgemeine musikalische Zeitung*, XIX (1817), 201–8.

16 *Sämtliche Schriften*, 129.

17 We read, for example, of Weber's preparation for the staging of Méhul's *Joseph*, his first production at Dresden. Not only did he conduct the rehearsals with unprecedented strictness and demands for precision, but he also spent long hours with the costumier, scene-painter, and carpenters. He directed their work in every detail basing his instructions on information he found while studying the volumes on ancient Egypt in the Royal Library. Max Maria von Weber, II, 61.

18 *Sämtliche Schriften*, 275

19 *Sämtliche Schriften*, 303.

20 He was, at various times, closely associated with such writers as E. T. A. Hoffman, Clemens Brentano and Ludwig Tieck.

JAN LaRUE

HAYDN LISTINGS IN THE REDISCOVERED LEUCKART SUPPLEMENTS: BRESLAU 1788-92

The discovery of a bibliographical rarity is like striking oil in one's own backyard: it is unlikely but never impossible. Even in these days of push-button bibliography we still feel a distinct excitement when we enter two areas of potential discovery: forgotten archives and neglected corners in well-known archives. Though famous for incunabula and early illuminated manuscripts, the Cathedral Archive of Gniezno in Poland is largely *terra incognita* in the annals of musicology. On a visit in 1964 to catalogue manuscripts of eighteenth-century symphonies, which in several respects resembled a voyage of discovery, the present writer pursued a special research technique familiar to all archivists, the 'search without plans,' which may appear to be mere aimless poking around, but is never entirely aimless if directed by an inquiring eye. By a fortunate accident resulting from this somewhat impressionistic technology, an apparently unique book turned up: the only surviving copy of ten supplements to the sale-catalogue of the music dealer and later publisher, F. E. C. Leuckart, a still-existing firm that just a few years ago celebrated its 175th anniversary. Leuckart opened his business as a dealer and importer of printed music in Breslau in 1787, later moving to Leipzig, where he became a rival of Breitkopf. The years of the newly recovered supplements (1787–92) represent an important documentary resource, since they begin just at the time when Breitkopf stopped issuing supplements to his own famous thematic catalogue, recently reprinted under the editorship of Barry S. Brook. Leuckart's supplements thus provide us with useful additions to the scanty evidence of publication dates for music in all parts of Europe, at the same time furnishing by implication a fascinating picture of the musical life of Breslau and its environs at the end of the eighteenth century. The part that Haydn played via long-distance but surprisingly efficient connections to this obviously burgeoning provincial culture can be estimated in an intriguing if partly reconstructive manner by studying the contents of Leuckart's lists as a reflection of his purchasers' tastes.

Although there is apparently no evidence of any contact between Leuckart and Haydn, nor indeed, of any direct Haydn contacts with Breslau, there is no doubt that Breslau was warmly alive to the attractions of Haydn's music. We could hardly expect less of a city that only a few years later was able to attract the 17-year-old prodigy, Carl Maria von Weber, as its *Theaterkapellmeister*. During the five-year span of Leuckart's supplements, the publisher offered the surprisingly large total of 134 separate Haydn publications. This considerably exceeds the total of 83 works by Mozart offered during the same period, but falls far below the listings for Hoffmeister and Pleyel. (I have elsewhere suggested that this 'catalogue popularity' undoubtedly owes something to the circumstances that both Hoffmeister and Pleyel were music publishers who 'pushed' their own compositions.) A numerical comparison of Haydn's listings with a suitable representation of important contemporaries may be seen in Table I.

Arranged in raw statistical order, the composers represented by twenty or more compositions rank as follows: *Pleyel, Hoffmeister, Haydn, Kozeluch, Mozart, Gyrowetz, Clementi, Wranitzky, Rosetti, Sterkel, Stamitz, Dittersdorf, Salieri, Vanhal.* The only slight surprises in this list are the relatively high ratings of Kozeluch (again a publisher) and Wranitzky, both of whom have received renewed attention from Czech musicologists in recent years. (See particularly Milan Poštolka, *Leopold Kozeluh*, Praha 1964, which contains a complete thematic catalogue, and *Thematisches Verzeichnis der Sinfonien Pavel Vranickýs*, in *Miscellanea Musicologica*, Praha 1967, pp. 101–28.)

Haydn's much lower statistical total in this list, compared with Pleyel and Hoffmeister, must be viewed in the light of these publishers' habit of issuing almost all of their personal compositions in numerous arrangements. A symphony, for example, after appearing in an edition of orchestral parts might also appear in arrangement for string quartet, piano quartet, piano trio, piano sonata with violin accompaniment, piano four hands, and finally as a piano reduction in a periodical such as the *Journal de Musique pour les Dames.* Though Haydn's works also appeared in various arrangements, since the publisher was supposed to pay Haydn new royalties for each new version (there were plenty of loopholes in this situation, however), usually only the most lucrative types of arrangements were produced for his works. If we therefore assume that a publisher

TABLE I

A Selective Comparison of Leuckart's Offerings

	I 1787	II 1788a	III 1788b	IV 1789a	V 1789b	VI 1790a	VII 1790b	VIII 1791a	IX 1791b	X 1792	TOTALS
Bach, C. P. E.	1	1		1		3		3	4		13
Bach, J. F. C.	2	6	2					3			13
Bach, W.						3					3
Benda	1	1	2	2	2	2			2	1	13
Boccherini									6		6
Cambini	1		3			6					10
Clementi	3	8	1	8	8	9	1	9	7		54
Devienne			1	1		6		6			14
Dittersdorf			3		9	1	2	3	3	4	25
Graun, C. E.	1										1
Gyrowetz				3		6	14	23	9	5	60
Haydn	2	29	18	8	14	14	17	20	8	4	134
Hoffmann	1					3					4
Hoffmeister	83	39	26	28	65	32	3	39	28	25	368
Kozeluch	10	19	10	6	3	9	10	6	6	6	85
Mozart	8	8	12	8	12	6	4	3	4	18	83
Pichl				4	3	1	9	2			19
Pleyel	48	24	58	41	62	60	41	56	57	34	481
Rosetti	9	11	6		7		1	3			37
Sacchini			1	2							3
Salieri		3	6	6			6	2		2	25
Sarti		9		3	1	1					14
Stamitz, C.				18	1	9		2			30
Sterkel	4	9	1	5	4	8		3			34
Vanhai	2	4	1	2	1	4	3	3		1	21
Viottl				1	1	8		1			11
Wranitzky							9	21	1	8	39

made at least twice as many arrangements of his own works as of Haydn's, the latter's total listing compares remarkably favourably with those of Pleyel and Hoffmeister. Furthermore, there is a considerable statistical gap between Haydn and the next most favoured composers, Kozeluch and Mozart.

Looking at Leuckart's supplements from another point of view, almost all of Haydn's works that became available in print by German publishers during this five-year period were offered to the Breslau public. Owing to political uncertainties in France, importation of French prints became exceedingly difficult at just this time, and probably for this reason, Leuckart relied almost exclusively on German publishers. A systematic summary of these astonishingly comprehensive listings appears in Table II.

TABLE II

Types of Haydn Works Listed by Leuckart

Symphonies	20	Duos 2 vns		6
Sym arrs.		Sonatas pf		10
org/hps/pf vn	6	Variations pf		4
pf fl vc	1	pf 4h		1
pf	7	Overture pf 4h		1
Concerto pf	1	Misc pf		6
Quartets str	33	Dance collections		4
Qt arrs. pf vn vc	3	Aria collections		4
Trios str	6	Vocal works incl. arrs.		7
pf vn vc	9			
pf fl vc	4			

Not all of the works listed above are actually different pieces, for Leuckart sometimes advertised the same Haydn work in two different editions, and at different prices. For example, the string quartet version of the *Seven Last Words* appeared first in the Artaria edition for two *Reichsthaler*; by the time of the next supplement, however, Hummel of Berlin had issued it with a lower opus number, and Leuckart, not to be outdone, offered it also at a lower price—only one *Reichsthaler/22 Silbergroschen/6 Pfennige*, about 12 per cent cheaper. (There may have been more favourable customs arrangements between Berlin and Breslau, of course.) Sometimes the competing editions appeared in the same catalogue: the first three 'Paris' symphonies (Haydn Collected Edition Nos. 82–84) occur on the first page of Leuckart's 1788a supplement as Viennese symphonies, 'opus 51', in the Artaria edition for 3/20/–. Immediately above, however, we find them as Berlin symphonies, 'opus 38', in the Hummel edition just slightly cheaper: 3/18/9. For most works the quality of Artaria engraving was well worth the additional cost for superior appearance and accuracy. As a general rule Leuckart added an importer's mark-up of approximately 10–15 per cent. For example, the three 'Paris' symphonies could be obtained for two florins each or five florins for the set in Vienna, which converted to *Reichsthaler* at the standard equivalency of 3:2 would be 3/10/–, but as we have just seen, Leuckart added 10 Sg. to the price.

Undoubtedly, the most popular work of Haydn in Breslau at this time was the *Seven Last Words*, which appeared in no less than six different publications, once in the original orchestral version (Artaria, Vienna 1787); next in two Artaria arrangements for string quartet and for piano solo (1788a); then in directly competitive publications by Hummel (Berlin) for quartet and piano (1788b); and finally in a Schmitt (Amsterdam) arrangement for piano (1789b). By this time perhaps even Leuckart himself became tired of so many listings, for in his final entry he abbreviated the Saviour's dying statement as 'die 2 (!) letzten Worte Christi im Clavier Auszuge Op. 49 Amsterd'.

This version by Schmitt also demonstrates an incidental modern service of the Leuckart Supplements: in a number of cases we can derive more precise dates for publications by reference to Leuckart's issues. In Anthony van Hoboken's *Joseph Haydn: Thematisch-bibliographisches Werkverzeichnis*, for example, the Schmitt publication is listed as '– 1790' (page 844). We can now fairly reliably push it back a year. Another Schmitt publication listed by van Hoboken (page 785), the *Caprice, Adagio & Deux Minuetts pour le Clavecin ou Piano Forte . . . Oeuvre 43*, until now undated, can be reasonably assigned to 1789, since it appears in Leuckart's second supplement for that year. A similarly minor doubt surrounds the dating of Artaria's *Recueil de différentes Pièces pour le Clavecin ou Piano Forte tirées des Simphonies . . . Oeuvre 56*. Since Leuckart lists this publication in his first supplement for 1789, it seems likely that it appeared at the end of 1788, though Artaria, contrary to his custom, apparently never advertised this publication, and Alexander Weinmann's *Vollständiges Verlagsverzeichnis Artaria & Comp.* leaves the dating open (though clear by implication of the plate number, which is surrounded by works that appeared at the end of 1788). In themselves these tiny clarifications of Haydn's publication history have little importance, but one can never tell when a bio-bibliographical determination of real significance may use a small detail of just this sort as the point of departure for a valuable chain of evidence.

SIEGMUND LEVARIE

THE CLOSING NUMBERS OF
DIE SCHÖPFUNG

The hearer following Haydn's *Die Schöpfung* in its entirety may be rightly puzzled by the manner in which the oratorio ends. The third part, centring on Adam and Eve in Paradise, consists of two halves of approximately equal length. In the first half, Uriel sets the scene; Adam and Eve, against the background of the Heavenly Host, sing 'one of the most inspired and powerful numbers of the entire work';[1] and a jubilant chorus establishes the tonic of C major in gigantic cadences praising God 'in eternity'. Neither the dramatic situation nor the music seems to demand a continuation. Yet there follows a parallel second half—recitative, duet, and chorus—which by its mere existence offers competition to its predecessor. The hearer who had no need to expect this second half is further puzzled by the musical substance, which Geiringer rightly calls 'commonplace' and 'somewhat conventional',[2] and even more so by the deflection to B flat major, the key in which the oratorio ends.

This apparent anticlimax has led to the frequent omission in performance of all numbers (31–34) after the huge C major chorus, a practice excused by Geiringer[3] and advocated by Tovey.[4] The latter goes so far as to imagine that Haydn (if he had only had a chance to read Tovey's essay) 'would, after some doubts, be glad' to make the suggested cut 'and would come to see that another Palladian double fugue in B flat, however grand, could add nothing'.

The purpose of the following few pages is to suggest that Haydn knew very well what he was doing (a safe assumption, in any case, with a master composer) and that some musical thoughts and expectations around 1800 were different from those of later generations.

A concern with proportion provides an opening argument for the validity of the structure as Haydn conceived it. Part III, compared to Parts I and II, is a bit short, anyway. Some balance is maintained by the intensity of man's appearance as conveyed by the accompanied E major recitative and the following duet and chorus ('the greatest thing in *The Creation* since the Chaos and the Light').[5] Nonetheless, the omission of the second half of Part III would make the disproportion so great—two numbers against thirteen and fifteen, respectively, in Parts I and II—as to dispute Haydn's special sense of balance and upset the hearer's. (The clocked discrepancy, here as elsewhere in music, should be understood as a symptom and not as a mechanical measurement of balance.) After the labour of the first six days, man—who, after all, is listening to the oratorio—would feel rightly shortchanged by relegation to just one number.

To Haydn, man was the crown of all creation. Man, therefore, has to be shown in both his aspects as partaking of divinity and succumbing to worldly pleasures. God has touched him, but the snake will get him. He is heroic but also pathetic. He is the protagonist but also his parody. The two halves of Part III demonstrate the point in clear musical terms. The superlatives universally bestowed on Nos. 29 and 30 testify to Haydn's successful portrayal of the divine character of man. The reluctance to accept Nos. 31 to 34 may merely indicate that, unlike Haydn, we do not like to recognize as equally real, if less attractive, our earthy counterpart.

The first and second halves of Part III follow and illuminate each other like main and secondary plots in a ·play. They necessarily supplement each other. The heroic action is immediately repeated but in parody. To Haydn and the audience which first heard *Die Schöpfung*, this technique was standard. It answered well-established expectations. The *commedia dell'arte* abounds in situations in which the fate of the serious lovers is comically mirrored by that of the 'lower' couple. *Opera buffa*, by origin and definition a kind of parody of *opera seria*, used the double plot as a stock device. Haydn showed his affinity to the Neapolitan style by choosing librettos by Goldoni for three of his operas. *Le pescatrici* of 1769—to give one example—enabled Haydn to explore the juxtaposition of serious and earthy couples in purely musical ways. The voices of the heroic couple, Prince Lindoro and his bride Eurilda, are bass and contralto; those of their plebeian counterparts (there are two comic couples in this opera), tenor and soprano. The many resulting ensembles are relevant to our inquiry.

The German *Singspiel*—particularly Mozart's work in this area—

points more directly to the last duet in *Die Schöpfung*. Belmonte and Constanze are precisely parodied by Pedrillo and Blondchen in a plot which Haydn, under the title *L'incontro improvviso*, had himself set to music a few years before *Die Entführung aus dem Serail*. The closest model for much of the general attitude of *Die Schöpfung*, we submit, is *Die Zauberflöte*. The problematic closing numbers of the Haydn oratorio become persuasively intelligible when understood as the *Singspiel* counterpart to the grander preceding scene. Geiringer, with his characteristic musical discernment, sensed a connection of this order when pointing out 'a slight resemblance between the last scene of *Don Giovanni* (after the death of the hero) and the last two numbers of *The Creation*'; but he did not pursue the thought.[6]

The *Zauberflöte* finale is a perfect example of the dramatic and musical representation of man's double personality by the parallel actions of two separate couples. Despair, attempted suicide, trial, and reunion of the lovers are shown twice—first seriously and then in parody. This order is essential for the parody to retain its rôle and not to presume serious character.[7] After the fire-and-water music, Papageno's panpipe may sound anti climactic but it provides deliberate relief. After the great C major ensemble (No. 30 in *Die Schöpfung*), the following love scene between Adam and Eve may sound ostentatious but not more so than Papageno's and Papagena's excessive concern with progeny.

The text—the basis for Haydn's music—defines the two levels on which Adam and Eve move. The first duet in Part III addresses itself to God and praises His creation: 'Heaven and earth are full of Thy goodness, o Lord. This great wonderful world is Thy work. All creation worships Thee eternally.' The following duet devotes itself entirely to earthy pleasures: 'Dearest spouse, at your side every moment is bliss. Precious husband, near you my heart swims in joy. What would be fruit, flowers, morning dew, evening breezes without your company? You make me enjoy everything double.' Can parody be more deliberate?

The music explores the given contrast in every possible way. Turned toward God, Adam and Eve join forces with the Heavenly Host in an ensemble that combines soloists and chorus throughout. Turned toward each other, they are suddenly alone; the chorus reacts after they have finished. As a reminder of the parallelism, both duets adhere to a similar structure: a slow lyrical section, oriented toward triple metre, leads to a faster joyous section in duple time. Within the structures, the music amply clarifies Haydn's intent to write, not two competing scenes, but an elevated main scene followed by its entertaining parody. Competition—particularly after the intensity of the C major ensemble—would be an error inconceivable to Haydn's masterly imagination and control. The devices singled out below make the lower level of the parody purposely audible.

The overall form of No. 30 is elaborate, best understood by the tripartite tonal plan C major – F major – C major. The modulations in the centre reach as far down as G flat major. The love duet that follows (No. 32) does not leave the tonic; the occurring accidentals serve merely to confirm the main harmonic function of E flat major. Even if one groups the closing chorus (No. 34) with this duet, the lack of harmonic adventurousness, compared to No. 30, conveys the sense of simplicity. The relative textures contribute toward defining the two different levels of experience. The lighter parody dispenses with trumpets, trombones, timpani, and double bassoon. After the imitative tight polyphony of Adam's and Eve's first vocalization, the voices now enter one at a time and join at the end in folkway parallel thirds and sixths. Whereas the first *adagio* sounds exalted, the second is merely sentimental (in the best eighteenth-century manner). Whereas in the first *allegro* the reappearance of the opening theme in a multitude of keys reminds one of the complexities of a typical C. P. E. Bach rondo, the organization of the second *allegro* into two almost identical strophes sounds homely.

This last *allegro* exchange between Adam and Eve displays every characteristic of the Vienna popular song of the time. The phrases run in symmetrical groups of four measures—easy amusement after the artful leaning in the serious duet toward phrases of six, seven, and more complex-numbered measures. The opening horn duo above a harmonic bass provides the atmosphere of a country dance, which becomes intensified by the

fiddling response eight measures later. The rhythm ♩ ♫ | ♫♩ | is that of an écossaise, which enjoyed its greatest popularity in Vienna precisely in the decades around 1800. Anybody hearing *Die Schöpfung* at that time had either danced it himself or witnessed it in surroundings associated with social enjoyment rather than with Paradise.[8] This rhythm, moreover, can be readily interpreted as a lighter version of the corresponding one in No. 30: ♪| ♩ ♫ | ♩ ♩ |. Nor can one help associate the rhythm of Papageno's opening song: ♪| ♩ ♫ | ♫♩ |.

The same Mozart piece comes to mind later in the duet when the flow of the dialogue is interspersed with airy bass-less little figures (bars 107 ff. and their strophic repetition in bars 209 ff.) not unlike the panpipe interruptions of Papageno's singing. Thrasybulos Georgiades, in his recent book on Schubert, calls this amusing device 'eine echt Wiener klassische Struktur' ('a true Vienna classical feature').[9] We can add a list of related devices, all of which the Vienna audiences in the 1790's knew, not from oratorios, but from the *opera buffa* and the *Singspiel*: the reversal of the reiterated 'ohne dich, ohne dich' to 'mit dir, mit dir' (*cf.* the duet of Susanna and the Count); the playful breaking up of a phrase by rests (bars 138 f.; *cf.* 'Silberglöckchen, Zauberflöten' of the Three Ladies); the jocular imitation of a short phrase (bars 148 ff.; *cf.* Papageno-Papagena); the sentimental preparation of the final cadence of each strophe (*cf.* similar tempo changes in the quartet from *Die Entführung aus dem Serail*); the effusive accents on an inarticulate exclamation (bars 78, 86, 180, 188; *cf.* Fiordiligi and Dorabella at the beginning of the first finale in *Così fan tutte*); and so forth.

Thus far we have reasoned that the commonplace conventionality of the musical substance of the second duet is a deliberate fall from the elevated level of the first duet and, in this sense, certainly not intended as its equal. The puzzle of the strange key relationship is thereby not answered. We may stipulate that many major works, like small works, of the eighteenth and nineteenth centuries centre on a well defined tonic key. Handel's *Israel in Egypt* begins and ends in C, as does Haydn's *Il ritorno di Tobia*; and this concern is totally documented by Haydn's and Mozart's Masses and the latter's operas (*Le nozze di Figaro* and *Don Giovanni* in D, *Così fan tutte* in C, *Die Zauberflöte* in E flat, *etc.*).

We may also stipulate that *Die Schöpfung* stands on C. The very first octave sound indicates the tonic; the entire introduction, representing the change from chaos to order, gropes for a gradual tonal clarification; and the long-expected full authentic cadence on 'Licht' (still part of the introduction!) illuminates the issue and establishes C once for all.[10] The tonic key appears four more times in the course of the oratorio, evenly spaced throughout, to mark significant moments: the end of the second day when the firmament is established; the end of the fourth day (and of Part I) when the creation of inanimate life is completed; the introduction of man in Part II; and the paradisiac scene in the first half of Part III. To conclude the oratorio with this last scene—'with the greatest design Haydn ever executed', to quote Tovey once more[11]—would seem possible if one chose to ignore the elements of overall balance and specific parody explicated above. The tonal arch must have been perfectly clear to the composer. Sketches reveal that Haydn first conceived of No. 30 as beginning in C minor and ending in C major, thus making the symmetry with the introduction all the more obvious.[12] But the tonal plan of the whole is subtle in a manner that reflects established eighteenth-century symbolism as much as it predicts new Romantic tendencies. The first *Figaro* finale, to give one example, portrays Figaro's cumulative troubles by successive drops of descending fifths all the way from G major to E flat major. After Haydn, Schubert thought of hiding the G major tonality of *Die schöne Müllerin* (as given by the second and next-to-last songs, the central dominant climax of 'Mein', *etc.*) by a less personal but symmetrical frame of which one side (No. 1, B flat) lies as far below the tonic as the other side (No. 20, E) lies above it. Wagner in *Tristan und Isolde* expresses the unachievable E major tonic of the lovers by beginning the opera in the subdominant and ending it on the dominant. Haydn was too much a man of this earth to conclude his vision of creation with undisturbed bliss in Paradise. The 'fall' from the tonic is well laid out. Part I begins and ends in C major. God and the cosmos are alone. Part II begins in F major and ends in B flat major. The subdominant push, first heard with the creation of the earth's flora (No. 8, B flat) and first confirmed with the creation of the earth's fauna (No. 15, F), leads unambiguously in the direction of this life on earth and not in heaven. Part III, finally, after Uriel's most exalted reminder of heavenly harmony in the highest key of the entire oratorio (E major, but only a recitative[13]) and the huge C major ensemble in which Adam and Eve are still in touch with God and in the company of the Heavenly Host, settles the descending trend definitively below the tonic, on E flat and B flat. The direction of the fall had been insinuated by the turn toward flats in the middle of even the C major ensemble as much as by the tonal courses of all the numbers. If Haydn's deliberate deflection from the perfection of the world needed extra-musical support, the last and rather unexpectedly threatening recitative (No. 33) spells it out. Uriel here begins in the dominant of the real tonic as a reminder of his origin but quickly descends into flats as he foretells man's fall from grace. The parody, as we have called it, appropriately remains in a lower key then the ideal.

   Why did Haydn choose to conclude his oratorio as he did? The question is typically 'modern'. One raises it only if one is conditioned (as we all have been) to expect a bang at the end. *Die Meistersinger von Nürnberg* and *Der Ring des Nibelungen* end in such a manner, but *Don Giovanni* and *Die Zauberflöte* do not. Nor does *Die Schöpfung*. Not only the tradition of eighteenth-century Vienna guided Haydn in this respect but probably even more so his own philosophic and religious convictions. The biblical account of creation leads up to the statement, frequently interpreted and commented upon, that God rested from all his works so that man might continue, and by his own acts perpetuate, creation (Gen. 2:3). Haydn must have known this common interpretation. It fits into his concept of man's relation to God, of man's imperfect emulation of God's perfect design. The open end of *Die Schöpfung* is a musical interpretation of this significant Bible sentence. Haydn, the man, continues God's creation but he neither completes it nor exults in his own fate. After indicating to us the glory of God and the bliss of Paradise, his music leaves us at the end in earthy uncertainty, where we belong.

Karl Geiringer has unceasingly advocated in his life work the indivisibility of the total musical experience. An intellectual speculation should be practically fertile. Our understanding of the closing numbers of *Die Schöpfung*, while possibly satisfactory in itself, should also contribute toward a proper performance of the entire oratorio. The omission of the last numbers runs counter, as we hope to have shown, to all of Haydn's explicit best intentions. In performance, these numbers must never try to compete with their predecessors. The more lightly they are treated by the conductor's hands, the more 'conventionally' they sound, the better they will serve the composer's spirit.

NOTES

1 Karl Geiringer, *Haydn: A Creative Life in Music* (New York: W. W. Norton & Company, Inc., 1946), p. 313.

2 *Ibid.*

3 *Ibid.*, p. 314.

4 Donald Francis Tovey, *Essays in Musical Analysis* (London: Oxford University Press, 1937), V, 124–5, 145–6.

5 *Ibid.*, p. 142.

6 *Op. cit.*, p. 314.

7 Alfred Lorenz has stressed this point and used it as a forceful argument against the occasional practice of opera houses to rearrange the sequence of scenes. *Cf.* 'Das Finale in Mozarts Meisteropern', *Die Musik*, XIX, no. 9 (June, 1927), 621–32.

8 Here are some telling examples:

Haydn, Englischer Tanz (Hoboken, I, 579)

Beethoven, Ecossaise für Militärmusik (Kinsky, p.461)

Beethoven, Ecossaise für Klavier (Kinsky, p.536)

9 *Schubert*: *Musik und Lyrik* (Göttingen: Vandenhoeck & Ruprecht, 1967), p. 114. For an analysis of Schubert's 'Volkstümlichkeit', Georgiades also uses Papageno's first song as a paradigm.

10 The famous effect of this spot, by the way, stems not so much from the dynamic change, which is an external trimming, as from the relief provided by the first clear tonic cadence thus far.

11 *Op. cit.*, p. 124.

12 Nationalbibliothek, Vienna, MS. 16835. *Cf.* Karl Geiringer, 'Haydn's Sketches for *The Creation*', *The Musical Quarterly*, XVIII, no. 2 (April, 1932), 299–308.

13 Note the Baroque melodic descent on the words, 'Vom himmlischen Gewölbe strömt reine Harmonie zur Erde hinab', after which E major is abandoned forever by a series of successive cadences falling through the cycle of fifths.

ALFRED MANN

HAYDN AS STUDENT AND CRITIC OF FUX

The student relationship of Haydn to Fux which is here suggested must be traced to the very beginning of Haydn's career. When the eight-year-old Haydn entered the choir at St Stephen's at the request of Karl Georg Reutter, court composer and choirmaster, Fux was still in charge of Imperial Court Music. Fux's *Singfundamente* served for the training of the choirboys. His Masses and Vespers formed the most important part of the choir's repertory. The thematic catalogue appended to Koechel's Fux biography (1872) includes a record of performance dates which were entered on the covers of the original part books. From this account we can gather an impressive choice of works which Haydn must have heard. 'Ich habe aber auch das Schönste und Beste in allen Gattungen gehört, was es in meiner Zeit zu hören gab. Und dessen war damals in Wien viel! O wie viel.'[1] The impact of the work and personality of the aged *Kapellmeister* must have been lasting.

In the formal sense, of course, Haydn had received no instruction in composition. In fact, no such instruction was offered at the Choir School, and G. A. Griesinger mentions in his *Biographische Notizen über Joseph Haydn* (1810) that Haydn remembered having had only two theory lessons 'von dem braven Reutter'.[2]

It was in the intense period of study which followed his choirboy days that Haydn became thoroughly acquainted with the theoretical instruction of Fux. Fux's *Gradus ad Parnassum* (1725), the celebrated manual of counterpoint, was apparently among the first works to which Haydn turned his concentrated attention once he had attained the cherished privacy of his attic room in the *Michaelerhaus*. 'Mit unermüdeter Anstrengung suchte sich Haydn Fuxens Theorie verständlich zu machen; er ging seine ganze Schule praktisch durch, er arbeitete die Aufgaben aus, liess sie einige Wochen liegen, übersah sie alsdann wieder, und feilte so lange daran, bis er es getroffen zu haben glaubte.'[3]

Haydn's copy of the work—'ein stark abgenutztes Exemplar', as it is described by Griesinger—has been discussed to some extent in Pohl's Haydn biography.[4] Evidently the Latin text of Fux's work presented no problems to the young Haydn: Haydn's marginal annotations, a few of which Pohl quotes, are written in Latin as well. Pohl mentions that Haydn corrected errors both in text and music, and he lists typical comments which Haydn made (*bene—melius*, *male*, *nihil valent*, etc.). Pohl touches also upon the interesting question that these comments seem to reflect both Haydn's study and his teaching, and he notes that some portions of Haydn's commentary were first written in pencil, or light ink, and were later retraced by Haydn. Although the choice of examples given in Pohl's text is scant, it suggests that Haydn's use of the copy covers a remarkably wide span of time. Drawing comparisons, Haydn refers to his early training (N.B. *et hunc usurparbunt veteres, etiam G. Reutter*) and to theoretical opinion published a generation later (*Kirnberger negavit; bene contra Ph. Kirnb.*). But beyond this Pohl's biography gives us no detail.

A recent search for this document of Haydn's work led to the report that it was destroyed during the Second ·World War. According to a communication received from the librarian of the Esterházy Archives, Dr Johann Hárich, the copy had been among the holdings of the Esterházy library that had been transferred to Budapest, but it was consumed by flames during the siege.

Through the kind help of the distinguished Haydn scholar in whose honour the present volume is compiled, my attention was called to the fact that the brief description in Pohl's biography is by no means the only extant account of the lost Haydn manuscript: Pohl had had the foresight to transfer, with utmost care, all of Haydn's marginal notes to corresponding pages in another copy of Fux's work. This copy passed from Pohl to Mandyczewski, his successor as Curator of the Archive of the *Gesellschaft der Musikfreunde in Wien*, and it now forms part of the Archive's valuable collection.[5]

Even a brief examination of this copy reveals a commentary of well-nigh incredible thoroughness and complexity. Haydn more than doubles

Fux's own extensive listing of errors and omissions. He elaborates upon point after point, interprets, clarifies, closes every possible gap, and traces every possible inconsistency in Fux's discussion.

In general we can discern two aspects of comment in Haydn's annotations: the comment of the corrector and revisor concerned with the text itself, and the comment of the practising contrapuntist concerned with the principles conveyed by the text, its underlying aims and tendencies. The second is bound to take its point of departure from the first, but it is in both that we can follow a gradual change from the young to the experienced reader, from student to critic.

Haydn's list of *errata*, for instance, is carried into Fux's own *errata* listing on which Haydn comments in several instances and to which he adds a page of his own notes. His correction of errors in the examples is carried into the excerpts from Fux's own works quoted at the end of the book (portions of a Mass and a separate Offertory, which were—and have remained—otherwise unavailable in print).[6]

In similar manner, Haydn applies the judgement that he has gained through the study of Fux's text to the examples of counterpoint and fugue which it contains. His mark *male* may simply underline what the author himself has said about a given example. Or it may contrast the author's opinion against that of others: Haydn adds *male juxta alios Authores* to the second of two examples of hidden fifths which Fux designates as acceptable (*Gradus ad Parnassum*, pp. 130 ff.; interestingly enough, this is the same example on which Beethoven later comments: 'Das letztere würde jedoch für mein Ohr nie zu entschuldigen sein.')[7] But in the majority of cases the statement is Haydn's own carefully weighed opinion, such as 'the open chord may pass, but the octaves in the seventh bar are bad'. (Comment upon a fugal entrance, *Gradus ad Parnassum*, p. 173, see Figure 1).

Thus Haydn differentiates and qualifies as he formulates his criticism. In various instances he points out a repetition in Fux's melodic lines as *monotonia*, but in one case he adds *monotonia unius tactus bona* (*Gradus*, p. 97); in another case he adds *Lic: in fine* (*Gradus*, p. 54); in a third he suggests an alternate solution *NB G melius fuisset* (*Gradus*, p. 92).

Such corrections appear frequently and at times a single change deals with more than one problem. With the annotation *melius fuisset h, loco a, in Sopr.*, Haydn not only improves a soprano line but also avoids hidden octaves (*Gradus*, p. 113). His particular interest is devoted to solutions for

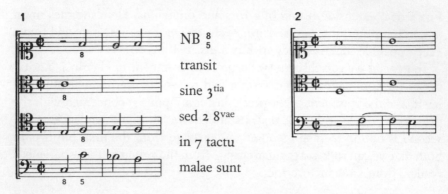

problems expressly stated in the text. Fux singles out the first two bars of a syncopation exercise (Figure 2) because of hidden fifths between the soprano and alto parts.[8] As a remedy, he suggests the use of a rest instead of the opening note of the alto part (Figure 3). Haydn changes this

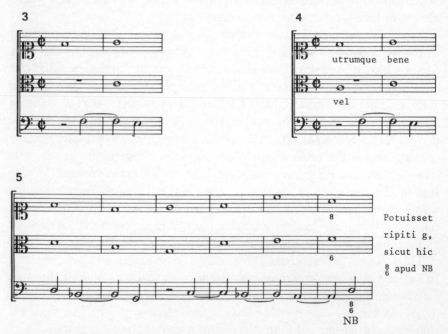

example (Figure 4), and then notes a similar change in another portion of the same exercise in which Fux had permitted the use of a rest to ease the part-writing (see Figure 5). Yet the following beginning of an example Haydn marks *bene* although Fux gives an alternate solution (Figure 6).

In discussing the same counterpoint species in four-part writing, Fux points out the possible conflict of dissonant resolution and four-part sound (Figure 7), advising a division of the whole note in the tenor part (Figure

8). Haydn again comments upon Fux's solution, adding the remark *vel tertia dupplicanda*, and adds the whole note *f* below the two half notes in the corrected tenor part.

A key concept that guides Haydn's emendations is consistency. His innumerable changes of slight inconsistencies may at first seem pedantic, but the sensitive way in which he handles the problem of *monotonia* is in itself an argument sufficient to invalidate such a reproach. He is concerned with the adherence to fundamental and unequivocal principles. Only when he finds inconsistencies that violate such principles will his remarks occasionally assume a tone of harsh criticism. *NB prohibuit et tamen ipse fecit. Etian duas quintas* he writes in one instance (Figure 9; *Gradus*, p. 180). This comment does not deal primarily with the suggestion of parallel fifths arising from the voice crossing but with the tritone formed by the tenor and bass progressions across the bar line, for a progression of this kind runs counter to one of the first laws Fux formulates in his text:

Mi contra fa
Est diabolus in musica

Earlier on the same page Haydn marks a similar progression and adds *Quando mi fa a 4^{tro} in duobus tactibus sequitur etiam dicitur erroneum.*

It is quite characteristic of Haydn's attitude how seriously he takes Fux's modal approach to the technique of part writing. We find frequent Haydn annotations in Fux's chapter on the modes, and such a problem as the progression V–IV is never judged by him upon harmonic considerations but invariably upon the consideration of the awkward *mi fa* progression from one voice to another which he often quotes in the examples. (This is an aspect of Haydn's theoretical thinking that may have alienated Beethoven; under Albrechtsberger's tutelage he was liberated from hexachordal and modal thought and used only *cantus firmi* in major and minor tonalities). Yet with respect to the *mi fa* progression, too, Haydn finds possibilities of qualifying the rule. In the passage shown in Figure 10 (*Gradus*, p. 181) he corrects the second note of the soprano part *a* to *b* (an error that had remained unnoticed by Fux) and marks the following downbeat in the soprano part *mi*; he adds *quando mi fa in transitu celeri venit non estimatur quà error.*

Haydn's correction in the preceding example directs our attention finally to one of the most interesting manifestations of his concern for consistency: consistency in the use of melodic material that has become thematic. A correction which resembles the one shown in Figure 10

10

occurs in the stretto of a four-part fugue. Similarly, Haydn changes the first note of the alto part in the last measure of Figure 11 (*Gradus*, p. 170) from *f* to *d*. (This is again an error not mentioned in Fux's *errata* listing, although the note in question—occurring in the original copy at the

11

beginning of a new line—is correctly indicated by Fux's *custos* in the preceding line.)

The significance of an exposed thematic entrance is eloquently described in Fux's text: '. . . it is necessary after a rest to introduce either the old subject or some new subject, which must then be taken up also by the other parts, if you do not want to make yourself open to the reproving words of the Gospel of St Matthew (22:12): "Friend, how camest thou in hither, not having a wedding garment?" '⁹

The point is amply and expertly illustrated in Fux's own fugal examples. But Haydn calls attention to two passages contained in the same chapter. In the first case (Figure 12; *Gradus*, p. 166) he marks a bass entrance through which a vexing problem is posed. Fux had explained the desirability of rhythmic changes in the use of thematic material, but his instruction suggests utmost caution where melodic changes are concerned, particularly since he deals in great detail with the logic of the tonal answer. His modification of the bass entrance—valid within the tonal structure—arises from the innate smoothness of his part writing. Yet Haydn is unquestionably right in marking it *Lic: non bona*, although within the given context he cannot write a better solution.

He does just that, however, in the other case (the fugue following the one containing the comment just quoted, Figure 13; *Gradus*, p. 167). Examining the alto passage which follows the second entrance of the soprano and which receives added prominence once the tenor part rests, he discovers the possibility of a thematic statement that had escaped Fux. This thematic statement, brought about by the change of one note, strengthens in effect the entire structural balance of the small work: anticipating in double counterpoint the more extensive stretto starting

12

Fuga à 3. Modi A

(etc.)

seven bars later, it enhances what had been a single entrance at the second introduction of the theme.

Thus, in improving upon Fux's text, Haydn refers to Fux's own thematic material, as he refers again and again to the framework of Fux's own teaching. He assumed the role of Fux's critic on the authority of being Fux's student.

13

Fuga à 3. Modi C

(Haydn)

NOTES

1 J. F. Rochlitz, quoting Haydn in *Für Freunde der Tonkunst*, see C. F. Pohl, *Joseph Haydn*, Leipzig, 1878, vol. 1, p. 63. In his edition of Haydn's letter (*Joseph Haydn: Gesammelte Briefe und Aufzeichnungen*, Kassel, 1965, p. 138), Dénes Bartha has pointed out the fact that Haydn had asked for the original score of a *Te Deum* which was preserved

in the Imperial Archives. One of the extremely rare autographs of Fux, it remained in Haydn's private library until his death.

2 New edition by F. Grassberger, Vienna, 1954, p. 10.

3 Griesinger, *loc. cit.*

4 *Op. cit.*, p. 176.

5 Class mark 101/37 *Duplicat.*

6 A choice of Haydn's comments specifically concerned with the revision of Fux's text was published for the first time in the Critical Notes for the new edition of the *Gradus ad Parnassum* within the Complete Works of Fux (Johann Joseph Fux, *Sämtliche Werke*, Ser. VII, vol. 1, ed. by A. Mann, Graz and Kassel, 1967); see also the present writer's study 'Eine Textrevision von der Hand Joseph Haydns' in *Musik und Verlag*, ed. by R. Baum and W. Rehm, Kassel, 1968 pp. 432 ff.

7 See G. Nottebohm, *Beethoveniana*, Leipzig, 1872, p. 181.

8 Fux writes *quae facilis auribus perceptu* to which Haydn adds *ob magnum saltum.*

9 See A. Mann, *The Study of Fugue*, New York, 1965, p. 97 (p. 161 of the original Latin text). The principle was first formulated in Thomas Morley, *A Plain and Easy Introduction to Practical Music* (1597), see new ed. by R. A. Harman, London, 1952, pp. 265 ff.

WILLIAM J. MITCHELL

MODULATION IN
C. P. E. BACH'S *VERSUCH*

In his *Versuch*,[1] C. P. E. Bach uses two complementary terms, *die Modulation* and *die Ausweichung* in a differentiated manner. In order to describe the differences accurately, it will be well to start with a review of the senses in which one of the terms, modulation, has been applied to music over a fairly inclusive span of time. This will be done without any desire to conduct a philological or semantic exercise, but simply to remind the reader of periodic shifts in the meaning of the word.

Probably all contemporary students of the theory of music learn the meaning of modulation early in life. Depending on the views of their instructors or textbooks they may particularize its sense, distinguishing or not between transient and enduring modulation, employing such terms as applied dominant or secondary dominant, classifying keys as closely, intermediately, or remotely related, or refining the broad structural implications of the technique. But in the end they know, as expressed by Willi Apel,[2] that modulation is solely, 'the change of key within a composition'. In brief, the term has acquired a single definition which all but obliterates its generic sense. In fact, it had become so sharply delimited by the beginning of the twentieth century that Max Reger,[3] in his widely used study of modulation, did not bother to define it. It was in the nineteenth century that the reduction in meaning became normal.

It was quite different in the seventeenth and earlier centuries. The one thing that modulation did not mean in the overwhelming number of cases was 'change of key' or mode. Rather, it referred in the main to proper musical shape, conduct, or context. The best that Thomas Morley[4] could offer was, 'going out of key' and, 'the bass is brought in out of

333

key'. About seventy years later, in 1673, Matthew Locke[5] wrote: 'I have annexed an example or two by way of Transition, or passing from one key to another.' Somewhat earlier, Christoph Bernhard[6] had written: 'One should not repeat *einerley Modulation*, although fugues and imitations retain their value', using modulation in the sense of figure or succession. It seems reasonably clear that 'modulation' had not come into more than isolated use to denote 'change of key' or mode.

During the eighteenth century the term began to include change of key among its meanings. It was still unavailable in Germany when Friderich Erhard Niedt[7] in 1700 introduced the subject as: '*Wie man manierlich aus einem Thon in den andern fallen sol.*' (How to move properly out of one key into another.) However, in France at about the same time, modulation had come into use in a new as well as the older sense. Of the older sense, going back to modal theory, Sebastien de Brossard[8] wrote: 'To modulate or modulation has been nothing more than to cause a melody to move between these two extremes [formed by the octave] in such a manner as to pass more frequently through the *essential sounds* than through the others and this always *diatonically.*' Elsewhere,[9] however, he wrote: 'To modulate is also to leave the mode at times, but in order to re-enter it properly and naturally.'

Modulation, now defined with two meanings, appears with increasing frequency throughout the remainder of the eighteenth century. Perhaps the case is most extensively treated by Jean Jacques Rousseau[10] who writes at the beginning of his entry on modulation: 'This is properly the method of establishing and treating the mode; but this word, at present, is more generally taken for the art of conducting the harmony and the air successively in several modes, by a method agreeable to the ear, and comformable to rules.' Five pages are given over to an explanation of the newer meaning.

An historian's critical approach to the technique, now expressly described as modulation, and his summary description of its operating principles can be found when Charles Burney[11] turns his attention to the Fitzwilliam Virginal Book. He writes: 'In the . . . tune, called Dr Bull's Jewel . . . the modulation from C natural to B flat, and from B flat to C, is sudden and violent in the first part. . . . And in the last strain . . . the modulating instantly into F, is such a violation of all present rules, as seems rude and barbarous.' Indeed, Bull seems to have had a bad taste in modulation. He then cites 'an Allemand by old Robert Johnson as a proof how much secular modulation was governed by ecclesiastical, and how undetermined the keys were, at this time, by any rules in present use. This short air begins in D minor; but in the first bar, we have the chord of C natural, as fifth of the key of F; then at the third bar, the author returns, in no disagreeable manner, to D minor, ending in the church style, with a sharp third.'

In uneasy summary, then: During the seventeenth century and earlier, modulation, for the musician, meant not 'change of key' but rather, among many other things, 'affirming or sustaining the key' or mode; in the nineteenth and twentieth centuries it has meant essentially 'change of key' and few other things, certainly not 'affirming or sustaining the key'; but in the eighteenth century it meant 'change of key' *and* other things, among which was 'affirming or sustaining the key'.

The modern theorist, working with eighteenth-century materials, encounters disturbing challenges when he comes face to face with the term. He must be prepared to forsake the tight later meaning, yet to bring it into play when it seems called for. He must be prepared also to search for an appropriate different word or expression when 'change of key' is not meant.

In the case of Emanuel Bach's *Versuch*, the modern reader will receive a degree of welcome assistance from the author, for as noted earlier, Bach uses *die Modulation* and *die Ausweichung* in perceptibly differentiated senses. When discussing the technical aspects of 'key change',[12] *die Modulation* is not once used. Rather he relies on *die Ausweichung*, a term in general use which can be taken to mean yielding or shunting, and its verb form, *ausweichen*, along with less formal expressions, such as: *'in andere Tonarten versteigen'*; *'die Haupttonart verlassen . . . wieder ergreifen'*; *'in entlegenere Tonarten gehen'*; or *'die Tonarten berühren'*. Yet in the remainder of the *Versuch*, *die Modulation* is employed quite frequently, and *die Ausweichung* only rarely.

This separation in use suggests a distinction in meaning: *Die Ausweichung* and its related forms stand exclusively for 'change of key' in its clinical sense; *die Modulation* and its related forms stand for context, shape, pattern, conduct, all in the earlier sense of the term. Certain difficulties arise, however, when 'modulation' is applied to passages which, in fact, include a key change in the narrowest sense. Nevertheless in the bulk of cases it clearly retains its older generalized meaning.

Insight into Emanuel Bach's differentiated uses of the terms can be gained by comparing two of his passages with parallel passages in Türk's *Klavierschule*,[13] a book modelled in large part on the *Versuch*. Bach writes:

'A fantasia is said to be free when it. . . changes keys more (*in mehrere Tonarten ausweichet*) than is customary in other pieces.'[14] *Ausweichet* means 'modulates' in the modern sense. Türk in 1789, who used *die Modulation* interchangeably with *die Ausweichung*, but prefers *die Modulation* in this case writes: 'A Fantasia is called free when the composer . . . luxuriates with respect to modulation' ('*In Ansehung der Modulation ausschweift*').[15] Clearly, Bach's and Türk's terms are synonymous and refer to key changes. In another case, however, in which Türk lifts almost bodily from Bach, there is an opposite kind of change. Bach, writing about the accessory, but unnotated accidentals to be used in the performance of trills and their suffixes, says: 'The performer must judge at times from the context' ('*so muss man sie . . . bald aus . . . der Modulation beurtheilen*').[16] Because Bach's illustration is not clearly a change of key, Türk, whose illustrations are also non-modulatory, after borrowing all other considerations literally, changes Bach's *Modulation* clause to: 'A practised player will surely judge . . . also for harmonic reasons' ('. . . *auch wohl aus harmonischen Gründen beurtheilen*').[17] In brief: For Bach, *die Modulation* and *die Ausweichung* had different meanings; for Türk they seem to have been close to identical when they referred to key changes. In the years that separated 1753, 1762 from 1789 modulation had begun to shed its generalized sense and to assume its more modern exclusive one. The double meaning lingered, however, for Heinrich Christoph Koch[18] still wrote in 1802: Modulation is 'the proper and varied conduct of notes generally . . . [and] the leading of notes from the chief tonality into another and back'. However, it was not long before the term assumed its modern meaning; and in German writings, *die Ausweichung* tended to acquire the sense of the English, 'transient modulation'. C. P. E. Bach was far removed from such a distinction.

Before turning specifically to Bach's prescriptions for a change of key, let us examine a few of the many cases to which he applies the various verbal forms of *die Modulation*.

In discussing the recitative, he comments[19] that singers sometimes substitute melodic forms such as those of Example 1a for a written form like that of 1b. The reasons, he writes, may be greater convenience of range

or forgetfulness, the latter, 'because the singer, in memorizing, easily interchanges the ever similar recitative patterns (*Recitativmodulationen*), being more mindful of the underlying harmonies than the written notes'. The sense of modulation, in this case is similar to that intended by Christoph Bernhard, cited earlier.

In another instance, Emanuel Bach, discussing the chord of the seventh, points to a passage in which a three part accompaniment is recommended, 'because the course of the principal part' ('*die Modulation der Haupt-stimme*') 'does not readily suffer a fourth part'.[20] Modulation as 'course' or 'nature' seems clearly indicated here, for if 'change of key' were intended, it would inevitably include the activity of all parts. Basically, the embellished chromatic changing notes are the cause of the difficulty.

Occasionally, the term is applied to a passage in which, from a particularized point of view, a 'change of key' occurs. In discussing the ascending trill, Emanuel Bach suggests that it can be employed with good effect 'when the modulation changes' ('*wenn die Modulation sich verändert*').[21] The passage contains one of the critical factors that Bach

includes under his description of the techniques of key change. Yet, when the various employments of the term are considered *in toto*, it becomes apparent that in the *Versuch*, *die Modulation* relates back to its earlier generalized sense, springing from modal theory. Hence, it is not surprising that it should be applied at times to musical passages that suggest its later exclusive sense.

In his treatment of the Free Fantasia,[22] Bach, using only *ausweichen* along with a few related expressions, turns to a detailed study of the techniques of key change. A new key, writes Bach, should be sought through its major seventh (*semitonium modi*) and a proper accompaniment.[23] Although this cannot be regarded as an epoch-making statement, the material that precedes and follows it sheds interesting light on the application of the precept.

Earlier[24] he suggests that a dependable procedure for those of limited ability is to preludize on the ascending and descending scale of a key, employing among other things, 'various thorough bass signatures'. In his musical illustrations, he introduces traditional settings for this 'rule of the octave', but includes others that are somewhat more luxuriant, as in Example 4.

Observe the presence of several leading notes. However, Emanuel Bach has made it clear that the scale of a single key is the guide. It would seem that he makes a distinction between inclusive structure and passing, often chromatic detail. The distinction is underlined when his 'various signatures' are compared with the stern diatonic procedures advocated by Rousseau when he prescribes the act of modulation in the older sense. He writes: 'To modulate well in the same tone . . . never . . . alter any of the sounds of the mode; for we cannot, without quitting it, make a diesis [a sharp] or a B flat [a flat] be heard, which does not belong to it, or remove any one that does belong to it.'[25] The difference is striking and further emphasized when Emanuel Bach states that, 'a tonic organpoint is convenient for establishing the tonality at the beginning and end'.[26] The illustrations, although based on widespread practice, might well have been disapproved by the French savant.

An *Ausweichung* consists not merely of a seeking out of leading tones, but rather of a broad march toward the new key along various chromatic by-paths. C. P. E. Bach, always strong for a controlled play of fancy in changing keys, writes: 'It is one of the beauties of improvisation when one feigns modulation to another key' (*'wenn man sich stellet . . . in eine andere Tonart auszuweichen'*) 'through a formal cadence, and then moves off in another direction. This and other rational deceptions make a Fantasia attractive'.[27] Elsewhere, he speaks of 'a skilful attaining' of the leading note, as well as the need to approach keys 'gradually'. Also, he describes his illustrations as being 'slightly circuitous' ways of changing keys.

All of this suggests strongly that for Emanuel Bach an *Ausweichung* is to be thought of as a long or middle range goal of musical activity, rather than an immediate or transient matter. It suggests further, that *die Modulation* is employed by him to denote many things, including those brief skirmishes with keys while en route to a broadly conceived goal.

The inclusive meaning of an *Ausweichung* is indicated, further, by his statement that when 'one wishes not merely superficially to touch upon (*obenhin berühren*) remoter keys, but formally to reach them (*darein förmlich ausweichen*), it is insufficient simply to reach for the leading tone in the belief that once it is found, the goal will have been attained. . . . The ear must be prepared for the new key by means of intermediate harmonic progressions.'[28]

An examination of one of his illustrations of key change will, perhaps, help to clarify the distinction between *moduliren* and *ausweichen*. He suggests a 'few special ways to come gradually to closely related keys'.[29] One of these is a motion from the tonic to the dominant key. He seems to start off in the wrong direction, striking an F chord, preceded by its

applied dominant, threatening to move to a D minor chord, approaching an A minor chord and then one on D, but major, through their respective leading notes, only to settle on the dominant. The *Ausweichung* is the overall change from C to G; the *Modulation* is the actual transition, involving several leading tones. The seeming discursiveness of the route followed is simply a particular fleshing out or prolongation of a firm ground plan. The nature of the plan can be neatly illuminated by superposing over Bach's *Ausweichung* an avowedly bare-boned modulation to the dominant written by Max Reger.[30] Reger, in his terms, presents *eine Modulation*; Bach, in paraphrase of his terms, presents *eine modulirende Ausweichung*.

In conclusion and summary, let us turn to an excerpt from one of C. P. E. Bach's compositions.[31] The nineteen bars, coming near the end of the piece, will be presented only in a terse thorough bass outline (Example 8a), since the music is readily available. Suffice it to say that the refrain under examination, having been stated several times earlier in the Rondo, is now repeated in a venturesome rhapsodic guise, embodying much that is chromatic. The first seven chords of Example 8a. illustrate Emanuel Bach's fondness for the diminished seventh chord 'as a means of reaching the most distant keys more quickly and with agreeable suddenness'.[32] Two *Ausweichungen* are thereby carried out, from C minor to F sharp minor, and to E flat minor. The chords from the seventh to the thirteenth bring us back 'gradually' to C minor by means of chromatic *Modulation*, in Bach's usage. The next goal in the plan of *Ausweichungen* is D flat major, reached, again by chromatic *Modulation*, at the nineteenth chord and extended through the twenty-first following which C minor is regained and affirmed by means of its subdominant and dominant chords.

In distinguishing between the meaning of modulation, as a reference to proper, but fanciful musical conduct, and *Ausweichung*, as a reference to inclusive key changing techniques, C. P. E. Bach was pointing the way toward levels of musical meaning. His differentiated usage is the rough equivalent of the more modern, immediate and intermediate levels of structure,[33] corresponding to Heinrich Schenker's *Vordergrund* and *Mittelgrund*. To facilitate the relating of these to a remote level, Schenker's *Hintergrund*, an inclusive linear-structural analysis of the passage has been subposed in Example 8b.

1 Carl Philipp Emanuel Bach, *Versuch über die wahre Art das Clavier zu spielen* (Part 1, 1753, Part 2, 1762, Berlin). All references will be to these editions. An English translation is available under the title, *Essay on the True Art of Playing Keyboard Instruments*, tr. and ed. Wm. J. Mitchell (New York, 1949).

2 Willi Apel, *Harvard Dictionary of Music* (Cambridge, Mass., 1955), entry on Modulation.

3 Max Reger, *Beiträge zur Modulationslehre* (Leipzig, 1903). It had attained its 24th printing by 1952, and has been translated into French and English.

4 Thomas Morley, *A Plaine and Easie Introduction to Practical Musicke* (London, 1597). A modern edition, ed. R. Alec Harman (New York, n.d.) is available. Morley's statements appear on pp. 249 and 261.

5 Matthew Locke, *Melothesia* . . . (London, 1673), as quoted by F. T. Arnold, *The Art of Accompaniment* . . . (New York, 1965), p. 157.

6 Christoph Bernhard, *Tractatus compositionis augmentatus* (1650–1660?), Ch. 2, Par. 8 in J. M. Mueller-Blattau, *Die Kompositionslehre Heinrich Schützens* . . . (Leipzig, 1926).

7 Friderich Erhard Niedt, *Musicalische Handleitung* (Hamburg, 1700), as quoted by Arnold, p. 235.

8 Sebastien de Brossard, *Dictionaire de Musique* (Mont-Parnasse, 1703), entry under Modo.

9 *Ibid.*, entry under *Modulatione*.

10 Jean Jacques Rousseau, *Dictionnaire de musique* (Geneva, 1767). The translation is from the English version by William Waring (London, 1770).

11 Charles Burney, *A General History of Music* (1776–89), New edition, ed. Frank Mercer (New York, 1957), vol. 2, pp. 98–9.

12 *Versuch*, Pt. 2, Ch. 41, Pars. 6–10.

13 Daniel Gottlob Türk, *Klavierschule* (Leipzig and Halle, 1789). Facsimile edition, ed. Erwin R. Jacobi (Kassell, 1962).

14 *Versuch*, Pt. 2, p. 325, Par. 1.

15 *Klavierschule*, p. 395, Par. 35.

16 *Versuch*, Pt. 1, p. 67, Par. 19.

17 *Klavierschule*, p. 264, Par. 42.

18 Heinrich Christoph Koch, *Musikalisches Lexikon* (Frankfurt am Main, 1802), entry under *Modulation*.

19 *Versuch*, Pt. 2, pp. 317–18, Par. 7.

20 *Versuch*, Pt. 2, p. 118, Par. 13.

21 *Versuch*, Pt. 1, pp. 70–1, Par. 25.

22 *Versuch*, Pt. 2, Ch. 41, pp. 325–41.

23 *Versuch*, Pt. 2, p. 330, Par. 8.

24 *Versuch*, Pt. 2, pp. 327–30, Par. 7.

25 Rousseau, *Dictionnaire* . . ., entry under Modulation, tr. Wm. Waring.

26 *Versuch*, Pt. 2, pp. 327–30, Par. 7.

27 *Versuch*, Pt. 2, p. 330, Par. 8.

28 *Versuch*, Pt. 2, p. 333, Par. 10.

29 *Versuch*, Pt. 2, pp. 331–2, Par. 9.

30 *Beyträge* . . ., p. 6, item 1.

31 The Rondo in C minor, bars 76–94, from the Fifth Collection of *Clavier-Sonaten und Fantasien . . . für Kenner und Liebhaber* (Leipzig, 1785. It also appears in *Four Hundred Years of European Keyboard Music*, ed. Walter Georgii (Köln, 1959)).

32 *Versuch*, Pt. 2, p. 335, Par. 11.

33 Cf. *The Music Forum*, ed. Wm. J. Mitchell and Felix Salzer (New York, 1967), vol. 1 Glossary, pp. 260–8.

LEONARD G. RATNER

ARS COMBINATORIA
CHANCE AND CHOICE IN
EIGHTEENTH-CENTURY MUSIC

———

Along the bypaths of later eighteenth-century music, many curiosities may be discovered. Of these, none is more intriguing than the musical games by which marches, minuets, polonaises, contredanses, and waltzes could be composed by throwing dice, spinning a top, or choosing numbers at random. In these pastimes, pre-fabricated musical figures are provided by the compiler of the game; the music for each measure is chosen by the player of the game as he makes his throw or spin.

From 1757 to 1813 more than a dozen such games were published. Some had a wide circulation, appearing in several editions and in various languages. Important figures, such as Mozart, Haydn, Kirnberger, and Emmanuel Bach amused themselves with these pastimes.

The first of these games to appear in print was Kirnberger's *Der allezeit fertige Menuetten—und Polonoisenkomponist*,[1] which was published in Berlin in 1757. In Kirnberger's game, the polonaise is laid out in two periods, respectively six and eight bars in length. The minuet and its trio are each eight bars long. The harmony for each measure is fixed; for example, the chord progression in the first reprise of the polonaise is:

1	2	3	4	5	6
I	V	I	I	I-V	I

Melody, of course, is the variable element. Each bar in the game has eleven possible melodic variants, corresponding respectively to the eleven numbers that can turn up on a throw of two six-sided dice.

343

Example 1 gives the table of numbers for the first reprise of the polonaise and a sample polonaise put together from Kirnberger's fragments:

Example 1

Kirnberger: Polonaise Composer: Table of Numbers

Zum ersten Theile

mit einem Würfel	1	2	3	4	5	6					
mit zwei Würfeln	2	3	4	5	6	7	8	9	10	11	12
1 Wurf	70	10	42	62	44	72	114	123	131	138	144
2 ,,	34	24	6	8	56	30	112	116	147	151	153
3 ,,	68	50	60	40	7	4	126	137	143	118	146
4 ,,	18	46	2	12	79	28	87	110	113	124	128
5 ,,	32	14	52	16	48	22	89	91	101	141	150
6 ,,	58	26	66	38	54	64	88	98	115	127	154

1

Kirnberger: Polonaise

For the first reprise of Kirnberger's polonaise 11^6 different melodies exist, and for the second reprise, 11^8. Together, 11^{14} polonaises await only the toss of the dice to come to life. The minuet and trio offer 11^{32} different possibilities. The entire population of eighteenth-century Europe, working a lifetime on these games could not exhaust the combinations that lie within Kirnberger's minuets and polonaises.

Other games have different methods of selection. Hoegi's[2] is completely random, allowing the player to choose a number from 8 to 48 for each of the two eight-bar reprises. *Le Tôton Harmonique*[3] and *Ludus Melothedicus*[4] use a nine-sided top. Having selected a number from 1 to 9 by a spin of the top, the player must piece out the melody from a set of two charts, the first numerical, the second musical. C. P. E. Bach's *Einfall*[5] uses a variant of the same method. Games by Mozart,[6] Haydn,[7] Stadler,[8] Callegari,[9] and Ricci[10] proceed in the same manner as that of Kirnberger.

Musically, the content of the short pieces constructed by means of such games is typical of eighteenth-century popular idioms. It does not betray its mechanical origins. While the minuets, waltzes, marches, and contredanses thus fashioned are not superb musical compositions, they possess coherence and validity of style because their harmonic, rhythmic, and melodic components are built of useful musical stuff. Many could well be incorporated into a light serenade or divertimento. Possibly, there was a factor of economy; a host could provide uncounted minuets for his dancing guests without having to rush out every few weeks to buy the newest collection being published.

The amusement afforded by these musical games of chance bespeaks pure dilettantism and, perhaps, decadence. Yet, the process by which the games were put together reflects a substantial view of musical construction, one that permeates the seventeenth and eighteenth centuries. In this view, the play of musical elements is controlled so as to achieve a coherent and persuasive flow of rhetoric. At this time in musical history, it was possible to codify the mechanical elements of musical composition more clearly than at any other time. Arrangements of such elements, though uncountable in practice, were intelligible and limited. Musical treatises of the seventeenth and eighteenth centuries contain many references to systematic arrangements of materials; such arrangements are subsumed under the term, *ars combinatoria*.

Ars combinatoria is a term that belongs properly to mathematics. Briefly, it deals with the number of different ways in which a given quantity of objects may be arranged or placed according to a given set of conditions. For example, the numbers 1, 2, 3, 4, taken two at a time may be arranged in twelve different ways. *Ars combinatoria* includes both *permutation*, in which a given number of objects is re-arranged, and *combination*, in which it is possible to substitute one object for another in a series. Permutation is illustrated as follows:

Three letters, A B C, may be arranged in six different ways:

| ABC | ACB | BCA | BAC | CAB | CBA |

Combination may substitute in the following way:

Given a three-term figure, with two alternatives for each term, there are eight possible combinations:

AB	CD	EF
A	C	E
A	D	E
A	C	F
A	D	F
B	C	E
B	D	E

345

B	C	F
B	D	F

The dice games represent this type of combination.

Prescriptions for the exercise of the permutatory and combinatory processes may differ but the spirit that moves these processes, the exploration of arrangements, is the significant point in the application of *ars combinatoria* to musical construction in the eighteenth century.

Many musical theorists in the seventeenth and eighteenth centuries refer to *ars combinatoria* or apply its principles in discussing musical construction. Glareanus,[11] still earlier, (1547) arrives at his *dodekachordon* by combining the four pentachords with the three tetrachords and then eliminating those that were not viable within the diatonic system. Mersenne[12] and Kircher[13] devote long sections to melodic and rhythmic permutations. Printz[14] applies combinatorial processes in demonstrating alternative melodies over a given bass. Brossard has the following entry:

'*Musica Combinatoria*, that part which teaches the manner of combining the sounds; that is, of changing their place and figure in as many manners as possible.'[15]

In addition, we find references in Mattheson,[16] Heinichen,[17] Adlung,[18] as well as in the theoretical treatises to be mentioned during the remainder of this article.

To illustrate the range covered by *ars combinatoria* in eighteenth-century theory and practice, the following classifications will be used:

1. Arrangement of notes into figures and motives
2. Alternatives in phrase and period structure
3. Alternatives in the order of keys in a piece
4. *Ars combinatoria* applied to complete movements

1. *Figures and motives*

Joseph Riepel, in his *Grundregeln zur Tonordunung*,[19] the second volume of his very important set of treatises on musical composition, begins the formal consideration of melody by investigating mathematical permutations. He then applies permutations to musical notes in series of three or four. The four-note series also incorporates rhythmic permutations of two crotchets and two quavers. Example 2 gives the twenty-four melodic permutations; had Riepel carried the permutational process to its end, there would have been 144 melodic-rhythmic variations.

Riepel: Melodic-rhythmic permutations (20)

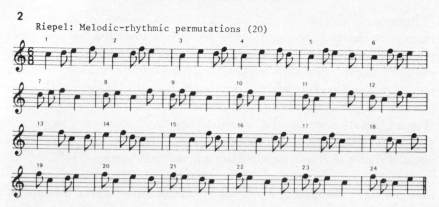

Riepel then proceeds to incorporate each of these twenty-four figures into phrase groups to demonstrate how they can become components of themes. First, he uses those fragments that begin on *C* as opening bars, pairing them with the *D* fragments which serve as third bars. Then he takes those that begin on *E* and *F* and shows how they can stand as third bars, the first two bars being identical in all twelve of this second group of themes. Example 3 quotes two of the first type and four of the second:

Example 3 Riepel: Permutations as parts of themes[21]

Riepel's rubric for this section, pages 25–32, in the *Inhalt*, not only states very clearly how important he regards permutation but also gives the colour of his views; he is concerned principally with the practical, the mechanical aspects of musical composition, with solid, effective musical rhetoric, and not with abstract mathematical speculations. He says:

'The unique ars permutatoria, by which one can invent many more than 99 themes in one day, is at least 99 times more healthy for musical composition than the above-mentioned mathematical speculations.'[22]

Later, in vol. 3 (*Gründliche Erklärung*),[23] Riepel turns to *ars combinatoria*, to discuss simple combinations of tones taken two, three, four at a time, illustrating some hundred or more combinations of bowing involving the relative positions of slurred or detached notes. Violinists, upon seeing these, may be reminded of their own early experiences as they struggled through the musical tongue-twisters that made up the bulk of Sevçik's studies for the violin.

Melodic permutation is treated even more thoroughly in a manuscripted treatise on musical composition by Ziegler.[24] Ziegler gives several hundred permutations and variations of the C major triad, showing how the student can invent motives in different metres, rhythms, contours, and styles. Example 4 illustrates Ziegler's method:

4

Ziegler: Melodic permutation (25)

Galeazzi[26] prepares the student for large-scale composition by first showing him how he can invent suitable figures out of combinations and permutations. This applies only to those who cannot invent their own. He says:

'We find many who can proceed with a given figure with little effort but who have insuperable difficulties when they have to invent new material. Here is something that can assist (in invention) with which one can discover a hundred, a thousand in the twinkling of an eye: it may appear puerile but first experiment with it and then judge.'[27]

Galeazzi then tells the student to write the letters of the tonic triad on cards and to choose one at random; next, the seven letters of the scale are written, and three or four are chosen at random. The tones represented by the letters are then put in order to form a simple musical figure. A typical rhythm is superimposed upon this figure; the figure is counterstated, and thus a theme is born. Example 5 quotes Galeazzi's illustrations, all of which reflect the familiar late eighteenth-century *galant* manner:

5 Galeazzi: Melodic invention by means of combinations (28)

Galeazzi explains the scope of his method by demonstrating permutations and combinations of four letters. He then says that if the eight notes of the octave are combined with values of minims and crotchets one can obtain 20922789888000 different melodies, and by adding quavers to the permutations the enormous sum of 62044840173323943936000 melodies is available.[29]

All the theorists who treat of permutation, from Mersenne to Galeazzi, do so for a practical reason—to unlock the imagination of the student. The method is mechanical; the materials are few and simple; but the possibilities are unthinkably vast. If we think of the device as a way of obtaining a *prius factus*, then it does not differ essentially from taking an *ostinato*, a *cantus firmus*, a motto or a known melody as a point of departure for composition. As such it need not be spurned even by the experienced composer.

2. *Phrase and period*

When we combine the permutations of a single set of notes and time values with other sets in order to work out phrases and periods of 4 to 16 bars in length, we arrive at sums that represent the powers or multiples of the permutations. For example, if we assume that Galeazzi's last sum stands for two-bar patterns, an eight-bar period could involve the number cited carried to its third power, a figure of 72 ciphers. Permutation is useless for teaching composition on this level; its principal value lies in the manipulation of a few components. For larger units of structure, *combination* is the method employed; this limits and prescribes the number of alternatives and the place where they may be put.

Riepel proceeds along these lines as he works out melodic combinations in the construction of minuets, concertos, and symphonies. Within a given model he seeks to achieve optimum effects by substituting figures, phrases, and cadences. The skill and taste of the student are challenged. Often Riepel will quote a two-bar beginning, then provide alternative continuations, as in Example 3 above. Koch, who was strongly influenced by Riepel, uses this same approach throughout the second and third volumes of his *Versuch*.[30]

For the beginning of the second reprise of a minuet, Riepel provides three alternatives, giving each a picturesque name that suggests its special kind of action:

1. *Monte*—a rise, signifying a sequential progression that moves upward;
2. *Ponte*—a bridge, signifying a pedal on the dominant or a progression centring around the dominant;
3. *Fonte*—a well or source (to which one descends) signifying a sequential progression that moves downward.

These are sketched in Example 6. Thus after the first period of a minuet, it would be possible to proceed at will with *monte*, *ponte* or *fonte*. Here is *ars combinatoria* that uses harmonic phrases as the pieces in the game.

6

Riepel: Monte, Ponte, Fonte (31)

Monte

Ponte

Fonte

Another line of instruction provides a bass and suggests alternate melodies upon this bass. Ziegler, in his *Anleitung*, provides a bass, fifteen bars in length; above this bass he has written six different melodies, incorporating a variety of rhythmic patterns and melodic configurations in each melody. When these melodies are reduced to their essential tones, they turn out to be basically the same. In Example 7, which gives seven measures of two of Ziegler's melodies, one could alternate figures between lines 1 and 2 or mix them at will without impairing the coherence of the music, this being the principle of the dice games. Here the combinatorial factor is a choice from the reservoir of memory and experience of the composer himself, not a throw of the dice or a spin of the top.

7

Ziegler: Alternate melodies over a bass (32)

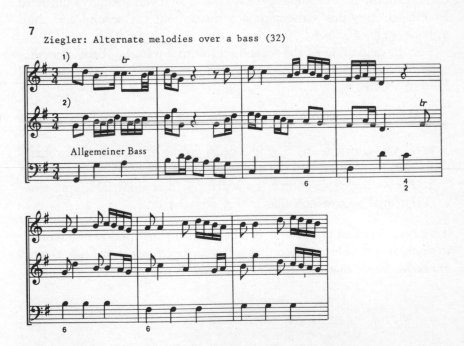

Langlé, in his *Traité de la basse sous le chant*[33] proceeds along the same lines. He gives a bass of four bars, with the following harmony: I, II⁷, V⁷, I. One hundred melodies are set to this bass. Example 8 gives the bass with two of the melodies.

Both Ziegler and Langlé exemplify their respective stylistic milieus. Ziegler's music is typically in the *galant* vein of the mid-century; it moves steadily, propelled by the *continuo* bass; its figures are congruent but there

8

Langlé: Melodies over a bass (34)

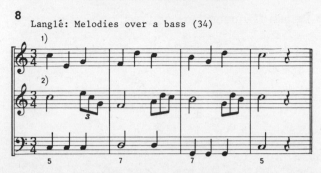

is relatively little symmetry, either in the figures themselves or in the overall phrase plan, apart from the two-bar punctuations; Telemann's music comes to mind. On the other hand, Langlé establishes a drastic symmetry and simplicity. The first three bars of each melody use similar figures; the fourth bar has but a single cadence tone. This music reflects the popular style of the classic period and the early nineteenth century; the second melody, especially, with its automatic sing-song restatements of the first figure, brings to mind the banality that renders deadly so much of the second-rate music of this time.

On the phrase and period level, the instructions of Ziegler, Riepel, Koch, Langlé, and others point to a characteristic of eighteenth-century musical construction often practised by composers and frequently sensed by listeners—the interchangeability of melodic components. This topic will be further investigated below.

3. *Alternatives in the order of keys in a piece*

For the classic style, the opposition of dominant to tonic is an axiomatic feature of harmonic structure. For the mid-century, when some remnants of ecclesiastical modal practice are still present, other alternatives are still available. Again, it is Riepel who spells this out systematically and thoroughly. On pages 112–21 of *Grundregeln*, he gives one hundred and twenty permutations of the tonal relationships that can exist in a piece in C major. Riepel takes the degrees that are related to C diatonically— G, F, e, d, and a;* these are the stations for intermediate cadences in the system of the ecclesiastical modes. One of Riepel's charts is given below, along with a scheme of tones that represents a compression of an actual harmonic form; in a full scale work there would be one or more periods between the formal cadences.

* Lower case = minor key, *e.g.*, d = D minor. Ed.

Example 9 Riepel: Harmonic permutation[35]

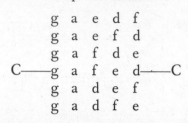

(36)

Riepel writes with a salty humour, introducing many colloquial expressions and topical references. In this vein, he assigns names to the keys centring around a tonic, names which give a clear picture of the distance, place, and authority of each key; his scheme is the counterpart of the social hierarchy of absolutism. The names are:

if *C* is the tonic

C = *Meyer* (landowner, farmer-master);
G = *Oberknecht* (chief servant);
a = *Obermagd* (chief maid);
e = *Untermagd* (second or kitchen maid);
F = *Taglohner* (day labourer);
d = *Unterläufferin* (female interloper, possibly; or a female worker in the salt factory);
c = *schwarze Gredel* (black Margaret; a local nickname for a Swedish Queen whose swarthy complexion made her look like a man)[37]

For what it is worth, it may be observed that only the first four keys belong to the *household* of *C*; the others may enter to do their bit but are apparently considered to be more remote in the key scheme. In a baroque concerto or fugue these relationships generally hold; the dominant, relative minor, and mediant are more likely to be included than the other keys.

4. *Complete movements: substitution and paraphrase*

For centuries paraphrase was a legitimate and honoured technique of musical composition, practised by the greatest masters. Parody masses,

Bach's reworking of Vivaldi concerti, Mozart's adaptation of keyboard sonatas into concerti are examples of this treatment of musical material. Variation is also a type of paraphrase. In most cases of paraphrase the basic harmonic and rhythmic structure is fixed; melody and texture are the variables. If we regard each step of the harmonic-rhythmic progression as a 'slot' into which a melodic figure can be placed, either by the choice of the composer, or, as in the dice games, by random selection, paraphrase can be taken as a kind of combinatorial play. In the case of the games, the number of available figures is fixed; when the composer draws upon his invention, there is no tallying the number of suitable figures.

Paraphrase is often recommended to the student as a means of learning how to put an entire piece together. Crotch, in his *Elements of Composition*,[38] recommends the following:

ist. To make variations to airs in the manner of different masters;
2nd. To put different basses to a given treble.
3rd. To put different trebles to a given bass;
4th. To put different trebles and basses to a given inner part.
5th. To write accompaniments on a ground bass'[39]

Galeazzi makes similar recommendations, using the term *mascherare*, i.e., to camouflage.[40] Later, Czerny, in his *School of Practical Composition*, says:

'the best method is undoubtedly that which Joseph Haydn recommended to his pupils:—Let the beginner, in the first place, exercise himself in little sonatas, which he must so compose according to the models chosen that the same key, time, form of the periods, number of bars, and even each modulation shall be strictly followed, but be it well observed, he must take pains to invent ideas, melodies, and passages as different as possible from each of the models chosen'.[41]

This was the method demonstrated by Kirnberger in his little pamphlet *Methode Sonaten aus'm Ermel ʒu schüddeln*.[42] This booklet explains a device by which the bass and treble parts of a given model are in turn recomposed or paraphrased, so that a new composition may result.[43] The same procedure is used by Daube in his *Anleitung ʒur Erfindung der Melodie*[44] to provide three variants upon sixteen measures of a symphonic movement. Daube also suggests that Haydn's music be used for models.

As an illustration of paraphrase, the following excerpt from Portmann's *Leichtes Lehrbuch der Harmonie*[45] will serve. On pages 39–56 of
the appended examples, Portmann sets down the following material:

1. A ground-plan of a sonata in D major, giving the measures, the
   actual bass notes and the fundamental bass. These are followed by:
2. A sonata by Portmann himself, composed according to this plan;
3. The source of the plan, the first movement of the sonata in D major,
   K.284, by Mozart.[46]

Mozart's sonata is a typical Italian opera *sinfonia* transferred to the keyboard; its unisons, its bold and simple figures, its well-defined contrasts
and unflagging momentum which hurries the music to its cadences are
familiar musical qualities in this *genre*. While Portmann's music retains
some of this quality, its figures are more decorative; its lines of action are
less direct; the integration of figures is less tight than Mozart's; the overall effect is more typical of pianism than of orchestral style. Example 10
reproduces a portion of each sonata.

10

Portmann: Paraphrase of a sonata by Mozart   (47)

Beyond this point, we can associate the well-known eighteenth-century habits of transcribing, borrowing, rescoring, adapting, and even *pasticcio* with the idea of *ars combinatoria*; these represent combinations, substitutions, and permutations in the field of musical performance.

Returning to the games, we find two cases in which the spirit of *galanterie* that led to their devising is associated with a more serious purpose. The first is Wiedeburg's *Musikalisches Charten-Spiel ex G dur*[48] whereby a musical composition can be easily put together for the pleasure and practice of keyboard players and for the use of organists in small towns and in the country. Wiedeburg's game will produce a *praeludium* of thirty-six measures; in his preface, Wiedeburg states that he is carrying out the project Kirnberger refers to in the *Menuetten-Componist*, to apply the method to larger compositions.

The second game that has more serious implications is C. P. E. Bach's *Einfall*.[49] His publication consists of twelve tables of musical tones, and the instructions for their use. When the material is put into normal musical formation we have nine treble melodies and nine bass melodies. Each first measure of the treble is invertible with each first bar of the bass; the same is true of all six bars of the game. Apart from the billions of invertible counterpoints that can be made, the striking feature of this exercise is its skeleton. When all the ornamental tones are removed, the result is a first species counterpoint in thirds and sixths. Example 11 gives a sample counterpoint to illustrate the type of ornamentation, and the basic progression upon which the game was built.

11

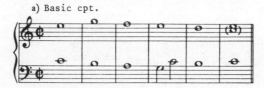

Bach must have begun with the ground plan, later adding the figuration. The species counterpoint in this example is not the counterpoint of J. S. Bach's fugues with its compact, uneven harmonic rhythm and its broadly-gauged lines of movement. Rather, it is the counterpoint of Fux and his school, based on a *cantus firmus* whose notes are long and of equal duration; in this technique, the phrases are short and the cadences clear and final. Species counterpoint was taken over bodily into the music of the classic style. We can find hundreds, if not thousands, of short passages in which one part elaborates against a line of half or whole notes in another part. Much classic music that is thoroughly *galant* in spirit will reveal a two part counterpoint in first or second species when the elaboration is lifted away, as in Example 11. The training of the classic master in the Fuxian tradition is well known, but the degree to which this training entered into their original work is yet to be assessed; the clues provided by C. P. E. Bach's *Einfall* and by many references to this technique in eighteenth-century musical theory suggest that species counterpoint had a deep and pervasive influence in classic music.

There is no way to assess the extent to which *ars combinatoria* might have entered into the composition of music in the eighteenth century. Dice games and instructions from music theory are specific; we can follow the process, step by step. But this is not the case with the composer's imagination. We cannot tell when and if he had recourse to combinations and permutations. But the spirit of the *ars combinatoria* can be felt throughout eighteenth-century music. The short, well-defined melodic stereotypes available to all composers; the few established paths taken by the harmonic-rhythmic periodicity—these invited the manipulations, the jugglings and substitutions that make up combinatorial play. The game was certainly not played formally, but we can easily presume an impalpable factor of chance as the composer reached into his reservoir of memory and experience to find a figure that would fit at a given place. Choice, based on skill and taste, would then modify any element of pure chance that may have influenced the selection of a figure. In any case, paraphrase bespeaks *ars combinatoria* very clearly, and who is to say that the principal structural layout in classic music, the I–V; X–I plan, which shapes the two-reprise dance form and its larger sibling, the sonata form, is not a framework within which composers were constantly creating fresh music by means of melodic combinatorial play?

Sometimes the composer tells us to pay heed to *ars combinatoria*. We would miss the finest points of rhetoric were we to overlook the permutations of melodic figures in the recapitulations of the first movements of Haydn's 'Oxford' (No. 92) and 'Drum Roll' (No. 103) Symphonies, as compared to their original order in the expositions. The following examples illustrate permutation and combination from the music of Mozart and Beethoven. Mozart loved to turn things topsy-turvy; in Example 12, he subverts the role of the authentic cadence. Ordinarily, it would appear in bars 3 and 4, and 7 and 8. Conversely, bars 3 and 4, and 7 and 8, having an upbeat or antecedent character, would appear at the beginnings of their respective phrases. Through permutation, Mozart has created an oddly comic effect. Furthermore, since the cadence is at the beginning of the period, it sounds as though it were an echo of the

12

Mozart: 'Jupiter' Symphony K.551, Menuetto (Trio)

a) Actual arrangement with permutations: answer-question; cadence-upbeat

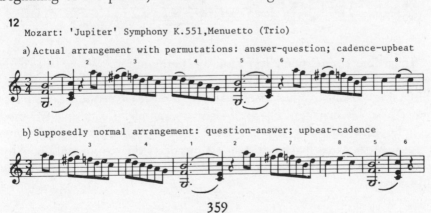

b) Supposedly normal arrangement: question-answer; upbeat-cadence

cadence of the minuet which precedes the trio. In fact, throughout this trio, the cadence never seems to find its proper place; it is used for everything *but* a cadence, and this would seem to have been the point of the trio—to put the cadence out of countenance.

In Example 13, we have the permuted version of the theme from the *Alla Tedesca* movement of Beethoven's Quartet in B♭ major, opus 130. This version appears near the end of the movement, having been heard eight times previously in its normal formation. Hence, we cannot miss the crazy-quilt effect created when the pieces are scattered and re-arranged, an impression enhanced by the pointillistic fragmentation in range. The rhythm of this movement has an automatic, clocklike regularity, expressed in long chains of four-measure phrases; but the dynamics and texture carry such detail of nuance as to approach preciousness of manner, a kind of parody of a German waltz. Thus, the oddness of the scattered form is prefigured, and when it is reached, the scattered form suggests that the wheels of the clock had momentarily gone wild, re-arranging themselves in some grotesque action. Immediately thereafter, several false starts toward correction are made; the true correction, *i.e.* the theme in its proper form, takes place in the final period of the movement.

13

Beethoven: Quartet in B♭ major, Op. 130, 'Alla Tedesca'

a) normal version

b) permuted version

Invertible counterpoint is a kind of permutation. When two parts are involved, no calculation is needed, since the permutation is limited to but a single change. When there are three or more elements, the composer must plan his changes. The best-known example of multiple inverted counterpoint occurs in the last movement of Mozart's 'Jupiter' Symphony. Mozart uses five figures; the strings carry the action, reinforced by wind and brass. Example 14 gives the table of permutations used by Mozart:

Example 14 Mozart: Permutation of counterpoint in the finale of the "Jupiter" Symphony

Violin I			2	1	3	4	5	1
Violin II		2	1	3	4	5	2	3
Viola	2	1	3	4	5	2	1	2
Violoncello	1	3	4	5	2	1	3	4
Contrabass			2	1	3	4	5	

Other instances of systematic permutation in multiple counterpoint are:

Mozart:	Quintet in C major, K. 515, first movement, development
Mozart:	Quintet in E♭ major, K. 614, finale, bars 111–150
Beethoven:	Symphony No. 6 in F major, opus 68, first movement
Haydn:	Quartet in C major, opus 20, No. 2, finale

From the foregoing material, the following points may be made in summary:

1. *Ars combinatoria*, explicitly or implicitly, was an important *modus operandi* in eighteenth-century musical construction, as indicated both by internal and external evidence.

2. *Ars combinatoria* could be applied to any element of musical construction—melody, harmony, rhythm, phrase structure, counterpoint, large-scale form.

3. Eighteenth-century musical materials were especially adaptable to the arrangements of *ars combinatoria*; the simple, clear, and symmetrical layouts that characterize the structure expedited permutation and combination; the component pieces could easily be joined, shifted, or substituted.

4. On the surface, *ars combinatoria* in eighteenth-century music appears to be schematic, mechanical, perhaps frivolous in its intentions. But it also helps us to recognize the point at which the schematic becomes vital. Thus, it reflects some important eighteenth-century views. As one makes a study of the numbers and kinds of relationships that can exist among a given number of factors, judgement is brought into play; skill and taste will decide which of the combinations have a greater felicity of effect. Thus, *ars combinatoria* is not composition but a resource in its

service; it is a rational, intellectual device that can help to spark musical feeling, to set the clockwork in motion, to stir the mechanical into life.

NOTES

1 Johann Philipp Kirnberger, *Der allezeit fertige Menuetten-und Polonoisenkomponist.* Berlin: Winter, 1757.

2 Piere Hoegi, *A Tabular System Whereby the Art of Composing Minuets Is made so Easy that any Person, without the least knowledge of Musick, may compose ten thousand, all different, and in the most Pleasing and Correct Manner.* London: Welcker (1770?).

3 E. F. de Lange, *Le Toton Harmonique ou Nouveau Jeu de Hazard.* Liege: Desoer, n.d.

4 [Anonymous], *Ludus Melothedicus ou Le Jeu de Dez Harmonique.* Paris: de la Chevardiere (176–?).

5 Carl Philipp Emanuel Bach, 'Einfall einen doppelten Contrapunct in der Octave von sechs Tacten zu machen ohne die Regeln davon zu wissen', in *Historisch–Kritische Beyträge zur Aufnahme der Musik,* Friedrich Wilhelm Marpurg, editor, vol. 3, part 1, pp. 167 ff. Berlin: Lange, 1754–78.

6 Wolfgang Amadeus Mozart, *Anleitung zum Componiren von Walzern so viele man will vermittlest zweier Würfel ohne etwas von der Musik oder Composition zu verstehen.* Berlin: Simrock (1793).

7 Franz Joseph Haydn, *Gioco Filarmonico, o sia maniera facile per comporre un infinito numero di minuettie trio anche senza sapere il contrapunto.* Naples: Marescalchi (1793).

8 Maximilian Stadler, *Table Pour Composer des Menuets et des Trios a l'infinie; avec deux Dez a Jouer.* Paris: Wenck, n.d. (1780 is the date given in E. L. Gerber, *Historisch-biographisches Lexikon der Tonkünstler* as the time of composition. Stadler's music is almost identical to that of Haydn's *Gioco,* except that Haydn's is scored for two violins and bass, while Stadler's is for keyboard. Nos. 6, 7, 8 listed in these notes employ the same dice table of numbers.)

9 Antonio Callegari, *L'Art de composer de la Musique Sans en Connaitre les Elémens.* Paris: Boudin, 1802.

10 Pasquale Ricci, *Au plus Heureux Jeux Harmoniques pour Composer des Minuets ou des Contredances au sort d'un dex.* (Apparently published by the composer, no place, no date.)

11 Henricus Glareanus, *Dodekachordon.* Basel, 1547.

12 Marin Mersenne, *Harmonie Universelle.* Paris, 1636.

13 Athanasius Kircher, *Musurgia universalis.* Rome, 1650.

14 Wolfgang Caspar Printz, *Phrynis Mytilenaeus oder der Satyrischer Componist.* Dresden, 1696.

15 Sebastian de Brossard, *Dictionnaire de Musique.* Paris: Ballard, 1703.

16 Johann Mattheson, *Der vollkommene Capellmeister.* Hamburg: Herold, 1739.

17 Johann David Heinichen, *Der Generalbass in der Komposition.* Dresden, 1728.

18 Jacob Adlung, *Anleitung zur der musikalischen Gelahrtheit.* Erfurt: Jungnicol, 1758.

19 Joseph Riepel, *Grundregeln zur Tonordnung insgemein.* Frankfurt, 1755.

20 p. 27.

21 pp. 28, 29.

22 Table of contents.

23 Joseph Riepel, *Gründliche Erklärung der Tonordnung insbesondere.* Frankfurt, 1757, pp. 15–21.

24 Christian Gottlob Ziegler, *Anleitung zur musikalischen Composition*. Quedlinburg, MS. 1739.

25 p. 84.

26 Francesco Galeazzi, *Elementi teorico-pratici di musica*. Rome: Puccinelli, 1791–6.

27 Vol. II, p. 248.

28 Vol. II, examples, Table VII.

29 Vol II, p. 250.

30 Heinrich Christoph Koch, *Versuch einer Anleitung zur Composition*. Rudolstadt and Leipzig: Böhme, 1782–93.

31 *Grundregeln*, pp. 45–7.

32 *op. cit.*, p. 157.

33 Honoré F. Langlé. *Traité de la basse sous le chant, precedé de toutes les regles de la composition*. Paris: Naderman, 1798.

34 p. 266.

35 p. 112.

36 p. 113.

37 p. 66.

38 William Crotch, *Elements of Musical Composition*. London: Longmans, 1812.

39 p. 136.

40 *op. cit.*, p. 251.

41 Carl Czerny, *School of Practical Composition*, opus, 600, 3 vols., tr. by John Bishop. London: Cocks and Co., 1848. Book I, p. 36.

42 Johann Philipp Kirnberger, *Methode Sonaten aus'm Ermel zu Schüddeln*. Berlin: Bernstiel, 1783.

43 William Newman, in the *Musical Quarterly*, October 1961, discusses this topic, quotes the introductory text, and gives the example itself, the model for which is the gigue from the 6th French Suite of J. S. Bach.

44 Johann Friedrich Daube, *Anleitung zur Erfindung der Melodie und ihrer Fortsetzung*. Vienna: Täubel, 1797. Daube's illustrations are quoted in part in the present author's article. 'Eighteenth-Century Theories of Musical Period Structure', Musical Quarterly, October, 1956, p. 445.

45 Johann Gottlieb Portmann, *Leichtes Lehrbuch der Harmonie, Composition und des Generalbasses*. Darmstadt: Will, 1789.

46 p. 39 of the musical examples.

47 p. 43, p. 50.

48 Michael Johann Fridrich Wiedeburg, *Musikalisches Charten-Spiel ex G dur*. Zurich: Winter, 1788.

49 E. Eugene Helm, in *Journal of Music Theory*, Spring, 1966, discusses Bach's *Einfall*, reproducing all the tables and the melodies that can be extracted from them.

GLORIA ROSE

FATHER AND SON:
SOME ATTRIBUTIONS TO J. S. BACH
BY C. P. E. BACH

Karl Geiringer has truly noted that 'the list of chamber music works attributed to J. S. Bach had to be drastically revised and curtailed in recent years'.[1] We are all indebted to the recent Bach scholarship so gracefully assimilated by Dr Geiringer; yet the list may in some directions have been curtailed too drastically. What starts as a cautious question-mark in the Neue Bach-Ausgabe or in Wolfgang Schmieder's monumental catalogue soon gets taken as an absolute rejection, and Bach is not even left with the benefit of the doubt.

I have suggested elsewhere[2] that J. S. Bach may still, on reasoned grounds, be thought the most likely author of the song 'Bist du bei mir' (BWV 508) and the Sonata in C major for two violins and *continuo* (BWV 1037). I should like to suggest here that the question of autho rship is still open as regards the Suite in A major for violin and harpsichord (BWV 1025), the Sonata in E flat major fo r flute and harpsichord (BWV 1031), and the Sonata in C major for flute and *continuo* (BWV 1033).[3]

In Schmieder,[4] the Suite in A major (BWV 1025) bears the note 'Echtheit angezweifelt', authenticity doubted. It is not, of course, strictly the authenticity of the music or the manuscripts which is doubted. 'Authenticity doubted' is understood as meaning 'authorship uncertain'.

Virtual certainty about the authorship of B WV 1025 is, however, just what other Bach scholars have ventured to express. Ulrich Siegele, for example, says without giving a reason: 'The work can hardly derive from J. S. Bach.'[5] Hans Eppstein says yet more emphatically, on grounds of musical style: 'Also this composition can on no account derive from Bach's hand.'[6]

Arguments from musical style are always legitimate and often weighty, but it is not always easy to know how much weight to give them in comparison with other considerations, and especially in comparison with reputable attributions contemporary or nearly contemporary with the music. This difficulty arises very conspicuously in the present case. As both Siegele and Eppstein point out, BWV 1025 was attributed to J. S. Bach by C. P. E. Bach. BWV 1025 was copied out in two partbooks by C. P. E. Bach, who gave it the title: 'A dur/Trio für's obligate Clavier und eine Violine/Von J. S. Bach.'[7] There is also an arrangement of BWV 1025 for harpsichord;[8] here the first brace of music is in the hand of J. S. Bach.[9]

The situation is similar with regard to BWV 1031 and BWV 1033. Eppstein says, again for stylistic reasons, that J. S. Bach's authorship of BWV 1031 'hardly comes into question'.[10] Yet one source of BWV 1031 (copied by an anonymous scribe) was entitled by C. P. E. Bach: 'Es d./Trio/Für's obligate Clavier ū. die Flöte/Von/J. S. Bach.'[11]

The authorship of BWV 1033 is also questioned by Bach scholars.[12] Yet this work, too, was copied out by C. P. E. Bach, who probably, according to Paul Kast, gave it the title: 'C dur/SONATA/a/Traversa/e/Continuo/di/Joh. Seb. Bach.'[13] Another copy of BWV 1033 was made by Michel, the chief copyist of C. P. E. Bach in Hamburg;[14] Michel gave it the title: 'Sonata/a/Traversa/e/Continuo/d./Joh. Seb. Bach.'[15]

Thus all three works—BWV 1025, 1031 and 1033—confront us with disagreement between a reputable original attribution and a reputable modern analysis of musical style. BWV 1025, BWV 1031, and perhaps also BWV 1033, were attributed to J. S. Bach by C. P. E. Bach; and all three works are considered by various Bach experts to be not in the style of J. S. Bach.

Sometimes an entire work makes so strong an overall impression of being by J. S. Bach that any unusualness of detail may have to be accepted as simply something that we did not previously know about his style. The overall impression made by BWV 1025, 1031 and 1033, however, is by no means of this convincing quality.

In detail, I should like to take up Eppstein's statement[16] that 'nowhere does the bass take part in the thematic work' of BWV 1031. On the contrary, it does so in bars 40, 42, 49, and 50 of the first movement; in bars 19 and 21 of the second movement; and in bars 46, 48, 53, 55, 70,

84, 128, 130, 135 and 137 of the third movement. The following examples are taken from Mus. ms. Bach P 649 in the Berlin Staatsbibliothek.

Music examples for 'Father and Son' by Gloria Rose

Ex. 1. BWV 1031, first movement, bars 40–42.
Ex. 2. BWV 1031, first movement, bars 49–50.
Ex. 3. BWV 1031, second movement, bars 19–21.

Ex. 4. BWV 1031, third movement, bars 46–48.
Ex. 5. BWV 1031, third movement, bar 70.

Nor would this point afford any proof, since not every movement by J. S. Bach uses thematic participation of the bass. In slow movements, especially, the bass may function chiefly as a harmonic support. It is too precarious to rely on this sort of detail for absolute certainty. We cannot be absolutely certain what a composer so versatile might not sometimes have done—short of something absolutely unmusical. Eppstein himself adds: 'That the kind of melody, especially in the slow movements, occasionally reminds us strongly of Bach, should not be misunderstood'.[17] But this precisely is the question. Is it being misunderstood?

It has been suggested that C. P. E. Bach composed BWV 1031 himself, but ascribed it to his father.[18] Now it seems that another son, W. F. Bach, really did ascribe one or two (but only one is certain) of his own compositions to his father, apparently for pecuniary reasons.[19] But Wilhelm Friedemann Bach and Carl Philipp Emanuel Bach were two different men, with different personalities, and in different financial and other circumstances. We cannot assume that motives which affected the one might equally affect the other. From all that we know of the character of C. P. E. Bach, and of the high admiration and respect in which he held his father's music,[20] it seems most improbable.

There is no external, contemporary evidence that BWV 1031 was composed by C. P. E. Bach; and there is no internal, musical evidence.[21] But suppose that C. P. E. Bach, not having composed the music, was genuinely misinformed as to who did compose it? Suppose that he sincerely but mistakenly believed it to be his father's music? This is possible; but again it seems not very probable.

C. P. E. Bach was a man of honest character and sound musical judgment. He stood very close to his father: closer than us by 200 years and the warmest of family ties. He was in a very good position indeed to know what his father had composed. An undoubted attribution in the hand of C. P. E. Bach is about as strong a piece of external evidence as we can hope to find, short of a signed autograph by the composer himself. This is not even a case of conflicting original attributions, since no source has been found in which BWV 1025, BWV 1031 or BWV 1033 is attributed to any other composer than J. S. Bach.

Should we ask how C. P. E. Bach could have ascribed music falsely to his father? Or should we not ask, instead, if we need to expand our conception of J. S. Bach's range of styles? It seems that modern scholars, in considering BWV 1025, 1031 and 1033, have put stylistic analysis before contemporary evidence: a reversal of the usual scholarly method. Whatever conclusions we may reach about the musical style of these works, the fact remains that at least two of them, and possibly all three, were attributed to J. S. Bach by C. P. E. Bach.

The older generation of Bach scholars accepted these attributions at full value, and though they were not always right, we have no new facts in this case on which to base an opposite conclusion. We may have hesitations, but we have no grounds for presenting them as certainties. It seems to me wisest, for the present, not to claim absolute certainty about the authorship of BWV 1025, 1031 and 1033. As Karl Geiringer says, writing about Bach research in general: 'even a confirmed optimist cannot assume that definite solutions will be achieved in the near future; indeed it seems more likely that certain answers will never be forthcoming.'[22] That is the realistic view of a very able and very honest scholar.

NOTES

1 Karl Geiringer, *Johann Sebastian Bach: The Culmination of an Era* (New York, 1966), p. 302, n. 1.

2 *Acta musicologica*, XL (1968), 203–19.

3 For their kind help in supplying information and microfilms of these works, I wish to thank Dr. Karl-Heinz Köhler, Director of the Music Division, Deutsche Staatsbibliothek, E. Berlin; and Dr. Heinz Ramge, Director of the Music Division, Staatsbibliothek, Preußischer Kulturbesitz, W. Berlin.

4 Wolfgang Schmieder, *Thematisch-systematisches Verzeichnis der musikalischen Werke von Johann Sebastian Bach* (Leipzig, 1950), p. 571.

5 Ulrich Siegele, *Kompositionsweise und Bearbeitungstechnik in der Instrumentalmusik Johann Sebastian Bachs* (unpublished doctoral dissertation, Eberhard-Karls-Universität, Tübingen, 1957), p. 117.

6 Hans Eppstein, *Studien über J. S. Bachs Sonaten für ein Melodieinstrument und obligates Cembalo* (Uppsala, 1966), p. 187.

7 W. Berlin, Staatsbibliothek der Stiftung Preußischer Kulturbesitz, Mus. ms. Bach St 462.

My authorities for the handwriting of C. P. E. Bach in this MS are Georg von Dadelsen, *Bemerkungen zur Handschrift Johann Sebastian Bachs, seiner Familie und seines Kreises* (Trossingen, 1957), p. 40; and Paul Kast, *Die Bach-Handschriften der Berliner Staatsbibliothek* (Trossingen, 1958), p. 88. When he copied St 462, C. P. E. Bach was young, according to Dadelsen; in his middle period, according to Kast.

8 E. Berlin, Deutsche Staatsbibliothek, Mus. ms. Bach P 226, pp. 33–40.

9 My authorities for the handwriting of J. S. Bach in this MS are Georg von Dadelsen, *Beiträge zur Chronologie der Werke Johann Sebastian Bachs* (Trossingen, 1958), p. 117; and

Kast, *Die Bach-Handschriften*, p. 15. Dadelsen dates the handwriting 'about 1744/46 to 1749'; Kast indicates 'late'.

10 Eppstein, *Studien*, p. 179.

11 W. Berlin, Staatsbibliothek, Mus. ms. Bach P 649.

My authorities for the handwriting of C. P. E. Bach in this MS are Dadelsen, *Bemerkungen*, p. 26; and Kast, *Die Bach-Handschriften*, p. 40 (there mistakenly listed as BWV 1032). Dadelsen specifies C. P. E. Bach as an older man.

12 See Hans-Peter Schmitz, NBA, Ser. VI, Bd. 3 (Kassel, 1963), p. vi.

13 W. Berlin, Staatsbibliothek, Mus. ms. Bach St 460.

My authorities for the handwriting of C. P. E. Bach in this MS are Dadelsen, *Bemerkungen*, p. 40; and Kast, *Die Bach-Handschriften*, p. 88. Both Dadelsen and Kast specify the young C. P. E. Bach. Kast indicates that the title page is probably in the hand of C. P. E. Bach.

14 Dadelsen, *Bemerkungen*, p. 24; Kast, *Die Bach-Handschriften*, p. 87.

15 W. Berlin, Staatsbibliothek, Mus. ms. Bach St 440.

16 Eppstein, *Studien*, p. 179.

17 Eppstein, *Studien*, pp. 180–1.

18 Hans-Peter Schmitz, in a letter to me of January 27, 1968.

19 Martin Falck, *Wilhelm Friedemann Bach: Sein Leben und seine Werke* (Leipzig, 1913), p. 53. Falck wrote that 'Friedmann's authorship for the Kyrie is not entirely certain'. Subsequent scholars have ignored this caution attached to the authorship of the Kyrie in G minor, BWV Anh. 168.

20 See the brilliant article by Dragan Plamenac, 'New Light on the Last Years of Carl Philipp Emanuel Bach', *Musical Quarterly*, XXXV (1949), 565–87. C. P. E. Bach's high regard for his father is also discussed by Karl Geiringer, *The Bach Family: Seven Generations of Creative Genius* (New York, 1954), p. 351.

21 Dr. E. Eugene Helm, the author of a forthcoming book on C. P. E. Bach, has very kindly considered this question for me. In Dr Helm's opinion (March 8, 1968), neither BWV 1031 nor BWV 1025 is in the style of C. P. E. Bach.

22 Geiringer, *Johann Sebastian Bach*, p. v.

LÁSZLÓ SOMFAI

A BOLD ENHARMONIC MODULATORY MODEL IN JOSEPH HAYDN'S STRING QUARTETS

Musicology has still to deal in depth with the bold harmonic experiments undertaken by Haydn. Tendencies which came to fruition in Romantic music may be noticed here. Karl Geiringer's often inspiring and thought-provoking monograph on Haydn draws attention to the slow movement of the String Quartet opus 76 in E flat major, which 'with its bold enharmonic changes, the unusual formal structure and the motion of the outer parts tying the different tonalities together, is to some extent removed from the classical way of expression'.[1] This study presents a specific model of modulation to be found in the movement in question. Our model anticipates the type of modulations introduced on the well-tempered piano by Schubert and Chopin. However—and this makes it unique!—with Haydn it originates within the confines of the 'pure' and 'tempered' string quartet texture. In this type of modulation, theoretically speaking, the *recapitulation does not start in the tonic key but in its enharmonic equivalent with flats in the signature* (e.g. B major—C flat major or E flat major—F♭♭ major). Although such devices were used by Mozart and even by Bach[2] in their keyboard compositions, Haydn pursued a method of his own to solve the problem. In this modulation he does not employ chords allowing enharmonic interpretations; in the course of the modulations there only occur diatonic or obvious chromatic progressions, and the tonal connection between the succeeding keys is clearly noticeable. However, instead of the logical succession of keys with many sharps or flats Haydn, thanks to small enharmonic deceptions, remains within the keys playable on strings and finally the recapitulation is sounded in the key of the exposition. The sequence of this fascinating alternation of fictional and real keys constitutes one of the great bravura achievements in Haydn's music. To perform such a piece with clean intonation seems even to-day a supreme challenge for masterly performers.

Among the many instances available we have selected five movements written between 1793 and 1803 (opus 71 in E flat/I; opus 76 in G/IV; opus 76 in E flat/II; opus 77 in F/I; opus 103/I). We shall present them not in chronological order, but start with rather simple types of modulation and proceed to more complicated ones.

To understand the latter a few general remarks have to be made. The 'tension' between the chords or keys placed next to each other without connecting modulations may be measured through their distance within the circle of fifths.[3] In the Viennese classical style of Haydn's period the most distant and therefore most 'modern' *direct* relationships in major or minor triads or tonalities do not in general exceed the distance for four or perhaps five fifths; for instance:

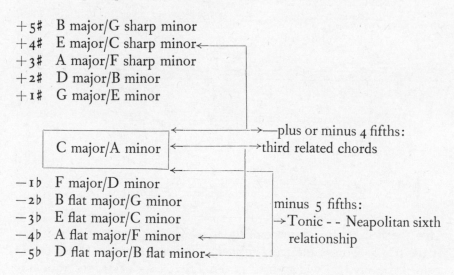

To this may be added that these comparatively distant connections may still be discerned by our ear. It is for instance impossible to 'hear' a sequence of 'third related chords' like C major—A flat major (−4) as C major—G sharp major (+8 fifths) or a change from major to minor like C major—C minor (−3) as C major—B sharp minor (+9 fifths).

To put it more cautiously: our tonal hearing is unable to recognize immediately an enharmonic change of +8, +9 fifths, if the same succession of keys without enharmonic change presents a well known, natural sequence of tonalities.

All this had to be mentioned because in the modulations to be discussed in this study, Haydn commits his small acts of enharmonic deceptions almost always with simple triads of −4 fifths (third relation) or −3 fifths (*maggiore—minore*) in order to stay within keys which are comparatively easy to play.

The purest, simplest realization of this modulatory model is to be found in the *Andante grazioso* in B flat major of the Quartet opus 103:

After the B flat major cadence of the first section (bar 28) the basic key of the trio section is the third related G flat major (−4). After the D major harmony,[4] so widely used in the Trio's conclusion, the recapitulation (bar 71) begins in B flat major, again a third relation (−4). The enharmonic 'deception' occurs in the middle of the Trio section. After the cadence in D flat major (bar 48) constituting a *maggiore*, we hear a *minore* (−3) of D flat minor, although Haydn actually wrote C sharp minor. (The continuation in C sharp minor is logical: modulation through E major and A minor to G major). Haydn takes care of the pure

372

intonation by having the D flat major chords followed by *melodic* C sharp minor broken chords, instead of C sharp minor chords. Under the leadership of the first violin, the different instruments appear in succession and thus have sufficient time to 'rectify' their intonation.

In the opening *Vivace* of the E flat major Quartet opus 71 the pure intonation of the passage spelled enharmonically is somewhat more problematic, though the quick tempo facilitates the transition. The plan of modulation of the development section starting in E flat minor is as follows:

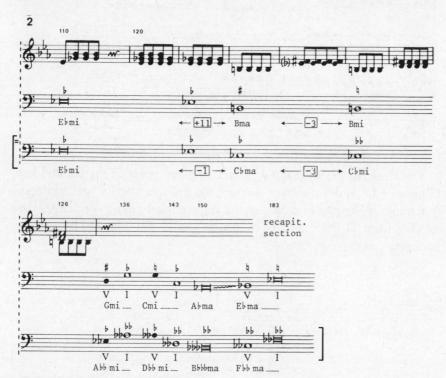

Here Haydn bridges the distance of −4 fifths from E flat minor to B minor (= E flat minor to C flat minor), third related keys, by 2 steps: they consist of −1 fifth and −3 fifth divided, E flat minor—C flat major —C flat minor. The transition to the enharmonic spelling proceeds stepwise and this ensures a comparatively clean intonation. This is Haydn's innovation: there are no enharmonic progressions from G flat to F sharp or from E flat to D sharp. The different instruments perform the intervals, familiar and relatively easy to perform, of an augmented second (E flat—

F sharp in the viola bar 121–123; in V. I bars 123–125) while the third (note D) of the B minor chords is entrusted to the open string (V. II bar 125, Va. bar 126). He even takes care that the third and fifth of the B major chords presented in the mixed spelling (B–E flat—F sharp) should not sound simultaneously with the root of the triad, *i.e.* with the basic note B (cf bar 123) so as to avoid a 'false' major triad:

The finale of the G major Quartet opus 76 starts in the parallel key, G minor.[5] In its development section, the enharmonically spelled deception appears likewise in a passage of third related keys (−4 fifths), thus turning from D flat minor to A major (= D flat minor—B♭♭ major, bars 100–102):

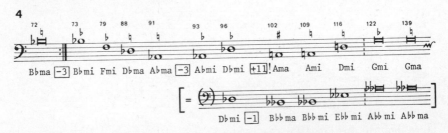

To achieve 'pure' intonation here means solving an extremely delicate problem. Though the melodically broken chords are entrusted at the critical moment to the first violin (and he may turn for support to the objective security of the open A string), the viola is forced four bars earlier (starting at bar 98) to fit the note E as third into a chord of D flat minor; the second violin plays the chromatic progression A flat–A, while the cello even performs the enharmonic exchange of D flat to C sharp:

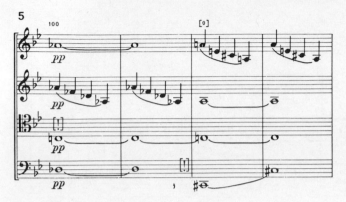

Yet this famous passage in the G major quartet is still much easier to handle than the fantastic B major 'Fantasia', the slow movement of the E flat major Quartet opus 76. A reduction of the modulatory model in bars 1–60 looks as follows (the continuation, the main section of the movement not being problematic from the tonal point of view):

```
6
 1              20          31                    49            60
 Theme 'scale' Theme 'scale' Theme   'modulation'   Theme 'scale' ‖ Theme ∿
                                 +10      -9            +9
 Bma- C#mi.....Ema,Emi- Gma..Bbma,Bbmi- Bma  G#mi Abma  ......   Bma
                                 -2                +3 [=G#ma!]  -3    [Cbma]
                              [=Cbma  Abmi    Abma               Cbma]
```

The modulation of −1 fifth to the relative major key in bars 16–20 from C sharp minor to E major, both presented scalewise, is surprising but, however, still easily playable. In bars 27–31 something similar occurs with a modulation from G major to B flat major (−3 fifths), third related keys. The first difficult moment occurs in bars 35–39 when the beginning of the theme appears after B flat major in B flat minor and with the help of a Neapolitan sixth = I⁶ in C flat major the modulation reaches—not C flat major but: B major. According to the spelling, the enharmonic change does not occur simultaneously in the four parts, but in three different steps.[6] (See Ex. 7, p. 376.)

This passage, which is also quoted in Karl Geiringer's book, offers one of the critical problems of 'pure' intonation to the quartet player.— The second enharmonic deception is to be found in bars 46–49 and is of special interest because Haydn (in order to avoid playing in G sharp

major) 'returns' to the logical tonality of A flat major. As a correction was just made in two neighbouring diminished sevenths, the pure intonation is not threatened:[7]

The last 'trick' of enharmonic spelling is the most obvious one: in bars 56–60, this time in the relationship A flat major to B major (= A flat major to C flat major) Haydn prescribes enharmonically the same modulation of keys a third apart of −3 fifths which he had employed in bars 27–31 where he was dealing with simple keys. This passage may, however, with a small correction of intonation by the cellist restitute the movement's basic key of B major.[8]

Possibly the oddest realization of the device demonstrated in four examples is to be found in the development section of the first movement of the F major Quartet opus 77. The development starting in C major modulates stepwise without enharmonic tricks to the key of E flat minor (bar 89). However, in bars 98 we are doubtlessly in the (written) key of E minor which logically should be F flat minor. (The remainder of the development recedes again stepwise to F major [written] which logically should be G♭♭ major). What happened in these few bars? Bars 92–95 would have been more rational in a modulation from E flat minor to F flat minor (−5 fifths) than in a modulation from E flat minor to E minor (+7 fifths). Without considering the point of view of logic or of musical orthography it seems truly remarkable that in an F major movement these two keys should appear next to each other. Let us see, however, how Haydn makes it appear plausible that a real E flat minor key may be followed by E minor. We are quoting the passage from the autograph score[9] with Haydn's own annotations. (See Ex. 10, p. 378.)

This is in fact a bolder, more modern, modulatory solution than Beethoven's well known 'quasi-modulation' with a stiff semitone direct jump which, incidentally, Haydn too liked to use.[10] First (bars 91–93) the tone E flat is the root of an E flat minor triad (reinforced by the 'Neapolitan leading tone' F flat). However, the same E flat, spelled as D sharp (bars 93–94), is considered the leading tone of the new key of E minor. A more extreme functional re-interpretation of two neighbouring notes half a note distant is inconceivable within the classical style. The fact that Haydn inscribed into the part of the cellist the remark 'l'istesso tuono' ('the same tone') between the notes E flat and D sharp is to be interpreted as a forced confession of enharmonic thinking within the tempered tonal system.[11] The remark 'das leere A' ('The open A string') is, as it were, an act of desperation: the motive A G G G favours playing on the D string.[12] Haydn, however, in the interest of pure intonation, refers to the open A string as the only firm point. This last 'irregular' type of modulation provides an excellent characterization of Haydn's

art. His imagination draws him into unknown, almost unrealizable, experimental adventures; but with the realism of the practical musician he clings to a solution allowing for 'pure' intonation. Out of a synthesis of these tendencies results an exciting, fantastic and still flexible new idiom.

We have reached the end of this brief analysis of a few selected instances of the modulatory type. One question yet remains to be answered. Why does the modulation 'descend' into the enharmonic flat range (-12) rather than 'rise' to the enharmonic sharp range ($+12$)? The answer we have to offer sounds rather commonplace; yet it seems to be the most likely one. This device is a precursor of Romantic thought, a trend from light to dark. Let us remember that in the 'golden age' of J. S. Bach's music the most widely employed type of modulation was as follows: evasion in the region of sharps ($+1$ or $+2$ fifths); then, towards the middle or in the second half of the movement, descent into the region of flats (-1 or -2) and hence 'rising up' again to the tonic key.[14] Haydn's typical model of modulation as described in this study consists of a single descent in ever darker regions which is not altered by the fact that somewhere in the course of the modulation the basis rises with the help of enharmonic means by + 12 fifths and then again continues its descent.

11

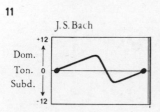
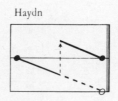

It should of course not be overlooked that the model of modulation in general occurs only in the development sections and that the large evasion toward the dominant always occurs somewhere as a needed counterbalance (*e.g.* in the exposition of the sonata form). The physiognomy of the whole movement or of the cyclical form is ultimately one imbued with 'classical' calm. Nevertheless the fact is that Haydn's music was full of remarkable bold Romantic features, and deserves far more attention in this respect. It provides a challenge to the musicologist to submit such 'modern' stylistic devices—among them those concerned with harmony—to a thorough and detailed scrutiny.

NOTES

1 Karl Geiringer: *Joseph Haydn.* Schott's Söhne 1959, p. 199.

2 *Cf., e.g.* the introductory *Adagio* and *Allegro* section of the Fantasia for Piano K. 475 in C minor by Mozart, the Organ Fantasia BWV 542 in G minor by J. S. Bach, etc.

3 *Cf.* A. von Oettingen: *Harmoniesystem in dualer Entwicklung*, 1866. With much more success this method is employed for analysis by my former professor of musical theory, Lajos Bárdos (*cf. Natürliche Tonsysteme*, Budapest 1956; *Egy romantikus moduláció* [A romantic modulation in Mozart's Piano Concerto K 453], Budapest 1957; *Modális harmóniák Liszt müveiben* [Modal harmonies in Liszt's works], Budapest, 1955; etc.).

4 As a matter of fact a dominant half cadence in G major: ♯ IV♭$_3^4$–V.

5 It is typical for the late Haydn that a Finale of a composition of a basic major key is started on purpose with the 'darker' *Minore* in order to achieve a very strong emotional effect with the *Maggiore* of the basic key in the recapitulation. (In the opus 76 set this happens apart from the G major work also in the 'Emperor' Quartet in C major.)

6 One may ask whether Haydn himself wrote it this way or whether the specific spelling occurred only in later editions. The autograph of the opus is lost. The National Széchényi Library owns, however, a score in Elssler's hand (MS. Mus. I. 126, formerly in the Esterházy Archives and before that in Haydn's private collection) which certainly constitutes a

copy of the autograph; also in this manuscript all enharmonic tricks of writing in this movement are expressed in the spelling known to us today.

7 However, Haydn's mixed spelling in bars 46–49 cannot be called correct from the view-
point of harmonic logic. Based on the relationship of G sharp minor to G sharp major or
else on the relationship of A flat minor to A flat major it ought to read:

8 The logical correct formation of B major at the beginning and C flat major at the end
of the movement has been complicated by the fact that after the final chords of the first
movement in E flat major we would automatically hear the beginning of the second movement as C flat major (relationship by a third of −4 fifths).

9 National Széchényi Library Budapest (MS. Mus. I. 46a, fol. 3b).

10 Cf., e.g. the gliding modulation from F minor to G flat major in the second movement
of the Quartet, opus 55 in F minor.

11 Similar remarks occur also in other Haydn autographs: 'the same Tone' in the second
movement of Symphony No. 102; 'Nb: the Same Tone', in *Scena di Berenice*, bar 129 (*cf.*
H. C. Robbins Landon: *The Symphonies of Joseph Haydn*, London 1955, p. 592), maybe
a meaning of this kind is provided by the remark 'sapienti pauca' in the first movement of
the 'Farewell Symphony', no. 49 (treated by Karl Geiringer in *Eigenhändige Bemerkungen
Haydns in seinen Musikhandschriften*, Anthony van Hoboken, *Festschrift zum 75. Geburtstag*,
Mainz 1962, p. 90).

12 Today the passage is usually performed on the D string by string quartet players.

13 Regarding the enharmonic modulation toward the *flats* at least a dozen other examples
could be mentioned from different types of Haydn's music; for modulation toward the
sharps I have found so far a single uncontestable example. The development section of the
first movement in sonata form of the piano Trio in F sharp minor (1795, or earlier, Hob.
XV: 26), reads in chordal simplification:

From F sharp major—following the repeat sign—Haydn reaches by means of *Minore–
Maggiore*, third relation, and other devices a logical recapitulation in E♯♯ minor (meas. 63).

It cannot be denied, however, that among the keys passed only that of D sharp minor written as E flat minor (minor parallel of the *Maggiore*) was established for 3 half measures (moreover the combination of [written] G sharp major to B minor at the end of the development), resulting in a modulation less striking and less noticeable than that towards flats. Incidentally, the modulation is carried out mainly by the tempered piano.

14 Important new results of research are to be found in a Hungarian book by Zoltán Gárdonyi about J. S. Bach's 2-part and 3-part Inventioned. (*J. S. Bach ellenpont-müvészetének alapjai* [The Foundations of J. S. Bach's Contrapuntal Art], Budapest 1967, p. 50 ff, 86 ff.).

BENCE SZABOLCSI

MOZART'S *GAGLIARDA*

What is a *gagliarda*? An old Italian dance form, to be sure; yet one whose roots reach far into a remote past, to the treasury of old Mediterranean rhythms. In all likelihood it already appeared as Versus Adonicus of the antiquity, as the concluding formula of the hexameter and the Sapphic stanza:

$$ - \cup \cup \cup / - \cup $$

wherefrom a modified, 'softer' version such as $\cup \cup \cup / - \cup$ might easily have ensued.

The *gagliarda* may be traced in old Italian proverbs, rhymes for children, songs, canzonets and subsequently in the entire European song literature. From the Middle Ages through the Renaissance it served as a dominant form of Latin-Italian-German dance songs, an international symbol, as it were, of convivial joy of life. *Chi la gagliarda vuol imparare* and *A lieta vita Amor c'invita* was sung in Italy since Gastoldi's days; *Lasset uns scherzen, liebende Herzen* resounded in Germany since Simon Dach's gay songs. It was, however, in Goethe's and Mozart's era that the *gagliarda* reached its classic bloom and culmination in Italian opera and German poetry as well. Its rhythm was crystallized in stanza formations such as

$$ 3-2-3-2 $$
$$ 3-2-3-1 $$
or
$$
\begin{array}{ll}
3-3-3-3- & \qquad 3-2 \\
3-3-3-1 \quad \text{and} & \qquad 3-3-\ 3-3 \\
& \qquad 3-2
\end{array}
$$

As examples we might mention:
From Rinaldo da Capua's *La Zingara* (1753):

> O dell 'Egitto
> Nume, custode
> La nostra frode
> Proteggi ognor.
> Opra è divina
> Punir l'avaro
> Cui solo è caro
> L'argento e l'or.

From Piccinni's *La buona figliola* (1760):

> Scenda Cupido
> Dio degli amori,
> Gli amanti cuori
> Venga a legar;
> E il bel diletto
> d'un vero affetto,
> No, non si veda
> Mai terminar.

The *gagliarda* seemed especially well suited for the 'chiusetta', an ensemble-finale, where (according to *commedia dell'arte* tradition) it 'deduces the moral from the story' (*cf. e.g.* Haydn in *Lo speziale*). The tradition was recaptured by young Mozart. However, before entering the operatic stage, we should like to point to classical Gagliarda forms in Goethe's workshop:

> Zwischen dem Alten,
> Zwischen dem Neuen
> Hier uns zu freuen
> Schenkt uns das Glück.
> Und das Vergangene
> Heisst mit Vertrauen
> Vorwärts zu schauen,
> Schauen zurück.
>
> (*Zum neuen Jahr*, 1802)
>
> Zündet das Feuer an!
> Feuer ist obenan,

Höchstes, er hat's getan,
Der es geraubt.
Wer es entzündete,
Sich es verbündete,
Schmiedete, ründete
Kronen dem Haupt.
(Pandora, 1807)

Christ ist erstanden!
Freude dem Sterblichen,
Den die verderblichen,
Schleichenden, erblichen
Mängel umwanden.
(Faust I)

(In this connection one might also refer to the English national anthem and other festive songs, hymns, *etc.* moreover to the chorus of the furies in Gluck's *Orfeo* and its parody in Paisiello's *Socrate immaginario*).

What meaning did this floating dance rythm of a hymn-like festive character have for Mozart? In which way did he use it in his music and especially in his dramatic works?

We should like first to examine three examples from Mozart's instrumental music. They are taken from the Divertimento K. 131 (1772) the Symphony K. 182 [166c] (1773) and the Divertimento K. 334 [320b] (1779), the two first ones being Finale allegros, the third a minuet.

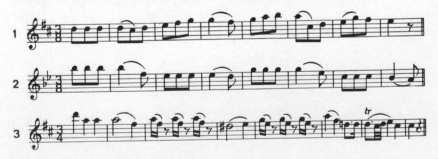

All three have a convivial character. They are conventional pieces in a solemn mood depicting a group of people meeting and greeting each other at a festive occasion. Something of the kind is also to be found on Mozart's stage; out of this type the formula of the concluding song, the 'lieto fine', a traditional feature of Italian opera.

The idea of the 'lieto fine' inspires the *gagliarda* motives in the finales of Mozart's youthful operas. Usually they proclaim a reconciliation, agreement, a softening or a clearing up of the 'imbroglio' mood; *cf.* in *Bastien und Bastienne* the duet No. 15: 'Komm, nimm aufs neue, Neigung und Treue' and the concluding Terzet 'O zum Geier, welch' trefflicher Mann' or in *La finta giardiniera* the final song 'Viva il conte, viva amore che fa tutti rallegrar' ('Wir sind glücklich und vergnügt. Liebe und Treue hat gesieget'). (A similar effect is to be found in the introduction 'Welches Vergnügen'). And yet the opposite may also be conveyed with this form: excitement, confusion, intrigues, stupefaction. This is the case in the first finale of *La finta giardiniera*, in the scene beginning with Podesta's indignation' Wo ist die Ehrfurcht, die mir gebühret' up to 'Wir wollen gehen, Und nun gleich sehen, Die Wahrheit zeigt sich dort oder da'. Likewise it occurs in the *Allegro* scene as conclusion to the Finale of the First Act: 'Unmensch, Verbrecher, Verräter' (*cf.* also Podesta's aria in the second act 'Wie was, ein Fräulein?' *etc.*).

In Mozart's later operas the *gagliarda* form appears on quite a different level. It expresses fervent lyricism in Belmonte's B major aria (*Allegretto* section) 'Dass wir uns niemals wiederfinden'

or soothing in Zerlina's comforting song 'Vedrai, carino'.

In both arias, the lilting dance rhythm contributes to the expressiveness of the diction. In both cases, the striking power of the melody is intensified and accentuated by its rhythmic pulsations.

Tense, very personal passion carried to the extreme is conveyed by the dance rhythm in Figaro's famous *cavatina* 'se vuol ballare' (where subsequently the identity of Adonicus and *gagliarda* rhythms is clearly stressed by the change of metre). The same is true of Don Giovanni's demoniac-pathetical ultimate toast.

Another sphere, that of playful irony, is touched in *Così fan tutte* with Despina's first aria and the pseudo-doctor's presentation.

The same opera offers a variant with a somewhat loosened melodic figure in Guglielmo's wooing:

Finally, like a message from the fairy-world of folk tales, the dance-like rhythms of the three *Knaben* (youths) in the *Magic Flute* soars toward us.

10 Seid uns zum zwei - ten - mal will-kom-men, ihr Män-ner, in Sa -

- ra - stros Reich

We have attempted to demonstrate in Mozart's work the different potentialities of expression, the different 'spheres of intonation' of a single rhythmic pattern chosen at random, restricting ourselves in this study to examples best known. It should be added that the *gagliarda* form often played a very important rôle in Romantic opera literature, especially so in Italy. We mention only two examples: Rossini's *Barber* and Verdi's *Trovatore*. Both conjure up on the stage worldly elegance as well as tragic poignancy, the wildly romantic as well as the 'folksy'—all by means of this 'irresistible rhythm'. They discovered what, in an even more decisive way, was clear to Mozart: that a single form used by a creative genius for the expression of divergent spheres in the 'human comedy' always stirs the same deep-lying chords in our reaction to dramatic music.

WILLIAM G. WAITE

BERNARD LAMY,
RHETORICIAN OF THE PASSIONS

———

It is well known that in the first half of the eighteenth century it was firmly held that the proper subject matter of music was an expression of the passions. These experiences of the soul were understood to be motions imparted to it from outside stimuli by means of the 'esprits animaux', the rarefied spirits that course through the veins according to principles enunciated by Descartes in 1650 in *Les Passions de l'ame*.[1] This emphasis upon the passions is in turn the result of a wide acceptance of the belief that music shared the goals of oratory: to teach, and in teaching, to delight and move the auditor. At first glance it would appear that a doctrine of the passions based upon mechanistic principles would be incompatible with the precepts of oratory whose roots extend back to humanistic literary expression. Nevertheless a fusion of the two did transpire in the seventeenth century, and this became the foundation of the musical systems of such great theorists as Marpurg, Scheibe, and Mattheson.

The importance of this reconciliation and of the man responsible for it has long been ignored, even though he is known to us through the writing of Johann Adolph Scheibe. In his periodical *Critischer Musicus* Scheibe wrote, 'Everyone will agree with me, if I state that it is the figures which give the greatest impression to musical style and lend it an uncommon strength. . . . It is the same in music as in oratory and poetry. Both of these fine arts would possess neither fire nor the power to move, if one took away from them the use of figures. Could one indeed arouse and express the passions without them? By no means. The figures are in fact themselves the speech of the affections, as is mentioned by Gottsched in his *Critische Dichtkunst* in imitation of Lamy'.[2] Johann Christoph Gottsched was the influential literary theorist and critic whose *Versuch einer Critischen Dichtkunst* (1730) was the model for Scheibe's own periodical. But who is this man, Lamy, so casually referred to by Scheibe? Bernard Lamy (1640–1715) was associated with Port Royal, the Cistercian Abbey outside of Paris which served as the centre of the Jansenist Movement in Fance.[3] From the beginnings of his studies there, Lamy was attracted to Cartesian philosophy. The first fruits of this interest was *L'Art de parler*, completed in 1670 but not published until 1675. This is a treatise on oratory written in the spirit of Descartes' methodology. Translated into English and German soon after its appearance, this book was widely disseminated. Benjamin Franklin recommended its adoption by the Philadelphia public schools. In 1740 Rousseau included it among the few works on rhetoric and logic in his 'Project sur l'éducation de M. de Sainte-Marie'.[4] It is the postulates of this work that were transmitted by Gottsched to his musical adherents.

When one opens Lamy's book, one is instantly aware of his radical departure from the accepted traditions of works dealing with oratory. Instead of endless illustrations drawn from classical authorities, one finds a lucid, rational explanation of the phenomena of language in terms of seventeenth-century science. Modelling himself upon Descartes, Lamy starts from what he takes to be first principles, and proceeds to reconstruct language from them. He postulates a band of 'New Men' without the gift of language and delineates the steps that would be necessary to create communication among them. This establishment of the structure of language is handled in Part I of the treatise, and need not detain us here. In the remainder of the book he covers more subtle aspects of language as an art: the use of tropes and figures, the pleasing arrangement of the sounds of language, and the question of style.

When Scheibe, in the quotation given above, informs us that figures are indispensable for moving the passions, he is faithfully following Lamy. The latter draws a sharp distinction between tropes and figures of speech. According to him, language is not fertile enough to provide us with individual words for all we wish to say. Consequently we have to make use of words that will allude to or suggest the specific idea we have in mind. 'The idea of a thing may be excited at the naming of any of those things, with which it has any resemblance. When to express a thing, we make use of an improper word, which Custom has applied to another Subject, that way of explaining ourselves is figurative; and the words so transported from their proper signification, and applied to other things than what they naturally mean, are called *Tropes*, or *Changes* of Custom, as the *Greek* Verb τρέχω imports.' (p. 97).

The use of tropes, such as metaphors and similes, is to enable us to express our thoughts more clearly. 'They must have two qualities,' Lamy tells us, 'one is, they must be clear, and contribute to the understanding of what we intend, seeing the only use of them is to make us more intelligible; the other is, that they hold proportion with the Idea we design to delineate' (p. 82). Tropes, then, serve to give our ideas the clarity and distinction that are required by Descartes in his *Discourse on Method* of ideas that are true. They are an expression of our will and of our thought.

On the other hand our passions, the motions of our soul, may also be reflected in our speech. 'We see in a Man's Face what passes in his Heart; the fire in his Eyes, the wrinkles in his Brow, the paleness in his looks, are evidences of more than ordinary commotion. The Circumstances of his Discourse, the new and sudden way of expressing himself (quite contrary to his way when he was cool and in peace) are certain characters of agitation, and imply disturbance in the person who speaks. . . . So our words answer to our thoughts: The Discourse of a Man that is moved, cannot be equal: Sometimes it is diffuse, and describes exactly the thing that is the Object of our Passion: Another time it is short; his expression is abrupt; twenty things said at a time; twenty Interrogations; twenty Exclamations; twenty Digressions together; he is alter'd by a hundred little particularities and new ways of signifying his mind, which ways are as different, and distinguishable from his ordinary way, as the Face of a Man is when he is angry, from his Face when he is quiet and serene. These ways of Speaking (which are Characters drawn by our Passions in our Discourses) are the famous *Figures* mentioned by Rhetoricians, and by them defin'd, *Manners of speaking, different and remote from the ways that are ordinary and natural* . . . ' (pp. 92–4).

Although the figures are associated with the passions rather than the rational faculties, they are nevertheless useful and necessary. We need to employ them for a number of reasons. When we are describing a person under the influence of a passion, we must imitate his discourse and use the figures appropriate to the particular passion. 'We cannot affect other people, without we appear to have some impression upon our selves. . . . *Si vis me flere, dolendum est* . . .' (p. 97). More importantly, figures are the 'Arms of the Soul'. 'The Body knows how to move, and dispose itself dexterously, for the repelling of Injuries; and the Soul may defend itself as well: Nature has not made her immoveable upon any insult; The Figures imploy'd by her in discourse, do the same, as Postures in defence of the Body. If Postures be proper for defence, in corporal invasions, Figures are as necessary, in spiritual attacks. Words are the Arms of the Mind which she uses to disswade or perswade, as occasion serves.'

Figures of speech are departures from normal speech. They are in a sense re-arrangements of the physical elements of speech, such as normal syntax. Lamy describes them in terms of the physical aspects of the Cartesian passions. Exclamation, for example, 'in my judgment, is not improperly to be plac'd in the Van of the Figures, seeing it is by that, our Passions do first exert, and discover themselves in discourse. *Exclamation*, is a violent extension of the Voice. When the Soul comes to be disturb'd, and agitated with a furious impulse, the animal Spirits passing through all the parts of the Body, and thronging into the Muscles that are about the Organs of the Voice, swell them up in such manner, that the passage being streight'ned, the Voice comes forth with more impetuosity, by reason of the Passion that propells it. Every Ebullition of the Soul is followed by an *Exclamation*; and therefore the Discourse of a Man in that condition, is full of these Exclamations, *Alas! Good God! O Heavens! O Earth! etc'*. (p. 101).

Now language is more than grammar and concept; it is also a form of sound. Lamy devotes the third part of his treatise to this factor and in Chapter II (p. 132 ff.) he lays down six conditions for making sound agreeable. Interestingly enough these turn out to be almost identical with the prescriptions given by Descartes in his *Praenotanda* at the beginning of his *Compendium musicae* written in 1618. Lamy's stipulations are as follows:

1. 'God has decreed . . . that whatever happens to the Body, and disturbs not its good disposition, should give him content. It is pleasing to see, to feel, to touch, to taste, etc. . . . The sense of a sound must then be pleasing to the ear, when it strikes it with moderation.' (Descartes: Sensus omnes alicuius delectationis sunt capaces. Ad hunc delectationem requiritur proportio quaedam obiecti cum ipso sensu.)

2. 'A Sound ought to be distinct, and by Consequence strong enough to be heard. . . . Whatever we discern clearly, whether by the sence or the mind, is pleasant.' (Descartes: Talis obiectum esse debet, ut non nimis difficulter & confuse cadat in sensum.)

3. 'The equality of sounds contributes to the rendering of them distinct. . . . Unequal Sounds that strike the Organs strongly or weakly, swiftly or slowly without proportion, trouble the mind. . . .' (Descartes: Illud obiectum facilius sensu percipitur, in qua minor est differentia partium.)

4. 'Diversity is as necessary as Equality. . . . Equality grows tedious and insupportable when continued too long. . . . A Sound tires the Ear by striking upon it too long.' (Descartes: Notandum est varietatem omnibus in rebus esse grattissimam.)

5. Numbers three and four must be united. 'In appearance the two last conditions are incompatible . . . but they agree very well, and equality and variety may consist without any confusion.' Lamy cites the elements of a formal garden as an example of how equality and diversity may be reconciled in a single object.

6. 'This agreement of equality and variety ought to be sensible, so as the temperament may be perceivable to the Ear. Wherefore all Sounds in which that Agreement is to be found, ought to be joyn'd, and the ear ought in like manner to hear them without any considerable interruption. . . . That the Ear may discern the order and proportion of several Sounds, it is necessary that they be compar'd: In all comparison 'tis supposed the terms of the Comparison are present, and joyn'd one with the other, and it is this union that makes the Beauty and Pleasure of Harmony.' (Descartes: Partes totius obiecti minus inter se differentes esse dicimus, inter quas est maior proportio. Illa proportio Arthmetica esse debet, non Geometrica. Cuius ratio est, quia non tam multa in ea sunt advertenda, cum aequales sint uibque differentie, ideoque non tantopere sensus fatigetur, ut omnia quae in ea sunt distincte percipiat. . . .)

Lamy is thus maintaining that the principles of musical sound and verbal sound are one and the same. 'These Conditions are necessary to all Sounds to make them agreeable, whether it be to the sounds of the voice, or of Instruments . . .' (p. 140). The first two considerations are easily fulfilled. The remaining four may be realized in speech in several ways. 'The ear judges of the measure of time in which each Letter, each Syllable, each Word, each expression is pronounc'd. Next it judges of the Elevations and Depressions of the Voice by which in speaking, each word, each expression, is distinguished. In the third place the Ear observes the silence or repose of the Voice at the ends of the Words or Sentences: when we joyn or separate words: when we cut off a Vowel, and several other things compriz'd under the name of Accents, the knowledge of which is absolutely necessary for pronunciation.' (p. 142)

All of these elements may be organized according to proportions and equality. We may dispose our words 'with such artifice, that the Measures of the time of our pronunciation be equal; that the pauses of the Voice be rais'd or debased with equal degrees. We may joyn Equality with Variety, by making several of these conjoyn'd measures to be equal, though the parts of which they are compos'd be unequal, and by ordering things so that the Ear may receive this temperament with pleasure. . . .' (p. 147) By establishing principles for oratory that are related to music Lamy has brought the two arts close together. But more importantly, he then proceeds to link these matters of proportion and variety to the Passions. The various proportions of speech, we are told, are called numbers. 'The Masters in the Art of Speaking have thought good to call *Numeros* whatever the Ear perceives of proportion in the pronunciation of a Sentence, whether it be the proportion of the measure of Time, or a just distribution of the Intervals of Respiration. . . . And *Numerosa Oratio* in Latin, is the same as an elegant or harmonious Discourse with us. The cadence of a studied discourse is likewise call'd a number.' Now there is a strange affinity between these numbers and the soul. 'Saint Augustine observes that our souls have a sympathy and allyance with these numbers; and that the different motions of the mind do correspond and follow certain Tones of the Voice, to which the Soul has a secret inclination.' (p. 202–3)

Lamy is not satisfied, however, with a mystical explanation of this phenomenon, but explains it in terms of the physiological causes of the passions as established by Descartes. So clear is his presentation and at the same time so fundamental for understanding the relationship of music and the passions as expounded in the rest of the Baroque era, the passage is worth quoting in its entirety. (p. 203 ff.)

'To search into the Causes of this marvellous sympathy betwixt Numbers and our Soul, and how they come to that power and Efficacy upon our passions, we must know that the motions of the mind do follow the motions of the Animal Spirits; as those Spirits are slow or quick, calm or turbulent, the mind is affected with different Passions: The least force is able to obstruct or excite the Animal Spirits, their resistance is but small; and their Levity is the cause that the least unusual motion determined them; the least motion of a sound puts them in agitation. Our Body is so dispos'd, that a ruff and boysterous sound forcing our

Spirits into the Muscles, disposes it to flight, and begets an aversion, in the same manner as a frightful Object begets horror by the eye. On the other side a soft and moderate sound, attracts and invites our attention. If we speak lowd or hastily to a Beast, it will run from us; by speaking gently, we allure and make it tame. From whence we may collect that diversity of Sounds do produce diversity of motions in the Animal Spirits.

'Every motion that is made in the Organs of Sense, and communicated to the Animal Spirits, is connext by the God of Nature, to some certain motions of the Soul: Sound can excite passions, and we may say, that every Passion answers to some sound or other; which it is, that excites in the Animal Spirits, the motion wherewith it is allyed. This connexion is the cause of our Sympathy with Numbers, and that naturally according to the Tone of the Speaker, our Resentment, [*i.e.* feeling] is different. If a tone be languishing and doleful, it inspires sadness; if it be lowd and brisk, it begets vivacity and courage; some Ayres are gay, and others Melancholly.

'To discover the particular Causes of this Sympathy, and explain how among the numbers, some produce sadness, some joy, we should consider the different motions of the Animal Spirits in each of our Passions. It is easy to be conceiv'd, that if the impression of such a sound in the Organs of hearing is follow'd by a motion in the Animal Spirits like that which they have in a fit of Anger (that is, if they be acted violently and with inequality), it may raise Choller, and continue it. On the contrary, if the impression be doleful and melancholy, if the commotion it causes in the Animal Spirits be feeble and languishing, and in the same temper as commonly in Melancholy, what we have sayd ought not to seem strange; especially if we reflect upon what has been deriv'd to us from many eminent Authors relating to the strange effects of Music.'

The implications of this passage for the future formulations of music theory in the Baroque era are extraordinarily important. Although he is dealing with a verbal art, Lamy is maintaining that the passions may be aroused by sound alone. It is sound as a quantity, sound as a form of matter in motion, that can stir the vital spirits and through them arouse the passions that command the actions of mankind. He even goes so far as to say: 'So the Cadence of Words is many times of more force than the words themselves. In short, we cannot doubt the efficacy of the Tone. A bold Tone begets an impression of Fear. A sorrowful Tone disposes to Compassion. . . .' (p. 199) It would appear that the proper organization of tones is the most efficacious way to effect the ends of art: to guide men through manipulating their passions.

Sounds as such cannot only arouse the emotions directly, they are also capable of presenting an idea to the mind. 'It is not to be doubted but sounds are significative; and of power to renew the Ideas of several things: The sound of a Trumpet, does it not have a secret Allyance and Connexion among themselves, and do excite one another. It is not to be question'd but certain sounds, certain Numbers, and certain Cadences, do contribute to awake the Images of things with which they have had allyance and connexion.' Lamy cites instances of how this may be done: onomatopoetic devices, slow and fast metres, long and short periods, *etc.* Here again there is an obvious application to music. If these manipulations of sound are effective in oratory, they should be just as effective in music, since we are presumably working with universal principles.

In 'A Discourse Presenting an Idea of the Art of Perswasion,' which is appended to the *Art of Speaking*, Lamy reaffirms the importance of the passions. 'Men are not to be acted, but by motion of their passions: Every man is carry'd away by what he loves, and follows that which gives him most pleasure: For which reason there is no other natural way of prevailing upon men, than this we have propos'd. . . . Whilst we are without passion, we are without action; and nothing moves us from this indifference, but the agitation of some passion.' Everything we do, all that we undertake, is dependent upon some motion of our passions. These in turn can be aroused by the organization of sounds to effect a certain movement of our vital spirits. The artist, be he orator or musician, can effect this end by control over the physical motions of his art.

Although it was not his intent, Lamy has laid out a solid theoretical basis for a rational approach to bringing musical techniques into line with the mechanistic principles of the new science. Since music is a tonal art, it is capable of arousing the passions of the soul by activating the vital spirits. It can produce a particular passion by utilizing motions and proportions of sound commensurable with the known movements of the passion. Adherence to these beliefs could only mean the subordination of tropes, be they literary or musical, to the figures. The metaphorical symbols of the music of the Renaissance and early Baroque, where individual words of the text are given a musical equivalent, will continue to be used as a means of conveying meaning, but these tropes will only be an adjunct to the figures, arrangements of physical sound, which alone are capable of effecting the highest aims of art, to move people to right actions through stirring their passions. It can truthfully be said that the elaborate theoretical systems of Mattheson and Scheibe owe much to the earlier work of Lamy. It was he who showed how art could be reconciled with the scientific theorems that were transforming the world. Rhetorical figures, transformed into matter in motion, have become the key to men's souls.

NOTES

1 The doctrine of the passions and its importance in the 17th and 18th centuries is well summarized in the article *Affektenlehre* in MGG.

2 *Critscher Musicus.* Neue, vermehrte, und verbesserte Auflage. Leipzig, 1745, p. 683. 'Man wird mir allerdings Recht geben, wenn ich behaupte, dass die Figuren der musikalischen Schreibart den grössten Nachdruck und eine, ungemeine Stärke geben. . . . Es ist damit in der Musik eben so, als in der Redekunst und Dichtkunst, beschaffen. Diese beyden zweyen Künste würden weder Feuer, noch rührendes Wesen behalten, wenn man ihnen den Gebrauch der Figuren entziehen wollte. Kann man wohl ohne sie die Gemüthsbewegungen erregen und ausdrücken? Keinesweges. Die Figuren sind ja selbst eine Sprache der Affecten, wie solches der Herr Professor Gottsched in seiner critischen Dichtkunst aus dem P. Lami ausführlich erinnert.'

3 For details on the life of Lamy consult the most recent work, François Girbal, *Bernard Lamy Etude biographique et bibliographique.* Paris, 1964. (Le mouvement des idées au xviie siécle, 2). My quotations for Lamy are taken from the first English edition, *The Art of Speaking:* in pursuance of a former treatise, intituled, The Art of Thinking Rendered into English, London. Printed by W. Godbid, and are to be sold by M. Pitt, 1676.

4 Oeuvres complétes de J. -J. Rousseau avec des notes historiques, III, Paris, Furne & Cie, 1846, p. 277, col. *a.*

EMANUEL WINTERNITZ

A HOMAGE OF PICCINNI
TO GLUCK

———◇———

Some years ago, browsing through Parisian book stores, I found a tiny, luxuriously bound music calendar for the year 1789,[1] a portentous year indeed. The contents, however, contained not the slightest hint that everything was not quiet around the Bastille. On the contrary, many "royal" virtuosi advertised their services. The calendar had evidently been printed well in advance of the beginning of the year, or probably at the beginning or the middle of 1788. This is also suggested by several obituaries on Gluck, who had died on November 15, 1787. They are followed by an undated letter from Piccinni to the editor. The obituaries are clichés; Piccinni's letter is not. In fact, it is such a noble and moving document that we will quote it here in full.

A few dates may illuminate the scene. Nicola Piccinni, born in Bari, went to Paris as late as 1774, in his 46th year. There Gluck was firmly established as an opera composer. 1777 saw the great success of Gluck's *Armide* at the Paris Opera, and one year later, Piccinni's first French opera, *Renaud*, was performed. In 1779, both Piccinni and Gluck prepared an *Iphigenie en Tauride*, but Piccinni's setting had to be postponed because of the performance of Gluck's opera in May, 1779, which was a triumph. Soon after, Gluck left Paris for good and spent his last years in Vienna.

In January 1781, Piccinni's *Iphigenie* was performed, also with great success, although the second performance, according to the chronique scandaleuse, was marred by a painful accident—the singer of the main rôle, Mlle. Laguerre, appeared on the stage in an intoxicated state, which led the public to add to the list of Iphigenies (*Iphigenie au Aulide*, *Iphigenie en Tauride*) a third one, 'Iphigenie en Champagne'.

397

Gluck's banner was taken over in Paris by another contestant, Antonio Maria Gasparo Sacchini, who, according to Burney's testimony, was one of the most famous Italian composers of the time. Only two days after Piccinni's *Didon*—no less than 250 performances—Sacchini's *Chime* was given at Fontainebleau, a performance which at once established Sacchini as a worthy successor of Gluck. The Gluckistes did their best to woo Sacchini and to alienate him from the Piccinnistes—how successfully, one can infer from the fact that Sacchini's *Renaud*, originally composed in 1772 for Milan under the title *Armida* and given in Paris in 1783, was criticized by the Piccinnistes as 'gluckine'.

Piccini left Paris ten years after Gluck, in 1789. The revolution had deprived him of his royal pension. He returned to Naples and devoted himself chiefly to church music, but he was still in Paris when he learned of Gluck's death in Vienna. Here is the text of his letter 'to the editors of the musical calendar':

MESSIEURS,

Ce n'est pas l'éloge du grand Compositeur, dont votre Journal nous a annoncé la mort, que je veux faire dans la Lettre que j'ai l'honneur de vous adresser. La guerre musicale dont cet homme célébre et moi fumes la cause, mais dont il ne fut pas la victime, feroit suspecter cet éloge par ceux qui ne me connoissent que par mes Ouvrages ou par mon nom. C'est à vous, Messieurs, historiens de cette guerre et de la révolution musicale qu'elle a opérée en France, à louer dignement l'homme à qui votre Théâtre lyrique doit autant que la Scène Françoise au *grand Corneille*. L'Italie vient de consacrer plus qu'en éloge, quelque bien fait qu'il puisse être, à la mémoire de *Sacchini*. Florence lui a décerné un buste dans sa Galerie; Rome a placé l'image de ce grand Compositeur dans le Panthéon; et le marbre retrace aux yeux d'un peuple qui aime véritablement la Musique, les traits d'un des hommes qui a le plus honoré cet art.

J'oserai vous proposer pour le Chevalier *Gluck*, un hommage qui peut durer plus que le marbre encore, et qui transmettra à la postérité la plus reculée, non ses traits, que le buste que vous lui avez élevé conservera, mais l'image du génie de l'homme que l'Art et la France doivent honorer. Je vous propose en conséquence de fonder, en l'honneur du Chevalier *Gluck*, un concert annuel qui aura lieu le jour de sa mort, si ce jour-là n'est pas jour d'Opéra, et dans lequel on n'exécuteroit que sa Musique. Cet établissement, qui honoreroit autant la France que le grand homme auquel elle décerneroit cet hommage, pourroit, ce me semble, être rendu immuable par une souscription dont le produit, placé en rente perpétuelle sur le Roi, seroit affecté à ce Concert, que le Directeur du Concert Spirituel s'engageroit à donner, et dont ce revenu annuel seroit à perpétuité la première rétribution. Une institution semblant me paroît la plus digne de consacrer la mémoire de *Gluck*, et elle joint à cet avantage celui de servir encore après sa mort, l'art qu'il professa d'une manière si éclatante pendant se vie. Vous savez, Messieurs, combien les traditions musicales se perdent et se corrompent plus facilement encore que celles du jeu et de la déclamation sur vos autre Théatres. Cette institution auroit l'avantage de conserver le mouvement, le caractère, l'esprit dans lequel *Gluck* avoit écrit ses savantes Compositions. Elle transmettroit le sentiment de ces parties qui constituent si particulièrement l'exécution d'un Ouvrage musical; et dans tous les temps on pourroit reprendre les chefs-d'oeuvre de ce Compositeur, et en retracer le génie à la postérité qui succédera à celle qui les vit naître. La philosophie de l'art y gagneroit encore. Vous savez que cet art, qui doit peut-être ses charmes à sa mobilité, et qui commande, j'oserai le dire, une sorte d'inconstance dans ses formes, change chez une nation en proportion de se qu'il perfectionne ou de ce qu'il s'y propage davantage. Peut-être ce besoin de variété, qui a corrompu l'art en l'Italie, vous gagnera; et la musique que vous ferez dans quarante ans ne ressemblera peut-être plus à celle qui fait actuellement vos délices. L'institution que je propose aura encore l'avantage de rappeller vos Compositeurs aux principes de l'art et à la sorte de vérité qu'exige celui de la musique. L'image des grands modèles que vous a laissé *Gluck* conservera, parmi ceux qui lui succéderont, le caractère et la marche de la musique dramatique, partie qui constituoit particulièrement le génie de ce grand Compositiuer.

Telles sont, Messieurs, les idées qui m'engagent à vous proposer mon projet de souscription. S'il vous paroît susceptible d'exécution, si la Souveraine qui protégea ce grand homme et ses rivaux, daigne d'agréer, j'oserai prier le Public de me permettre de consacrer les derniers accens d'une voix qui s'éteint, à célébrer dans le premier Concert qui sera l'effet de cette souscription, les talens d'un homme de génie, dont la mort ne m'a fait éprouver d'autre sentiment que le désir d'immortaliser la mémoire d'un Compositeur dont le nom servira d'époque à la révolution qui s'est opérée sur un des plus beaux Théatres de l'Europe.

Signé, PICCINI.

P. S. J'ignore trop les formes à employer pour faire réussir ce projet, et je compte trop sur votre attachement à la mémoire et à la gloire du Chevalier *Gluck*, pour n'espérer pas que vous me suppléerez à cet égard.

Piccinni's reaction to the death of his old adversary was highly unusual. On the whole, musical party lines have an unwholesome effect on the leaders, who are forced to represent the dogma in its extreme rigour, often far beyond their own aesthetic credo. One century later, Wagner hardly took notice of the existence of Verdi; Verdi was visibly shaken when, during a rehearsal, he learned of Wagner's death, and he abruptly terminated the rehearsal. Towards Brahms, Wagner maintained a cool, ironical attitude with occasional facetious critical outbursts; Brahms, in turn, unlike the Brahmsians, respectfully recognized the merits of Wagner's music, if not the man. But in Gluck's and Piccinni's time, the feud was confined to one comparatively narrow scene, one single court and one city, and this, of course, made the battle more intense and colourful, and inflamed the temperaments by the day or the week. It speaks for the leaders that both, as noble characters and not without a sense of humour, did not let themselves be degraded to lower intrigues or vulgar invectives. If this in itself is unusual, Piccinni's letter to the calendar is of unique greatness, for Piccinni not only recognizes warmly the artistic merits of his dead adversary—for an Italian to compare a German to Corneille is a supreme and imaginative laudation—but he suggests an immensely practical way to perpetuate Gluck's glory by recommending something like a Bayreuth for Gluck.

NOTES

[1] Calendrier Musical Universel pour l'an de Grace 1789; A Paris Chez l'Auteur, maison de M. le Duc, au Magasin de Musique et d'Instruments, rue du Boule, no. 6.

HELLMUTH CHRISTIAN WOLFF

THE FAIRY-TALE OF THE
NEAPOLITAN OPERA

Although the conception of a Neapolitan Opera was strongly criticized by
a group of opera experts at the I.M.S. Congress of 1961 in New York and
the erroneous use of such a designation was refuted, there appear again
and again studies which unhesitatingly repeat the earlier formulation and
pay no heed to the results of recent research in opera. For this reason I
should like strongly to draw attention to two papers read at the Congress
in question by Helmuth Hucke and Edward O. D. Downes and to the
ensuing discussion which is presented in the second volume of the Report
of this Congress.[1] In the course of the discussion, it was proved that the
term of 'Neapolitan Opera' cannot be used in the former way; it can at
best be employed for Neapolitan dialect comedies, but will certainly not
serve for the characterization of the whole Italian opera from about 1700
to 1750. As early as 1912 Hugo Riemann had offered in his *Handbuch der
Musikgeschichte* convincing arguments in this respect and suggested
merely to speak of the 'Italian Opera' of that time. In 1937, I was able to
prove that a large part of the so-called 'innovations' of the 'Neapolitan
School' were already achieved in the Venetian opera of the second half
of the seventeenth century, *viz.* the *da capo* aria, the employment of great
vocal coloratura, the arias with concertizing solo instruments, the song
or dance-like character of the aria themes and, on the other hand, the
formation of independent comic scenes within the opera seria. The form
of the intemezzi, as well as the extensive cultivation of large comic operas
and musical comedies, were likewise started in Venice, a fact which has
mostly been overlooked so far.[2]

Helmuth Hucke gave a historic survey regarding the use of the concept of a 'Neapolitan Opera' and a Neapolitan style. He was able to prove that the erroneous use of this designation was started through a book by Francesco Florimo entitled *La scuola musicale di Napoli ed i suoi Conservatorii*, Naples 1880/82. In this work Florimo merely described musical life in Naples, but did not establish a general stylistic concept. This was done by German musicologists—Otto Jahn, Hermann Kretzschmar, Robert Haas—who believed in the fairy tale of a 'Neapolitan Opera'. They misinterpreted a remark by Charles Burney in his *A General History of Music* (London 1789, vol. IV, p. 57 and 539 ff.).

Here Burney, while clearly proving the superior significance of Venice for eighteenth-century opera, had on the other hand made Alessandro Scarlatti the head of a 'Neapolitan School'. It is true that Scarlatti was of greatest significance for the musical life of Naples. However, it was not Burney's intention to see in Scarlatti the head of the important new Italian opera which was subsequently given the label of 'Neapolitan Opera'. Scarlatti's operatic style was by and large much more indebted to the Italian, especially the Venetian, opera in the second half of the seventeenth century; through in his last opeas such as *Mitridate Eupatore* performed at Venice in 1707 (not in Naples), he employed larger aria forms and widely contoured melismata, thus approaching the new operatic style. Incidentally, this Scarlatti opera supplied strong stimulatiom to Handel, who was then in Venice and wrote his *Agrippina* for that town. Like Agostino Steffani, Handel carried on the contrapuntally founded style of such Venetian composers as Legrenzi and Sartorio. Through his whole life he maintained this older stylistic idea, which suited his German training in strict counterpoint better than the purely vocal idea of the Italian opera after 1720.

The establishment of a new homophonic style for the aria, without reliance on contrapuntal devices, the use of large coloratura and the expansion of the aria evidently originated in Venice. Downes has pointed out that such arias are to be found in Venice as early as 1716–19 in works by Giovanni Porta, Giuseppe Orlandini, Stefano Andrea Fiore and Fortunato Chelleri. Before them, however, Antonio Vivaldi had, ever since his opera *Orlando finto pazzo* (Venice 1714), employed this style of singing with a purely harmonic accompaniment, as I was recently able to demonstrate.[3] The stylistic evolution from the late Baroque of the seventeenth century to the gallantry or sensibility of the eighteenth probably took place all over Europe; it can be shown for instance in the Hamburg opera. Here Reinhard Keiser had composed the first version of his opera *Croesus* of 1710 in a pathetic and agitated style that one has to characterize as 'late Baroque'. Some twenty years later, in 1732, the work was performed again in Hamburg with widespread revisions. Keiser adjusted the composition to the new style of sensibility, using as models composers like Francesco Conti and Orlandini, whose works had meanwhile been heard in Hamburg.[4] In the new *Croesus*, the instrumental bass did not supply contrapuntal counterparts any more and had been turned into purely harmonic accompanying figures. The vocal parts, on the other hand, were given a more refined rhythm and ornamentation, often reminiscent of instrumental technique. The accompanying instruments of the opera orchestra now lost their independence and moved *unisono* with the singers; the vocal melody easily dominated and was brought to the foreground. At the same time, this melody was refined and bravura parts were created, supported by the expressive declamation of the text and its changing interpretation; the singers supplied further improvisatory elaboration, especially in the *da capo* of the first aria section. The change of style brought forth a change of vocal technique which was not tied to specific compositions but generally cultivated. Older composers like Scarlatti and Keiser adopted the new ideal or transformed it; the younger ones followed and developed it further. In this way, the new generation of such men as Antonio Vivaldi, Leonardo Leo, Nicolo Porpora, Domenico Sarri, Francesco Feo or Francesco Mancini took part in the shaping of the form; and Pergolesi as well as Hasse were able to start from this point. Most of these composers were not connected with Naples, or only temporarily so; their operas were played in many towns of Italy, especially in Venice which, throughout the whole eighteenth century, remained an operatic centre. In Venice, more operas were performed than in Naples; it had more opera theatres and held a leading position in this field.[5] It would constitute an urgent task for future musicologists to investigate in depth the Venetian operatic culture in the eighteenth century and thus explore, from this standpoint as well, the fairy-tale of the Neapolitan opera's predominance.

While in earlier times the 'Neapolitan Opera' was often regarded as a product of artistic decadence with emphasis on the external glitter of the singing voices and the 'virtuosovanity', one has recently learned to appreciate the positive aspects of this style. It was the soloist bent on expressive interpretation of the text who used to insert into the arias ornaments and coloratura in order to achieve a melodic as well as expressive climax. Before our time, an unjustified tendency had prevailed to consider some vocal coloratura of a particularly instrumental character as typical for the whole style. However, these were exceptional instances conceived by virtuoso singers of unusual ability such as Carlo Broschi Farinelli. It is true that an enhanced coloratura technique prevailed and that the art of improvisation reached a peak at that time. All this was not, however, quite as new as scholars used to believe; indeed the madrigals of the late sixteenth century were already given improvisatory ornamentation of this kind. This was a Mediterranean, southern feature of solo singing which had been cultivated for centuries in Italy, and at the beginning of the eighteenth century was enlisted for the 'number opera'. Such an elemental southern type of music making has remained a feature so strange to the Europeans of more northerly regions that it was regarded with mistrust and even contempt as something too superficial. This was the source for so many unjustified verdicts about the Italian coloratura technique in eighteenth-century operas. Today we know that it was principally the vocal delivery by the soloist which gave these old operas an attraction; this was true even for Handel who secured the most renowned and superb Italian singers for London. In our time, after experiencing the overemphatic expression and the pathetic declamation in late Romantic and expressionistic operas we feel particularly attracted to the pure vocal art of the eighteenth century. Likewise the strict forms of the old 'number opera' are again welcomed by composers of our time. We might refer in this connection to Hindemith, who received direct stimulation for his *Cardillac* of 1926 from performances of Handel operas in Göttingen. In the second version of this work (1952), Hindemith even included a whole act from Lully's opera *Phaeton* (Paris 1683). Igor Strawinsky, too, used ideas from old operas in his *The Rake's Progress* (1951) for which he found models in works by Monteverdi, Handel and Mozart. Thus the old art of Baroque opera is interesting not only for the historian and scholar, but for the practical musician as well. All the more reason to achieve clarity about the stylistic changes in the history of seventeenth and eighteenth century opera and avoid working with wrong concepts like that of the 'Neapolitan Opera'. It is easy to understand the error, for the *cantabile* melody, the bravura coloratura seemed to fit so well into Southern Naples. However, this concept cannot prevail against the sober facts of history. It was the whole of Italy that put the new style to use, especially Venice.

Rudolf Gerber has already stated that Metastasio's personality was of the greatest importance for the understanding of the new operatic style. He even suggested speaking of a 'Metastasio style' instead of a 'Neapolitan style'. There is much to be said for such a concept, although Metastasio lived and worked up to 1782, that is, up to a time which again set itself different artistic goals. Nevertheless the concept of the 'Metastasio opera' should be kept in mind. Through his librettos he became one of the leading figures in this field and the vocal ornaments in the operas merely served the interpretation of his texts. Apart from the arias the recitatives played a much larger rôle than was often formerly assumed. In the recitatives, Metastasio's beautiful verses were expressively declaimed and scenically represented, texts which to the audience of that time were often more important than the compositions. For this reason, Metastasio's librettos were again and again set to new music. Together with the re-evaluation of the old 'number opera', a re-evaluation of Metastasio's poetry has therefore proved necessary. Metastasio was not the representative of a courtly convention, as he is so often described; he attempted to evoke in his operatic librettos general human virtues and to achieve effects of an ethical nature. As late as 1786 Metastasio was praised by Johann Adam Hiller as a 'teacher of virtue, loyalty, obedience, patriotism, the duties of every profession' (in *Über Metastasio und seine Werke*, Leipzig 1786). The poet invented and skilfully characterized a multitude of different personalities; one cannot speak to-day any more of schematism in his librettos.[7] For Metastasio the drama, not the music, had its prominent place in opera; without him Gluck's so highly praised operatic reform would have been impossible.

The future may decide whether to designate the Italian opera of 1720–50 (or even up to 1780) as 'Metastasio Opera' or whether to revert to the customary stylistic notions of 'gallantry', 'sensibility', 'preclassicism'; anyway the term of 'Neapolitan Opera' for a stylistic designation of a general nature should definitely be shelved.

NOTES

[1] *Report of the Eighth Congress of the IMS*, New York, 1961, vol. I, p. 253–84, and vol. II p. 132–39.

2 *Cf*. Hellmuth Christian Wolff, *Die venezianische Oper in der zweiten Hälfte des 17. Jahrhunderts*, Berlin 1937. *Cf*. also Hans Nietan, *Die Buffoszenen der spätvenezianischen Oper* (1680–1700). Diss. Halle, 1924 (only typescript).

3 *Cf*. H. C. Wolff, 'Vivaldi und die Oper,' in *Acta Musicologica*, XL, 1968, fasc. II.

4 A complete new edition of the two versions of *Croesus* by Reinhard Keiser was offered

by Max Schneider in DDT 37/38. A detailed report is to be found in H. C. Wolff, *Die Barockoper in Hamburg*, Wolfenbüttel, 1957, vol. I, p. 269–76.

5 *Cf.* H. C. Wolff, 'Das Opernpublikum der Barockzeit,' in *Festschrift Hans Engel*, Kassel, 1964, p. 443 f.

6 Rudolf Gerber, *Der Operntypus Johann Adolf Hasses und seine textlichen Grundlagen*, Leipzig, 1925.

7 *Cf.* H. C. Wolff, *Musikgeschichte in Bildern—Oper, Szene und Darstellung von 1600 bis 1900*. Leipzig, 1968, p. 116.

A SELECTED BIBLIOGRAPHY
OF THE WORKS OF
KARL GEIRINGER
IN HONOUR OF HIS
SEVENTIETH BIRTHDAY

COMPILED BY
MARTIN A. SILVER

University of California, Santa Barbara

A SELECTED BIBLIOGRAPHY OF KARL GEIRINGER

BOOKS AND TRANSLATIONS

BACH FAMILY

Lost portrait of J. S. Bach. New York, Oxford University Press, 1950. [10] pp.

The Bachs: A family portrait. Boston, Boston University Press, 1953, 23 pp.

Symbolism in the music of Bach; a lecture delivered in the Whittall Pavilion of the Library of Congress, May 23, 1955. Washington, 1956, 16 pp. (Louis Charles Elson Memorial Lecture).

Music of the Bach family, an anthology. Cambridge, Harvard University Press, 1955, 248 pp.

Johann Sebastian Bach: the culmination of an era, in collaboration with Irene Geiringer. New York, Oxford University Press, 1966, 382 pp.

London, Allen and Unwin Ltd., 1967, 382 pp.: *Johann Sebastian Bach*, i samarbete med Irene Geiringer. Stockholm. Bokförlaget Pan/Norstedts, 1969, 344 pp. (French and German editions in preparation.)

The Bach family; seven generations of creative genius, in collaboration with Irene Geiringer. London, Allen and Unwin, 1954, 514 pp.

New York, Oxford University Press, 1954, 514 pp.

Bach et sa famille; 7 générations de génies créateurs. En collaboration avec Irene Geiringer. Traduit de l'Anglais par Marguerite Buchet et Jacques Boitel. Paris, Correa, 1955, 557 pp.

Hun naam was Bach; zeven generaties muzikale scheppingkracht, in samenwerking met Irene Geiringer. Arnhem, Van Loghum Slaterus, 495 pp.

Die Musikerfamilie Bach: Leben und Werken in drei Jahrhunderten, unter Mitarbeit von Irene Geiringer. München, Beck, 1958, 571 pp.

La familia de los Bach, en colaboracíon con Irene Geiringer. Traducción del Inglés por Guillermo Sans Huelin y María Teresa de Llanos de Sans. Madrid, Espasa-Calpe SA., 1962, 592 pp.

BRAHMS

Johannes Brahms; Leben und Schaffen eines deutschen Meisters. Wien, Rudolf M. Roher, 1935, 325 pp.

Brahms, his life and work, translated by H. B. Weiner and Bernard Miall. London, Allen and Unwin, 1936, 352 pp.

Boston, Houghton Mifflin Co., 1936, 352, pp.

Brahms, his life and work. 2d ed. rev. and enl., with a new appendix of Brahms' letters. New York, Oxford University Press, 1947, 383 pp.

London, Allen and Unwin, 1948, 383 pp.

New York, Anchor Books, 1961, 344 pp.

Brahms, sua vita e sue opere, traduzione italiana de Gianni Gai e Maffeo Zanon. Rome, Ricordi and Co., 1952, 315 pp.

Brahms. [Hebrew version] Tel Aviv, Ledori, 1955, 320 pp.

Brahms, translated by Ginji Yamane. Tokyo, Ongaku no tomo-sha, 1952, 466 pp.

Johannes Brahms: sein Leben und Schaffen, 2. erweiterte und verbesserte Auflage. Zürich Pan Verlag, 1955, 380 pp.

Kassel, Bärenreiter Verlag, 1958, 380 pp.

Iogannes Brams, translated by G. Nasatyr. Moskva, Muzyka, 1965, 432 pp.

HAYDN

Joseph Haydn. Potsdam, Akademische Verlagsgesellschaft Athenaion m.b.H., 1932, 160 pp. (Bücken, Ernst, ed. Die Grossen Meister der Musik.)

STUDIES IN EIGHTEENTH-CENTURY MUSIC

Joseph Haydn: der schöpferische Werdegang eines Meisters der Klassik. Mainz, Schott, 1959,
    368 pp.
Haydn, a creative life in music. New York, W. W. Norton and Co., 1946, 342 pp.
    London, Allen and Unwin, 1947, 342 pp.
    Haydn: ett liv av musikaliskt skapande, translated by Gereon Brodin. Stockholm, P. A.
    Norstedt and Söners, 1953, 352 pp.
    Haydn den: sono hito to shôgai, translated by Tetsugoro Yamamotŏ. Tokyo, Gekkan
    Myûjikku-sha, 1961, 237 pp.
Haydn: a creative life in music, in collaboration with Irene Geiringer. 2d ed. rev. and enl.
    New York, Anchor Books, 1963, 430 pp.
    3d. ed. Berkeley, University of California Press, 1968, 434 pp.
    (Hungarian edition in preparation).

MUSICAL INSTRUMENTS

'Die Flankelwirbelinstrumente in der bildenden Kunst des 14.–16. und der 1. Hälfte des 17.
    Jahrhunderts.' Dissertation, 1923 (manuscript).
'Alte Musik-Instrumente im Museum Carolino Augusteum Salzburg.' Leipzig, Breitkopf
    und Härtel, 1932, 45 pp.
Musical Instruments; their history from the stone age to the present day, translated by Bernard
    Miall. London, Allen and Unwin, 1943, 339 pp.
    New York, Oxford University Press, 1945, 278 pp.

CATALOGUES

Hugo Wolf. 'Katalog einer Jubiläumsausstellung'. Wien, 1928.
Gesellschaft der Musikfreunde in Wien. 'Führer durch die Joseph Haydn Kollektion im
    Museum der Gesellschaft der Musikfreunde in Wien', in collaboration with H. Kraus,
    Wien, 1930, 56 pp.
'Joseph Haydn. Katalog einer Zentenarausstellung', in collaboration with H. Kraus, Wien,
    1932.
Philadelphia. Free Library. 'Edwin A. Fleisher music collection.' Philadelphia, privately
    printed, 1933–45. 2 v. 'The information for the majority of compositions has been sup-
    plied by Karl Geiringer.'
'Johannes Brahms. Katalog einer Zentenarausstellung,' in collaboration with H. Kraus
    and V. Luithlen. Wien, 1934, 121 pp.
'*125 Jahre Gesellschaft der Musikfreunde.*' Katalog einer Ausstellung, in collaboration with
    H. Kraus. Wien, 1937.
'A thematic catalogue of Haydn's setting of folksongs.' Superior, Wisconsin, Research
    Microfilm Publishers, 1953, 438 pp. (Studies in Musicology, Series A).

TRANSLATIONS

Wagner, Richard. *Briefe. Die Sammlung Burrell.* Hrsg. und kommentiert von John N.
    Burk. Einl., Kommentar u. Anhang übertr. von Karl und Irene Geiringer. Frankfurt
    a.M., S. Fischer, 1953, 825 pp.
Drinker, Sophie Lewis. *Die Frau in der Musik. Eine Soziologische Studie.* Deutsche Über-
    tragung von Karl und Irene Geiringer. Zürich, Atlantis Verlag, 1955, 192 pp.

A SELECTED BIBLIOGRAPHY OF KARL GEIRINGER

ARTICLES

BACH FAMILY

'Artistic interrelations of the Bachs' (in *Musical Quarterly*, 36/3, 1950, pp. 363–74).

'Unbeachtete Kompositionen des Bückeburger Bach' (in *Festschrift Wilhelm Fischer zum 70*. Geburstag, 1956), (Innsbrucker Beiträge zur Kulturwissenschaft, Sonderheft 3), Innsbruck, Sprachwissenschaftliches Seminar der Universität Innsbruck, 1956, pp. 99–107.

'Unbekannte Werke von Nachkommen J. S. Bachs in amerikanischen Sammlungen' (in *Bericht über den Siebenten Internationalen Musikwissenschaftlichen Kongress*. Köln, 1958, pp. 110–112).

'The impact of the Enlightenment on the artistic concepts of Johann Sebastian Bach' (in *Studies on Voltaire and the 18th century*. Geneva, 1967, pp. 601–610).

BEETHOVEN

'La prima missa di Beethoven' (in *Il Pianoforte*, 7/1926).

'Bemerkungen zum Bau von Beethovens "Diabelli Variationen"' (in Heussner, Horst, ed., *Festschrift Hans Engel zum 70*. Geburstag. Kassel, Bärenreiter, 1964, pp. 117–24).

'The structure of Beethoven's Diabelli Variations' (in *Musical Quarterly*, 50/4, 1964, pp. 496–503).

BRAHMS

'Johannes Brahms im Briefwechsel mit E. Mandyczewski' (in *Zeitschrift für Musikwissenschaft*, 15/8, 1932–33, pp. 337–70).

'Brahms as a reader and collector' (in *Musical Quarterly*, 19/2, 1933, pp. 158–68).

'Brahms' zweites "Schatzkästlein des jungen Kreisler"' (in *Zeitschrift für Musik*, 100/1933, pp. 443–46).

'Brahms als Musikhistoriker' (in *Die Musik*, 25/8, 1933, pp. 571–78).

'Brahms and Wagner' (in *Musical Quarterly*, 22/2, 1936, pp. 178–89).

'Brahms' Mutter, Briefe von Christiane Brahms an Johannes Brahms aus den Jahren 1853–56' (in *Schweizerische Musikzeitung und Sängerblatt*, 76/1, January 1, 1936, pp. 1–6; 76/2, January 15, 1936, pp. 43–47; 76/4, February 15, 1936, p. 107–12).

'Brahms and Henschel: Some hitherto unpublished letters' (in *Musical Times*, 79/ March 1938, p. 173–4).

'Brahms and Chrysander with unpublished letters' (In *Monthly Musical Record* 67/68 1937/38: 1, June 1937, p. 97–99, 2, July–August 1937, pp. 131–32, 3, October 1937, pp. 178–80, 4, March–April 1938, pp. 76–79)

'Brahms und Dvořák (mit ungedruckten Briefen Anton Dvořáks)' (In *Der Auftakt* 17/7–8 1937, pp. 100–102)

'Brahms' prickly pet' (In *Etude 59* 1941, pp. 82, 134, 139)

HAYDN

'Das Haydn-Bild im Wandel der Zeiten' (In *Die Musik*, 24/6, 1932, pp. 430–36)

'Haydn's sketches for "The Creation"' (In *Musical Quarterly* 18/2 1932. pp, 299–308)

'Joseph Haydn und die Oper' (in *Zeitschrift für Musik*, 99/4, 1932, pp. 291–94).

'Haydn and the oratorio' (in *Musical Opinion*, 62/ 1938).

STUDIES IN EIGHTEENTH-CENTURY MUSIC

'Haydn, Joseph' (in Thompson, Oscar, ed. *International cyclopedia of music and musicians*, New York, Dodd, Mead, 1939, pp. 764–69).

'Haydn as an opera composer' (in *Proceedings of the Musical Association*. London, 1939–40, 66, pp. 23–32).

'Haydn and the folksong of the British Isles' (in *Musical Quarterly*, 35/2, 1949, pp. 179–208).

'Sidelights on Haydn's activities in the field of sacred music; small works of church music in Eisenstadt' (in *Bericht über die Internationale Konferenz zum Andenken Joseph Haydns*. Budapest, Ungarische Akademie der Wissenschaften, 1959, pp. 49–56).

'The small sacred works by Haydn in the Esterházy Archives at Eisenstadt' (in *Musical Quarterly*, 45/4, 1959, pp. 460–72).

'Joseph Haydn als Kirchenmusiker; die kleineren geistlichen Werke des Meisters im Eisenstädter Schloss' (in *Kirchenmusikalisches Jahrbuch*. Köln 1960, 44, pp. 54–61).

'Eigenhändige Bemerkungen Haydns in seinen Musikhandschriften' (in Schmidt-Görg, Joseph, ed. *Antony van Hoboken, Festschrift zu seinem 75*. Geburtstag. Mainz, Schott, 1962, pp. 73–86).

'Gluck und Haydn' (in Gerstenberg, Walter, ed. *Festschrift Otto Erich Deutsch zum 80*. Geburtstag. Kassel, Bärenreiter, 1963, pp. 75–81).

'Joseph Haydn, protagonist of the Enlightenment' (in *Studies on Voltaire and the 18th Century*, Geneva 1963, pp. 683–90).

MOZART FAMILY

'Leopold Mozart' (in *Musical Times* 78/ May 1937, pp. 401–4).

W. A. Mozart the younger' (in *Musical Quarterly*, 27/4, 1941, pp. 456–73).

'The Church Music of Mozart' (in Landon, H. C. Robbins and D. Mitchell, eds. *The Mozart Companion*. London, Rockliff, 1956, pp. 361–76).

'Schumann in Wien' (in *Zeitschrift für Musik*, 98/3, 1931, pp. 208–15).

'Eine unbekannte Klavierkomposition des jungen Schumann' (in *Die Musik*, 25/10, 1933, pp. 721–26).

'Ein unbekanntes Blatt aus Schumanns Endenicher Zeit' (in *Anbruch*, 17/1935, pp. 273–78).

'Le Feuillet d'Endenich' (in *La Revue Musicale*, December 1935, pp. 54–60).

'New Light on Schumann's last years' (in *The Listener*, June 8, 1939, pp. 1237).

(in Aprahamian, Felix, ed. *Essays on Music: an anthology from the Listener*. London, Cassell, 1967, pp. 228–31).

WOLF

'Hugo Wolf, der musikalische Parteigänger; zum 30. Todestag am 22 Februar, 1933' (in *Zeitschrift für Musik*, 100/1933, pp. 126–28).

'Hugo Wolf and Frieda von Lipperheide; some unpublished letters' (in *Musical Times*, 77/August, 1936, pp. 701–2, September, pp. 793–97).

MUSICAL INSTRUMENTS

'Der Instrumentenname "Quinterne" und die mittelalterlichen Bezeichnungen der Gitarre, Mandola und des Colascione' (in *Archiv für Musikwissenschaft*, 6/1924, pp. 105–10).

'Musikinstrumente' (in Adler, Guido, ed. *Handbuch der Musikgeschichte*. Frankfurt a M., 1924, pp. 515–71).

(2d ed., Berlin, H. Keller, 1930, 2 vol., v. 1, pp. 573–634).

A SELECTED BIBLIOGRAPHY OF KARL GEIRINGER

'Das Problem des Musikbildwerkes. Eine Einführung' (in *Die Musik*, 19/10, 1927, pp. 708–13).

'Eine Geburtstagkantate von Pietro Metastasio und Leonardo Vinci' (in *Zeitschrift für Musikwissenschaft*, 9/5 1927, pp. 270–83).

'Gaudenzio Ferraris Engelkonzert im Dome von Saronno; ein Beitrag zur Instrumentenkunde des 16. Jahrhunderts' (in *Kongressbericht der Beethoven-Zentenarfeier*. Wien, March 1927, pp. 378–81).

'Vorgeschichte und Geschichte der europäischen Laute bis zum Beginn der Neuzeit; eine ikonographische Studie' (in *Zeitschrift für Musikwissenschaft*, 10/9–10, 1928, pp. 560–603).

'I quadri musicali olandesi e fiamminghi del secolo XVII' (in *La Rassegna Musicale*, 2/1–4, 1929, pp. 36–47, 90–100, 154–63, 203–11).

MISCELLANEOUS

'Renaissance and Gothic analogies in modern music' (in *The Dominant*, 2/2, 1929, pp. 11–15).

'Paul Peuerl (in *Studien zur Musikwissenschaft*, 16, Wien, Universal-Edition, 1929, pp. 32–69). (Beihefte der Denkmäler der Tonkunst in Österreich).

'Christoph Strauss; ein Wiener Künstlerdasein am Beginn des 17. Jahrhunderts (in *Zeitschrift für Musikwissenschaft*, 13/2, 1930, pp. 50–60).

'Isaac Posch' (in *Studien zur Musikwissenschaft*, 17, Wien, Universal-Edition, 1930, pp. 53–76). (Beihefte der Denkmäler der Tonkunst in Österreich).

'Curt Sachs; zum 50. Geburtstag 29. Juni [1931]' (in *Zeitschrift für Musikwissenschaft*, 13/9–10, 1931, pp. 491–92).

'The Friends of Music in Vienna (1812–1937).' (in *Musical Quarterly*, 24/3, 1938, pp. 243–48).

'Strauss, Richard' (in Ewen, David, ed. *The Book of Modern Composers*. New York, Knopf, 1942, pp. 56–63).

'Gluck und Haydn' (in Gerstenberg, Walter, ed. *Festschrift Otto Erich Deutsch zum 80. Geburtstag*. Kassel, Bärenreiter, 1963, pp. 75–81).

'Es ist genug, so nimm Herr meinen Geist; 300 years in the history of a Protestant funeral song' (in Reese, Gustave, ed. *The Commonwealth of music, in honour of Curt Sachs*. New York, Free Press, 1964, pp. 283–92).

Anton Bruckners Vorbilder' (in Grasberger, Franz, ed. *Bruckner-Studien*, Leopold Nowak zum, 60. Geburtstag. Wien, Musikwissenschaftlicher Verlag, 1964, pp. 27–31).

'Anthony van Hoboken zum 80. Geburtstag' (in *Neue Zürcher Zeitung*, March 23, 1967, pp. 9).

C. CONTRIBUTIONS TO LARGER WORKS

Colles, H. C. ed. *Grove's dictionary of music and musicians*. 4th ed. London, Macmillan, 1940, 6v.

Among the numerous articles contributed by Karl Geiringer are the following:
Brahms, Johannes
Caldara, Antonio
Haydn, Joseph
Neidhart von Reuental

Schumann, Robert
Starzer, Josef
Strauss, Christoph
Wolf, Hugo

Posch, Isaac (in Blume, Friedrich, ed. *Die Musik in Geschichte und Gegenwart*. Kassel, Bärenreiter-Verlag, 1948–68, v. 10, pp. 1509–11).

Haydn, Joseph (in Riemann, Hugo. *Musik-Lexikon*, 12th ed., edited by Wilibald Gurlitt. Mainz, Schott, 1959–1968, v. 1, pp. 750–54).

Schubert, Franz (in Riemann, Hugo. *Musik-Lexikon*, 12th ed., edited by Wilibald Gurlitt. Mainz, Schott, 1959–68), v. 2, pp. 638–42).

IN PRODUCTION

'The rise of Chamber music' (in *New Oxford History of music*, v. 6, London, New York, Oxford Univesity Press, 1954–).

MUSICAL CONTRIBUTIONS TO MONUMENTS AND GESAMTAUSGABEN

Peuerl, Paul and Isaac Posch, 'Neue Paduanen, 1611; Weltspiegel, 1613; Ganz neue Paduanen, 1625; Isaac Posch, Musikalische Tafelfreud, 1621, Nebst Anhang (in *Denkmäler der Tonkunst in Österreich*, 36/2, Band 70, Wien, Universal-Edition, 1929, 133 pp.).

Caldara, Antonio, 'Kammermusik für Gesang, Kantaten, Madrigale, Kanons,' in collaboration with E. Mandyczewski (in *Denkmäler der Tonkunst in Österreich* 36/, Band 75, Wien, Universal-Edition, 1932, 108 pp.).

Haydn, Joseph, 'Volksliedbearbeitungen Nr. 1–100, Schottische Lieder' (in *Joseph Haydn Werke*, 32/1,München-Duisburg, Henle, 1961, 105 pp.).
'Kritischer Bericht unter Mitarbeit von Paul G. Buchloh,' München-Duisburg, Henle. 1961, 32 pp.

IN PRODUCTION

'Haydn, Joseph, Orlando Paladino' (in *Joseph Haydn Werke*).
'Gluck, Christoph Willibald, Il Telemaco' (in *Gluck sämtliche Werke*).

EDITIONS OF MUSIC

1923 Bach, Johann Sebastian. *Brandenburg Concertos* (6), Wien, Wiener Philharmonischer Verlag, 1923.

1925 Pergolesi, Giovanni Battista. *La serva padrona: poesia di G. A. Federigo*. Wien, Wiener Philharmonischer Verlag, 1925. 166 pp.
Tanzbrevier: *Weise, Bild und Meinung aus vier Jahrhunderten* (compiled with W. Fischer), Wien, Wiener Philharmonischer Verlag, 1925. 70 pp.

1927 Beethoven, Ludwig van. *Mass in C Major*, Op. 86. Wien, Wiener Philharmonischer Verlag. 1927, 199 pp.

1931 Haydn, Joseph. *Divertimento, Es dur, für vier Streichinstrumente*. Hannover, A. Nagel, 1931, 8 pp. (Nagels Musik Archiv, no. 84).

Haydn, Joseph. *Notturno 5° für zwei Violinen, Flöte und Oboe, zwei Hörner, zwei Violen, Violoncello und Kontrabass.* Wien, Universal-Edition, 1931, 23 pp.

Peuerl, Paul. *5 Variationensuiten und 2 Canzonen für Streichinstrument.* Wolfenbüttel, Georg Kallmeyer Verlag, 1931, 31 pp.

1932   Haydn, Joseph. *Allegro con variazoni* (in *Haydn-Festschrift.* Wien, 1932, pp. 44–45).

Haydn, Joseph. *Amors Pfeil für Sopran und Klavier oder Orchester,* deutscher Text von Irene Geiringer. Berlin, Edition Adler, 1932, 11 pp.

Divertimento in G dur (1786). Berlin, Edition Adler, 1932, 43 pp.

Partita in F per flauto, oboe, 2 corni, 2 violini, 2 viole, violoncello e contrabasso. Wien, Universal-Edition, 1932, 32 pp.

Divertimento (Feldpartita) B dur für 8 stimmigen Bläserchor, Leipzig, Fritz Schuberth, 1932, 7 pp.

1933   Bach, Johann Sebastian. *Choral aus der Kantate Nr. 60 'O Ewigkeit du Donnerwort',* *Konzerteinrichtung von Johannes Brahms.* Transcribed by Karl Geiringer (in *Zeitschrift für Musik,* 1933, Heft 5 Notenbeilage).

Caldara, Antonio. *Ein Madrigal und achtzehn Kanons zu 3–6 Stimmen.* Wolfenbüttel, Georg Kallmeyer Verlag, 1933, 16 pp. (Das Chorwerk, no. 25).

Gassmann, Florian Leopold. *Symphonie H-moll.* Wien, Universal-Edition, 1933, 30 pp.

Haydn, Joseph. *Trio für Violine, Viola und Cello (Barytontrio Nr. 82),* Kopenhagen, W. Hansen, 1933 (Das Hauskonzert, no. 10).

Schumann, Robert, *Sechs frühe Lieder für Gesang und Klavier op. posth.,* Wien, Universal-Edition, 1933, 12 pp.

8 Polonaises für Klavier zu vier Händen (1828), Wien, Universal-Edition, 1933, 35 pp.

1934   Brahms, Johannes. *Five songs of Ophelia to poems from Shakespeare's Hamlet.* New York, G. Schirmer, 1934, 11 pp.

Haydn, Johann Michael. *Türkische Suite aus der Musik zu Voltaires "Zaire" (1777),* Wien, Universal-Edition, 1934, 64 pp.

Stamitz, Karl, *Orchesterquartett F dur, opus 4, no. 4,* Wien, Universal-Edition, 1934, 15 pp. (Continuo).

Wagenseil, Georg Christoph. *Triosonate F dur,* Wien, Universal-Edition, 1934, 12 pp. (Continuo).

1935   Caldara, Antonio. *Suonata da camera,* Wien, Universal-Edition, 1935, 8 pp. (Continuo).

Wiener Meister um Mozart und Beethoven, Wien, Universal-Edition, 1935, 53 pp.

Schubert, Franz. *Tantum Ergo op. posth. (August, 1816),* Wien, Universal-Edition, 1935, 11 pp.

Stamitz, Karl. *Konzertante Symphonie F dur.,* Wien, Universal-Edition, 1935, 74 pp.

1936   *Die Alten Meister* (Ausgewählt von Karl Geiringer), Herausgegeben von Emil von Sauer, Wien, Universal-Edition, 1936, 107 pp.

Die Familie Bach, 1604–1845, Wien, Universal-Edition, 1936, 48 pp.

1937   *Alte Meistersonaten für Geige und Klavier.* Wien, Universal-Edition, 1937, 48 pp.

Boccherini, Luigi. *Sinfonia (A major), 1787,* Wien, Universal-Edition, 1937, 75 pp.

1939   Schumann, Robert, *Variations on an original theme (1854),* London, Hinrichsen, 1939, 8 pp.

1940   Haydn, Joseph, *Adagio and Presto for Strings, Flute and Horn,* London, Novello, 1940, 13 pp.

1941   Gluck, Christoph Willibald, *God is Good, Anthem for mixed voices, a cappella*. Philadelphia, Theodore Presser, 1941, 4 pp.

Old Masters of Choral Song, 20 vols., New York, G. Schirmer, 1941.

1. Palestrina, Giovanni Pierluigi. Jehovah did make this holy day (Haec dies quam fecit), 7 pp.
2. Senfl, Ludwig. My hunting-horn sad notes doth play (Ich schell' mein Horn in Jammers Ton), 10 pp.
3. Praetorius, Jacob. Wake, O Wake! the watch is calling (Wachet auf ruft uns die Stimme), 4 pp.
4. Marenzio, Luca. Zephyrus calls the nymphs (Zeffiro torna), 8 pp.
5. Marenzio, Luca. Liquid were those bright pearls (Liquide perle), 8 pp.
6. Hasler, Hans Leo. Now start we with a goodly song (Nun fanget an), 7 pp.
7. Stoltzer, Thomas. All leafless is the forest (Entlaubet ist der Walde), 4 pp.
8. Hasler, Hans Leo. A Song of the Rose-Garden (Ein Lied vom Rosengarten), 11 pp.
9. Hofhaimer, Paul. If thou dost say (Nach Willen Dein), 4 pp.
10. Hofhaimer, Paul. O picture fair (Herzliebstes Bild), 4 pp.
11. Bach, Johann Michael. I know that my Redeemer lives (Ich weiss dass mein Erlöser lebt) 7 pp.
12. Marenzio, Luca. When your eyes are concealed (Quando i vostri), 10 pp.
13. Eccard, Johannes. Over the hills Maria went (Über's Gebirg Maria geht), 8 pp.
14. Senfl, Ludwig. The bells at Speyer (Das G'leut zu Speyer), 11 pp.
15. Senfl, Ludwig. Hans Beutler must ride out one day (Hans Beutler, der musst' reiten aus), 8 pp.
16. Lasso, Orlando di. Though deep has been my falling (Aus Meiner Sünden Tiefe), 4 pp.
17. Gallus, Jacobus [Jacob Handl]. Lo now, so is the death of the just man (Ecce, quomodo moritur), 7 pp.
18. Issac, Heinrich. O World, I must be parting (O Welt ich muss dich lassen), 4 pp.
19. Bach, Johann Christoph. The Righteous (Der Gerechte), 16 pp.
20. Bach, Johann Christoph. I will not let Thee go (Ich lasse dich nicht), 19 pp.

1946   Haydn, Joseph. *Harmony in Marriage,* text by J. N. Goetz, English words by Henry S. Drinker. New York, Music Press Inc., 1946, 14 pp.

From the 'Song of thanks to God', text by J. F. Gellert, trans. by Henry S. Drinker, New York, Music Press Inc., 1946, 12 pp.

Schubert, Franz. *Five German Dances and Seven Trios* (for string orchestra or string quartet), New York, Music Press Inc., 1946, 14 pp.

1947   Haydn Joseph, *La Canterina* (piano-vocal score), Deutsche Fassung von Karl und Irene Geiringer, New York, Music Press Inc., 1947, 47 pp.

1949   Haydn, Joseph, *Evensong to God (Abendlied zu Gott)*, trans. by Henry S. Drinker, New York, Boosey & Hawkes, 1949, 15 pp.

1951   Haydn, Joseph, *To the Women* (An die Frauen), trans. by Henry S. Drinker, New York, G. Schirmer, 1951, 14 pp.

1955   Handl, Jacob. *I ascend unto my Father (Ascendo ad Patrem meum)*, trans. by Henry S. Drinker, Boston, C.C. Birchard, 1955, 9 pp. (Birchard Boston University Series of Early Music).

Music of the Bach family, an anthology. Cambridge, Harvard University Press, 1955, 248 pp.

Peuerl, Paul. *I must be Gay (Frölich zu seyn)* trans. by Henry S. Drinker.

Boston, C.C. Birchard, 1955, 9 pp. (Birchard Boston University Series of Early Music).

O Melody (*O Musica*), trans. by Henry S. Drinker. Boston, C.C. Birchard, 1955, 8 pp. (Birchard Boston University Series of Early Music).

1956   Bach, Carl Philip Emmanuel. *Heilig* (*Holy is God*), vocal score English-German, trans. by Henry S. Drinker, St. Louis, Concordia, 1956, 30 pp.

1958   Haydn, Joseph, *Eloquence,* New York, Carl Fischer, 1958, 11 pp.

The old man, New York, Carl Fischer, 1958, 11 pp.

1960   Brahms, Johannes. *Fünf Ophelia-Lieder für eine Sopranstimme und Klavierbegleitung.* Wien, Schönborn Verlag, 1960, 23 pp.

Haydn, Joseph, *We seek not God, our Lord for Glory* (*Non nobis Domine*), St. Louis, Concordia, 1960, 15 pp. (Concordia Motet Series).

1964   Bach, Johann Ludwig, *Zwei Motetten*, Wolfenbüttel, Möseler Verlag, 1964, 23 pp. (Das Chorwerk, no. 99).

1968   Posch, Isaac. *Harmonia Concertans I* (1623) 14 Cantiones Sacrae for Voices and Instruments. Ann Arbor, Michigan, University Microfilms, 1968. 49 pp. (University of California, Santa Barbara—Series of Early Music, Vol. 1). (Vol. II in preparation.)

SELECTED BOOK REVIEWS

Bach, Johann Sebastian, Adventskantaten ('Neue Ausgabe sämtlicher Werke') 1/1, Kassel, 1954 (in Music Library Association *Notes,* 12/4, 1955, pp. 628–31).

Bach, Johann Sebastian. Magnificat ('Neue Ausgabe sämtlicher Werke' 2), Kassel, 1955 (in Music Library Association *Notes,* 12/4, 1955, pp. 628–31).

Bach, Johann Sebastian. Messe in h-Moll, BWV 232 ('Neue Ausgabe sämtlicher Werke',) 2/1 Kassel, 1954 (in Music Library Association *Notes,* 12/4, 1955, pp. 628–31).

Besseler, Heinrich, '*Fünf echte Bildnisse Johann Sebastian Bachs.*' Kassel, 1956 (in Music Library Association *Notes,* 14/2, 1957, pp. 260–1).

Hoboken, Anthony van, '*Joseph Haydn thematisch-bibliographisches Werkverzeichnis*', Band 1, Mainz, 1957 (in Music Library Association *Notes,* 14/4, 1957, pp. 565–6).

Hoboken, Anthony van, '*Joseph Haydn thematisch-bibliographisches Werkverzeichnis.*' Band 1, Mainz, 1957 (in *Neue Zeitschrift für Musik,* 118/2, 1957, pp. 644).

Hummel, Walter, W. A. Mozarts Söhne, Kassel, 1956 (in Music Library Association *Notes,* 14/3, 1957, pp. 372–3).

van Serooskerken, Baron van Tuyll, 'Probleme des Bachporträts'. Bilthoven, 1956 (in Music Library Association *Notes,* 14/2 1957, pp. 260–61).

Haydn, Joseph, 'Messe B-Dur, Schöpfungs-Messe (Faksimile)' München-Duisburg, 1957 (in Music Library Association *Notes,* 15/4, 1958, pp. 644).

Haydn, Joseph, 'Sextet no. 14, Eb, for violin, viola, violoncello, oboe, horn and bassoon.' London, 1957 (in Music Library Association *Notes,* 15/4 1958, p. 644).

Haydn, Joseph, 'Barytontrios 49–72, 73–96 (Joseph Haydn Werke, 14/3–4)', München-Duisburg, 1958–59 (in Music Library Association *Notes,* 17/1, 1959, pp. 127–29).

Haydn, Joseph. 'Kanons (Joseph Haydn Werke 31), München-Duisburg, 1958 (in Music Library Association *Notes,* 17/1, 1959, pp. 127–29).

Haydn, Joseph. 'Mehrstimmige Gesänge (Joseph Haydn Werke 30) München-Duisburg, 1958 (in Music Library Association *Notes,* 17/1, 1959, pp. 127–29).

Haydn, Joseph, 'Lo Speziale (Joseph Haydn Werke 25/3)', München-Duisburg, 1958 (in Music Library Association *Notes,* 17/1, 1959, pp. 127–29).

Haydn, Joseph. Messen 5–8 (Joseph Haydn Werke 23/2) München-Duisburg, 1958 (in Music Library Association *Notes* 17/1 1959, pp. 127–29).

Haydn, Joseph, 'La Canterina (score) (Joseph Haydn Werke 25/2), München-Duisburg, 1959 (in Music Library Association *Notes*, 23/1, 1960, pp. 125–26).

Haydn, Joseph. 'Die Sieben letzten Worte unseres Erlösers am Kreuze.' Orchesterfassung, 1785 (Joseph Haydn Werke 4), München-Duisburg, 1959 (in Music Library Association *Notes*, 23/1, 1960, pp. 125–26).

Bartha, Dènes. 'Haydn als Opernkapellmeister.' Budapest, 1961 (in Music Library Association *Notes*, 19/1, 1961, pp. 67–9).

'Bericht über die internationale Konferenz zum Andenken Joseph Haydns.' Budapest, 1961 (in Music Library Association *Notes*, 19/1, 1961, pp. 67–9).

'Haydn Compositions in the Music Collection of the National Széchényi Library.' Budapest, 1960 (in Music Library Association *Notes*, 28/2, 1961, pp. 230–32).

'International Musicological Society: Report of the Eighth Conference', New York, 1961; Kassel, 1961 (in Music Library Association *Notes*, 18/4, 1961, pp. 569–70).

Haydn, Johann Michael, 'Te Deum in C (1770) (Collegium Musicum 3)', New Haven, 1961 (in *Journal of the American Musicological Society*, 16/3, 1963, pp. 407–9).

Deutsch, Otto Erich. 'Mozart; die Dokumente seines Lebens', (W. A. Mozart: Neue Ausgabe sämtlicher Werke, Serie 10, Werkgruppe 34), Kassel, 1961 (in Music Library Association *Notes*, 19/3, 1962, pp. 432–4).

Gal, Hans, 'Brahms: his work and personality', New York, 1963 (in Music Library Association *Notes*, 20/4, 1963, pp. 635–36).

Haydn, Joseph, 'Londoner Sinfonien, 4. Folge (Joseph Haydn Werke 1/18)', München-Duisburg, 1962 (in Music Library Association *Notes*, 20/4, 1963, pp. 556–8).

Haydn, Joseph, 'Die sieben letzten Worte unseres Erlösers am Kreuze (Vokalfassung) (Joseph Haydn Werke 28/2)', München-Duisburg, 1962 (in Music Library Association *Notes*, 20/4, 1963, pp. 556–58).

Haydn, Joseph, 'Streichquartette, Opus 9 und Opus 17 (Joseph Haydn Werke 12/2)', München-Duisburg, 1962 (in Music Library Association *Notes*, 20/4, 1963, pp. 556–8).

Haydn, Joseph, 'Symphony no. 89, F major', London, 1962 (in Music Library Association *Notes*, 20/4, 1963, pp. 556–58).

Haydn, Joseph, 'Gesammelte Briefe und Aufzeichnungen, Kassel, 1965 (in *Journal of the American Musicological Society*, 19/2, 1966, pp. 251–54).

Haydn, Joseph, 'L'incontro improvviso (Joseph Haydn Werke 25/6)', München-Duisburg, 1963 (in Music Library Association *Notes*, 22/4, 1966, pp. 1308–11).

Haydn, Joseph, 'L'infedeltà delusa (Joseph Haydn Werke 25/5)', München-Duisburg, 1964 (in Music Library Association *Notes*, 22/4, 1966, pp. 1308–11).

Haydn, Joseph, 'Messen, Nr. 9–10 (Joseph Haydn Werke 23/3)', München-Duisburg, 1965 (in Music Library Association *Notes*, 22/4, 1966, pp. 1308–11).

Haydn, Joseph, 'Sinfonien 1764 und 1765 (Joseph Haydn Werke 1/4)', München-Duisburg, 1964 (in Music Library Association *Notes*, 22/4, 1966, pp. 1308–11).

'Musica Rinata, nos, 1–8.' Budapest, 1964–65 (in Music Library Association *Notes*, 23/4, 1967, pp. 824–26).

SELECTED RECORD ANNOTATIONS

Bach, J. S., *Brandenburg Concertos*, Epic SC6008.
RCA, LSC7038.
Chromatic Fantasy and Fugue, Capitol P8348.
Clavier Partitas (6), Capitol PRR8344.
Concertos for Harpsichord, No. 1, 4 and 5, Haydn Society HSL92.
Concertos for Two Harpsichords, Haydn Society HSL113.

Concertos for Two Harpsichords and Orchestra, Haydn Society HSL93.
Partitas and Sonatas for Unaccompanied violin, Capitol PCR8370.
Suites for Orchestra (4) Haydn Society HSL90–91
Toccatas (7) *and Fantasias* (4) Capitol PBR8354.
Works for Organ, Haydn Society HSL104.
Music of the Bach Family; an anthology, Boston Records BUA1 (B402–405) [a complete
    recording of the music of the Harvard University Press anthology, 1955.]
Organ Music of the Bach Family, RCA LSC2793.
Beethoven, Ludwig van, *Sonata in A major, opus 47*, Capitol 8430.
Brahms, Johannes, *Concerto for Violin and Violoncello, opus 102*, RCA LDS2513.
Handel, Georg Friedrich, *Flute Sonatas* (10), Westminster WAL218.
Haydn, Joseph, *Arianna a Naxos and English Songs*, Haydn Society KSL2051.
    Concerto in Eb major for Trumpet, Angel 36148.
    Missa Brevis Sancti Joannis de Deo, Haydn Society HSL2064.
    Missa Sancti Bernardi de Offida, Haydn Society HSL2048.
    Piano Sonatas (1–10), Haydn Society HSLP3037.
    Songs for Mixed Voices (1796), Haydn Society HSL2064.
    String Quartets, opus 20, Haydn Society HSQ–F.
    String Quartets, opus 33, Haydn Society HSQ–G.
    String Quartets, opus 50, Haydn Society HSQ–H.
    String Quartets, opus 51, Haydn Society HSQ–39.
    String Quartets, opus 76, Haydn Society HSQ–L.
    Symphony No. 49 and 73, Haydn Society HSL1052.
    Symphony No. 61, Haydn Society HSL1047.
    Symphonies 93–98, Westminster WM1002.
    Symphonies 93–104, Capitol GCR7127,–7198.
    Symphonies 1–19, 46–59, Musical Heritage Society OR H 201–6, OR H 219–25.
Mozart, W. A., *Concertos for Horn and Orchestra*, Boston Records B401.
Strauss, R., *Sonatina in F for 16 Winds*, Boston Records 1016.

PROGRAMME NOTES

Karl Geiringer wrote the programme notes for the Los Angeles Philharmonic Orchestra for
    five seasons from 1955 until 1960. His annotations covered a wide spectrum of musical
    literature.

ARTICLES ABOUT KARL GEIRINGER

Scott, Marion M., 'Dr. Geiringer and Dr. Haydn' (in *Musical Times*, 89/1948, pp. 9–11).
Landon, H. C. R. (in Blume, Friedrich, ed., *Die Musik in Geschichte und Gegenwart*. Kassel,
    Bärenreiter, 1949–v., 4 pp. 1616–17).
Grove, Sir George, *Grove's dictionary of music and musicians*. 5th ed., edited by Eric Blom,
    London, Macmillan, 1954, 9 v. pp. 589, v. 3.
Baker, Theodore, *Baker's biographical dictionary of musicians*, 5th ed. revised by Nicolas
    Slonimsky, New York, G. Schirmer, 1958, p. 545).
Riemann, Hugo, *Musik-Lexikon*, 12th ed., edited by Wilibald Gurlitt, Mainz, Schott,
    1959–68, 3 v. p. 601, v. 1.
Westrup, Jack A. and F. L. Harrison. *The new college encyclopedia of music*. New York,
    1960, p. 270.
Thompson, Oscar, ed. *The international cyclopedia of music and musicians.*, 9th ed.,
    revised by Robert Sabin, New York, Dodd, Mead, 1964, p. 780.

o*

INDEX